LEARNING & TEACHING CENTRE
UNIVERSITY OF VICTORIA
PO BOX 1700 STN CSC
VICTORIA BC V8W 2Y2
CANADA

Best Practices for Teaching Beginnings and Endings in the Psychology Major

Best Practices for Teaching Beginnings and Endings in the Psychology Major

Research, Cases, and Recommendations

Edited by
Dana S. Dunn, Bernard C. Beins, Maureen A. McCarthy and
G. William Hill, IV

OXFORD
UNIVERSITY PRESS

2010

OXFORD
UNIVERSITY PRESS

Oxford University Press, Inc., publishes works that further
Oxford University's objective of excellence
in research, scholarship, and education.

Oxford   New York
Auckland   Cape Town   Dar es Salaam   Hong Kong   Karachi
Kuala Lumpur   Madrid   Melbourne   Mexico City   Nairobi
New Delhi   Shanghai   Taipei   Toronto

With offices in
Argentina   Austria   Brazil   Chile   Czech Republic   France   Greece
Guatemala   Hungary   Italy   Japan   Poland   Portugal   Singapore
South Korea   Switzerland   Thailand   Turkey   Ukraine   Vietnam

Visit the companion Web site at www.oup.com/us/dunn.

Published by Oxford University Press, Inc.
198 Madison Avenue, New York, New York 10016

www.oup.com

Oxford is a registered trademark of Oxford University Press.

Library of Congress Cataloging-in-Publication Data
Best practices for teaching beginnings and endings in the psychology
major / edited by Dana S. Dunn . . . [et al.].
p.   cm.
Based on a conference held in Oct. 2007.
Includes index.
ISBN 978-0-19-537821-4   1. Psychology—Study and teaching
(Higher)—United States—Congresses.   2. Psychologists—Training of—United
States—Congresses.   I. Dunn, Dana.
BF80.7.U6B47 2010
150.71'173—dc22
2009021111

ISBN: 978-0-19-537821-4

9 8 7 6 5 4 3 2 1

Printed in the United States of America
on acid-free paper

For our colleagues and students: May they always have strong beginnings and happy endings

Foreword

C. James Goodwin
Western Carolina University

There is no special reason that the October 2007 Best Practices conference titled "Beginnings and Endings" should have reminded me of my doctoral dissertation, completed long ago during a time of disco, bad hair, and Watergate. But it did. I spent a year and slogged through five different experiments teasing out the effects of practice on the "serial position effect of free recall," surprising no one with the results. It did eventually get published (you could look it up!), but it had no effect on the subsequent history of memory research. Of course, everyone knows the important message of the serial position effect—beginnings and endings, even in single-trial free recall, matter. The Best Practices conference on how we start and end the psychology major drove this "it matters" point home. If you missed the conference, or if you went but the effects of time have taken their inevitable toll on your memory, this book will either show you or remind you of the importance of how we start our young students on the road to being a successful psychology major and how we help them finish the journey (I initially just wrote "polish them off at the end," but aside from the issue of a mixed metaphor, it somehow sounded dire).

Beginnings

It used to be that everyone who wound up being a psychology major started the process by taking a general psychology course. That is still true in many places and the recruitment function of Psych 100 always will be an important way in which we attract bright students and convince them that psychology is for them. Having taught the course since disco days, my best rewards have *not* come from that rare student who actually understood negative reinforcement. Rather, it was during those occasional times when a bright biology major took my course and decided to switch to psychology.

In recent years, however, a movement has developed among psychology departments to go beyond hoping that the introductory course would sufficiently introduce students to the psychology major. Instead, thoughtful teachers and departments have taken a more proactive approach and either developed specific programs or courses for introducing the student to the psychology major or more finely tuned the department's existing efforts (e.g., the nature of early advising of majors and potential majors). One goal is to never again have to figure out what to say to those seniors who wander into our office in March of their senior year and, looking puzzled, ask, "So what's this about graduate school?"

The intent of these "beginnings" efforts is clearly metacognitive—it is to make psychology majors more consciously aware of a number of things:

1. what they are getting themselves into → yes this is a science, you'll be taking stat and methods, graduate schools are more likely to require these courses than any other ones in the psychology curriculum, get used to it.
2. typical misconceptions → just because everyone likes to tell you their problems and thinks you're a "good listener" does not mean you'll get into a clinical graduate program and become the next Dr. Phil (one Dr. Phil is plenty, thanks).
3. the advantages of being a psychology major, even if they won't be going to graduate school (which, of course, is true of the vast majority of psych majors) → this major includes all the advantages of a strong liberal arts degree, plus you'll be able to evaluate empirical data *better* than your English major buddy.
4. how best to plan for their immediate futures as a psychology major for the next 3 or 4 years → don't wait for senior year to take stat and methods; they are the foundation for all else, and by taking them early, you will have a better chance of becoming involved in some professor's research (and get yourself free rides to neat conferences).

5. how best to plan for their distant futures, perhaps as a professional psychologist of one type or another → there are dozens of fascinating things for psychologists to do besides psychotherapy.

So beginnings are important, and psychology departments are increasingly taking deliberate steps to get students off to a good start. The conference was, and this book is, full of good ideas about how to accomplish what an old memory researcher would think of as a primacy effect.

Endings

The manner by which we end the education of our psychology majors matters just as much as how we start them out. In fact, maybe "recency" matters even more (in free recall, recency is always greater than primacy, but only for practiced subjects—my dissertation again!—you could look it up!). For our psychology majors, from these final experiences with us, we launch them into the world of work or into graduate school. Endings are usually conceived of by psychology departments as "capstone" courses. The term invokes a construction metaphor, the "finishing stone" of some building, according to my online dictionary. Capstone courses have a longer history than specialty courses (i.e., non-intro psych) designed to begin the major. They are diverse, and their variety—from a senior seminar on contemporary issues in psychology, to a history of psychology course, to an independent research project—was well represented at the conference and is reflected nicely in the chapters in this book. The form of the course matters less than the fact that one exists in a psychology curriculum. The presence of a capstone means that the department has given some thought to the question of how to achieve closure in the curriculum.

I believe you will find this book extremely useful. If you are in a department that does not do much to start their students on the metacognitive path to success as a psychology major or/and doesn't have a clear idea about how the curriculum ought to conclude, I am confident you will find ideas in here that will help strengthen your program. If you are already doing things at both the start and end of your curriculum, the book will give you some food for thought about how to improve those efforts. Beginnings (primacy) and endings (recency) matter. You could look it up!

Contents

Part III   Coda

Contributor List

Jeffrey T. Andre
Associate Professor
Department of Psychology
James Madison University
Harrisonburg, VA

Drew C. Appleby
Professor
Department of Psychology
Indiana University-Purdue University
Indianapolis, IN

Suzanne C. Baker
Professor and Assistant Department Head
Department of Psychology
James Madison University
Harrisonburg, VA

Kenneth E. Barron
Associate Professor
Department of Psychology
James Madison University
Harrisonburg, VA

Bernard C. Beins
Chair and Professor
Department of Psychology
Ithaca College
Ithaca, NY

Victor A. Benassi
Faculty Director
Center for Teaching Excellence
Professor
Department of Psychology
University of New Hampshire
Durham, NH

Ludy T. Benjamin, Jr.
Professor
Department of Psychology
Texas A&M University
College Station, TX

Kim K. Buch
Associate Professor
Department of Psychology
University of North Carolina-Charlotte
Charlotte, NC

William Buskist
Professor
Department of Psychology
Auburn University
Auburn, AL

S. Lynn Cameron
Coordinator of Library Instruction
James Madison University
Harrisonburg, VA

Stanley H. Cohen
Professor Emeritus
Department of Psychology
West Virginia University
Morgantown, WV

Brennan D. Cox
Doctoral Student
Department of Psychology
Auburn University
Auburn, AL

Francis W. Craig
Professor
Department of Psychology
Mansfield University
Mansfield, PA

Kristin L. Cullen
Doctoral Student
Department of Psychology
Auburn University
Auburn, AL

Dana S. Dunn
Professor
Department of Psychology
Moravian College
Bethlehem, PA

Eric A. Goedereis
Assistant Professor
Department of Behavioral and Social Sciences
Webster University
St. Louis, MO

C. James Goodwin
Department of Psychology
Western Carolina University
Cullowhee, NC

Joann H. Grayson
Professor
Department of Psychology
James Madison University
Harrisonburg, VA

Regan A. R. Gurung
Chair, Human Development
Professor, Department of Psychology
University of Wisconsin, Green Bay
Green Bay, WI

Jane S. Halonen
Dean, College of Arts and Sciences
University of West Florida
Pensacola, FL

Charles M. Harris
Professor
Department of Psychology
James Madison University
Harrisonburg, VA

Paul Hettich
Professor Emeritus
DePaul University
Chicago, IL

G. William Hill, IV
Professor
Department of Psychology
Kennesaw State University
Kennesaw, GA

Peter A. Keller
Provost
Division of Academic Affairs
Mansfield University
Mansfield, PA

R. Eric Landrum
Professor
Department of Psychology
Boise State University
Boise, ID

Brian T. Loher
Professor
Department of Psychology
Mansfield University
Mansfield, PA

Neil Lutsky
William R. Kenan Jr. Professor of Psychology
Department of Psychology
Carleton College
Northfield, MN

Maureen A. McCarthy
Professor
Department of Psychology
Kennesaw State University
Kennesaw, GA

Wayne S. Messer
Associate Professor
Department of Psychology
Berea College
Berea, KY

David B. Porter
Professor
Department of Psychology
Berea College
Berea, KY

Monica J. Reis-Bergan
Associate Professor
Department of Psychology
James Madison University
Harrisonburg, VA

Sherry L. Serdikoff
Professor
Department of Psychology
James Madison University
Harrisonburg, VA

Randolph A. Smith
Professor and Chair
Department of Psychology
Lamar University
Beaumont, TX

Sue Spaulding
Lecturer
Department of Psychology
University of North Carolina-Charlotte
Charlotte, NC

Michael L. Stoloff
Professor and Head
Department of Psychology
James Madison University
Harrisonburg, VA

Karri B. Verno
Assistant Professor
Department of Psychology
Mansfield University
Mansfield, PA

Phil D. Wann
Professor and Chair
Department of Psychology
Missouri Western State University
St. Joseph, MO

Georjeanna Wilson-Doenges
Associate Professor and Chair
Department of Psychology
University of Wisconsin, Green Bay
Green Bay, WI

Tracy E. Zinn
Associate Professor
Department of Psychology
James Madison University
Harrisonburg, VA

About the Editors

Dana S. Dunn, a social psychologist, is professor of psychology and director of the Learning in Common Curriculum at Moravian College, Bethlehem, Pennsylvania. He received his PhD from the University of Virginia, having graduated previously with a BA in psychology from Carnegie Mellon University. A Fellow of the American Psychological Association, Dunn served as president of the Society for the Teaching of Psychology in 2010. Former Chair of Moravian's Department of Psychology, Dunn writes frequently about his areas of research interest: the teaching of psychology, social psychology, and rehabilitation psychology. Dunn is the author of five previous books—*Research Methods for Social Psychology, The Practical Researcher: A Student Guide to Conducting Psychological Research, Statistics and Data Analysis for the Behavioral Sciences, A Short Guide to Writing about Psychology,* and *Psychology Applied to Modern Life* (with Wayne Weiten, Margaret Lloyd, and Elizabeth Y. Hammer)—and the co-editor of four others—*Measuring Up: Educational Assessment Challenges and Practices for Psychology* (with Chandra M. Mehrotra and Jane S. Halonen), *Best Practices for Teaching Introduction to Psychology* (with Stephen L. Chew), *Best Practices for Teaching Statistics and Research Methods in the Behavioral Sciences* (with Randolph Smith and Bernard C. Beins), and *Teaching Critical Thinking in Psychology: A Handbook of Best Practices* (with Jane S. Halonen and Randolph Smith).

Bernard C. Beins, an experimental psychologist, is Chair and Professor of Psychology at Ithaca College. He earned his bachelor's degree in psychology at Miami (Ohio) University and his doctorate at the City University of New York. He is a Fellow of the American Psychological Association and of the Association for Psychological Science and served as president of the Society for the Teaching of Psychology in 2004. Beins has written two editions of *Research Methods: A Tool for Life* and co-authored (with Agatha Beins) *Effective Writing in Psychology: Papers, Posters, and Presentations.* In addition, he has co-edited *Best Practices for Teaching Statistics and Research Methods in the Behavioral Sciences* (with Dana Dunn and Randolph Smith), *Promoting the Undergraduate Research Experience in Psychology* (an e-book with Richard Miller, Robert Rycek, Emily Balcetis, Steve Barney, Susan Burns, Roy Smith, and Mark Ware), *Teaching Psychology in Autobiography: Perspectives from Exemplary Psychology Teachers* (an e-book with Trisha Benson, Caroline Burke, Ana Amstadter, Ryan Siney, Vincent Hevern, and William Buskist), *Teaching Psychology in Autobiography: Perspectives from Exemplary Psychology Teachers, vol. 2* (an e-book with Jessica Irons, Caroline Burke, William Buskist, Vincent Hevern, and John Williams), *Preparing the New Psychology Professoriate: Helping Graduate Students Become Competent Teachers* (an e-book with William Buskist and Vincent Hevern), and the *Gale Encyclopedia of Psychology* (with Susan Gall and Alan Feldman). In addition, during his career, his students have given over 75 presentations at research conferences.

Maureen A. McCarthy, a quantitative psychologist, is a professor of psychology at Kennesaw State University and served as president of the Society for the Teaching of Psychology in 2008. Former Associate Executive Director of the APA Precollege and Undergraduate Programs, McCarthy writes about program evaluation, assessment, and the scholarship of teaching and learning. Together with Dunn, Baker, Halonen, and Hill, McCarthy authored the seminal article "Quality Benchmarks in Undergraduate Programs," published in the *American Psychologist.*

G. William (Bill) Hill, IV, an experimental psychologist, earned his PhD at the University of Georgia. He is a professor of psychology at Kennesaw State University and director of the Kennesaw Center for Excellence in Teaching and Learning. A Fellow of the American Psychological Association (APA) and past president of the Society for the Teaching of Psychology, he also received the 2004 American Psychological Foundation Charles L. Brewer Distinguished

Teaching Award. His professional activities and research have primarily revolved around teaching-related issues such as grading practices and strategies, incorporating cross-cultural issues into the psychology curriculum, and program assessment. In 2001–2002, he was a member of the APA Board of Educational Affairs task force that developed expected learning outcomes for the undergraduate major in psychology as well as an accompanying online *Assessment CyberGuide*. In 1989 he founded, and continues to coordinate, the annual Southeastern Conference on the Teaching of Psychology. During his term as the STP Director of Programming, he coordinated the first seven annual "Best Practice" in teaching psychology conferences, including the conference on which this book is based.

Preface

We and our authors cover two timely and interconnected issues in psychology pedagogy in this book: What are the most effective ways to introduce the psychology major to undergraduates? Four years—and many psychology courses—later, what are the most effective practices for helping students apply their disciplinary knowledge in capstone experiences and post-graduate life? Providing the right beginnings and endings in psychology education is increasingly a concern for teachers, department chairs, program directors, and even deans. Orientation courses and capstone courses are now routine topics in conference and listserv discussions. Further, both courses have become increasingly important as sources for gathering pre- and post-course work assessment data for demonstrating degree learning outcomes (e.g., Halpern, 2004).

Psychology teachers (and their students) benefit from innovative and effective strategies for starting off the major. The strategies found in this book will help educators examine issues related to teaching the introductory course or a careers course and develop a psychology-specific orientation program. Currently, the books available on this topic are written for a student, which is laudable, except that these books provide little guidance for teachers who are interested in developing a course or courses that familiarize students with opportunities that open up to them by majoring in psychology (e.g., Kuther, 2005; Landrum & Davis, 2006; Sternberg, 2007).

What about advice on how best to design courses for bringing closure to the major? Such courses include capstone experiences designed to fit the needs of a department, its pedagogical philosophy, or even the educational agenda of the larger institution wherein the department resides. Senior seminars, research-intensive experiences (for solo students or research teams), the history and systems course, or courses designed around applied/internship experiences fit here, too. In addition, many psychology programs are also focusing on the capstone course both as a culminating experience and as a primary venue for gathering assessment data on student achievement of learning outcomes. Despite the aforementioned interest in the topic, there are no books that address these issues in contemporary terms, and only a few articles do so (Ault & Multhaup, 2003; Gibson, Kahn, & Mathie, 1994; Sullivan & Thomas, 2007; Weis, 2004; Zechmeister & Reich, 1994).

We believe that our book fills these two resource voids quite well. We recruited well-regarded teachers of psychology with expertise in course development for both the beginnings and the endings in the psychology major. These authors approached their task with a practical purpose, writing chapters containing guidance, clear examples, and concrete suggestions for improving the teaching and learning activities at the start and finish of the psychology major. We are happy to report that our authors also made serious efforts to connect their teaching and pedagogy ideas to assessment initiatives, as is now routinely advocated in psychology education (e.g., Dunn, Mehrotra, & Halonen, 2004; Halonen et al., 2003; see also Dunn, McCarthy, Baker, Halonen, & Hill, 2007).

Our book has several outstanding features that will make it appealing for teachers of psychology. Chapters in this book discuss a variety of timely issues concerning the best way to begin and end a student's education in psychology at the undergraduate level, including

- *Orientation and advising.* The chapters offer thoughtful guidance regarding ways to help students becomes acclimated to the psychology major via advising and orientation courses.
- *Mentoring relationships.* We present ways to foster close ties between students and faculty at the start of college so that student learning about psychology can be deep and directed rather than superficial and haphazard.
- *Developmentally appropriate practices.* The writers discuss application of developmental knowledge (i.e., first-year students

are qualitatively different from sophomores, sophomores from juniors) to course design and pedagogical practice as important.

- *Learning communities.* We discuss the use of learning communities as a means to introduce psychology to interested students and potential majors.
- *Active learning exercises.* We provide effective practices and strategies for helping students become engaged by the discipline both in and outside the classroom.
- *Capstone opportunities and issues.* We present capstone experiences in psychology that reflect departmental philosophies, take into account resources, and play to teacher strengths.
- *Alternative capstone experiences.* Some authors introduce innovations to make stand-alone courses (e.g., history of psychology) or particular student experiences (e.g., participating in a research team, writing an honors thesis, doing a field project) fulfill the roles and needs of the capstone course.
- *Planning endings in the major.* We identify the advantages and common pitfalls associated with creating a final course experience in the curriculum.
- *Assessment.* Several chapters place emphasis on considering, collecting, and using assessable information when developing courses for the start and finish of students' education in psychology.
- *Future employment.* The chapters offer readers concrete advice on counseling psychology graduates about how to use what they have learned in course work in the workplace.
- *Scientific reasoning across the major.* A closing chapter encourages use of a rubric for scientific reasoning to improve beginning and ending experiences in the psychology major.

Who will benefit most from reading and using the strategies presented in this book? Our primary audience consists of college-level psychology teachers, department chairs or heads, and other psychology program administrators; this group wants to fine-tune its efforts at orienting students to their institution by helping them plan for their futures after graduation 4 years later (or after 2 years in the case of community colleges). This book will also draw colleagues who are interested in using pedagogically sound designs for capstone experiences and who want to assist students in understanding the interconnections of their course work; it will also attract those who want to assess student learning outcomes in the psychology major. High school teachers of psychology may find the ideas and issues presented in the book helpful when it comes to rethinking and redesigning aspects of their courses. We imagine some teachers in related social science disciplines, for example, in sociology, may also be interested in the book.

We believe that the ideas in this book will provide the basis for innovation in psychology departments in higher education. The suggestions that readers will see in this volume reflect the work of individuals and departments in the forefront of emerging ideas in the teaching of psychology. By following the guidance provided here, readers can benefit from the successes of psychology teachers across the country and use the information to guide the development of their own programs. As such, students everywhere will benefit from the zeal and commitment of the psychology teachers who help them begin and end their undergraduate psychology education.

References

Ault, R. L., & Multhaup, K. S. (2003). An issues-oriented capstone course. *Teaching of Psychology, 30,* 46–48.

Dunn, D. S., McCartney, M., Baker, S., Halonen, J. S., & Hill, G. W., IV. (2007). Quality benchmarks in undergraduate psychology programs. *American Psychologist, 62,* 650–670.

Dunn, D. S., Mehrotra, C., & Halonen, J. S. (Eds.) (2004). *Measuring Up: Educational Assessment Challenges and Practices for Psychology.* Washington, DC: American Psychological Association.

Gibson, P. R., Kahn, A. S., & Mathie, V. A. (1994). Undergraduate research groups: Two models. *Teaching of Psychology, 23,* 36–38.

Halpern, D. F. (2004). Outcomes assessment 101. In D. S. Dunn, C. M. Mehrotra, & J. S. Halonen (Eds.), *Measuring up: Educational assessment challenges and practices for psychology* (pp. 11–26). Washington, DC: American Psychological Association.

Halonen, J. S., Bosack, T., Clay, S., & McCarthy, M. (with Dunn, D. S., Hill, G. W., IV, McEntarfer, R., Mehrotra, C., Nesmith, R., Weaver, K., & Whitlock, K.). (2003). A rubric for authentically learning, teaching, and assessing scientific reasoning in psychology. *Teaching of Psychology, 30,* 196–208.

Kuther, T. L. (2005). *The psychology major's handbook.* Belmont, CA: Wadsworth.

Landrum, R. E., & Davis, S. F. (2006). *The psychology major: Career options and strategies for success* (3rd ed.). Upper Saddle River, NJ: Prentice-Hall.

Sternberg, R. J. (2007). *Career paths in psychology* (2nd ed.). Washington, DC: American Psychological Association.

Sullivan, B. F., & Thomas, S. L. (2007). Documenting student learning outcomes through a research-intensive senior capstone experience: Bring the data together to demonstrate progress. *North American Journal of Psychology, 9*, 321–330.

Weis, R. (2004). Using an undergraduate human-services practicum to promote unified psychology. *Teaching of Psychology, 31*, 43–46.

Zechmeister, E. B., & Reich, J. N. (1994). Teaching undergraduates about teaching undergraduates: A capstone course. *Teaching of Psychology, 21*, 24–28.

Acknowledgments

Collaborating can be a pleasure, especially when your collaborators are also your good friends and confidants. We four know each other well; we enjoy the all-too-rare times we are all together in one place, just as we genuinely like the frequent e-mails and occasional phone conversations about "the project." It helps, too, when you genuinely want to improve the teaching and learning process in our ever-growing discipline. All of us read and commented on the contributions found in this book. We are very pleased to have worked with such an array of committed teachers who, like ourselves, worry about conveying the maximum amount of advice and guidance in as few pages as possible. This is our first publishing venture with Oxford University Press and we hope that it will not be the last. Our editor, Abby Gross, has been helpful and given us the time to complete the project. During the production process, we were pleased to work with Suwathiga Velayutham. Finally, we thank those colleagues who reviewed our proposal: Elizabeth Yost Hammer, Robert Reeves, Peter Giordano, Bryan Saville, and Randolph Smith.

We are especially grateful to our friends and colleagues at Kennesaw State University's Department of Psychology and Kennesaw's renowned Center for Excellence in Teaching and Learning (CETL). KSU provides a wonderful place where serious teachers of psychology can meet and discuss current topics that advance the teaching, learning, and development of students as well as faculty.

We are also very thankful for the leadership of the Society for the Teaching of Psychology who, with the KSU, have developed and funded the many successful "Best Practices" conferences that led to this and earlier books on pedagogy in psychology. We also want to thank our friends at the National Institute for the Teaching of Psychology (NIToP), especially Doug Bernstein, for the generous support directed toward enhancing teaching and learning in psychology.

Without the love and support of his family—Sarah, Jake, and Hannah—Dana would accomplish little. He is grateful for the freedom and understanding they offer for his work. Moravian College provided Dana with the necessary resources to plan and complete this book, including a Faculty Development and Research Committee Stipend for Summer 2008. Maureen is grateful for the opportunity to work with some of the best colleagues in the teaching community—Dana, Barney, and Bill. Barney thanks his family—Linda, Agatha, and Simon—for the support they provide in ways they don't even know about and wants to point out that, without them, these endeavors would not matter nearly as much as they do. Bill is grateful for the support and encouragement of his friends and colleagues in the Society for the Teaching of Psychology, a community of dedicated teachers who have made a tremendous difference in the teaching of psychology.

Dana S. Dunn, Bethlehem, PA
Bernard C. Beins, Ithaca, NY
Maureen A. McCarthy, Kennesaw, GA
G. William Hill, IV, Kennesaw, GA

Best Practices for Teaching Beginnings and Endings in the Psychology Major

1 Undergraduate Education in Psychology

All's Well That Begins and Ends Well

Dana S. Dunn, Bernard C. Beins, Maureen A. McCarthy, and *G. William Hill, IV*

One of the editors of this volume recalls his first day at college. After moving into his dormitory and seeing his parents off, he wandered about the campus with his roommate. Shortly thereafter he experienced a nagging epiphany: He realized he had no idea where anything was on the campus and that he knew precious little about the university. He had accepted the offer of admission virtually sight unseen, deciding to matriculate there without having much sense of the institution's layout or physical plant, let alone its curriculum. Although he knew the school's reputation was quite good, what did he really know about the university before arriving? Had he made the right choice? What was he going to study as a first-year student? Was psychology the right major? If he pursued psychology (and he did), what lay ahead in the future? His experience, the soul-searching and the questions, is by no means unique.

Psychology is a popular major. Yet even after they declare a major, many students feel similarly adrift. Indeed, for many students, deciding to major in psychology is only half the battle. In the short term, they wonder what their choice will mean in terms of course selection: Are statistics and research methods really necessary? If I want to work with people, why does psychology demand so much research and writing? Across the next 3 or so years, they wonder how their choice of major will shape their future lives. Is graduate school necessary? What sorts of careers can and do psychology majors pursue? Will all of the discipline-related tools and skills be transferable from course and campus to office and field? These are important questions, and students need—deserve—helpful, educationally sound answers sooner rather than later.

For their part, psychology faculty members take their teaching responsibilities very seriously and they want to present the discipline as providing a wide variety of opportunities for interested and motivated majors. Yet psychology teachers often focus on presenting their specialty area in the context of one class (e.g., cognitive psychology, social psychology, industrial/organizational psychology) or a cluster of courses they regularly teach (e.g., infancy, childhood, adolescence). Unless they have an administrative role as a department chair or program director, they are less likely to consider the "big picture" of being a psychology major that students face. A key aspect of this big picture is creating coherence between beginnings and endings, that is, both the early work in the major and the critical last courses (Dunn et al., 2010). We and our author colleagues conceived this book to provide perspective on how to help students have a strong start in psychology as well as a balanced finish.

Why Best Practices for Beginnings and Endings in Psychology?

We developed the concept for this book to reflect and respond to important concerns raised by colleagues who routinely teach undergraduates: What can be done early in the psychology major to help students learn better as they progress through it? What can be done later in the major, prior to graduation, so that students have an opportunity to integrate and synthesize the discipline-based knowledge they have acquired? We viewed these and related questions as a call for considering developmentally appropriate activities that build upon one another, thereby informing teaching and learning from the beginning to the end of the psychology program. As our chapter title suggests, we believe that a good start predicts a great educational finish.

This handbook has three main sections. The first section deals with foundational issues in the psychology major, that is, "Beginnings," such as helping novice students become oriented to the psychology major and identifying the appropriate learning outcomes that will help them to succeed. Besides such traditional topics, newer ones, such as the advent of learning communities at many colleges and universities are also considered. The book's next section, "Endings," profiles various ways to properly close the learning experience in the major, such as different conceptions of capstone courses, gaining experience on a research team, or doing fieldwork. True closure from the college experience is also considered by way of helping undergraduates make the transition to the workplace. The third and final section of the book, "Coda," contains one chapter that offers a framework for helping students develop and refine their scientific reasoning skills over the course of their careers as psychology majors. We now consider the contents of each of these three sections in greater detail.

Beginnings

So-called millennial students pose particular challenges for higher education, particularly where academic support and intellectual guidance are concerned. Many faculty routinely comment on the lack of preparation they find in recent cohorts of students. Psychology students are no different from their peers: Some matriculate to college with a serious work ethic and concrete plans while others struggle with the foreign demands of higher education, self-reliance, and the pressures of planning for the future. Perhaps now more than ever, helping students start the psychology major by providing solid support and opportunities to seek guidance as they plan for their college years and beyond is a good idea. In this first section of the book, our contributors provide psychology teachers and program chairs with ideas about how best to familiarize students to the discipline and their institution's psychology curriculum.

Teaching introductory psychology is a challenge, especially now, when both textbooks on the topic and research in the discipline continue to grow almost exponentially. How can one course satisfy the demands of a general or liberal education course elective while still providing would-be majors with the information they need for upper level courses in the psychology department's curriculum? Michael Stoloff (James Madison University) discusses the particular demands introductory psychology teachers face and suggests some approaches for making the course a manageable and meaningful arena for student learning. Developing learning objectives, organizing the course material, and perhaps the biggest hurdle, effectively teaching first-year students, are key issues Stoloff considers. The practical guidance he offers will help novice and experienced teachers of this important beginning course improve the ways they structure and teach the course.

Introductory psychology is a foundational course, but how should psychology programs coordinate other "beginning" and "ending" experiences within the larger curriculum? A group of colleagues from Mansfield University—Brian Loher, Karri Verno, Francis W. Craig, and Peter A. Keller—focus on how best to integrate an orientation course and a capstone effort into a curriculum. The reasons for doing so are really twofold: New students often need firm guidance as they make the transition from high school to college or university life. A solid orientation to psychology as their chosen major can set them up for the rest of their work therein, creating realistic educational expectations in the process. As their undergraduate education winds down, an effective capstone experience can prepare them for the next phase of their lives, whether it is a subsequent transition to graduate education or a direct move into the world of work. As the authors suggest, the ideal circumstance is one in which psychology faculty agree with the precepts of the courses and plan accordingly so that orientation and capstone experiences, respectively, share important qualities no matter who is teaching the class.

Drew Appleby (Indiana University-Purdue University, Indianapolis) also believes that a good orientation can prepare students for the future—however, the future he focuses on is connected to career exploration in the context of an orientation to the psychology major course. Appleby describes an intriguing career exploration course designed to help junior- or senior-level psychology majors understand their choice of major, possible future careers, and themselves. How can such a broad set of goals be achieved in one course? Appleby cleverly devised an exercise in which students craft a book about themselves, their career aspirations, and the strategies they intend to use to achieve their goals in the future. The exercise is a terrific example of self-assessment, one that both motivates students and steers them toward thoughtful decisions regarding post-graduate life.

Creating an ideal orientation experience for undergraduates is also a primary concern for authors Brian Loher (Mansfield University) and Eric Landrum (Boise State University), the authors of chapter 5. Their main goal is to counter media-based images and myths about what psychologists do by providing accurate career information. To counter popular views, Loher and Landrum present some classroom exercises. They also provide some savvy advice on the administrative issues involved in launching and establishing an orientation course for first-year students interested in becoming psychology majors.

General orientation courses are designed to provide all students with a positive transition to the college experience. These interdisciplinary courses may also serve as an entry into the major. Regan Gurung (University of Wisconsin-Green Bay) and Georjeanna Wilson-Doenges (University of Wisconsin-Green Bay) describe a psychology-focused seminar course and data supporting first-year programs as beneficial to student engagement. They also offer specific recommendations for using first-year courses as an entry point for the major.

In the early 1990s learning communities, or cohort-based course scheduling, gained popularity in U.S. colleges and universities. A collaborative team, from two different schools, offer insights into their respective learning communities as an entry point for the psychology major. Kim Buch and Sue Spalding (University of North Carolina at Charlotte) describe a discipline-based, psychology learning community (PLC) and they provide data that offer support for retaining students. Kenneth Barron and Jeffery Andre (James Madison University) describe their residential discipline-based learning community. Together they offer interesting perspectives on how a learning community can serve as an entry point for the major and they suggest that the learning community may strengthen the capstone experience.

The APA Guidelines for the Undergraduate Major in Psychology stipulate that students graduating with a degree in psychology should possess information literacy skills. Charles Harris and Lynn Cameron (James Madison University) examine student approaches to obtaining information—specifically Wikipedia as a reputable resource. Their curricular approach provides students with skills for evaluating credibility of resources. They offer specific learning modules that can easily be used to strengthen information literacy.

Eric Goederis and Stanley Cohen provide specific recommendations for crafting an orientation to the major course. They describe the West Virginia University course—career exploration, career information, and program planning—as a vehicle for efficiently moving students through the major. The WVU model serves as a blueprint for programs that use a comprehensive psychology careers course as an entry point for the major.

Endings

Education in psychology is often like a funnel: Early academic experiences are broad, but as a student progresses through the major, the focus narrows and becomes more topically specialized. Should the expected outcome of an undergraduate education in psychology be represented by one or more specialized courses? Isn't such specialization best saved for graduate education in the discipline? The consensus of many teachers is that specialization is fine as long as the course work and skills acquired earlier in the major are brought together in some culminating intellectual experience. This and related philosophies accounts for the increasing appeal of so-called capstone courses. Knowledge acquired in the psychology major can be integrated into a meaningful academic experience in other ways besides a formal capstone course. Several authors in this section of the book suggest competing alternatives, including a history of psychology course, fieldwork, career courses, and research opportunities.

Dana Dunn (Moravian College) and Maureen McCarthy (Kennesaw State University) provide context for the endings section of this book. They provide a rationale for the capstone experience as an essential component of the undergraduate major in psychology. They also provide an overview of capstone courses that are typically offered by departments. Ultimately, Dunn and McCarthy provide the theoretical foundations for such a course and they conclude with recommendations for how the capstone can be used as a summative assessment of the major.

The history of psychology course represents one of the best ways for psychology programs to address the clear need for capstone experiences in the psychology major. On the other hand, the history course can also serve as a thoughtful, rich, and organizing framework for orienting students to the discipline. Ludy T. Benjamin, Jr. (Texas A&M University) gives a brief overview of the history course in psychology and then proceeds to offer a compelling rationale for teaching and treating the history course as either a starting or an ending point for undergraduate education in psychology. This course flexibility means that the history of psychology class may be an ideal way for departments to expand the intellectual rigor of their curricula while improving the breadth and depth of student learning in the major.

Bernard Beins (Ithaca College) and Phil Wann (Missouri Western State University) remind us that empirical research done in the context of controlled settings is what sets psychology apart from both the humanities and many of the other social sciences. Despite the fact that many undergraduate curricula are predicated on the idea that psychology is a science, not all departments or programs are able to offer students the opportunity to conduct an experimental research project from start to finish. There are many legitimate reasons that prevent departments from ensuring that all students perform some discipline-related empirical work. To address this problem, Beins and Wann provide detailed guidance for creating research teams within courses or departments. Besides exposing students to the rigors of psychological research, another benefit of the team approach is that faculty members can keep their methodological skills fresh even if their careers lead them to less-research intensive institutions.

Sherry Serdikoff (James Madison University) has documented the use of the senior thesis as the capstone experience for students. She describes the process that students undergo to create and complete an empirical research project and the outcomes that follow. Further, she points out that the senior thesis can provide information about the extent to which such a project fosters attainment of the goals and outcomes that a department has established.

Wayne Messer and David Porter (both of Berea College) also identify the capstone experience in their department as the culmination of the research focus that psychologists value. Half of the student experience in their psychology program involves research-based courses. As such, it seems fitting to apply the skills developed in such courses to demonstrate the students' proficiency as empiricists. In their chapter, they outline the benefits and goals associated with research as a capstone experience. Because offering this experience to all majors is time- and resource-intensive, they offer suggestions for dealing with common problems that occur in creating and conducting research. Finally, they provide a sense of student reactions as indicated in the undergraduates' reflections on the capstone experience.

One of the main reasons that capstone courses are not (yet) universal offerings is because they are by no means easy to develop or teach effectively. Three colleagues who teach at James Madison University—Tracy Zinn, Monica Reis-Bergan, and Suzanne Baker—adopt a tongue-in-cheek approach to the challenge of the capstone course. By reviewing some pressure points associated with teaching a capstone course in psychology, the three authors are able to offer helpful and considered solutions to the common pitfalls linked to this important course offering. Further, they counter the challenges posed by capstones by discussing several qualities they believe will make readers want to develop and teach this final course in the psychology major.

What are best methods for ensuring that students learn to write effectively and well? How should writing be taught in the variety of courses found in the typical psychology program's curriculum? Bernard Beins (Ithaca College), Randolph Smith (Lamar University), and Dana Dunn (Moravian College) discuss how writing assignments can vary depending upon whether a course is pitched to a beginning, intermediate, or advanced-level student. Besides the course level issues, these authors discuss different types of writing, revising and peer contributions, collaborative writing projects, and the place of teaching, learning, and using APA style.

Students spend a remarkable amount of time in classes, so much so that they may regard the classroom as their natural environment. However, as Joann Grayson (James Madison University) points out, students can gain a greater appreciation of what they learn in the classroom by leaving their version of the ivory tower and engaging in fieldwork. She has developed a capstone experience that takes students into the field so they can consolidate their theoretical knowledge with the complex, practical world. Grayson highlights the gains that students can make through fieldwork, along with the difficulties that she (and her students) has encountered in the creation and maintenance of fieldwork opportunities.

Paul Hettich (DePaul University) notes that the end of students' undergraduate education marks the beginning of a very different life, that of the workplace. Although students must work to develop their competence in the academic realm, they typically face very different expectations and circumstances after their college years. As Hettich points out, students are often unprepared for the new demands on their time and lives. He illustrates the importance of taking the initiative in the workplace; in their classes, students can succeed (although that may not be the best word) through a passive approach if they are good test takers. This example is only one of the issues that Hettich raises to differentiate college from career. He stresses how important it is for students to be aware of the changes they will face once they graduate. Their professors can play a major role in effecting a smooth transition.

What about those majors who decide to pursue graduate education immediately rather than entering the workforce after graduation? The authors of chapter 19—Brennan D. Cox, Kristin L. Cullen, William Buskist (all of Auburn University), and Victor A. Benassi (University of New Hampshire) offer useful guidance for them as well as their major advisors. As these chapter authors point out, most resources pertaining to graduate education in psychology focus on gaining admission. In contrast, this chapter focuses on the important, if often overlooked, transition from the end the psychology major to the new beginning in graduate school. How should budding graduate students approach their new experience after completing four years of undergraduate education in psychology? Cox and colleagues characterize the experience of graduate school so that academic advisors and mentors can help students keep their eyes—and minds—wide open to the challenges and opportunities of more focused study in the field.

To provide closure to closure, Neil Lutsky (Carleton College) harkens back to his introductory psychology class when he poses four claims: (a) we experience and navigate the world psychologically, (b) psychology can be studied scientifically, (c) we have much to gain from psychological science, and (d) Carleton College is a great school (which, he points out, is not merely a self-congratulatory assertion). By the time students finish their undergraduate education, it is useful to let them reflect on the four claims cited above. By looking at student opportunity, development, and attainment, one can encourage students to reflect on what they have gained, a fitting way to end, rather than merely to stop.

A Seamless Whole: Psychology as a Science

One idea that should appear throughout the undergraduate psychology curriculum is the simple fact that psychology is a science (cf., Dunn et al., 2010). Thus, the scientific method as a means to understand thought and behavior should appear with increasing depth and detail as students move from foundational to advanced offerings in the discipline. In this book's closing chapter, Suzanne Baker (James Madison University), Maureen McCarthy (Kennesaw State University), Jane Halonen (University of West Florida), Dana Dunn (Moravian College), and Bill Hill (Kennesaw State University) offer a framework for conceptualizing and organizing the scientific tools and techniques students learn across the three or so years they spend as psychology majors. By doing so, these authors highlight the differences in the habits of mind in psychology that students display at the beginning, middle, and toward the end of their undergraduate careers. Discussion of these differences will allow readers to adapt and adopt methods for improving instruction in psychology as a science at various points throughout the undergraduate major in psychology.

Continuity as Key: Linking Beginnings to Endings in Psychology

Too often we view the major as a collection of courses that comprise a curriculum in psychology. Although it is important to consider the breadth and depth of our curricular offerings (Dunn, McCarthy, Baker, Halonen, & Hill,

2007), less emphasis is placed on the coherent structure and sequence of the major. In this book we describe a variety of beginning courses that serve as a gateway to the major. We also provide a comprehensive set of capstone experiences. Together, the beginnings and endings offer the first step toward delivering an integrated educational experience.

References

Dunn, D. S., McCarthy, M., Baker, S., Halonen, J. S., & Hill, G. W., III. (2007). Quality benchmarks in undergraduate psychology programs. *American Psychologist, 62,* 650–670.

Dunn, D. S., Brewer, C. L., Cautin, R. L., Gurung, R. A., Keith, K. D., McGregor, L. N., Nida, S. A., Puccio, P., & Voight, M. J. (2010). The undergraduate psychology curriculum: A call for a core. In D. Halpern et al. (Eds.), *Undergraduate education in psychology: A blueprint for the future of the discipline* (pp. 47–51). Washington, DC: American Psychological Association.

Part I

Beginnings

2 Addressing the Multiple Demands of Teaching Introductory Psychology

Michael L. Stoloff

Introductory psychology is one of the most difficult courses in the psychology curriculum to teach in a manner that is effective for all enrolled students. For psychology majors, the course needs to help them develop a conceptual framework that can serve as a solid foundation for later learning in future courses. What is the most effective way to introduce the discipline of psychology to psychology majors? This chapter will identify the special demands of teaching introductory psychology and will provide tips on how to orchestrate successful learning.

Virtually every college offers introductory psychology (Pearlman & McCann, 1999), and many students take this course in high school (Ernst & Petrossian, 1996). Introductory psychology is required for the psychology major at 98% of colleges in North America, and it is a prerequisite to all other required courses at 82% of them (Stoloff et al., 2010). However, most of the students enrolled in this class are not psychology majors. Instead, students take introductory psychology to fulfill requirements of general education and other majors. Many students take it as an elective that they anticipate will be easier or more interesting than alternatives (Miller & Gentile, 1998). Introductory psychology needs to serve all enrolled students equally well by being both the foundation upon which all knowledge of psychology is built and as a student's only formal college experience in the discipline.

Misconceptions About Psychology

Introductory psychology students expect this course to focus on the topics covered on television talk shows. They often expect the primary emphasis to be on "self-help" topics such as dealing with social relationships, raising children, and the treatment of mental disorders. Students rarely expect a tremendous focus on fundamentals such as the biological basis of behavior, sensation, perception, cognition, learning, and empirical methods. They do not expect psychology to be a science. Students expect the information conveyed in their psychology class to be consistent with common knowledge and common sense, and therefore easy. Many students believe they have a sound grasp of the causes of various behavioral phenomena (Bernstein, 1997; Pittenger, 2006), and for behaviors they do not understand, they expect psychologists to have the answers.

But "introductory" does not mean easy; it means broad in coverage and designed for students without prior experience. Our science often discovers that people do not typically behave in ways that common knowledge and common sense predict. Many students are concrete thinkers and they have difficulty dealing with ambiguity (Halonen et al., 2003). In other words, they expect to learn the correct answer and students may not cope well with contradictory data and unresolved issues. Other students are slow to accept one perspective over another. Thus, fundamental differences in cognitive development among late adolescents present a challenge to the introductory psychology instructor (McKeachie & Svinicki, 2006).

Introductory psychology instructors need to explain what the field of psychological science is really all about. Students do not need to necessarily adopt the psychologist's perspective, but they need to understand and appreciate our way of knowing about the world. Students need to challenge their beliefs, begin to understand how those beliefs were formed, and understand what information can be used to inform and change beliefs. Psychology classes should not oversimplify; information needs to be presented realistically even when findings are ambiguous and do not lead to clear conclusions. Students should be changed as a result of having taken this course, but do not expect them to change dramatically. The empirical data suggest that measurable change can occur during introductory psychology courses, but gains are likely to be very small (Gutman, 1979; McKeachie, 1950) even after direct discussion of material that contradicts prior beliefs (Vaughan, 1977).

Learning Objectives for Introductory Psychology

What should students who complete introductory psychology learn from the overall experience? Many have written about the goals of this course (Brewer, 1993; Halonen et al., 2003; Matlin, 1997; McInish & Coffman, 1970; McKeachie & Svinicki, 2006; Smith & Fineburg, 2006; Sternberg, 1997; Walker & McKeachie, 1967; Zimbardo, 1997). Most suggest that the goals should include helping students to

1. Master a wide range of theoretical and applied psychology topics, findings, theories, and concepts.
2. Appreciate why psychology is interesting and relevant.
3. Think like psychologists about behavior, using scientific, creative, and practical approaches to answer questions and test hypotheses.
4. Master the ability to use empirical evidence to judge the truth, understand that naming is not explaining, distinguish between facts and inferences drawn from facts, become a critical consumer of new information distinguishing between reasonable and unreasonable evidence upon which generalizations are based.
5. Recognize how one's own biases and values impact perception and action, becoming more objective when interpreting the behavior of others and more tolerant of individual and group differences, embracing the richness of human diversity.

Introductory psychology objectives are similar to the goals of the psychology major and many of the objectives of the liberal arts curriculum, especially with respect to higher level thinking necessary to fulfill the last two objectives listed above.

Helping students master the fundamental psychology topics is a goal for the introductory course, but which topics are fundamental? If you look at the chapters in introductory psychology textbooks there appears to be substantial agreement about the topics that are included in this course. Introductory psychology is generally organized into 16 to 19 chapters in most texts (Griggs, Jackson, Christopher, & Marek, 1999), and there is broad agreement among instructors regarding the content areas that should be included (Miller & Gentile, 1998). However, examination of textbook glossaries shows that there is only marginal agreement about which details are fundamental; only

2.5% to 5% of glossary terms are common to most books (Griggs, Bujak-Johnson, & Proctor, 2004; Landrum, 1993; Narin, Ellard, Scialfa, & Miller, 2003; Quereshi, 1993; Zechmeister & Zechmeister, 2000). When instructors rated the importance of 2,505 terms on a 5-point scale, only 5.8% received mean ratings of 4.5 or above (Zechmeister & Zechmeister, 2000).

Introductory textbooks are encyclopedic rather than focusing on the information that textbook authors feel is most essential. According to Kalat (2002), whenever he tried to deemphasize topics in his introductory psychology text, potential adopters accused him of dumbing down the book, and his response was to retain the content. As a result, instructors must identify the most important content. Bernstein (1997) suggested that introductory psychology instructors should consider themselves to be like museum guides. Knowing that visitors will not have the time to explore everything in detail, museum guides design their tours to encourage future visits and bring good reviews. The role of the instructor is to introduce psychology in a way that students are likely to enjoy, appreciate, and understand. Help students learn as much psychology as they have time for. There may be some fundamental topics that should be covered in every introductory psychology course (e.g., the brain), but it is probably more important to select fewer topics and cover some of them in greater depth.

Engaging students in a scientific inquiry about psychological processes was the top goal for introductory psychology listed by faculty in a study of 490 institutions (Miller & Gentile, 1998). Rather than simply accumulating facts, students need to think deeply about that content. What does it mean to think deeply? When establishing educational objectives, many authors refer to Bloom's Taxonomy (Anderson et al., 2001), a system that classifies educational objectives in terms of two dimensions: Knowledge and Cognitive Processes. From simplest to most complex, the knowledge domain includes

1. Factual knowledge (terminology, elements, and details)
2. Conceptual knowledge (interrelationships between the basic elements within a larger structure that enables them to function together)
3. Procedural knowledge (how to do things, methods of inquiry, skills, and techniques)
4. Metacognitive knowledge (awareness and knowledge of one's own cognition and knowing how we know, learn, or remember)

Within the cognitive process dimension, from simple to complex, students should be able to

1. Remember (recognize and recall)
2. Understand (interpret, classify, summarize, infer, compare, and explain)
3. Apply (execute and implement)
4. Analyze (differentiate, organize, and attribute)
5. Evaluate (check, critique, and judge)
6. Create (generate, plan, and produce)

Although it will be unrealistic to expect students to have a high level of achievement in both dimensions as a result of a single introductory course, it would be a mistake to design a course that focuses exclusively on only the lowest levels.

How Do You Organize Your Course?

How do you design a course that meets the full range of educational objectives for introductory psychology? A broad range of pedagogical techniques is available (e.g., Dunn & Chew, 2006). Select an array of activities that support the objectives you adopt for your class. Given that preferred learning style varies among students and different approaches better address various learning objectives, include a variety of techniques.

Lecturing is by far the modal instructional approach. For skilled instructors this method can be an effective way of presenting course content. When selecting the subject matter for each class, identify the primary purposes of discussing that content, and address those purposes in your presentation. Focus on a few key issues and cover them in some depth (Benjamin, 2002). Organize each class around a central idea. Set up your class with an issue, and then organize your class around a discussion of that issue (Benjamin, 2002; Gray, 1997). For example, consider why we discuss brain structure and function in introductory psychology. I believe it is because we see the brain as the system that creates perception, cognition, emotion, and behavior, and therefore provides an important foundation for virtually every topic covered in this course. For the neuroscience unit, a possible organizing theme might be "What happens to a person if his or her brain is damaged?" Use this theme throughout the unit to help students understand why it is important to remember the details. Students may not remember all the brain structure-function relationships that are described during this unit, but they will remember what neuroscience brings to our understanding of behavior.

Pascarella and Terenzini (2005) concluded that instructional methods that emphasize small, modularized units of content, mastery of one unit before moving to the next, timely and frequent feedback to students, and active learning processes are very effective. Recall, recognition, and self-perceived learning are enhanced when teachers (a) structure and organize class time well, (b) are clear and unambiguous in their explanation of concepts, (c) have good command of the subject matter and are expressive and enthusiastic in its presentation, and (d) have good rapport with students and are accessible outside of class.

McKeachie and Svinicki (2006) suggested that to lecture in a way that can improve students' thinking quality, (a) be explicit about your goal of helping students improve their thinking and explicitly discuss Bloom's taxonomy, (b) think out loud to model higher level thinking and provide students with opportunities to recognize good thinking, (c) do not answer every question yourself, (d) show excitement for higher level thinking even if it produces only partial answers or new questions, and (e) acknowledge and reward examples of good thinking by students. For an excellent discussion of effective lecturing see chapter 2 in Forsyth (2003).

Approximately 98% of introductory psychology courses require students to purchase a textbook (Miller & Gentile, 1998), and faculty should expect students to learn many things from reading their book. Books vary in terminology, detailed content focus, level of difficulty, and number and type of pedagogical aids (Griggs, 1999; Griggs & Marek, 2001). Select a textbook that complements your focus and includes pedagogical aids you feel will be effective. Use class time to discuss how these tools should be used.

Classes should encourage students to actively process information in new and personally relevant ways, and help students to construct their own understanding. Pascarella and Terenzini (2005) reviewed the literature on effective learning strategies, and their analysis makes clear that many innovative pedagogical approaches can be effective. Effective approaches include active learning; learning for mastery; computer-assisted instruction; collaborative, cooperative, and small-group learning; and constructivist-oriented approaches such as problem-based learning. Interpretation of studies that demonstrate the effectiveness of particular strategies is difficult because instructors who are testing these new methods are excited about their innovative strategies. Enthusiasm, and a match between the instructors' dispositions, skills, and strategy might contribute significantly to the effectiveness of the approach. I believe that introductory psychology instructors should pick strategies that match their personality and skills, that they will enjoy implementing, and these are likely to be effective.

Teaching strategies constitute only one component of the larger introductory experience. To determine whether we are successful in introducing the discipline of psychology to majors and nonmajors we must assess student performance. Many assessment options are available including multiple choice, short answer, and essay exams; journals; reflection and application papers; literature reviews; research reports; laboratory exercises; presentations; participation; and attendance. What types of assessment should you include? Treat assessment as not only a method for determining grades but also as an opportunity for students to engage with course material, a chance for you to clarify what is important, and an opportunity for you to receive feedback about the pacing of the course (McKeachie & Svinicki, 2006). The relative weight of an assessment, with respect to the determination of final grades, should be proportional to the importance of that activity in your course. In classes with large enrollments, practical considerations may limit your options; however, even if you rely heavily on machine-graded multiple-choice examinations, you can still design questions that encourage higher level thinking. As suggested by Bernstein (1997), rather than asking "Which of the following substances is not a neurotransmitter?" consider asking "Leshon has been severely depressed lately. According to the biological approach to psychopathology, which of the following neurotransmitters is most likely to be involved in his disorder?"

The Challenge of Teaching Freshmen

Introductory psychology will be among the first college courses taken by many students, many of whom are unprepared for college. Some students possess poor reading or quantitative reasoning skills. They may not have previously experienced the level of academic challenge required in college and they are likely to be overwhelmed by large classes and instructors who do not monitor their daily behavior. In the past, students may have often felt that they are in charge, and they might be shocked by limitations imposed on them by college teachers. Students may have received exclusively positive feedback throughout their lives and may believe that you are wrong if you suggest that their work needs improvement. They have long fantasized about going to college and they completed a competitive process to be admitted; many will now be anxious about whether they will succeed. Students may also have competing motivations and poor time-management skills exacerbated by a lack of daily parental control. They may miss many classes, fail to prepare for class in advance, be inattentive during class, and fail to take useful notes; they may not read the textbook at all or they may wait until the last possible moment. They might surprise you by unexpectedly responding with anger, hostility, or discouragement in response to class activities, or they might be sensitive when selected topics are discussed. Some may have psychological disorders that are not under stable control.

Little work outside of the classroom is necessary for high school students to be successful. The typical high school student spends 6 hours a weekday on school work (U.S. Department of Labor, 2006), including about 1 hour a day on homework (Gill & Schlossman, 2003; Porterfield & Winkler, 2007), and the student does not recognize the importance of homework for academic success (Warton, 2001). College freshmen do not realize that to achieve the same level of success they had in high school, in addition to going to class, they need to spend much more time completing homework. The average college student spends only 3.2 hours a day on all educational activities (U.S. Department of Labor, 2006). Many students feel that textbooks are not necessary; those who purchase them use them infrequently, perceiving that studying class notes and attending lectures is more important than reading the text to get a good grade (Sikorski et al., 2002). On average, introductory psychology students read 27% of the assigned readings before class and 66% before an exam (Clump, Bauer, & Bradley, 2004). Typically they spend less than 3 hours a week reading their textbook, and most reading begins only 3 days prior to the exam (Sikorski et al., 2002).

Instructors need to make their expectations clear. Don't let your students set the difficulty level of your class. Expect students to face the challenge of meeting your high standards. But also make your expectations clear. College students need to understand that learning requires more activity from the learner than the teacher. Spending time discussing study skills is not a waste of valuable class time. An effective class will help students understand what they need to do to be successful not only in introductory psychology but also in all the college classes that will follow.

How Do You Motivate Students to Put in a Good Effort?

Students attend college for many reasons and only one of these reasons is to learn from course experiences. How do you get students to come to class, complete assignments, and study? How do you motivate them to put in their best effort when there are so many other exciting and immediately rewarding alternate activities competing for their attention? Here are my suggestions (based primarily on McKeachie & Svinicki, 2006):

1. Recognize students' need for self-determination and autonomy. Give students some control over which assignments they will complete and/or the time periods in which they must work most intensely.
2. Foster intrinsic motivation by arousing curiosity and providing challenge. Take time to describe your own intrinsic motivation for the subject matter. Model motivation for students by being well prepared for every class.
3. Make the value of your course explicit. Take time to help students understand why what they are learning matters.
4. Students will work for points, so design your evaluation scheme to give students points for what you most want them to accomplish. Let them know how they can earn more points in advance, so that this can be an incentive to put in the effort. (For an example, see Marchant, 2002).
5. Create conditions that enable all students to expect to succeed. Adopt a criterion-referenced approach to grading rather than a normative one. Foster mastery by encouraging students to revise their writing. Test frequently to give students the opportunity to become accustomed to your format and learn from their mistakes. Consider dropping questions missed by most students, and reteach that material.

The Challenge of Class Size

The number of students enrolled in introductory psychology classes is typically larger than the enrollment in more advanced classes. There is some evidence that students learn better in smaller classes than larger ones; however, this finding may depend on the primary goals of the class (Pascarella & Terenzini, 2005). The challenge of a large class can be overcome with effective pedagogy, but discovering the methods that are effective creates a challenge for instructors.

Especially in larger classes, to maintain student attention, instructors must be interesting and entertaining. An occasional surprise, use of humor, and statements charged with emotion help sustain interest. Precise communication is essential because each individual student can ask only a few questions. Imprecise or incorrect assignment instructions can have catastrophic consequences for an instructor because this can trigger a flood of questions when students attempt the assignment. The time required to grade assignments can limit the range of activities that can be included in a large class. However, large classes also provide some unique opportunities. For example, in a large class it is possible to collect anonymous data about sensitive issues such as the prevalence of symptoms of mental disorders, sexual preferences, or substance use. Rare events are likely to be represented in samples. College students are very interested in themselves, so by including data collected in class surveys, you can make many topics instantly fascinating.

Dealing With Academic Dishonesty

Although over 90% of students report that it is wrong to cheat, 76% of students report that they cheated in high school, college, or both (Davis, Grover, Becker, & McGregor, 1992). About half of all students admit that they have cheated in college and 25% admit doing so more than once (Davis & Ludvigson, 1995). Students say they cheat because of intense academic and family pressures, societal expectations, desire to excel, pressure to get high grades, pressure of getting a good job or acceptance into graduate school, high levels of stress, competitive environments, laziness, lack of preparation, and apathy (McCabe, Trevino, & Butterfield, 1999). Cheating is especially a problem in larger classes and those that rely heavily on multiple-choice exams, and therefore is likely to be a problem in many introductory psychology classes.

What can instructors do to reduce cheating and promote the learning process in their classes? Start by caring about whether students are cheating. Students want you to care (Davis, Grover, Becker, & McGregor, 1992). Remind students of your college's honor code, and even if your school does not have one, institute one within your own class. Incorporate a discussion of ethics into your class (Handelsman, 2006). When it is unclear whether a particular activity is cheating, many students take advantage (McCabe, Trevino, & Butterfield, 1999). For example, collaboration may be essential for group activities, but instructors may expect other assignments in the same class to be completed individually. Clarify your expectations for each assignment. Help students understand the value of learning rather than focusing on grades. Encourage the development of good character by being supportive, respectful, consistent, and fair when dealing with students—but also punish cheating. For additional suggestions about reducing cheating, see McCabe, Trevino, & Butterfield (2001).

Conclusions

All college courses are difficult to teach well, but after considering all of the issues discussed in this chapter, it may be clear that introductory psychology is among the most challenging. To teach it competently, instructors need to be proficient in all domains of psychology. How do instructors acquire the range of knowledge necessary to explain complex concepts, theories, and research; put content into proper context; and competently answer questions on virtually any topic? Graduate programs typically focus on specialty areas, so introductory psychology instructors must work hard to become generalists. Given the unique challenges of this course, is it logical that introductory psychology is often a new instructor's first teaching assignment? Explicit training in college teaching can certainly help address this concern (Forsyth, 2003).

The course clearly presents challenges, but when overcome, introductory psychology can be an important contributor to the overall college experience for all enrolled students. A course is successful if students completing the course do the following:

1. Demonstrate mastery of the instructor's curriculum objectives.
2. Complete the course feeling that they have learned something.
3. Appreciate that psychology can help us understand our world, improve the quality of life of individuals, and contribute to society.
4. Be able to produce examples of how some things that they learned during the course have impacted, or may impact, their personal and professional lives.

5. Make decisions about future directions as a result of the course (including choosing to take additional psychology courses, major in psychology, or not major in psychology).

Recommended Readings

Forsyth, D. R. (2003). *The professor's guide to teaching: Psychological principles and practices*. Washington, DC: American Psychological Association.

McKeachie, W. J., & Svinicki, M. (2006). *McKeachie's teaching tips: Strategies, research, and theory for college and university teachers* (12th ed.). Boston, MA: Houghton Mifflin.

Sternberg, R. J. (1997). *Teaching introductory psychology: Survival tips from the experts*. Washington, DC: American Psychological Association.

References

Anderson, L. W., Krathwohl, D. R., Airasian, P. W., Cruikshank, K. A., Mayer, R. E., Pintrich, P. R., et al. (2001). *A taxonomy for learning, teaching and assessing: A revision of Bloom's taxonomy of educational objectives*. New York: Longman.

Benjamin, L. T. (2002) Lecturing. In S. F. Davis & W. Buskist (Eds.), *The teaching of psychology: Essays in honor of Wilbert J. McKeachie and Charles L. Brewer* (pp. 361–368). Mahwah, NJ: Erlbaum.

Bernstein, D. A. (1997). Reflections on teaching introductory psychology. In R. J. Sternberg (Ed.), *Teaching introductory psychology: Survival tips from the experts* (pp. 35–47). Washington, DC: American Psychological Association.

Brewer, C. L. (1993). Curriculum. In T. V. McGovern (Ed.), *Handbook for enhancing undergraduate education in psychology* (pp. 161–182). Washington, DC: American Psychological Association.

Clump, M. A., Bauer, H., & Bradley, C. (2004). The extent to which psychology students read textbooks: A multiple class analysis of reading across the psychology curriculum. *Journal of Instructional Psychology, 31*, 227–232.

Davis, S. F., Grover, C. A., Becker, A. H., & McGregor, L. N. (1992). Academic dishonesty: Prevalence, determinants, techniques, and punishments. *Teaching of Psychology, 19*, 16–20.

Davis, S. F., & Ludvigson, H. W. (1995). Additional data on academic dishonesty and a proposal for remediation. *Teaching of Psychology, 22*, 119–121.

Dunn, D. S., & Chew, S. L. (Eds.). (2006). *Best practices in teaching introductory psychology*. Mahwah, NJ: Erlbaum.

Ernst, R., & Petrossian, P. (1996). Teachers of psychology in secondary schools (TOPSS): Aiming for excellence in high school psychology instruction. *American Psychologist, 51,* 256–258.

Forsyth, D. R. (2003). *The professor's guide to teaching: Psychological principles and practices.* Washington, DC: American Psychological Association.

Gill, B. P., & Schlossman, S. L. (2003). "A nation at rest:" The American way of homework. *Educational Evaluation and Policy Analysis, 25,* 319–337.

Gray, P. (1997). Teaching as a scholarly activity: The idea-centered approach to Introductory Psychology. In R. J. Sternberg (Ed.), *Teaching introductory psychology: Survival tips from the experts* (pp. 49–64). Washington, DC: American Psychological Association.

Griggs, R. A. (1999). Introductory psychology textbooks: Assessing levels of difficulty. *Teaching of Psychology, 26,* 248–253.

Griggs, R. A., Bujak-Johnson, A., & Proctor, D. L. (2004). Using a common core vocabulary in text selection and teaching the introductory course. *Teaching of Psychology, 31,* 265–269.

Griggs, R. A., Jackson, S. L., Christopher, A. N., & Marek, P. (1999). Introductory psychology textbooks: An objective analysis and update. *Teaching of Psychology, 26,* 182–189.

Griggs, R. A., & Marek, P. (2001). Similarity of introductory psychology textbooks: Reality or illusion? *Teaching of Psychology, 28,* 254–256.

Gutman, A. (1979). Misconceptions of psychology and performance in the introductory course. *Teaching of Psychology, 6,* 159–161.

Halonen, J. S., Bosack, T., Clay, S., & McCarthy, M. (with Dunn, D. S., Hill, G. W. IV, McEntarfer, R., Mehrotra, C., Nesmith, R., Weaver, K., & Whitlock, K.). (2003). A rubric for authentically learning, teaching, and assessing scientific reasoning in psychology. *Teaching of Psychology, 30,* 196–208.

Handelsman, M. M. (2006). Teaching ethics in introductory psychology. In D. S. Dunn & S. L. Chew (Eds.), *Best practices for teaching introduction to psychology* (pp. 159–175. Mahwah, NJ: Erlbaum.

Kalat, J. W. (2002). Teaching biological psychology to introductory psychology students. In S. F. Davis & W. Buskist (Eds.), *The teaching of psychology: Essays in honor of Wilbert J. McKeachie and Charles L. Brewer* (pp. 361–368). Mahwah, NJ: Erlbaum.

Landrum, R. E. (1993). Identifying core concepts in introductory psychology. *Psychological Reports, 72,* 659–666.

Marchant, G. (2002). Student reading of assigned articles: Will this be on the test? *Teaching of Psychology, 29,* 49–51.

Matlin, M. W. (1997). Distilling psychology into 700 pages: Some goals for writing an introductory psychology textbook. In R. J. Sternberg (Ed.), *Teaching introductory psychology: survival tips from the experts* (pp. 73–90). Washington, DC: American Psychological Association.

McCabe, D. L., Trevino, L. K., & Butterfield, K. D. (1999). Academic integrity in honor code and non-honor code environments: A qualitative investigation. *Journal of Higher Education, 70,* 211–234.

McCabe, D. L., Trevino, L. K., & Butterfield, K. D. (2001). Cheating in academic institutions: A decade of research. *Ethics and Behavior, 11,* 219–232.

McInish, J. R., & Coffman, B. (1970) *Evaluating the introductory psychology course.* Reading, MA: Addison-Wesley.

McKeachie, W. J. (1950). Changes in scores on the Northwestern Misconceptions Test in six elementary psychology courses. *Journal of Educational Psychology, 51,* 240–244.

McKeachie, W. J., & Svinicki, M. (2006). *McKeachie's teaching tips: Strategies, research, and theory for college and university teachers* (12th ed.). Boston, MA: Houghton Mifflin.

Miller, B., & Gentile, B. F. (1998). Introductory course content and goals. *Teaching of Psychology, 25,* 89–96.

Narin, S. L., Ellard, J. H., Scialfa, C. T., & Miller, C. D. (2003). At the core of introductory psychology: A content analysis. *Canadian Psychology, 44,* 93–99.

Pascarella, E. T., & Terenzini, P. T. (2005). *How college affects students: A third decade of research* (2nd ed.). San Francisco, CA: Jossey-Bass.

Pearlman, B., & McCann, L. I. (1999). The most frequently listed courses in the undergraduate psychology curriculum. *Teaching of Psychology, 26,* 177–182.

Porterfield, S. L., & Winkler, A. E. (May, 2007). Teen time use and parental education: Evidence from the CPS, MTF, and ATUS. *Monthly Labor Review,* 37–56.

Pittenger, D. J. (2006). Teaching psychology when everyone is an expert. In W. Buskist & S. F. Davis (Eds.), *Handbook of the teaching of psychology* (pp. 181–185). Boston, MA: Blackwell.

Quereshi, M. Y. (1993). The contents of introductory psychology textbooks: A follow-up. *Teaching of Psychology, 20,* 218–222.

Sikorski, J. F., Rich, K., Savile, B. K., Buskist, W., Drogan, O., & Davis, S. F. (2002). Student use of introductory texts: Comparative survey findings from two universities. *Teaching of Psychology, 29,* 312–313.

Smith, R. A., & Fineburg, A. C. (2006). Standards and outcomes: Encouraging best practices in teaching introductory psychology. In D. S. Dunn & S. L. Chew (Eds.), *Best practices for teaching introduction to psychology* (pp. 170–194). Mahwah, NJ: Erlbaum.

Sternberg, R. J. (1997). Teaching students to think as psychologists. In R. J. Sternberg (Ed.), *Teaching introductory psychology: Survival tips from the experts* (pp. 137–149). Washington, DC: American Psychological Association.

Stoloff, M. L., McCarthy, M., Keller, L., Varfolomeeva, V., Lynch, J., Makara, K., Simmons, S., & Smiley, W. (2010). The undergraduate psychology major curriculum: An examination of structure and sequence. *Teaching of Psychology.*

U.S. Department of Labor, Bureau of Labor Statistics. (2006). *American time use survey.* Retrieved July 7, 2008, from: http://www.bls.gov/tus/charts/students.htm.

Vaughan, E. D. (1977). Misconceptions about psychology among introductory students. *Teaching of Psychology, 4,* 138–141.

Walker, E. L., & McKeachie, W. L. (1967). *Some thoughts about teaching the beginning course in psychology.* Belmont, CA: Brooks/Cole.

Warton, P. W. (2001). The forgotten voices in homework: Views of students. *Educational Psychologist, 36,* 155–165.

Zechmeister, J. S., & Zechmeister, E. B. (2000). Introductory textbooks and psychology's core concepts. *Teaching of Psychology, 27,* 6–11.

Zimbardo, P. G. (1997). A passion for psychology: Teaching it charismatically, integrating teaching and research synergistically, and writing about it engagingly. In R. J. Sternberg (Ed.), *Teaching introductory psychology: Survival tips from the experts* (pp. 7–34). Washington, DC: American Psychological Association.

3 Reading From the Same Page

Building an Integrated Curriculum

Brian T. Loher, Karri B. Verno, Francis W. Craig, and *Peter A. Keller*

Managing transitions and creating realistic expectations are important objectives in many settings, including higher education (Fouad & Bynner, 2008; Nicholson, 1984). Orientation and capstone courses are consistent with these objectives. Orientation courses help new psychology majors to manage the transition into an undergraduate program and learn about the expectations in their department and field of study. Capstone experiences often include content to help participants successfully negotiate the transition to the workforce or graduate school.

To increase their effectiveness, orientation and capstone courses should not stand in isolation (McCarthy, 2008). Coordination of beginning and ending courses with program content, field experiences, and advising provides opportunities to consistently emphasize connections between program and participant goals. The purpose of this chapter is to describe our ongoing efforts at Mansfield University to build an integrated undergraduate curriculum that maintains a common core while responding to students' growing expectations for a customized educational experience.

Case Example

Mansfield University is a public university located in north-central Pennsylvania with approximately 3,300 students. The psychology department has eight tenure-track faculty positions. For the spring 2008 semester there were 154 undergraduate psychology majors spread across five concentrations (General, Counseling, Life Span Development, Mind/Body Health, and Human Resource Management [HRM]). Students come from across Pennsylvania and bordering states and include a small but growing cadre of international students. Part of Mansfield's mission is to provide access to higher education for our rural region of Pennsylvania. Roughly two-thirds of our majors enter the workforce upon receipt of their undergraduate degrees. The remaining students typically apply to master's-level programs in psychology, education, or HRM. As a department, we design and deliver courses and programs that are challenging but also realistic in terms of the abilities, skill levels, and interests of this student population.

During the early 1990s, our department began to develop and implement orientation and senior seminar courses (e.g., Launius, Loher, & Keller, 1995), complemented by a strategic planning process. A subsequent challenge has been the coordination of expectations and content in between these two "bookends." An integral part of this process was a commitment to ongoing assessment for the purpose of program improvement (Keller, Loher, Launius, Craig, & Cooledge, 2002; Loher, Keller, Craig, Launius, & Murray, 2007). We identified learning goals relevant to the undergraduate psychology major (e.g., McGovern, Furumoto, Halpern, Kimble, & McKeachie, 1991), and specified the courses in which artifacts for each goal would be generated. Our current goals include all of the expected competencies for undergraduate psychology programs from the American Psychological Association (APA, 2007) plus local goals of (a) understanding the language of the discipline, (b) knowing legal regulation of HRM and psychological services, and (c) participating in civic engagement and community service.

We begin by reviewing the primary objectives and content examples from the Orientation and Senior Seminar classes, and then we describe changes that have occurred in the Orientation and Senior Seminar classes over the last 5 years. We briefly review the objectives for two courses that have become key steps between the beginning and ending classes. The chapter concludes with a discussion of critical programmatic issues that have arisen over time and our responses to those issues.

The Bookends: Orientation Course and Senior Seminar
Orientation Course

Our orientation course began as a one-credit-hour class focused around a series of invited speakers. In spring 1991, it began the transition to a more structured experience targeting development of skills for student success within the undergraduate psychology program. Initiation of the psychology department student portfolio in the orientation course first occurred in spring 1995. The class increased to three credit hours in fall 1996 as its objectives and content continued to expand. At present, we offer three, 25-seat sections of the course per academic year (two in the fall semester and one in the spring semester). The class is intended to be as low stress as possible and the instructor grades all assignments on a pass/no pass basis, with students having an opportunity to revise most exercises. To generate the student's course grade the instructor sums the number of passed assignments and compares the total to an a priori grading scale. With these contingencies, final grades usually range from "A" to "F" and historically about 30% of the incoming students decide to leave the psychology major during or shortly after taking the orientation course.

Objectives. There are five major objectives for the orientation course:

1. Provide exposure to realistic information about the competencies and experiences required for psychology-related careers, including graduate school.
2. Introduce American Psychological Association paper formats, writing style requirements (APA, 2001), and research literature search tools.
3. Expose students to the APA Ethical Principles and Code of Conduct (APA, 2002).
4. Review and respond to questions about university and psychology department policies and procedures.
5. Begin development of a psychology department portfolio and measure baseline skills for program assessment.

Sample content. The spring 2008 version of the orientation course includes 25 assignments consistent with the course's objectives. For the first objective, the goal in the orientation class is to guide students to accurate information about psychology-related careers. We use specific information about a real psychology-related job to focus a student's choices and actions during time in the psychology program. Several exercises used in this process appear else-where (see Loher & Landrum, Chapter 5 of this volume).

Several interconnected exercises target the second objective regarding research search tools, APA paper formats, and writing style requirements. To illustrate, an exercise using EBSCOhost to search for empirical articles in the

PsycINFO database is in Appendix 3A. We use output from the assignment in a subsequent exercise to generate an APA-style reference list. We also use the list of articles in a visit to the periodicals room and book stacks to give students practice on how to find hard copies of articles or books in the main library.

Rather than lecture about the APA Ethical Principles and Code of Conduct (2002), we break students into groups to argue an ethics case for the third objective. For example, participants read a case about a student client who made a threat to commit suicide during a counseling session conducted by a predoctoral intern (see APA, 1987, p. 68). The supervising psychologist subsequently decided to contact the client's parents, which led to an involuntary hospitalization. The client filed a complaint alleging a breach of confidentiality. For the exercise, one group serves as "prosecutor," a second as the defense, and the third acts as the Ethics Panel. Students develop their arguments, identify supporting sections of the Ethics Code, and write opening and closing statements. In order to "win," some participants delve into the Code with considerable enthusiasm.

The instructor becomes an unofficial advisor for the fourth objective concerning university and department policies and procedures. Students in the orientation course develop a course plan that not only meets all minimal graduation requirements for the university but also includes classes that might give them a competitive advantage when applying for a job or graduate school. There is an advantage here for a course that meets throughout the semester compared to a one-time orientation session. Many procedural questions arise as students experience the undergraduate academic calendar for the first time (e.g., "How do I register for courses for next semester," "Do we have our regular classes during finals week"?).

The fifth objective, baseline assessment, begins when students take a "knowledge of psychology" test during the second class meeting. This exam is the same one given at the end of Senior Seminar. We introduce the APA and departmental learning goals and begin development of students' psychology department portfolio in the orientation course. Keller, Craig, Launius, Loher, and Cooledge (2004) describe the categories and process for introducing the portfolio.

Changes. Driven by feedback from the program assessment process and also by the implementation of additional classes that now serve as mandatory steps along the path to Senior Seminar (e.g., Research Methods I, PSY 2206, and Career Planning, PSY 3353), there have been several major changes in the orientation course since 2002. We reduced the number of assignments in the class. Exercises on some software (e.g., Word$^©$, PowerPoint$^©$) are less critical because most recent incoming students already have training and experience with these tools. Statistical Package for the Social Sciences (SPSS) and survey research are now covered extensively in the Research Methods courses. Perhaps reflecting changes in students described by Twenge (2006), there is more structure in the form of templates and scoring rubrics than in the past. While seeking to be independent, our students want to know exactly what is expected of them.

A final change in the orientation class is the delivery of materials. In 2002, students purchased a three-ring course binder that contained all of the major department handbooks and many of the orientation class exercises. This binder became the shell for the students' portfolios. Today, all of the same materials are available as Internet downloads. Within certain parameters, students choose the color, style, and vendor for their portfolio binders. It is not yet clear if this is increasing or decreasing willingness to read the documents, but it reduces initial costs for the student and makes updating materials easier for the department and the orientation course instructor.

Senior Seminar

Our typical student enrolls in Senior Seminar during the last semester of her or his final year. This class is considered the concluding course for the program regardless of which of the five concentrations a student has declared (e.g., counseling, human resource management), which allows some participants to enter and exit the program together. We try to maintain an intimate "seminar feel" with 15 or fewer students per section. We expanded the number of sections in 2003 to create more seats and to provide greater scheduling flexibility for students. Due to heavier than desirable enrollments, we experimented with offering Senior Seminar in summer 2008 for seniors seeking to graduate by August 2008 or December 2008.

Objectives. Senior Seminar, in part, seeks to sum up and advance content from the orientation and other core classes (see Dunn & McCarthy, this volume). It thus serves as a meaningful endpoint or capstone course. Based on years of assessing our students' needs and interests, we also approach this course as an important opportunity to prepare our departing seniors for the challenges that await them beyond the bachelor's degree. Senior Seminar documents the satisfactory completion of program goals first outlined in the orientation course and it helps to prepare students for the transition that lies ahead.

Table 3-1

Comparison of Selected Assignments in Orientation and Senior Seminar Classes

Orientation assignments	Senior Seminar assignments
Exploration of career options with psychology degree	Investigate educational/employment interests
Goal planning	Goal planning/assessment
Course planning	Job skills/preferences assessment
Beginning skills assessment	General knowledge examination
Ethics introduction	Learning ethical analysis
Presentation in class	Presentation to Mansfield community
Community service/citizenship	Community service/citizenship
Portfolio initiation	Portfolio completion/submission

Sample content. See Table 3-1 for a comparison of assignments between the orientation course and Senior Seminar. In Senior Seminar we emphasize the continued development of critical thinking and presentation abilities. Participants complete a literature review paper on a topic according to his or her interests (e.g., stress management). We require use of the professional research literature. The student presents the core issues and conclusions of her or his literature review at the end of the semester in a symposium that is open to the university and larger community. As part of our program assessment process, all faculty attend these presentations and use a simple evaluation tool to rate student performance (see Appendix 3B).

Exercises and activities intended to give students an edge as they enter the workforce or head to graduate school are the most popular. One example is the interview preparation section of the course. Over several classes, students sharpen their resumes, construct cover letters based on published job announcements (e.g., from a newspaper or Monster.com), attend a lecture on "smart interviewing," and discuss articles on interviewing procedures, techniques, and expectations. The exercise culminates when participants, in groups of three, engage in a round of mock interviews on the positions for which they have tailored their cover letters and resumes. ("Yes, you do have to dress up!" is the answer to one of the most common student questions about this class session.) In addition to being the interviewee, each student serves as an interviewer, which includes preparing structured questions for the inter-viewee prior to the meeting. A third student acts as an outside observer.

The interviewee assesses herself or himself at the end of each mock interview using a structured scoring sheet. The "interviewer" and "observer" also provide ratings and feedback.

Changes. Growth in student enrollment led us to offer more sections of Senior Seminar. This increase in the number of sections created a challenge to maintain consistency across instructors. As a department, we agreed that certain Senior Seminar activities are fixed regardless of the instructor (e.g., completion of the portfolio, seminar paper and presentation). Outside of these core exercises, the class is expected to address issues related to ethics, community engagement, workplace success, and personal exploration of values and goals. To encourage student engagement, each instructor may choose the means to address these issues. For example, in a recent section a majority of students felt that the most engaging reading and discussion of the semester concerned a chapter titled "Workplace Productivity," a reading the professor hesitated to include because of its overt associations with traditional economics rather than psychology.

With this flexibility, we adapt parts of Senior Seminar to fit the needs and interests of faculty and current students. For instance, fall 2007 participants asked that some attention be given in future sections to a discussion of debt management and personal finance. Debt management is a particularly important issue to the current generation of students (Twenge, 2006) and is clearly related to our goal of facilitating a successful transition from the university to the workplace or graduate school. With the structure of the class, there is the possibility for "customizing" aspects of the course to student needs and interests while maintaining a psychological perspective. Customization keeps the class fresh for the instructor and also delivers a more tailored experience to the students.

We recently added a "Foreword" section to the portfolio. The foreword is a multipage writing exercise made up of student reflections on their experiences as psychology majors. The exercise structure leads students to specifically describe experiences that connect to the department's learning objectives. It is an opportunity for students to consider their growth as a psychology major.

Adding "Steps": Research Methods I and Career Planning

Over the last 5 years our formal program assessment measures (e.g., Senior Seminar focus groups, alumni and student surveys) and informal conversations with students suggested a perceived gap between the orientation and capstone courses. After introduction of the learning goals in the orientation course, most subsequent classes include program outcomes in their syllabi and identify potential course artifacts for the portfolio. Advisors ask about career goals and examine portfolios-in-progress each semester. However, the faculty felt a need to address the perceived gap as we underwent a mandatory 5-year review. Our response, implemented for the fall 2007 semester and presented in a simplified form in Table 3-2, was the creation of a program incorporating a "Core" and specific "Concentrations." Two classes in the Core, Research Methods I and the Career Planning course, serve as mandatory "steps" to keep students on track in the overall program. Career Planning also serves as an alternative point of entry into the program for transfer students.

Research Methods I

Program assessment results indicated that our students struggled with research fundamentals. Research Methods I is a three-credit-hour class that is geared toward giving students a solid foundation in the basics of understanding psychological research. The content evolved over the last 5 years from an earlier, elective introduction to research methods course. Research Methods I is required as a core course for the new program and is a key step between the orientation and Senior Seminar classes. It is also a prerequisite for many other courses in the program. Originally, we offered two sections of the course during fall semester. However, due to recent increases in the number of

Table 3-2
Mansfield University Psychology Curriculum

Psychology core courses		Concentrations
Introduction to General Psychology	*Plus*	General
Orientation to Psychology[a]	*Choose a*	Mind/Body Health
Research Methods I	*Concentration*	Counseling
Career Planning	*(or Two)[b]*	Lifespan
Senior Seminar		Development
Internship or Research Apprenticeship		Human Resource
or Independent Study		Management

[a] Waived for students entering the program with 45 or more semester hours completed.
[b] Majors who choose General Psychology may not choose a second concentration.

psychology majors, we increased this to three 20-seat sections in fall 2007. Junior-level transfer students who begin the program during the fall semester must take this course during their first semester on campus in order to complete the program on time.

Objectives. There are five major objectives for the Research Methods I course:

1. Introduce fundamentals of psychological research.
2. Introduce basic research designs and corresponding statistical analyses.
3. Build skills to perform a literature search and prepare a bibliography of sources using APA style.
4. Provide students with the opportunity to apply psychological research concepts to real-life problems.
5. Learn to critically evaluate psychological research.

Sample content. The course consists of an integration of lecture and in-class group activities. The activities are a way for students to self-assess their own understanding of the material and provide an opportunity to learn through hands-on, peer-to-peer teaching demonstrations.

An annotated bibliography exercise is the artifact associated with the third course objective and the component that most clearly bridges the gap between the orientation and Senior Seminar courses. By the time students come to Research Methods I, they are reasonably prepared to conduct their own literature searches due to the introduction received during the orientation class. The assignment builds this competency when students locate, compile, and evaluate articles via the annotations. We require students to highlight the article's main points, strengths, and weaknesses. An integrative summary of the annotations serves as a measure of critical thinking.

Given its emphasis on research methodology and software (i.e., SPSS), Research Methods I is critical to student success across our Concentrations and classes (e.g., Learning & Cognition, Research Methods II, Independent Study). The literature search, reviewing, and small-scale public presentation requirements of Research Methods I all help to build student proficiencies related to our program learning goals (i.e., research methods, critical thinking, communication skills, and technology literacy). The competencies developed during this key step are essential to the successful completion of the research paper and presentation in Senior Seminar.

Career Planning Course

Objectives. This is a new (spring 2007) one-credit-hour course. The course's three target audiences are (a) continuing majors in their third year of study, (b) advanced internal transfer students (>45 credits completed), and (c) advanced external transfer students. An analysis indicated that the majority of recent majors entered the program as transfer students. Some internal and external transfer students were dissatisfied with being required to take the 1100-level orientation course. Focus group participants also felt that certain Senior Seminar material would be more useful if presented during the junior year (e.g., in-depth information about application to graduate school). Students who complete the orientation course do take the Career Planning class. Career Planning is intended as a booster shot to keep continuing students on track toward graduation. It is also required because we moved content out of Senior Seminar and into this course.

The objectives for the course include the following:

1. Self-assess interests and values.
2. Develop more specific career goals and search for job information and specific organizations.
3. Update or create a curriculum plan.
4. Compile in-depth information on specific graduate programs in psychology.
5. Update or create a department portfolio.
6. Review university and department policies and procedures regarding internships, independent study, and graduation requirements.

The Career Planning course is a work-in-progress as we sort out the needs of its three constituencies.

Sample content. One of the major unique artifacts from the Career Planning course is the creation of a personal strategic plan. This plan is supposed to have clear connections to self-assessment results as well as exercises on graduate school, careers, and a field interview. Students also update or create a cover letter and resume and participate in an ethics case analysis. The personal strategic plan becomes an artifact for the Career Planning section of the department portfolio.

Critical Issues

Several critical issues have emerged during the past 5 years that have affected the orientation and Senior Seminar courses. The first issue has to do with the timing of information and experiences. For the last 17 years, all students entering the major were required to take the orientation course. Recently, more of our new majors are either internal or external transfer students. These students have greater experience with college survival skills and different expectations from those of first-semester students. Portions of the orientation class did not seem appropriate for this cohort (e.g., introductory-level information about advising, creating a first resume, understanding basic university graduation requirements). Questions about the timing of information also pertained to Senior Seminar. One objective of Senior Seminar is to help students think about and plan for their "next step." However, focus group feedback indicated that some material was occurring too late to be functionally useful. For example, in light of changes that have occurred in deadline dates for graduate school applications, students felt that information about this process should be reviewed during the junior year. The junior-level Career Planning course was created in part to respond to both of these concerns.

A second major issue is how to maintain consistency with changes in faculty. Staffing changes are inevitable given retirements, reassignments to administrative activities, illnesses, and so on, all of which have affected our program over the last 5 years. Discussions must occur to identify the essential objectives or exercises for these core classes from the department's viewpoint while still supporting each new instructor's academic freedom. This is a very delicate balance and we find it a difficult one to maintain. Remembering the bigger picture through learning goals and program assessment combined with ongoing conversations can help departments deal with this issue. For example, five different faculty have led sections of Senior Seminar over the last 3 years. Each faculty member had his or her own ideas about what issues were important and how to conduct the class. Discussions at department meetings and retreats and requirements of the department's program assessment process (e.g., collection and evaluation of portfolios, community presentations of a literature review) generated the essential structure for the Senior Seminar course. As noted before, we agreed that individual faculty are free to experiment with different readings and instructional techniques.

A growing expectation on the part of students for a customized educational experience is a third critical issue. More than in the past, students like to pick and choose classes and skills based on their own preferences (Twenge, 2006). Familiarizing participants with external standards and expectations, as is done in the orientation and Senior Seminar courses, is one avenue to counter this trend. The Concentrations presented in Table 3-2 reflect another part of our response. We created clearer professional identities but with sufficient overlap so that motivated students can complete more than one concentration. Early results have been very positive, with a surprising number of majors completing the official paperwork to declare a second concentration.

Conclusion

Keeping faculty and students "reading from the same page" in any curriculum requires an extraordinary amount of energy from faculty as well as students. Faculty need to experience a collegial environment that feels safe and supportive, has consistent program-level goals and learning objectives, and is transparent in its operation. Getting to and maintaining such a state requires shared leadership based on a clear vision for the program's future educational effectiveness and continuing improvement. Specific times for shared reflection and planning are critical to program success.

Students can read from the same page only when they hear consistent expectations and values from their faculty. A shared faculty commitment to pursue program goals and learning objectives is one step in this direction. Using multiple venues (e.g., program Web sites, academic advisors, instructors, contacts with more experienced students) to explain and discuss program expectations is a second step. We and many other programs find that the orientation and other core courses are very useful in this regard, but only if taught in a consistent manner.

Finally, it is important to listen carefully to our ever-changing students regarding their perceptions and needs as they move through a curriculum. One way we choose to do this is through focus groups and other forms of program assessment. The design of a curriculum that is responsive to student needs while still being faithful to internal and external learning objectives is difficult. Where should students entering at midstream start? How will we make sure they receive a consistent picture of expectations and appropriate advising? How much latitude do we have to customize a curriculum? How flexible can we be? These are but a few of the questions that need to be addressed. An identifiable program mission accompanied by well-publicized and clearly stated goals and learning outcomes helps alleviate miscommunications regarding student expectations and answer faculty questions about what is appropriate. An integrated curriculum from beginning to end, with clear steps in between, is one way to keep everyone on the same page.

Recommended Readings

Keller, P. A., Craig, F. W., Launius, M. H., Loher, B. T., & Cooledge, N. J. (2004). Using student portfolios to assess program learning outcomes. In D. S. Dunn, C. M. Mehrotra, & J. S. Halonen (Eds.), *Measuring up: Educational assessment challenges and practices for psychology*. Washington, DC: American Psychological Association.

Lucas, A. F. (2000). A collaborative model for leading academic change. In A. F. Lucas (Ed.), *Leading academic change: Essential roles for department chairs* (pp. 33–54). San Francisco: Jossey-Bass.

References

American Psychological Association. (1987). *Casebook on ethical principles of psychologists*. Washington, DC: Author.

American Psychological Association. (2001). *Publication manual of the American Psychological Association* (5th ed.). Washington, DC: Author.

American Psychological Association. (2002). Ethical principles of psychologists and code of conduct. *American Psychologist, 57,* 1060–1073.

American Psychological Association. (2007). *APA guidelines for the undergraduate psychology major*. Washington, DC: Author. Retrieved from www.apa.org/ed/resources.html.

Fouad, N. A., & Bynner, J. (2008). Work transitions. *American Psychologist, 63,* 241–251.

Keller, P. A., Craig, F. W., Launius, M. H., Loher, B. T., & Cooledge, N. J. (2004). Using student portfolios to assess program learning outcomes. In D. S. Dunn, C. M. Mehrotra, & J. S. Halonen (Eds.), *Measuring up: Educational assessment challenges and practices for psychology*. Washington, DC: American Psychological Association.

Keller, P. A., Loher, B. T., Launius, M. H., Craig, F. W., & Cooledge, N. J. (2002, September). *Ignition to liftoff: Building an integrated curriculum with assessable outcomes*. Presented at Measuring Up: Best Practices in Assessment in Psychology Education, Atlanta, GA.

Launius, M. L., Loher, B. T., & Keller, P. A. (1995, October). *From cradle to grave: Keeping the psychology major on track.* Presented at the Second Annual Northeastern Conference for Teachers of Psychology, Ithaca College, Ithaca, NY.

Loher, B. T., Keller, P. A., Craig, F. W., Launius, M. L., & Murray, J. D. (2007). *Designing a multimethod system for undergraduate program assessment and improvement.* Continuing Education Workshop presented at the 115th Annual Convention of the American Psychological Association, San Francisco, CA

McCarthy, M. A. (2008). Beginning and endings: A reprise. *Teaching of Psychology, 35,* 59–60.

McGovern, T. V., Furumoto, L., Halpern, D. F., Kimble, G. A., & McKeachie, W. J. (1991). Liberal education, study in depth, and the arts and sciences major—psychology. *American Psychologist, 46,* 598–605.

Nicholson, N. (1984). A theory of work role transitions. *Administrative Science Quarterly, 29*(2), 172–191.

Twenge, J. M. (2006). *Generation me.* New York: Free Press.

Appendix 3A   EBSCOhost Exercise for

Orientation Course

Name: Date:

1. In the space below, write out your RESEARCH QUESTION. (Note: It
    must be phrased as a complete question)

2. Using EBSCOhost, identify at least **5** articles that pertain to your research
    question. Use PsycINFO and PsycARTICLES as your databases. After
    choosing the databases, make sure you **click on the "Advance
    Search" tab** at the top of the page!

3. Create pages with **ONLY** the following information (you will need to
    change or modify the standard printout):

    A. A record of your **SEARCH HISTORY**
        (Appears as a tab underneath where you typed in your search
        terms. To print, click on "Print Search History" immediately below
        the tabs)

    B. For **EACH** article: (You will see the labels on the left as tags for what
        you need)

Author(s)	Author(s) name(s)
Title	Complete title of article
Source	If for a journal article, it includes 1) year in which article was published, 2) name of journal in which article was published, 3) volume number for journal where article was published, 4) pages on which article appears (begin – end)
Publisher	This is important for referencing a book or edited volume
Abstract	Short summary of the article, book, etc.

WARNING: Attach this page as a cover sheet. Other than the research question on
this page, the rest of the assignment must be typed.

Appendix 3B Senior Seminar Presentation Rating Form

Student _____ Date ___/___/___Rater Initials_____

Title of Presentation _____

Rate each area in reference to what you believe would be a reasonable expectation for a senior student completing their college education as a psychology major. (3=Meets Expectations)

Area Rated	Substantially below Expectations (1)		(2)	(3)	(4)	Substantially Above Expectations (5)
Content & Critical Thinking						
Thesis, direction provided to audience						
Logical organization of material						
Review of literature						
Coverage of major points						
Use of data						
Supportable conclusions based on evidence						
Ability to think critically about topic						
Communication Skills & Delivery						
Visual design of PowerPoint						
Appropriate headings & main points (clarity & consistency)						

(continued)

Clarity in communicating major
     points
Appropriate pace and use of time
     allotted
Effective responses to questions
Overall professional demeanor
Overall clarity of communication
Other:

Global Rating of Presentation

Place Comments on Reverse Side:

4 Advising in the Classroom

A Career Exploration Class for Psychology Majors

Drew C. Appleby

The school-to-work transition is often abrupt for graduates with a

bachelor's degree, in part because they receive little information

regarding career opportunities within psychology and little guidance in

how to structure their educational experience to help them obtain their

goals.

The epigraph above by Maynard, Maynard, and Rowe (2004, p. 37) serves as the perfect introduction to this chapter because it describes the plight of approximately 88,000 psychology majors who graduate each year from American colleges and universities (Snyder, Dillow, & Hoffman, 2008). According to Ware (1999, p. 188), the two questions students most frequently ask their advisors concern their "career opportunities and post-baccalaureate educational alternatives". When these two questions are multiplied by 88,000, it becomes obvious within the context of this book that we should begin the process of providing our students with opportunities to explore these questions as early as possible so they can end their undergraduate careers with the knowledge base and critical thinking skills necessary to answer them. The purpose of this chapter is to explain how academic advising can be incorporated in a classroom setting that has been purposely designed to enable students to construct competent answers to these two crucial questions.

Two Types of Academic Advising

Crookston (1972) distinguished between two types of academic advising. He used the term *prescriptive* to describe advising whose purpose is to provide information to advisees that will enable them to fulfill their requirements and graduate in a timely manner. This approach has two problems. First, advisees remain dependent upon their advisors and do not develop responsibility for their academic plans. Second, although this type of advising enables students to graduate in a timely manner, it does not necessarily prepare them for life after graduation. Prescriptive advisors seek to credential their advisees (i.e., to ensure they earn their diploma) rather than to mentor students on the path to their post-baccalaureate goals.

Crookston (1972) used the term *developmental* advising to describe a process designed to help students identify their personal and occupational goals and then utilize their educational resources and opportunities to accomplish these goals. This model of academic advising is consistent with the broader developmental approach to the educational process. Academic advising occurs in many settings such as one-on-one advising (Appleby, 2002b), psychology club meetings (Satterfield & Abramson, 1998), and informal seminars (Lammers, 2001). Books (Appleby, 2007; Kuther, 2006; Landrum & Davis, 2007; Morgan & Korschgen, 2009), Web sites (Lloyd, 2004a), and classes (Lloyd, 2004b) can also facilitate advising. This chapter describes a class at Indiana University-Purdue University Indianapolis that provides psychology majors with developmental advising and teaches them to think critically about themselves, their major, and their career goals in the process.

The Structure of the Class

Orientation to a Major in Psychology (OMP) is a one-credit-hour class required of all majors in our department. There are two forms of this class, one designed for freshmen and sophomores and one (the subject of this chapter) for juniors and seniors. The description of this form of the class is the following:

> This class is for psychology majors—or those who are considering changing their major to psychology—who are classified as juniors or seniors. It provides opportunities for students to understand themselves, their major, their future careers, and the complex interactions that exist among these three domains. Students create a plan that will enable them to achieve their educational and career goals.

According to Landrum, Shoemaker, and Davis (2003), over one-third of all psychology departments in the United States offer a similar course. Studies have reported that students who complete these classes are aware of what they can and cannot do with a bachelor's degree in psychology (Dillinger & Landrum, 2002); possess career knowledge and demonstrate career exploration and decidedness (Thomas & McDaniel, 2004); and rate themselves as knowledgeable about themselves, their skills, and their job opportunities (Ware, 1987).

OMP enables students to become savvy psychology majors (Appleby, 2002a) who possess the ability to construct educational plans that increase their chances of successfully attaining their occupational goals. OMP accomplishes this by requiring its students to (a) select a realistic career goal; (b) identify the knowledge, skills, and characteristics (KSCs) necessary to enter and engage successfully in that career; (c) create an educational plan to develop these KSCs; (d) develop strategies to convince important others that these KSCs have been attained; and (e) select a mentor who can facilitate this career quest.

What Students Do in OMP

The pedagogical strategy of OMP is straightforward. I require my students to write an eight-chapter, APA-style book about their career aspirations and their strategies to actualize these aspirations. I provide them with eight basic questions that become the titles of their chapters. Each of these basic questions also contains a set of subquestions (see Appendix 4A) that requires them to investigate and write about themselves, their major, their career choices, and their strategies to attain their careers.

My students are initially terrified and/or outraged at the prospect of having to write a book, especially in a class that will earn them only one hour of academic credit. However, as the semester progresses, they begin to understand the value of this arduous task as demonstrated by the following anonymous comment taken verbatim from one of my recent end-of-semester student evaluation forms. "The book I wrote in B103 has been unbelievably informative. It was like four years of advising appointments rolled into a 16-week class. For the first time in my academic career I feel like I have a sense of where my education should be leading me, and I am now ready to reach my goal!"

The Role of Undergraduate Teaching Assistants (TAs) in the OMP

OMP is extremely work-intensive. I evaluate hundreds of chapters each semester and provide their authors with constructive feedback about both content and style. The use of TAs reduces my workload and creates a powerful opportunity for successful OMP students to continue productive contact with me and further sharpen their APA-style writing skills. TAs serve as academic case managers for students by acting as counselors, referral agents, evaluators, advocates, teachers, and encouragers. The first letters of each of these roles form the acronym CREATE, which is the title of the model of academic case management my TAs use to create success in OMP students (Appleby, 2008).

The enrollment limit in each of the two sections of OMP I teach each semester is 35, and I usually have eight or nine TAs per section, each of whom is responsible for a small family of approximately four students. They evaluate their family members' (FMs) chapters for APA style and format with a detailed scoring rubric, which they staple to their FMs' chapters before they give them to me to evaluate for content. TAs keep detailed records of their FMs' progress during the semester and write a case report on each of their FMs at the end of the class. I choose a lead TA for each section, and each of the other TAs volunteers for a specific duty (e.g., recruiting participants for the graduate student panel). The primary duty of the lead TA is to ensure that the other TAs carry out their duties in a professional, harmonious, and competent manner.

TAs write a detailed end-of-semester report that explains how their TA experience changed them personally, socially, and professionally. They must also create an entry for their resume or curriculum vita describing their responsibilities as a TA and write a paragraph that they can include in a personal statement for graduate school. The hard work, diligence, and caring my TAs exhibit make it easy for me to write them exceptionally strong letters of recommendation for graduate school and job applications (see Appendix 4B for a section of a letter of recommendation I wrote for one of my TAs that describes her performance in OMP).

The TA Selection Process

The TA selection process is crucial to the success of OMP. When I first taught the class, I selected the TAs for the following semester, and I usually made good choices. I now give my TAs the responsibility of nominating TAs for the following semester from the members of their student families, and I then contact these nominees to determine their willingness to accept their nominations. I provide nominees with a detailed application that requires (a) a personal statement describing why they want to become a TA and what they believe they will derive from their TA experience and (b) a letter of recommendation from their TA created with a set of instructions similar to those provided to faculty when they are requested to write letters of recommendation for graduate school applicants. Although this is a complicated and time-consuming process both for TAs and for their nominees, it serves as good practice for the arduous task of applying to graduate school. This process has produced a steady supply of competent TAs who are honored to be nominated, eager to gain professional experience, and enthusiastic about helping their fellow psychology majors. They require little or no formal training because they have proven their competence by performing well enough in the class to gain the nomination of their very demanding TAs who are well aware of their personal characteristics and abilities.

Assessment of Student Learning Outcomes

I collect both quantitative and qualitative data each semester so I can make data-informed changes to improve the class. I have listed the nine student learning outcomes (SLOs) of OMP below with the quantitative methods I use to assess how well my students accomplish them.

1. *Identify, clarify, and investigate a potential career, and create a realistic strategy to attain it.* The scores students receive on the books they submit at the end of the semester reflect the accomplishment of this.
2. *Write in APA style.* TAs evaluate the APA style and format of their FMs' book chapters with a detailed rubric containing 26 APA-style rules (e.g., correct citation of sources, margins, and the absence of contractions).
3. *Follow directions.* Students receive specific directions for writing their chapters and the TAs award them points for the directions they followed correctly.
4. *Use feedback to improve your writing.* The TAs and I provide students with abundant written feedback on their book chapters. The TAs award two, one, or zero feedback points on each chapter

depending upon the extent to which their students used this feedback from the previous chapter to improve their current chapter.

5. *Submit assignments when they are due.* TAs record the number of times students submit book chapters after their deadline has passed.

6. *Collaborate with a group of classmates on an oral presentation that contains a PowerPoint presentation.* I use an 11-item rubric to evaluate the quality of this presentation.

7. *Engage in psychology-related activities that will increase your involvement with the Psychology Department.* Students are required to engage in at least two psychology-related activities (e.g., attend a Psychology Club meeting, have an information-gathering interview with a psychology faculty member about a psychology-related career, or visit the Psychology Advising Office). Students must obtain the signature of the faculty or staff member who is in charge of each activity they attend.

8. *Become familiar with the resources in the Psychology Advising Office, the university's Career Center, and the library.* Students must identify three resources provided by each of these locations and explain how they will utilize these resources to help them explore their future careers.

9. *Use the Psychology Department's listserv to identify an opportunity that can help you attain your career goals.* Students submit a copy of a listserv message they received accompanied by a brief report of how they used this opportunity to attain one of their career goals.

Approximately 20 minutes of the final class period are devoted to an informal discussion during which I ask students to suggest ways I can change the content of the course to improve the attainment of its SLOs. The TAs take careful notes during this discussion and include these student recommendations, as well as their own recommendations, in their final reports. I use the most frequent and most feasible of these recommendations to make changes in OMP for the next semester. For example, one suggestion I implemented last semester was to allow those students who are employed in a job they wish to continue after graduation to explain how they plan to develop the

KSCs they will need to advance in their current position. I also make changes each semester based on the quantitative assessment data I collect about the specific SLOs (e.g., If I discover that my students are committing an unusually high number of mistakes on a particular aspect of APA style, I include more instruction about that aspect the following semester).

The final—and most personal—assessment data I collect relate to the implicit goal of OMP to provide a mentoring experience for its enrollees. These data take the form of the responses to the question on the School of Science senior exit survey, which asks graduating psychology majors if they have had a mentor during their undergraduate career and, if so, at what level did that mentor operate for them. During the past 6 years, 289 graduating psychology majors have reported that I served as a mentor to them, and 120 of these indicated I have served in this capacity at the highest level, which is defined on the survey as "having influenced the whole course of my life and this person's effect upon me has been invaluable."

Concluding Remarks

This is the most rewarding class I teach and, judging by the answers I receive to the final question in the book (i.e., "What conclusions have I come to about myself, my major, and my future career as a result of writing this book?"), my students find it equally rewarding. The following is one such answer.

> Before I started writing this book, I had absolutely no idea of what I wanted to do with my life; I only knew I wanted to help people. Writing this book made me think long and hard about my future career. It forced me to seek out answers to important questions that I have been ignoring and to learn what I have to do in order to succeed in life. I now possess knowledge about my career and how to achieve it. This class has made me fully aware of the fact that it is now up to me to actively utilize this knowledge and to begin the process of becoming the person I want to become. Writing this book, along with the research it required, has been the most valuable experience of my entire undergraduate career.

In a recent edition of *Carnegie Perspectives*, Studley (2004, p. 2) wrote, "Our students want to know how to connect their values and goals, their intellectual passions and capacities, the myriad of learning experiences in which they engage during college, and the work of their lives." That is precisely the opportunity I offer my students in OMP. I want them to engage in what Piaget called meaning making by engaging in active attempts to make sense of their world and their experiences (Kuhn, 1992). Piaget did not believe children passively soak up their environmental experiences like sponges, and I believe the same thing about college students. My students want to prepare themselves for their future careers, and they also want to believe their college experience can help them do that. Unfortunately, "the problem is that these career development processes are not woven into students' central educational endeavors where they could provide powerful material and expand motivation for learning" (Studley, 2004, p. 2).

OMP is my attempt to solve this problem. This class provides an opportunity for our psychology majors to begin to make meaning of their undergraduate experience by (a) identifying, clarifying, and exploring a career goal and (b) devising a carefully crafted and professionally written plan that will enable them to attain this goal when their undergraduate education comes to an end. It is also a valuable opportunity for a smaller subset of our majors to continue to strengthen the skills they acquired in the class by acting as OMP TAs and developing a new set of professionally relevant skills as they carry out their roles as counselors, referral agents, evaluators, advocates, teachers, and encouragers.

Author's Note

If you would like to receive a copy of my syllabus, one of my students' books, a set of responses to the final question my students answer in their books (i.e., What conclusions have I come to about myself, my major, and my future career as a result of writing this book?), my TA recommendation form, and one of my TA's end-of-semester reports, please contact me at dappleby @iupui.edu. I will send you the documents you request as attachments. I encourage you to use the information contained in these documents in any way that will facilitate your students' undergraduate journeys toward their professional goals.

Correspondence Information

Drew C. Appleby
Director of Undergraduate Studies in Psychology
Department of Psychology
Indiana University-Purdue University Indianapolis
402 North Blackford Street
Indianapolis, IN 46202-3275
317-274-6767
dappleby@iupui.edu

Recommended Readings

Gordon, V. N. (2006). *Career advising: An academic advisor's guide.* San Francisco: Jossey-Bass.

Gordon, V. N., Habley, W. R., Grites, T. J., & Associates. (2008). *Academic advising: A comprehensive handbook* (2nd ed.). San Francisco: Jossey-Bass.

Hettich, P. I., & Helkowski, C. (2005). *Connect college to career: A student's guide to work and life transitions.* Belmont, CA: Thompson Wadsworth.

Keith-Spiegel, P., & Wiederman, M. W. (2000). *The complete guide to graduate school admission: Psychology, counseling, and related professions* (2nd ed.). Mahwah, NJ: Erlbaum.

Kuther, T. L., & Morgan, R. D. (2004). *Careers in psychology: Opportunities in a changing world.* Belmont, CA: Thompson Wadsworth.

References

American Psychological Association. (2001). *Publication manual of the American Psychological Association* (5th ed.). Washington, DC: Author.

Appleby, D. C. (2002a). The savvy psychology major. *Eye on Psi Chi, 7,* 28.

Appleby, D. C. (2002b). The teaching-advising connection. In S. F. Davis & W. Buskist (Eds.), *The teaching of psychology: Essays in honor of Wilbert J. McKeachie and Charles L. Brewer* (pp. 121–139). Mahwah, NJ: Erlbaum.

Appleby, D. C. (2007). *The savvy psychology major* (4th ed.). Dubuque, IA: Kendall/Hunt.

Appleby, D. C. (2008). *Fall 2008 B103 Orientation to a Major in Psychology syllabus.* (Available from dappleby@iupui.edu)

Crookston, B. B. (1972). A developmental view of academic advising as teaching. *Journal of College Student Personnel, 13,* 12–17.

Dillinger, R. J., & Landrum. R. E. (2002). An information course for the beginning psychology major. *Teaching of Psychology, 29,* 230–232.

Kuhn, D. (1992). Cognitive development. In M. H. Bornstein & M. E. Lamb (Eds.), *Developmental psychology: An advanced textbook* (3rd ed.). Hillsdale, NJ: Erlbaum.

Kuther, T. L. (2006). *The psychology major's handbook* (2nd ed.). Belmont, CA: Thompson Wadsworth.

Lammers, W. J. (2001). An informal seminar to prepare the best undergraduates for doctoral programs in psychology. *Teaching of Psychology, 28,* 58–59.

Landrum, R. E., & Davis, S. F. (2007). *The psychology major: Career options and strategies for success* (3rd ed.). Upper Saddle River, NJ: Prentice-Hall.

Landrum, R. E., Shoemaker, C. S., & Davis, S. F. (2003). Important topics in an introduction to the psychology major course. *Teaching of Psychology, 30,* 48–51.

Lloyd, M. A. (2004a). The case for requiring a "careers" course for psychology majors. In W. Buskist, V. W. Hevern, B. K. Saville, & T. Zinn (Eds.), *Essays from E-xcellence in teaching* (Chap. 8). Retrieved August 20, 2004, from the Society for the Teaching of Psychology Web site: http://teachpsych.lemoyne.edu/teachpsych/eit/eit2003/index.html

Lloyd, M. A. (2004b). *Marky Lloyd's careers in psychology page.* Retrieved May 27, 2008, from www.psychwww.com/careers/

Maynard, A. M., Maynard, D. C., & Rowe, K. A. (2004). Exposure to the fields of psychology: Evaluation of an introductory psychology project. *Teaching of Psychology, 31,* 37–40.

Morgan, B. L., & Korschgen, A. J. (2009). *Majoring in psych? Career opportunities for psychology undergraduates* (4th ed.). Boston: Allyn & Bacon.

Satterfield, C. D., & Abramson, C. I. (1998). The undergraduate psychology club: Possibilities and suggested activities. *Teaching of Psychology, 8,* 67–71.

Snyder, T. D., Dillow, S. A., & Hoffman, C. M. (2008). *Digest of educational statistics 2007* (NCES 2008-022). Washington, DC: National Center for Education Statistics, Institute of Education Sciences, U.S. Department of Education.

Studley, J. S. (2004, March). Vocation is not a dirty word. *Carnegie perspectives: A different way to think about teaching and learning.* Retrieved September 11, 2004, from http://www.carnegiefoundation.org/perspectives/perspectives2004.Mar.htm.

Thomas, J. H., & McDaniel, C. R. (2004). Effectiveness of a required course in career planning for psychology majors. *Teaching of Psychology, 31,* 22–27.

Ware, M. E. (1987). Evaluating a career development course: A two-year study. In M. E. Ware & R. J. Millard (Eds.), *Handbook on student development: Advising, career development, and field placement* (pp. 94–95). Hillsdale, NJ: Erlbaum.

Ware, M. E. (1999). Academic advising for undergraduates. In B. Perlman, L. I. McCann, & S. H. McFadden (Eds.), *Lessons learned: Practical advice for the teaching of psychology,* Washington, DC: American Psychological Society.

Appendix 4A   The Eight Basic Questions That Become the Titles of Chapters Written by OMP Students and the Sets of Subquestions That Clarify Each of These Basic Questions

Chapter 1: What is psychology, why have I chosen it as my major, and why is it the most appropriate major for me?

- What is the definition of psychology, and what are its four goals? What are two specific reasons that caused me to choose psychology as my major? Are my reasons for choosing psychology in agreement with its definition and goals? Why or why not?
- Identify and explain two of the five skills for success in psychology described in the textbook I will need to develop or strengthen in order to become a more successful psychology major. What specific strategies will I use to develop or strengthen each of these skills?
- Does procrastination ever cause problems in my academic and/or personal life? If so, explain which procrastination style(s) identified in the textbook describe(s) me most accurately. What strategies can I use to decrease my tendency to procrastinate?
- Identify and define three areas of specialization in psychology that interest me, and explain my interest in them
- What are my three most important work values? What are psychology's five ethical principles? Explain why my work values and these ethical principles are or are not a good match by comparing each of my three work values with at least one of the ethical principles.
- Identify and explain the stage of separation from original knowledge in which I am currently operating. What specific critical thinking skills must I develop so I can reach the final stage by the time I graduate?

- What three famous quotations describe a savvy psychology major, and what nine specific skills does a savvy psychology major possess? Am I a savvy psychology major now on the basis of these quotations and skills? Why or why not? If I am not, what must I do to attain the skills and characteristics of a savvy psychology major?

Chapter 2: For what specific career am I preparing, and what resources at IUPUI can help me explore my career?

- For what specific career am I preparing, and what specific tasks and/or duties will I carry out on the job in this career?
- Will I need to go to graduate or professional school for this career? If so, what specific type of graduate degree will I need and approximately how long will it take me to attain this degree?
- Identify and describe three specific types of resources available in the IUPUI Career Center that can help me explore my career and/or graduate school options. In what specific ways will I use each of these three resources to enable me to become a more savvy psychology major?
- Identify and describe three specific types of resources available in the Psychology Advising Office that can help me explore my career and/or graduate school options. In what ways will I use each of these three resources to enable me to become a more savvy psychology major?
- Who is my academic advisor, and how have I utilized her/his advice in the past? Is this person the most appropriate advisor for me on the basis of the specific career for which I am preparing? If not, who would be a more appropriate advisor?
- What would I like to be able to say about myself after I write this book?

Chapter 3: How must I prepare myself for graduate/professional school if my career requires a degree beyond the bachelor's?

(Chapters 3 and 4 are your plans for the future. Chapter 3 deals with graduate school and Chapter 4 identifies a job you could obtain with a bachelor's degree. Whichever idea is your Plan A, label it Plan A. Whichever is your second choice, label it Plan B.)

- What specific degree must I earn to enter my chosen profession?
- What are the skills and characteristics of successful graduate students? Do I possess these skills and characteristics now and, if I do not, what are my specific plans to acquire them?
- What is the GRE (or the test I must take to qualify for admission into my graduate/professional program), what type(s) of questions does this test contain, what skills and knowledge does it measure, and how can I prepare for it? When do I plan to take this test, what must I do to register for it, and when must I register so I can take it at the appropriate time?
- What steps must I take and what documents must I create and request to apply to the graduate/professional school I plan to enter?
- What skills and characteristics of applicants do graduate admission committees want to read about in letters of recommendation?
- Is becoming a professional psychologist (or another professional who is required to earn a graduate degree) a realistic goal for me in terms of my academic record; my performance on standardized tests; my resources; and my personal skills, attitudes, and characteristics?

Chapter 4: What are my career options if I decide to end my education with a bachelor's degree?

(Begin your Chapter 4 title with Plan A: if you plan to enter the workforce or remain in your current job after you receive your bachelor's degree. If you plan to remain in the same job you have now, explain how the KSCs you can acquire during your undergraduate education can help you to advance in your current job (e.g., earn a promotion or salary increase). Begin your Chapter 4 title with Plan B: if you plan to attend graduate school immediately after you receive your bachelor's degree.)

- Identify and describe the skills and abilities needed by the American worker in the 21st century as identified in the federal government's 1991 SCANS Report.
- Identify and describe the skills employers look for when they interview psychology majors.
- Identify and describe the skills IUPUI psychology majors can develop if they take advantage of their undergraduate opportunities. In what ways do you plan to develop these skills?

- What specific occupational fields can a psychology major
  with a bachelor's degree successfully prepare for and enter?
  Why should these fields be considered "psychology-major-
  related" even if they do not deal with specific psychological
  knowledge?

Chapter 5: How must I change to prepare myself for my career? Who can help me make these changes?

- For what specific career am I preparing (from Chapter 2)? What are
  three specific types of knowledge, three specific types of skills, and
  three specific characteristics (KSCs) possessed by a person who is
  successfully employed in this career?
- What is the work environment of a person employed in this career in
  terms of workload, daily schedule, flexibility of work schedule,
  deadlines and other time pressures, and amount of social interaction?
  What is the outlook for this career in the future? What can I expect to
  earn in this career? How much and what kind of education will I need
  to enter this career?
- Why is this career a good fit for me in terms of my KSCs,
  my work values, and my preference for a particular work
  environment?
- What is the covert curriculum? What four skills from the covert
  curriculum must I develop more fully before I can succeed in my
  career, and how will I develop each of them? How will I use each of
  these skills in my career, and what specific negative consequence
  would occur if I am not able to perform each of these skills?
- What is a mentor, what three needs do I possess that a mentor can
  help me to fulfill, who would be a good mentor for me, and how can
  she or he help me to fulfill my three needs?
- Bonus Option: You may earn up to two bonus points if you include
  information in this chapter gathered during an informational
  interview or job shadow experience with a person who is employed
  in the career you wish to enter. Ask this person about the specific
  KSCs necessary to enter and succeed in this career and how she/he
  suggests you can use the remainder of your undergraduate
  education to achieve these KSCs.

Chapter 6: How can I use my education to change myself so I am prepared for my career?

- What are the four specific differences in requirements between the BS and BA degree in psychology at IUPUI? With which of these degrees do I plan to graduate, and why will the degree I have chosen prepare me better for my career than the one I did not choose?
- Under what bulletin was I accepted into the School of Science? What is my semester-by-semester plan to graduate? (This plan should include the departments, numbers, and titles of specific classes you have taken and those you plan to take, their credit hours, the semester in which you took or plan to take them, and the specific requirements they will fulfill [i.e., general education, psychology major, or elective].)
- What were my academic advisor's answers to the following questions I asked at the end of our required advising session? Is my semester-by-semester plan to graduate with a BA or BS in psychology complete? Will the courses contained in this plan prepare me for my graduate school and/or career goal(s)? What advice do you have for me that will enable me to get the most benefit from the remainder of my undergraduate career?
- Does my academic advisor act as a mentor to me? If not, who would be a better choice?
- Which of the 11 transcripts described in the textbook does my transcript resemble most closely, and why does it resemble it? What would a potential employer or graduate school admissions committee conclude about me if they read my current transcript? What specific things can I do to improve my transcript or their perceptions of it if these people draw a negative conclusion about me from my transcript?
- Identify two of IUPUI's Principles of Undergraduate Learning and two of the IUPUI Psychology Department's Student Learning Outcomes that will enable me to succeed in my career. Explain (a) why each of them will help me to succeed in my chosen career and (b) the negative consequences that would occur in my career if I do not attain each of them.
- List five of the specific elective classes I have taken or I will take. Explain how each of these courses will prepare me for my career.
- Would pursuing one of the Psychology Department's four track concentrations be advantageous for me? Why or why not? If I am

pursuing a concentration, how will each of the courses I must take to fulfill its requirements help me to accomplish my career goal?

Chapter 7: What strategies can I use to convince an employer to hire me or a graduate/professional school to accept me?

- What will my resume or curriculum vitae look like at the end of my undergraduate education? (Do not simply describe how your resume or curriculum vitae will look; create an actual resume or curriculum vitae.) What specific things must I do to make my resume or curriculum vitae look like this by the time I graduate?
- What three criteria should I use to choose people who can write me strong letters of recommendation for a job or graduate school? What three specific people would be good choices for me on the basis of these criteria?
- In what two extracurricular activities will I participate during my undergraduate career, and in what specific ways will each of these activities help me prepare for my career?
- What will be my very specific, multiple-part answer to one of the following interview questions: Why should our company, organization, or agency hire you rather than the other 100 people who have applied for this position? Why should our admissions committee accept you into our graduate or professional program rather than the 100 other applicants?

Chapter 8: Is psychology still the most appropriate major for me?

- Identify and describe three specific types of resources available in the university library that can help me explore my career and/or graduate school options. In what specific ways will I use each of these resources to enable me to become a more savvy psychology major?
- Is psychology still the most appropriate major for me? Why or why not?
- Is the occupation I said I wanted to pursue in Chapter 2 still the best choice for me? Why or why not? If it is not, then what is the occupation I would like to pursue now, and why is it a better fit for me than the one I chose in Chapter 2?

- Have I become a more savvy psychology major as a result of taking B103?
- Did I have any "awakening" experiences in B103 during which I suddenly realized I have been unaware of an important component of my journey to my future career? If so, what was it, how did I become aware of it, and what am I doing to address or attain it now?
- Am I able to say what I wanted to say about myself now that I have written this book?
- The Final Question: What conclusions have I come to about myself, my major, my undergraduate education, my future career, and my life from writing this book? (This is probably the most important question you will answer in your book, so please give it some very serious thought. I will be passing this information on to next semester's B103 students, so be sure to provide them with sincere and valuable wisdom about the effect that B103 can have on their present and future lives.)

Appendix 4B Section From a Letter of Recommendation I Wrote for One of My TAs

Carrie used her strong academic, communication, and interpersonal skills in her role as a teaching assistant (TA) to my B103 Orientation to a Psychology Major students by providing them with insightful and constructive feedback on their weekly writing assignments. She performed her role in exactly the manner I demand; she was unwilling to allow her protégés to write in less-than-perfect APA style but did so in a positive and supportive manner. I have professionalized the TA position in this class by requiring my TAs to assume the role of academic case managers who use the CREATE model to produce and sustain academic success in my students. CREATE is an acronym I constructed that represents the following six roles performed by my B103 TAs: Counselor, Referral agent, Evaluator, Advocate, Teacher, and Encourager. Carrie was responsible for a small "family" of B103 students, and she successfully carried out these six roles in the following manner.

1. In her role as a Counselor, Carrie developed an understanding of her family members (FMs) and used this knowledge—paired with her experience as a successful B103 student—to help them adapt to and succeed in this very demanding class by utilizing their strengths and strengthening their weaknesses. She also helped her FMs understand things about themselves that could prevent them from performing well in the class (e.g., that they can no longer procrastinate and expect to perform as well as they have in the past). She accomplished this by developing a trusting relationship with her FMs, which permitted honest and insightful examinations of dysfunctional academic behaviors (e.g., procrastination, carelessness, and an inability or refusal to use feedback to improve performance) and the development of more functional behaviors.

2. In her role as a Referral agent, Carrie identified her FMs' academic challenges and their subsequent need for assistance that required

the utilization of specialized campus resources. She was then able to connect them with these resources to eliminate or decrease the severity of these challenges (e.g., Adaptive Educational Services, the Advising Office, the Career Center, the Writing Center, and the Office of Counseling and Psychological Services).

3. In her role as an Evaluator, Carrie assessed the quality of the APA style and format of her FMs' book chapters and provided them with constructive and supportive feedback that enabled them to improve the quality of their chapters. Part of this role involved careful record keeping and the production of a comprehensive end-of-semester case report of each of her FMs' academic accomplishments.

4. In her role as an Advocate, Carrie supported her FMs when their busy and complicated lives made it difficult or impossible for them to meet the demands of B103. In these instances, Carrie acted as an advocate to lessen the academic cost of not meeting the requirements of the class by explaining the causes of an FM's poor performance to me so I could determine whether an exception in policy should be made (e.g., the extension of a deadline).

5. In her role as a Teacher, Carrie used the strong knowledge of APA style she developed in B103 to assist her FMs in the acquisition of this challenging and demanding professional skill. She also taught her FMs "by example" by modeling the characteristics of a successful psychology major such as involvement in departmental activities, the establishment of productive relationships with faculty, and the ability to set academic and professional goals and create and implement strategies to achieve these goals.

6. In her role as an Encourager, Carrie motivated her FMs to perform up to their optimal levels by helping them understand the value of the class, identifying and reinforcing their academic progress, and providing the support they need to complete B103. Although this is perhaps the least academic of the six TA roles, it is nonetheless one of the most crucial in this very demanding class. It is the role in which Carrie's exceptionally strong interpersonal skills enabled her to excel as a TA.

5 Building a Psychology Orientation Course

Common Themes and Exercises

Brian T. Loher and R. Eric Landrum

Psychology is one of the most popular majors in higher education. According to the National Center for Education Statistics, in the latest year data are available (2005–2006), 88,134 students earned psychology baccalaureate degrees in the United States (Snyder, Dillow, & Hoffman, 2008). Given that "degrees awarded" represents only those who successfully complete a program, the overall number of psychology undergraduate majors is undoubtedly much higher.

As with many academic programs, students frequently enter psychology with relatively little fact-based information about the knowledge, skills, abilities, and career options associated with the discipline. This small amount of information may be based on personal experiences (e.g., positive experiences with introductory psychology, school guidance counselors, and therapists) or media stereotypes (e.g., "psychologists" portrayed on television or in movies). For example, many new majors declared that they wanted to work as FBI profilers after the appearance of the movie *Silence of the Lambs* (1991) and the television show *Profiler* (1996–2000). More recently the popularity of forensic programs such as *CSI* has again increased the number of students interested in majoring in psychology.

The American Psychological Association has made a significant effort to address students' lack of information through its PsycCAREERS Web site (http://psyccareers.apa.org/). Another avenue adopted by a growing number of psychology departments has been an orientation course for new majors. For example, in a national sample of psychology departments, Landrum, Shoemaker, and Davis (2003) found that about one-third reported having a psychology major orientation course. Although the models differ for implementing and administering the courses, many of these courses appear to share several common assumptions and themes. The purpose of this chapter is to describe these assumptions and themes and to present several sample exercises used in our courses. We conclude by briefly reviewing some of the administrative issues related to implementation of orientation courses.

Assumptions

Orientation courses are designed to help inform, guide, and motivate students as they begin an undergraduate degree program. In this regard, orientation courses make the assumption that it is useful to "work backward." Rather than waiting until graduation, orientation students try to identify a future goal that would follow completion of the degree (e.g., a particular career or successful application to a specific graduate program) and then work backward to identify the competencies and experiences required to reach that objective. As with all goal setting (Locke & Latham, 1990), the expectation is that this process will help direct the student's actions and increase motivation to overcome the hurdles to the desired objective.

A second assumption is that motivation and learning will improve if we take active steps to help students make "connections." The authors link future career goals and present competencies, speakers, or experiences to connect class content with the "real" world, connections between courses within a program so students are less likely to view each class in isolation, and connections between exercises within the orientation course, so students will perceive that they are building toward some identifiable outcome rather than engaging in the dreaded "busy work."

A third assumption is that orientation courses should equip students with the tools and knowledge of the processes required to be a successful undergraduate student or "learning how the game is played." Appleby (2007) provided a number of useful how-to guides that fit this assumption, including information on dealing with freshman stress, time management, "how to receive weak letters of recommendation," and differences between unsuccessful and successful undergraduate students.

A final assumption for orientation courses is that student self-selection in *or* out of psychology as a result of the orientation course is an important accomplishment. Our students frequently tell us that the reason they entered the major was "to help people." Similar to employment recruiting (e.g., Barber, 1998), the orientation course may provide enough information about the required expectations, educational process, and competencies for new students to make a more informed choice regarding pursuit of psychology as a major. Whereas reducing the number of students majoring in psychology may not be a popular objective for some administrators, it is often a reality that can provide an initial voluntary (or involuntary) screening when a department is faced with large numbers of new majors and a finite number of staff and higher level course sections.

Common Themes

A number of themes appear across the content of psychology orientation courses. Table 5-1 presents the frequency of occurrence among some of the more prevalent themes drawn from a review of 10 syllabi based on our earlier work (Landrum & Loher, 2007). These results are consistent with an extensive survey of psychology departments by Landrum et al. (2003) as well as our

Table 5-1
Themes from a Sample of Orientation and Careers in Psychology Syllabi[a]

Themes	% Covering[b]
Careers	100
Self-assessment	90
Resumes and cover letters	70
Job competencies	60
Interview with subject matter expert	50
Class visits to off-campus sites	10
Graduate school	90
What happens in graduate school	50
Application process	50
Goals & curricular planning	90

(continued)

Table 5-1 (*continued*)

Themes	% Covering[b]
Skills for success	60
APA style	60
Finding information	40
How to read literature	20
Time management	10
Encouraging involvement	70
Community service	40
Internships	30
Assistantships	10
Ethics & values	60
APA Code of Conduct	30
Avoiding plagiarism and academic misconduct	20
Other themes	60
Resource awareness	60
University and/or department policies & procedures	40
Department baseline assessment activities	30
Administrative issues	
100 – level[c]	50
50 minutes per week class time	60

[a] See Appendix 5F for syllabi included.

[b] Percentage of syllabi that indicated theme—in some cases while the overall theme was present it was not possible to determine more specific elements.

[c] Appleby (2005) was identified as 100-level but required completion of 24 credits to enroll.

own experiences. For instance, the themes presented in this chapter nicely overlap with the important items indicated by instructors that Landrum et al. (2003) identified for the course. We describe subcomponents or elements of these themes and we offer example exercises.

Case Examples

Careers in Psychology

All of the courses in our sample included content regarding psychology-related careers (e.g., different specializations, jobs requiring advanced degrees versus undergraduate degrees). Given that 80% of these classes were offered at the first- or second-year level, the prevalence of the careers theme is consistent with our four assumptions. This theme frequently includes activities to encourage comparisons between a student's current status and the interests, competencies, and experiences required to become a competitive candidate for an entry-level job or graduate program.

Self-assessment. As part of the careers theme, most orientation courses include self-assessment activities. These may be informal or more structured exercises to assess interests, values, personal strengths, and weaknesses. The basic idea is to help students clarify their vocational interests and generate lists of jobs or occupations that require similar attributes.

The "Career Interests Game" at the University of Missouri Career Center (http://career.missouri.edu/students/explore/thecareerinterestsgame.php) is at the less-formal end of the continuum and, at present, is free for outside users. This site is based on Holland's Theory of Vocational Choice (Holland, 1997). The game begins with simple descriptions of the six Holland categories (i.e., realistic, investigative, artistic, social, enterprising, and conventional). Clicking on a category takes the student to representative lists of personality characteristics (e.g., are you friendly, outgoing, empathic), hobbies (e.g., volunteering with social action groups, playing team sports), and other descriptors. There is also a list of job titles that are consistent with each category. The job titles have been hyperlinked with the appropriate online section of the Federal Occupational Outlook Handbook (OOH; http://www.bls.gov/oco/home.htm). The OOH site contains summative descriptions about the nature of the work, education and training requirements, working conditions, job outlook, earnings, and other information. The FOCUS program (available at http://www.focuscareer.com/) is an example of a more formal assessment tool. It generates detailed personal reports with recommended occupations. To ease in the interpretation of these detailed reports, we recommend guidance from career counselor professionals.

Resumes. The next most common element in the Careers theme is the creation of a professional resume. Development of a resume may help students better understand the expectations of potential employers. This is arguably the best example of "learning how the game is played." There are many acceptable resume formats (e.g., see Kuther, 2006; Landrum & Davis, 2010); however, for consistency and feedback purposes, it is best if students use the same format in a class or psychology department.

A useful exercise is to ask class participants to generate two resumes to encourage thinking about the future and its relation to the present. Whereas our recent experience suggests that students require more structure and guidance than in the past, at a certain point there is a danger that some students will treat resume writing as a "cut-and-paste" job. By assigning a "Future" resume in addition to the "Current" resume, one can better identify whether students understand the underlying structural expectations for resumes and encourage their thinking about how one creates a path to a future job or career. The Future resume includes additional academic degrees required for the desired occupation (in their appropriate order), examples of relevant internships or work experiences (including time frame), and similar changes. Ideally, the changes should all reflect realistic information derived from earlier exercises on psychology-related careers.

A sample resume scoring guide is presented in Appendix 5A of this chapter. This exercise uses the "chronological" resume format presented in Kuther (2006). The resume template and scoring guide are available to students online in advance of submitting the assignment. The scoring guide can reinforce the information covered during class sessions and provides a structure for generating feedback to students. It is not intended to be comprehensive but can greatly reduce some of the most common resume mistakes and shortens the grading time required to provide student feedback.

Job competencies. Another common element is to encourage students to consider the competencies required for an occupation or by an undergraduate psychology program. Lists of expected competencies (e.g., APA, 2007; Landrum & Harrold, 2003) often demonstrate considerable overlap (e.g., listening skills, ability to work in teams, problem solving). Instructors should supplement the discussion of "what employers want" from job candidates by emphasizing APA's expected learning outcomes for undergraduate psychology programs (APA, 2007; http://www.apa.org/ed/psymajor_guideline. pdf) or locally developed program goals. Connecting what employers want to what teachers teach helps students see the reasoning and rationale behind curricular decisions and also demonstrates that program goals exist in a broader context. Confronted with this overlap, students may see their degrees as a stepping stone to a variety of career tracks. Appleby (2006) offers an extensive list of job titles with hyperlinks to relevant occupational information. An advanced Careers in Psychology exercise that uses the federal O*NET Web site (http://www.onetcenter.org/content.html) is available from Rajecki (2007). He provides step-by-step instructions for how to search in O*NET for occupational descriptors and examples for how to interpret the output. Rajecki (2008) recently questioned how realistic it is to go from an undergraduate psychology degree to certain jobs. His concerns highlight the importance of discussing job requirements in an orientation course. Armed with an early knowledge of position requirements, it may be possible for a student to craft an academic plan and relevant experience to become a competitive candidate for a desired career. Consistent with our assumption that an orientation course is useful if it helps with self-selection in or out of the major, job competency exercises may also help a student to understand that there is a more direct path to an intended career.

Interviews. Half of our sample of orientation courses included an interview with a job incumbent to obtain career-related information. Sample items for an interview are presented in Appendix 5B of this chapter. If conducted on site, a field interview can provide enhanced information about context as well as the content of a job. If travel to the site is not possible, students often conduct the interview via e-mail or telephone. Students present the responses in class. In this manner, the other participants learn about a range of occupations. For information on interview structure and techniques, see Stewart and Cash (2008).

A desirable bonus is that students may use an interview as an initial contact for future job shadowing, volunteering, or internships. They also discover that some psychology-related jobs are easier to find than others. For example, school psychologists are much easier to identify and interview than FBI profilers.

Graduate School

Many new psychology majors assume they will go to graduate school for an advanced degree but have little knowledge about graduate school content or processes. This student assumption must face a reality check given the number of matriculating students currently receiving baccalaureate degrees (again, almost 90,000 in 2005–2006) and the number of openings in graduate programs (57,412 enrolled at all levels in 2005; cf. APA-CPWAR, 2008). If students enter thinking the first year in college is the "13th grade" (Appleby, 2007; Hettich & Helkowski, 2005), they apparently infer that they can obtain a PhD by continuing on to grade 17 or 18. In reality, there were 19,770 master's degrees awarded in 2005–2006 and only 4,921 psychology doctorates awarded in 2005–2006 (Snyder et al., 2008). Even for those students with a master's degree wishing to pursue doctoral education, the demand would clearly outnumber the supply.

In our sample, almost all of the orientation courses included content on graduate study in psychology. The role of graduate coverage in an orientation course is to provide early realistic information about (a) the typical hurdles and other processes in a graduate program (e.g., class expectations, research participation, thesis process, comprehensive exams), (b) the application process (e.g., GRE, grades, research participation, letters of reference, community service, interviews), and (c) the competitive nature of the graduate school application process (e.g., see Appleby & Appleby, 2006). To help students organize their requests for letters of recommendation, see Appendix 5C for a sample letter of recommendation request worksheet.

A sample graduate school exercise is included as Appendix 5D. This assignment uses APA's *Graduate Study in Psychology* (2008) manual and requires students to respond to questions regarding the admission requirements of two specific programs. As students process the exercise, discussion can center on the number of programs available in the area of interest, admission emphases, financial support, or terminology (e.g., tuition remission, thesis versus nonthesis). Once again, a faculty mentor can emphasize the need to start preparing for graduate school early in one's undergraduate career.

Goals and Curricular Planning

Development of a curricular plan can encourage students to form connections between specific careers in psychology, graduate school application criteria, and local program requirements. Nine out of the ten syllabi in our sample included development of some sort of curricular document. The creation of a two- to four-year plan that not only meets local graduation requirements but also lays the groundwork to become a competitive applicant for a job or graduate school is often very challenging. The curricular plan can encourage students to think beyond meeting minimum requirements and is an excellent way for students to demonstrate their understanding of the local "rules of the game." We have found the curricular plan generated in the orientation course to be extremely useful during subsequent student advising.

Skills for Success

Orientation courses often present a variety of skills-for-success components. The most frequent of these elements is an introduction to APA writing style and paper formats (see chapter 9 in this volume). Many courses also include information about library and technology-based search skills. Time management can also be a useful skill for new students to learn.

APA writing style. Some entering psychology majors have the advantage of prior exposure to APA style (e.g., at the secondary school level). For many others, the orientation course can provide an initial encounter for what is likely to be the required style in their future psychology department courses. For example, new students are often confused about the difference between an "empirical" versus a "literature review" paper. Many are unsure of how to cite another author's work or how to prepare a references section. In our classes the objective is not to produce APA experts but to introduce basic expectations for document structure, preparation rules, citations, and references. After providing a range of introductory information we ask students to evaluate and correct a sample "bad" paper to conclude the module on APA style (e.g., see Freimuth, 2008).

Finding information. We might have alternatively labeled this element "Beyond Google and Wikipedia." For years we assumed that each new wave of entering students would be more advanced than their predecessors in regard to technological sophistication. However, although the breadth of technology that incoming students use is remarkable, the depth of their understanding is sometimes quite superficial. For example, although students can readily click on presented lists of links, they may be stymied if they have to type in a URL. Finding science-based information in the library or on the Internet is one area where this issue becomes apparent. At present, a Google search is unlikely to identify empirical articles in the *Journal of Applied Psychology* or similar science journals.

Some students receive training on electronic search engines at the secondary school level. Others are very familiar with popular search sites like Google or Yahoo. With appropriate motivation, this existing knowledge can be transferred to the use of databases like PsycINFO or the Social Sciences Citation Index. In our courses, a classroom demonstration is followed by an exercise requiring use of a specific database (usually PsycINFO) and output, including a search history. Boise State University, for example, includes a library "scavenger hunt" to familiarize students with the library's resources. (For further discussion of emerging information literacy among students, see chapter 8 in this volume.)

Encouraging Involvement

Seventy percent of the orientation courses in our sample included content regarding involvement in either the department or the community. The most frequent element was some form of a community service requirement. Off-campus community service can help students form contact networks and connections between classroom and applied issues. Some students find the intrinsic rewards of community service to be so positive that they continue to work as volunteers at the site well beyond the class requirements.

A smaller number of orientation courses include information about internships and assistantships. At Mansfield University, students must complete an internship, a research apprenticeship, or an independent study in order to fulfill degree completion requirements. Over 90% elect to do the internship. Because this is such a popular option we introduce the subject during the orientation course. Students complete an in-class group exercise that forces them to use the Department's Internship Manual (available at http://mansfield.edu/psychology/media/files/Psychology%20Internship% 20Manual%2006-18-07%20Fall%202007%20Version.pdf). The resulting discussion can help surface student questions regarding the internship process.

At Boise State, the orientation course includes information about teaching and research assistantships. The presentation describes the roles (e.g., what a research assistant does) and benefits (e.g., acquisition of additional skills, familiarization with research techniques) of assistantships as well as how to negotiate landing an assistantship. These tips help students to understand the range of opportunities available for becoming involved in psychology beyond the classroom. We include an exercise to assist students in the development of an "Outside of Class Activities Plan" at the end of this chapter, in Appendix 5E.

The benefits of becoming involved in career-relevant clubs (e.g., Psi Chi, Psychology Club) or organizations (e.g., becoming a student affiliate of APA or regional associations) can also be part of the orientation course. Student officers visit to describe the group and encourage participation in the club or in specific community service projects.

Ethics and Values

Over half of our sample indicated that they included material on ethics and values as part of the orientation course. Introduction of the APA Ethical

Principles and Code of Conduct (APA, 2002) and information on avoiding academic misconduct (e.g., plagiarism) were the two most common topics. A case study exercise requiring opposing parties to identify and apply relevant sections of the Code of Conduct can be very involving for new students. New majors often find it challenging to move beyond their feelings or opinions and instead argue based on the particulars of the case in relation to the Code.

The need to define and discuss plagiarism and other forms of academic misconduct appears to be increasing. The OWL site (http://owl.english. purdue.edu/owl/resource/589/01/) at Purdue University and the Writing Tutorial Services page at Indiana University (http://www.indiana.edu/ ~wts/pamphlets/plagiarism.shtml) contain definitions, examples, and recommendations for how to avoid the most common forms of plagiarism. A list of links to additional sites dealing with plagiarism is available from Stanger (http://keithstanger.com/estyle_2.htm).

Other Themes

Depending on the amount of available time, several other themes may be included in an orientation course for psychology majors. Most common among these is information to increase awareness of available resources, ranging from concrete needs (e.g., location of the computer lab, copy machines, faculty mailboxes, and department microwave) to recommendations regarding poten-tial advisors in relation to students' interests and career goals. For some courses another important element is coverage of university and department policies and procedures. For example, new students often have many "how do I . . . ?" questions regarding the registration process. They may see the orientation course instructor as an unofficial advisor in regard to general education requirements, timing of courses, or other details for successfully navigating campus life. Finally, some departments use the orientation course as a time to collect baseline data for their program assessment activities (e.g., initial con-struction of a department portfolio, baseline exams, and video samples).

Conclusion

It is clear that a growing number of psychology departments offer an orienta-tion course as part of their curriculum. In addition to course content, there are several administrative issues that need to be addressed. One issue is the timing of the course in the curriculum. Only 50% of the syllabi in our sample had a course number at the 100-level or its equivalent. One of these required completion of 24 credits prior to enrolling in the class (Appleby, 2005). Our recommendation is that the earlier orientation-type information is presented to students, the greater impact this information can have on students' decision-making processes. The downside to this strategy is that the course instructor may have to deal with some students who are unlikely to survive academically beyond the first year of college or those with minimal commitment to psychology. Another issue is the number of credit hours for the course. The range of credits in our sample was from zero to three. A related issue is the amount of contact time. Whereas once per week was the most common model, some departments may find that more frequent contact is necessary with new students.

Departments with large numbers of incoming students will inevitably have different formats from smaller departments. Access to teaching assistants can help with evaluation and feedback on assignments when dealing with larger enrollment numbers. One syllabus in our sample listed the names of 19 teaching assistants for the orientation sections (Appleby, 2005).

No matter what decisions are made regarding the initial structure and content for an undergraduate psychology orientation course, this is a course that often grows over time. Our experience is that colleagues, students, and alumni continuously suggest additional themes or exercises. In the future, the growing literature on issues relevant to orientation courses (e.g., Harris & Queen, 2007; Landrum & Mulcock, 2007; Rajecki, 2008; Thomas & McDaniel, 2004) should help us to refine our objectives and techniques so the orientation course can effectively inform and motivate our new undergraduate psychology majors. Given the recent growth in the psychology major, it is imperative that we work to improve the quality of information we provide and continue a "truth in advertising" approach to best serve our students.

Recommended Readings

Harris, P. B., & Queen, J. S. (2007). Link to the future: Web page design in a psychology careers course. *Teaching of Psychology, 34,* 129–134.

Kuther, T. L. (2006). *The psychology major's handbook* (2nd ed.). Belmont, CA: Thomson Wadsworth.

Landrum, R. E., Shoemaker, C. S., & Davis, S. F. (2003). Important topics in an introduction to the psychology major course. *Teaching of Psychology, 30,* 48–51.

Thomas, J. H., & McDaniel, C. R. (2004). Effectiveness of a required course in career planning for psychology majors. *Teaching of Psychology, 31,* 22–27.

References

American Psychological Association. (2002). Ethical principles of psychologists and code of conduct. *American Psychologist, 57,* 1060–1073.

American Psychological Association. (2007). *APA guidelines for the undergraduate psychology major.* Washington, DC: Author. Retrieved from www.apa.org/ed/resources.html

American Psychological Association. (2008). *Graduate study in psychology 2008.* Washington, DC: Author.

American Psychological Association-Center for Workforce Analysis and Research (2008). *Psychology education pipeline.* Retrieved May 30, 2008 from http://research.apa.org/PipelineGraphic.pdf

Appleby, D. C. (2006). *Occupations of interest to psychology majors from the Dictionary of Occupational Titles.* Retrieved April 22, 2008 from http://teachpsych.org/otrp/resources/appleby06.pdf

Appleby, D. C. (2007). *Four developmental tasks of understanding psychology majors: Surviving, thriving, striving, and arriving.* CD distributed with Keynote Address at the Sixth Annual Beginnings & Endings Conference, Atlanta, GA.

Appleby, D. C., & Appleby, K. M. (2006). Kisses of death in the graduate school application process. *Teaching of Psychology, 33,* 19–24.

Barber, A. E. (1998). *Recruiting employees: Individual and organizational perspectives.* Thousand Oaks, CA: Sage.

Freimuth, M. (2008). *A self-scoring exercise on APA style and research language.* Retrieved April 22, 2008 from http://teachpsych.org/otrp/resources/freimuth08.rtf

Harris, P. B., & Queen, J. S. (2007). Link to the future: Web page design in a psychology careers course. *Teaching of Psychology, 34,* 129–134.

Hettich, P. I., & Helkowski, C. (2005). *Connect college to career: Student guide to work and life transition.* Belmont, CA: Thomson Wadsworth.

Holland, J. L. (1997). *Making vocational choices: A theory of vocational personalities and work environments* (3rd ed.). Odessa, FL: PAR.

Kuther, T. L. (2006). *The psychology major's handbook* (2nd ed.). Belmont, CA: Thomson Wadsworth.

Landrum, R. E., & Davis, S. F. (2010). *The psychology major: Career options and strategies for success* (4th ed.). Upper Saddle River, NJ: Pearson Prentice Hall.

Landrum, R. E., & Harrold, R. (2003). What employers want from psychology graduates. *Teaching of Psychology, 30*, 131–133.

Landrum, R. E., & Loher, B. T. (2007). *Designing a psychology orientation course: Common themes and sample exercises.* Pre-Conference Workshop presented at the Sixth Annual Beginnings & Endings Conference, Atlanta, GA.

Landrum, R. E., & Mulcock, S. D. (2007). Use of pre- and post-course surveys to predict student outcomes. *Teaching of Psychology, 34*, 163–166.

Landrum, R. E., Shoemaker, C. S., & Davis, S. F. (2003). Important topics in an introduction to the psychology major course. *Teaching of Psychology, 30*, 48–51.

Locke, E. A., & Latham, G. P. (1990). *A theory of goal setting and task performance.* Englewood Cliffs, NJ: Prentice Hall.

Rajecki, D. W. (2007). *A job list of one's own: Creating customized career information for psychology majors.* Retrieved April 22, 2008 from http://teachpsych.org/otrp/resources/rajecki07.pdf

Rajecki, D. W. (2008). Job lists for entry-level psychology baccalaureates: Occupational recommendations that mismatch qualifications. *Teaching of Psychology, 35*, 33–37.

Snyder, T. D., Dillow, S. A., & Hoffman, C. M. (2008). *Digest of education statistics 2007* (NCES 2008-022) (Table 303). National Center for Education Statistics, Institute of Education Sciences, U.S. Department of Education, Washington, DC.

Stewart, C. J., & Cash, W. B. (2008). *Interviewing: Principles and practices* (12th ed.). New York: McGraw-Hill.

Thomas, J. H., & McDaniel, C. R. (2004). Effectiveness of a required course in career planning for psychology majors. *Teaching of Psychology, 31*, 22–27.

Appendix 5A   Sample Resume Scoring Checklist

	Issue	Yes	No
1.	Appropriate Psychology Department format?	_____	_____
2.	Name? Centered? Appropriate font size?	_____	_____
3.	Complete address(es), including zip code(s)?	_____	_____
4.	Phone number(s) with area code(s)? E-mail?	_____	_____
5.	Objective? Two sentence maximum?	_____	_____
6.	Education? Highest degree first? Includes location? Dates?	_____	_____
7.	Experience? Most recent first? Includes job title, location, major duties, and dates?	_____	_____
8.	Skills? Includes relevant courses and computer skills? Most relevant first?	_____	_____
9.	Activities? Most relevant first? Includes dates?	_____	_____
10.	References available on request?	_____	_____
11.	Uses action words and short phrases? Avoids "I" statements?	_____	_____
12.	One or fewer spelling or grammar or formatting errors?	_____	_____
13.	Two pages or less in length?	_____	_____
14.	Typed with appropriate margins, font size, etc.?	_____	_____
15.	Appropriate changes to "Future" version?	_____	_____

Appendix 5B Sample Job Incumbent Interview Template

Interviewer:_____   Interviewee:_____

Date of Interview:_____   Job Title:_____

                                     Organization:_____

1. What is the connection between your desired job and your interviewee's position?
2. How did you go about selecting the person you interviewed?

THE JOB
3. How long have you been employed in this field?
4. How long have you worked in your present position?
5. How did you get into your current job?
6. What educational requirements are needed for this position?
7. What are your major duties and responsibilities?
8. Please describe what you do on a typical day.
9. What issues do you deal with the most on a day-to-day basis?
10. How many hours do you work during a typical day?
11. Do you use any sort of special techniques or tests as part of your work?
12. What do you like most about your job?
13. What do you like least about your job?
14. How would someone locate an entry-level job in this occupation?
15. How does one advance in this occupation?
16. How do you keep up on new ideas and issues?

NONWORK ISSUES
17. How do you balance your work and nonwork roles?

ADVICE
18. What classes or training did you find helpful in preparing you for your career?

19. What experiences should I get before I enter the job market in this occupation?
20. What skills should I develop in order to enter this profession?
21. What areas of this profession seem to have the most opportunities for employment?
22. What one book would you recommend for someone who wants to enter this career?

Remember to **THANK** the interviewee for her or his time and effort. Send the person a thank-you note or e-mail after the interview.

Appendix 5C   Letter of Recommendation

Request Work Sheet

Adapted with permission from Landrum, R. E., & Davis, S. F. (2007). *The psychology major: Career options and strategies for success* (3rd ed.). Upper Saddle River, NJ: Pearson Prentice Hall.

In this exercise, use this form to organize the letter of recommendation. This can be used for employers as well as graduate school applications. There are lots of details to attend to, so use the checklist to make sure you don't forget everything and that your letter writer has everything he or she needs to write you the strongest possible letter. Remember, paying attention to details is important; if you can't follow the instructions for applying to graduate school, many graduate schools will figure that you couldn't follow the instructions once you were admitted to graduate school (so why bother?).

Category	Check √	Details
Initial Contact		Discuss the letter of recommendation with each faculty member/letter writer face-to-face.
		Ask "would you be willing to write me a strong letter of recommendation?"
		Make this contact as soon as possible—no later than 1 month before the first letter is due.
Demographic Information		Provide the letter writer with your name, campus and permanent address, e-mail address, and phone numbers (including cell phone)
Academic Information		List your major, minor, GPAs, test scores, academic awards, honor society memberships
		State the nature of the relationship, the length of time the letter writer has known you
Experiences		Describe internships, independent study, directed research, senior thesis, work experiences, extracurricular activities (e.g., Psi Chi, Psychology Club)
Accomplishments		Give some details about your skills, talents, abilities, personal qualities, and relevant accomplishments
		List relevant accomplishments with details, dates, etc.
		List relevant scholarships, recognitions (e.g., Dean's List)
Personal Characteristics		Describe academic strengths and weaknesses, why you are qualified for graduate school
		Provide concrete examples of skills, such as dependability, intellect, drive and motivation, written and oral communication skills, interpersonal skills
Wrap Up		State how you can be reached by the letter writer if he or she needs more information
		Clearly tell the letter writer if the letter is to be mailed directly to the graduate school or returned to you (sign on the flap?)
		Thank the letter writer formally with a hand-written card
		Keep the letter writer informed about the progress of your efforts

Appendix 5D   Sample Graduate School Exercise

The purpose of this assignment is to seek realistic information about graduate programs in your chosen career area. You will need to consult a copy of *Graduate Study in Psychology - 2008*. Two copies of this book may be found in the Psychology Reading Room. The books are a shared resource, so please remember not to remove them from the rooms.

Obtain and record the following information for <u>TWO</u> graduate programs:

1. Name and address and Web site address of the graduate program
2. Address for application materials (if different from #1)
3. Title of the program and degree level relevant to your interests
4. List <u>all</u> admission requirements for the program of interest (e.g., GRE, GPA, letters of recommendation, interviews, personal statement)
5. (A) Minimum scores and (B) average or median scores among those accepted in the area of interest on any required standardized tests (e.g., GRE) AND on GPA, if presented
6. List the types and levels ($ amounts) of available financial assistance

Appendix 5E   Sample Outside of Class

Activities Plan

Use the planning sheet below to map out your strategy for completing out-of-class activities while finishing your undergraduate degree (Landrum & Davis, 2007). Try to be as specific as possible in whom you are planning to work with, making contact, duration of work, and outcomes. The shaded regions are examples of how you might use this planning tool.

TEACHING

Specific Type of Activity	When Do I Make Initial Contact?	Whom Do I Contact?	Duration of Time Spent on Activity	Outcomes	Notes to Myself
Teaching Assistant, General Psychology	November 2008 (prior to Spring 2009 semester)	Dr. Smith	1 semester	– make connection with faculty member – review general psychology info	If this works out, maybe I'll ask Dr. Smith about being an RA.

RESEARCH

Specific Type of Activity	When Do I Make Initial Contact?	Whom Do I Contact?	Duration of Time Spent on Activity	Outcomes	Notes to Myself
Research Assistant	May 2008 (at the end of Research Methods)	Dr. Davis	2 semesters	– gain research experience – conference presentation	Let Dr. Davis know I'll be asking him for a letter of recommendation.

(Continued)

SERVICE

Specific Type of Activity	When Do I Make Initial Contact?	Whom Do I Contact?	Duration of Time Spent on Activity	Outcomes	Notes to Myself
Volunteer at Psychiatric Ward at Hospital	After completing Abnormal Psychology (Fall 2009)	Dr. Jones, VA Hospital	2 semesters	– make a professional connection – gain valuable out-of-class experience	This might turn into an internship next summer.

Appendix 5F   Syllabi Included in Our Sample

Appleby, D. C. (2005). *B103: Orientation to a Major in Psychology*. Indiana University – Purdue University Indianapolis.

Bates, S. C. (n.d.). *Psychology 2950 – Orientation to the Psychology Major*. Utah State University.

Ferraro, F. R. (2007). *PSY 120 – Orientation to the Psychology Major*. University of North Dakota.

Landrum, R. E. (2007). *PSYC 120: Introduction to the Psychology Major*. Boise State University.

Lloyd, M. A. (n.d.). *Psychology 2210 – Careers in Psychology*. Georgia Southern University.

Loher, B. T. (2007). *PSY 1151W: Orientation to Psychology*. Mansfield University.

Malacos, J. A. (2007). *Orientation to Psychology, PSYC 128.01*. University of Findlay.

Miller, R. L. (2007). *Orientation to Psychology: Psychology 300*. University of Nebraska at Kearney.

Mosteller, L. H. (2007). *Careers in Psychology: Psychology 2200*. Appalachian State University.

Prehar, C. (2006). *Psychology of Careers, 42.304.01*. Framingham State College.

6 Engaging Students in Psychology

Building on First-Year Programs and Seminars

Regan A. R. Gurung and *Georjeanna Wilson-Doenges*

How can you optimize student engagement in the psychology major? Regardless of how one measures success or engagement, it is clear that engaged students are successful students (Carini, Kuh, & Klein, 2006; Keup, & Stoltzenberg, 2004; Kuh, Kinze, Schuh, & Whitt, 2005). Engagement has been defined in a variety of ways, including active involvement in the classroom and with the university, interactions with faculty and other students, positive affective responses to courses, and a desire to achieve academically (Conner-Greene, 2006). Retention rates serve as one measure of student engagement (Swing, 2001) and other outcome measures may include grade point average (GPA), campus involvement (e.g., student government, residence hall assistant), relationships (e.g., faculty-student interaction, student organizations), perceptions of individual courses, and the college experience in general. The National Study of Student Engagement (NSSE) provides a standardized measure of student engagement.

Whereas increasing student engagement is a worthy goal, it is a difficult proposition to actually do so, one that calls for action at the level of the class, the department, and even the university. This chapter will present an effective strategy to engage students at the level of the class and the university. Designed to energize students with a passion for learning and to better connect them to the university, this strategy engages students with the curriculum.

Looking at a Small Part of the Big Picture

If you want to engage your introductory psychology students or your majors in the department, you do not have to do it by yourself. It is important to make yourself aware of universitywide initiatives. Many colleges and universities offer specific programs to help students adjust to college, especially in the first year (Tobolowsky, Mamrick, & Cox, 2005; e.g., orientation, majors fair, student organizations fair). Many of these programs are courses taken in the first semester. For example, University 101 is a type of course that helps students succeed at college. The University 101 model is normally a one-credit course focused on skill development (e.g., how to study, take tests, manage time) without embedding those skills in academic content. Alternatively, many schools offer first-year seminars that are interdisciplinary and academic in nature, with varying amounts of content-based skill development. These courses, called first-year seminars, often have catchy titles (e.g., Gods, Ghosts, and Goblins: Understanding Belief; Google and Ye Shall Find?) and are frequently guided by faculty interests (correspondingly, these courses are referred to as "passion courses"; Bartell, Wilson-Doenges, Gurung, Furlong, & Amenson-Hill, 2008). Approximately 70% of institutions offer some form of seminar (Barefoot, 2005). Instead of using a textbook, as seen in many "Introduction to . . . " courses, first-year seminars focus on contemporary issues that span disciplines, use readings that are rigorous but more accessible (e.g., Fast Food Nation; Schlosser, 2001), and involve active pedagogies. The amount of content-based skill development and connection to college orientation programs or student life programming varies across universities.

Tapping into existing college programs for first-year students provides a wonderful venue both to assess the level of student engagement in a college and to optimize first-year experiences for students who may be future psychology majors. Psychology departments could adapt the psychology curriculum to draw on existing university programming by offering introductory psychology as a first-year seminar with an added University 101 component, or by having psychology faculty develop psychology-focused "passion" seminars for first-year students such as the Psychology and Health freshman seminar at the University of Wisconsin in Milwaukee and the courses described later in this chapter. Reaching first-year students with engaging psychology courses connected to a larger universitywide engagement effort is a win-win proposition.

One important source of information about student engagement is the NSSE. Many universities participate in this nationwide survey, and data suggest that although student engagement with the university as a whole is a critical variable in retention, many universities show low levels of engagement (Kuh et al., 2005).

Improving student engagement with the whole university requires the coordinated effort of all aspects of the university, especially the academic programs. As psychology is one of the most popular majors on college campuses and approximately 1.3 million students take introductory psychology every year (T. Beesley, personal communication, May 27, 2008), our discipline's participation in these efforts is paramount. Consequently, designing introductory courses that are truly engaging can be pivotal—not just to develop strong psychology majors but also to help shape students' engagement with college in general. Can optimizing the introductory psychology course increase student engagement with the department and the college while also increasing NSSE scores? Absolutely.

Measuring Engagement

Most universities assess engagement by comparing grade point averages (GPAs) and retention rates of students, especially first-year students. Even though instructors may grade differently or institutions may have different grading standards (Robbins, Carlstrom, Davis, Langley, Lauver, & Le, 2004), GPA is the most common measure of student performance and is thought to be the best predictor of key success markers such as graduation rate and graduate school enrollment (Pascarelli & Terenzini, 2005).

Although retention rates are commonly used as a factor to measure engagement, measuring retention rates usually occurs only after the first semester or the first year. Many larger institutions are attracted to this technique as an easy assessment but it provides us with only one small piece of a larger college experience. Although some schools conduct more in-depth studies of a seminar group or cohort, generally cross-sectional data cannot capture the dynamic nature of college retention or engagement. For example, at Northern Michigan, GPAs and retention rates are taken into consideration for up to 7 years (Tobolowsky et al., 2005). Assessing retention rates over a long period of time may make the findings more useful to institutions trying to track engagement throughout the college experience.

Measuring engagement with GPA and retention rates as proxies, although commonly used, may not be the best way to assess engagement. As referenced earlier, the NSSE measures student engagement within the classroom and the institution and may well be able to get at the root of engagement rather than by GPA or retention proxies. Items on the NSSE focus on various possible measures of engagement including getting involved in class discussions, discussing class material with instructors and other students outside of class, and getting involved with various campus activities. Activities are also important as motivation to learn, and learning is accomplished by participating in campus activities that can positively influence motivation to learn (Covington, 2000).

The NSSE consists of 100 items divided into 29 sections and five different domains: *supportive campus environment, enriching educational experiences, student-faculty interaction, level of academic challenges,* and *active and collaborative learning* (See Table 6-1 for a summary of topics covered and example items from the five domains). These domains cover the aspects that are currently thought to be the backbone of student engagement. Items also assess student demographic information.

The NSSE can help with identifying the strengths and weaknesses of an institution's educational program, analyzing areas that may need more focus in order to improve student learning and sorting out the aspects of the program

Table 6-1

NSSE Domains and Sample Items

Domain	Topics covered
Supportive Campus Environment	Institutional assistance with and commitment to the success of its students. E.g., helps students cope with nonacademic responsibilities (work, family, and so forth).
Enriching Educational Experiences	Student exposure to diversity, new ideas, technology and work outside of the classroom. E.g., talking with students of a different race or ethnicity.
Student Interaction with Faculty Members	Student contact with faculty members outside of the classroom. E.g., discussing ideas from readings or classes with faculty members outside of class.
Level of Academic Challenge	Assigned course work and cognitive tasks that students may use to complete assignments. E.g., working harder than students thought they could to meet an instructor's standards.
Active and Collaborative Learning	Students are actively involved with their education by working with others. E.g., making class presentations.

that are not in line with the goals of the program (Kinzie, 2007). A modified version of NSSE is available to assess engagement with a class. The Classroom Survey of Student Engagement (CLSSE) developed by Smallwood and Ouimet (cited in Kinzie, 2007) is a questionnaire measuring student involvement in a particular class.

Standardized assessments such as the NSSE and in-house surveys (often administered in pre-post designs or cross-sectionally only at the end of a semester) provide useful quantitative data. Qualitative data are also useful to assess and improve introductory courses and seminars. Colleges and universities also use first-year seminar students as a focus group to obtain qualitative data for their assessments. For example, Bryant University, Indiana University–Purdue University at Indianapolis, and Millersville University are among the many institutions that use focus groups to aid in assessing their first-year seminars (Tobolowsky et al., 2005). These institutions found that students enjoyed interacting with other students and used and benefited from all of the resources in the seminars (e.g., direct connection to tutoring services, campus mental health professionals). The students also reported that they appreciated the skills they acquired throughout the program, including time management and study skills. Though focus groups and open ended questions can provide enriched data, having both quantitative and qualitative data is necessary for the best assessments (Mullendore, Biller, & Busby, 2003).

Revitalizing the Introductory Course: First-year Seminars in Psychology

A variety of first-year seminars exist on a wide range of college campuses. Barefoot (2005) classified freshman seminars into five major types:

1. *Extended orientation seminar.* Sometimes called a freshman orientation or student success course. It often covers issues of campus resources, time management, academic and career planning, and other topics.
2. *Academic seminar with generally uniform academic content across sections.* An interdisciplinary or theme-oriented course, which may be part of a general education requirement. Focus of the course is on the academic theme but will often include academic skill components such as critical thinking and writing.

3. *Academic seminars on various topics.* Similar to number two above, except the academic content varies from section to section.

4. *Pre-professional or discipline-linked seminar.* Designed specifically for students within a specific major or discipline.

5. *Basic study skills seminar.* Offered typically to academically underprepared students. Focus is on basic skills such as grammar, note taking, and test taking.

Institutions use seminars to create highly engaging classroom experiences for first-year students and to provide exposure to academic content in a novel structure (Kuh et al., 2005). An extensive literature (Barefoot, 2005; Pascarella & Terenzini, 1991, 2005; Tobolowsky et al., 2005) indicates that first-year seminars are strongly related to degree completion and outcomes such as improved retention and graduation rates, and in some cases, improved academic performance.

The freshman year is also commonly the time students first encounter the field of psychology. There is extensive research focusing on the content of the introductory psychology course and pedagogy (Dunn & Chew, 2006), but less on course design and structure. Furthermore, most research, both historically and presently, examines the content of introductory psychology textbooks and the core concepts covered (Griggs, Bujak-Johnson, & Proctor, 2004; Quereshi & Zulli, 1975). Building on the rich research on student development and the first-year experience (National Resource Center for the First-Year Experience and Students in Transition, 2008), the University of Wisconsin-Green Bay (UWGB) built and offered first-year seminars to incoming students. We will describe our program and identify the key components of a seminar that you can use to modify your own introductory psychology classes.

Case Example

In fall 2006, six University of Wisconsin-Green Bay faculty pilot tested six sections of a first-year seminar designed to promote engagement among a host of goals, such as promoting students' understanding of interdisciplinarity. We used an introductory psychology class and an introductory human development class capped at 25 students and limited to new entering fall first-year students. The seminars integrated traditional general education curricula with a range of engaging curricular and co-curricular elements including extensive writing, discussion, and active learning elements. These smaller general education classes were made available to all first-year students on a first-come first-served basis. Both classes used standard introductory textbooks.

Faculty took special pains to facilitate class discussion and provide students with opportunities to apply, evaluate, and synthesize the course material. For example, students in the introductory psychology class were asked to write comments, criticisms, or questions about each reading on index cards. The instructor then had students read items from their card to catalyze class discussion. Having the card in front of them provided a prop for the student and cut down on possible anxiety from being called on and having to generate an oral response without prior warning. The cards also motivated students to read the material and fostered deeper processing of the content.

The seminars met for 75 minutes on Mondays and Wednesdays, covered essentially the same content as similar larger section courses, and had scheduled co-curricular activities. Co-curricular activities included a seminar-relevant film series with follow-up discussions led by seminar faculty and campus speakers. These required activities and films related to each seminar, and faculty made explicit connections between each activity and psychological themes. For example, after viewing one of the films, *Good Will Hunting* (featuring Robin Williams as a clinical psychologist), students completed an annotated bibliography assignment reflecting on a selected psychological theme from the film. Common scheduling also enabled the faculty to implement a common lesson plan specifically designed to enhance students' understanding of the meaning and value of interdisciplinarity, one of the UWGB's core values. The common lesson involved the students in an interdisciplinary problem-solving task with students from other seminar classes. For two class periods students in all the seminars met together in groups of six, with one student from each seminar in each group, to solve a common problem. Each student then reflected on the experience by writing an essay on the value of interdisciplinary teams in solving problems (for complete details on the common lesson see Bartell, Gurung, Furlong, Kersten, & Wilson-Doenges, 2007).

The primary goal of the first-year seminars, both in psychology and the other disciplines, was to improve the quality of the first-semester experience. Prior to the implementation of the first-year seminars, UWGB freshmen campuswide scored statistically lower than students at other similar colleges, both in the UW System and nationwide, on virtually all aspects of educational engagement measured by the NSSE. With a student-faculty ratio over 23-to-1, and introductory level general education courses averaging over 90 students, the university has struggled to identify ways to connect first-year students with their faculty.

We used a between-subjects experimental design comparing first-year students in the seminars with other first-year students enrolled in at least one small class. All students completed selected items from the NSSE, focusing on the concepts of active and collaborative learning, student-faculty interaction, the supportive campus environment, and self-reported intellectual development (see Table 6-1 for item examples). We also compared fall 2006 scores with previously collected spring 2006 NSSE scores.

We found that seminars significantly increased student engagement. Seminar participants reported higher levels of various types of engagement and intellectual development than members of their cohort unable to take a seminar. In-class behaviors such as asking questions, making presentations, and working with classmates in class showed the largest differences. Seminar participants often reported significantly higher levels of interaction with faculty than did nonparticipants. For example, seminar students were almost twice as likely to discuss grades or assignments with faculty as were nonparticipants, and the percentage of participants who "never" talked about career plans with faculty was 18% lower than the corresponding percentage of nonparticipants. Seminars significantly and positively impacted participants' relationships with other students, faculty members, and university staff. In all three cases, participants reported friendlier and more supportive relationships than nonparticipants. The largest improvement occurred in their relationships with faculty members.

The university reflected on these and other assessment results from the first-year seminar pilot during its strategic budgeting process and devoted additional faculty resources to expand the number of seminars to 13 in fall 2007 and 16 sections in fall 2008.

Recommendations

So, how should instructors modify introductory courses in psychology to promote student engagement? Based on our findings and the wealth of research conducted on the first-year experience (e.g., Kuh et al., 2005;

Tobolowsky et al., 2005), we suggest the following critical guidelines to advance student engagement:

1. *Connect with first-year programs.* Even if your university does not currently offer first-year seminars, you can still tap into existing orientation programs to increase engagement. One easy route is to have the university students who are registered for introductory psychology also be in the same first-year orientation groups. If there are orientation groups of 20 to 25 and all students are in the same class when the semester begins, there is an automatic sense of group identity and a built-in support network. The instructor of the psychology class can make an appearance during orientation and touch base with each group so as to make the first day of class a little less intimidating for the students. If possible, the instructors of introductory psychology should be faculty orientation group leaders as well.

2. *Rely on existing institutional level measures.* Given the wealth of information provided by NSSE and the availability of validated tools, such as the CLASSE, departments can capitalize on these measures and apply the results of the same to inform department-level evaluation (Dunn, McCarthy, Baker, Halonen, & Hill, 2007). Departments in universities using the NSSE are entitled to use and modify any of the items from the NSSE for additional assessment of student engagement. Rewriting the measure for use in the introductory psychology courses will provide a rich new source of data for instructors and department chairs.

3. *Establish first-year seminars.* Although it may not be logistically possible for all first-semester first-year students to simultaneously take a small introductory psychology class, establishing at least some small sections of introductory psychology or using graduate or undergraduate teaching assistants to conduct special activities (see below) in small groups could be beneficial. If your university supports first-year passion seminars, maximize the number offered in the field of psychology or taught by your psychology faculty. Passion courses can cover many of the basic topics covered in an introductory psychology course in a more flexible format. Such courses may serve as useful gateways to the major. Many universities do have first-year seminars for all first-year

students. If this is the case, the more seminars that can be offered by psychology faculty, the better will be the connections made with new students to the department. Additional resources for the creation of and the optimization of first-year seminars can be found at the NRC-FYE Web site (http://www.sc.edu/fye/).

4. *Develop explicit learning outcomes.* Research from the last 10–15 years on the first-year experience suggests key learning outcomes for first-year courses. In addition to standard course goals (e.g., expose students to the breadth of the field of psychology, major theories, the scientific method), we developed the following seminar objectives:

   a. Promote engagement (in class, with faculty, with peers, with the university) and a positive adjustment to college
   b. Foster an understanding of interdisciplinarity
   c. Develop critical thinking/problem-solving skills
   d. Develop written and oral communication skills
   e. Develop information literacy

   We worked to meet these objectives through a combination of in-class collaborative learning, co-curricular activities, and the common lesson. Meeting these learning outcomes in introductory psychology classes can increase students' engagement with your psychology department as well as better prepare future psychology majors early on. Furthermore, many of the skill-based learning outcomes used in first-year seminar courses map nicely onto the American Psychological Association (APA) guidelines for undergraduate education (APA, 2007).

5. *Develop common elements.* To ensure consistency of the student experience across seminars, both across instructors within a department and across departments, we found that it is critical to establish common elements that serve to better reach the learning objectives. Some common requirements for engagement often include the use of active learning strategies such as structured and unstructured group discussion, writing opportunities, and venues for the practice of communication skills (Hunter & Skipper, 1999). Requiring a presentation is manageable in a small class and having students work together

(or alone) to present information serves many purposes. In the introductory psychology course, we took topics that are usually the most interesting to students (e.g., sleep, hypnosis, substance use) and had students present on these topics in groups in lieu of having the instructor lecture or present the material. In this way presentations were spread across the semester and provided a nice change of pace for the students.

6. *Focus on faculty development.* Teaching first-year students is not business as usual. If an instructor has never taught first-year students or normally teaches only large classes, special training from the departmental chair or from a teaching and learning center is recommended. It is also beneficial for all faculty teaching first-year seminars to have opportunities to communicate with each other to share experiences and perhaps troubleshoot issues of concern (e.g., dealing with student disruptions). It is also prudent to educate faculty on cohort differences and the mind-set of incoming first-year students. Substantial research suggests that "millennials" (our first-year students) are very different from first-year students even 10 years ago (Twenge, 2007). Hunter and Skipper (1999) have provided a detailed description and recommendations for faculty development for first-year seminars.

Developing first-year seminars is not easy. Most of the active learning techniques work better in smaller classes but often require additional effort on the part of the instructor designing the course. Creating smaller class sizes or the feel of a smaller class and implementing some of these strategies for engagement can also necessitate reallocation of resources and faculty development. Redirecting funds focused on smaller classes rather than on the more traditional large introductory class may be necessary. Hiring adjunct instructors to provide the necessary smaller classes may also be necessary. In addition to the issue of funding, there is often a sense of inertia in departments and on campuses that may make it difficult to develop new formats for student instruction. We have found that some issues such as the difficulty of covering all of the content while still participating in collaborative learning and co-curricular and common activities are actually not as problematic as they may seem. In addition, taking the time to engage students in their learning can paradoxically increase the amount of content covered. Research on introductory courses in disciplines such as biology suggests that the time taken to work on objectives such as critical thinking can actually help with content coverage (Nelson, 1999). Having students present material as suggested above is just one way of covering content while also increasing engagement.

Despite the expected bumps in the road, first-year seminars can engage both first-year students and the faculty teaching them (Hunter & Skipper, 1999; Troxel & Cutright, 2008). It is well worth the effort to get faculty interested in teaching such courses and convincing key administrators that these courses will serve the university (and the major). Do not forget that there are existing resources in other areas of campus such as Student Life or a similar office. There are also existing models of successful engagement initiatives that can be modified to fit a specific institution (Kuh et al., 2005). Attending the national conference for the First-year Experience is a beneficial way to access some of these options. Pilot a course. Build incrementally. Our experiences and a wide wealth of similar success stories nationwide suggest that reworking the introductory psychology class as a special seminar or teaching first-year psychology passion seminars has many benefits.

Suggested Readings

Kuh, G. D., Kinzie, J., Schuh, J. H., & Whitt, E. J. (2005). *Student success in college: Creating conditions that matter.* San Francisco: Jossey-Bass.

Pascarella, E. T., & Terenzini, P. T. (2005). *How college affects students: A third decade of research.* San Francisco: Jossey-Bass.

Troxel, W. G., & Cutright, M. (Eds.). (2008). *Exploring the evidence: Initiatives in the first college year.* [Monograph No. 49]. Columbia: University of South Carolina, National Resource Center for the First-Year Experience and Students in Transition.

References

American Psychological Association. (2007). *APA guidelines for the undergraduate psychology major.* Washington, DC: Author.

Barefoot, B. O. (2005). "Foreword." In B. F. Tobolowsky with M. Mamrick & B. E. Cox, *The 2003 National Survey on First-Year Seminars.* National Resource Center for the First-Year Experience and Students in Transition, Columbia: University of South Carolina.

Barefoot, B. O., & Fidler, P. P. (1992). *The 1991 national survey of freshman seminar programming: Helping first-year college students climb the academic ladder* [Monograph No. 10]. Columbia: University of South Carolina, National Resource Center for the Freshman Year Experience.

Bartell, D., Gurung, R. A. R., Furlong, S., Kersten, A., & Wilson-Doenges, G. (2007). An interdisciplinary lesson plan to foster student engagement. *Teaching Forum, 3*, [www.uwlax.edu/teachingforum/index.html].

Bartell, D., Wilson-Doenges, G., Gurung, R. A. R., Furlong, S., & Amenson-Hill, B. (2008, February). *Purpose and passion in first-year experience courses: Comparing interdisciplinary and traditional general education seminars.* Paper presented at the meeting of the First-year Experience conference, San Francisco, CA.

Carini, R., Kuh, G., & Klein, S. (2006). Student engagement and student learning: Testing the linkages. *Research in Higher Education, 47,* 1–33.

Conner-Greene, P. A. (2006). Problem-based learning. In W. Buskist & S. F. Davis (Eds.), *Handbook of the teaching of psychology.* Malden, MA: Blackwell.

Covington, M., 2000. "Goal theory, motivation and social achievement: An integrative review," *Annual Review of Psychology, 51,* 171–200.

Dunn, D. S., & Chew, S. L. (Eds.). (2006). *Best practices for teaching introduction to psychology.* Mahwah, NJ: Erlbaum.

Dunn, D. S., McCarthy, M.A., Baker, S., Halonen, J. S., & Hill, G. W., III. (2007). Quality benchmarks in undergraduate psychology programs. *American Psychologist, 62,* 650–670.

Griggs, R. A., Bujak-Johnson, A., & Proctor, D. L. (2004). Using common core vocabulary in text selection and teaching the introductory course. *Teaching of Psychology, 31,* 265–269.

Hunter, M. S., & Skipper, T. L. (Eds.). (1999). *Solid foundations: Building success for first-year seminars through instructor training and development* [Monograph No. 29]. Columbia: University of South Carolina, National Resource Center for the First-Year Experience and Students in Transition.

Keup, J., & Stoltzenberg, E. (2004). *The 2003 Your First College Year (YFCY) survey: Exploring the academic and personal experiences of first-year students* [Monograph No. 40]. Columbia: University of South Carolina, National Center for the First-Year Experience and Students in Transition.

Kinzie, J. (2007). *Measuring and managing student engagement: Why it matters in the first year of college.* Madison, WI, OPID Spring Conference.

Kuh, G. D., Kinzie, J., Schuh, J. H., & Whitt, E. J. (2005). *Student success in college: Creating conditions that matter.* San Francisco: Jossey-Bass.

McKeachie, W. (2005). *Teaching tips: Strategies, research, and theory for college and university teachers.* Boston: Houghton Mifflin.

Mullendore, R. H., Biller, G., & Busby, R. (2003). Evaluating and assessing orientation programs. In J. A. Ward-Roof & C. Hatch (Eds.), *Designing successful transitions: A guide for orienting students to college* (pp. 177–186). Columbia: University of South Carolina Press.

National Resource Center for the First-Year Experience and Students in Transition, 2008. http://www.sc.edu/fye/

Nelson, C. (1999). On the persistence of unicorns: The trade-off between content and critical thinking revisited. In B. Pescosolido & R. Amizade (Ed.), *The social worlds of higher education: Handbook for teaching in a new century* (pp. 168–184). Boston: Pine Forge Press.

Pascarella, E. T., & Terenzini, P. T. (1991). *How college affects students : Findings and insights from twenty years of research*. San Francisco: Jossey-Bass.

Pascarella, E. T., & Terenzini, P. T. (2005). *How college affects students: A third decade of research*. San Francisco: Jossey-Bass.

Quereshi, M. Y., & Zulli, M. R. (1975). A content analysis of introductory psychology textbooks. *Teaching of Psychology, 2,* 60–65.

Robbins, S., Carlstrom, A., Davis, D., Langley, R., Lauver, K., & Le, H. (2004). Do psychosocial and study skill factors predict college outcomes? A meta-analysis. *Psychological Bulletin, 130,* 261–268.

Schlosser, E. (2001). *Fast food nation*. New York: Perennial.

Swing, R. L. (Ed.). (2001). *Proving and improving: Strategies for assessing the first college year* [Monograph No. 33]. Columbia: University of South Carolina, National Resource Center for the First-Year Experience and Students in Transition.

Tobolowsky, B. F., Mamrick, M., & Cox, B. E. (2005). *The 2003 national survey on first-year seminars: Continuing innovations in the collegiate curriculum*. Columbia: University of South Carolina Press. National Resource Center for the First-Year Experience and Students in Transition.

Troxel, W. G., & Cutright, M. (Eds.). (2008). *Exploring the evidence: Initiatives in the first college year*. [Monograph No. 49]. Columbia: University of South Carolina, National Resource Center for the First-Year Experience and Students in Transition.

Twenge, J. M. (2007). *Generation me: Why today's young Americans are more confident, assertive, entitled—and more miserable than ever before*. New York: Free Press.

7 Learning Communities as an Innovative Beginning to the Psychology Major

A Tale of Two Campuses

Kenneth E. Barron, Kim K. Buch, Jeffrey T. Andre, and *Sue Spaulding*

I never imagined the incredible impact that the Psychology Learning Community would have on my freshman year, not only academically but socially as well. The opportunities with psychology are endless, and the Psychology Learning Community makes you aware of everything that you can become involved in. You create great relationships with professors, and meet fellow students who have the same passion for the major as you do. Applying for the Psychology Learning Community was one of the best decisions I ever made. It puts you in a position to succeed.

The Psychology Leaning Community establishes a group of friends, a network of connections to various professors, and a greater understanding of the field of psychology. Being a member of it is an amazing experience that every psychology major should undertake. I've been really lucky to be a part of such a group. When I first started it, I didn't know exactly what I was getting into, but now that I've been in it for almost a whole year, I know that I wouldn't have wanted to do my freshman year any other way.

—EXAMPLE END-OF-THE-YEAR COMMENTS FROM PSYCHOLOGY LEARNING COMMUNITY STUDENTS

If you were approached to create a *learning community* in psychology, what would your response be? First, would you be able to define what a learning community is and would your definition encompass the variety of learning community models that now exist? Second, would you see value in creating a learning community and appreciate how it could be an innovative way to begin an undergraduate major in psychology? Third, would you know how to develop and sustain a learning community given the departmental and universitywide resources available on your campus?

These were exactly the kinds of questions that we faced a little over 5 years ago when we developed Psychology Learning Communities (PLCs) on our respective campuses at the University of North Carolina Charlotte (UNC Charlotte) and James Madison University (JMU). In the current chapter, we have joined forces to share our experiences. We begin by providing a brief review of learning community initiatives in higher education. Then we present two models of PLCs that we currently coordinate along with assessment data evaluating the impact of our learning communities. We conclude by highlighting a list of additional resources on learning communities that we found particularly helpful in developing our programs.

Learning Communities in Higher Education

The first use of the term *learning community* in higher education is credited to the educational reform efforts of Alexander Meiklejohn in the late 1920s (Smith, MacGregor, Matthews, & Gabelnick, 2004). Meiklejohn created the Experimental College at the University of Wisconsin, which involved an ambitious restructuring of both the curriculum and living experiences for small cohorts of students. Students participating in the Experimental College enrolled in common general education courses during their first 2 years of college while living together in the same residence hall. Faculty teaching in the Experimental College stressed active and collaborative learning and worked closely to better integrate students' different curricular and co-curricular experiences. Although this first attempt at creating a learning community lasted just 5 years, it inspired many others to experiment with learning communities in the 1960s and 1970s.

During the past 10 to 20 years, learning community initiatives have experienced unprecedented growth. By recent estimates (Henscheid, 2007; Smith et al., 2004), over 500 colleges and universities now have implemented some form of learning community, cutting across all types of academic institutions (2-year vs. 4-year, liberal arts colleges vs. research-oriented, public vs. private, and residential vs. commuter). Efforts range from campuswide interventions involving a majority of students to small-scale interventions for just a few students. Learning community proponents (e.g., Cross, 1998; Shapiro & Levine, 1999; Smith et al., 2004) have suggested that widespread interest in the learning community movement is fueled by a learning community's ability to promote the type of academic and social experiences that researchers have linked to college student success (e.g., Astin, 1993; Chickering & Gamson, 1987; Zhao & Kuh, 2004). In particular, Astin (1985) noted how learning communities can facilitate increasing the three factors that he found most highly associated with student success: (a) student-student interaction, (b) student-faculty interaction, and (c) time-on-task. Furthermore, a number of recent national policy reports endorse learning communities as a key intervention for improving higher education (e.g., the Association of American Colleges and Universities National Panel Report in 2002).

The learning community movement also has led to many variations of what constitutes a learning community since the first attempt of Meiklejohn in the 1920s. Lenning and Ebbers (1999) classified learning communities into four general types—those centered on a classroom, the curriculum, campus living arrangements, or a particular student group. Classroom-based learning communities adopt active, cooperative/collaborative teaching pedagogies that promote greater interaction and sense of community between students and faculty in a given class. Curricular-based learning communities move beyond a single classroom experience and enroll the same cohort of students in two or more courses together, typically organized around a particular theme. Residential-based learning communities house students with common curricular (or co-curricular) interests in close proximity. Finally, student-based learning communities focus on bringing together a particular subpopulation of students, such as honor students, minority students, or students with a particular academic interest (like psychology) to facilitate interaction among the group.

However, although Lenning and Ebbers (1999) proposed four different types, definitions used for learning communities on most campuses and in most writing about learning communities center predominantly on curricular-based initiatives (or a combination of curricular- and residential-based initiatives). For example, in one of the most comprehensive reviews of the learning community movement to date, Smith et al. (2004) provided the following definition for learning communities:

> We use the term *learning communities* to refer to a variety of curricular approaches that intentionally link or cluster 2 or more courses, often around an interdisciplinary theme or problem, and enroll a common cohort of students. They represent an intentional restructuring of students' time, credit, and learning experiences to build community, enhance learning, and foster connections among students, faculty, and disciplines. . . . On residential campuses, many learning communities are also living-learning communities, restructuring the residential environment to build community and integrate academic work with out-of-class experiences. (p. 20)

Within curricular-based initiatives, three basic versions exist that vary in the degree of coordination and integration of the course work and whether courses are open only to learning community students. The first version, *student cohorts embedded within existing courses,* is often the easiest to implement. Small groups of students are enrolled into a set of larger, existing courses that contain learning community and non–learning community students. Because learning community students are taking courses with other students, faculty typically do not coordinate or integrate what is being taught across courses. However, to facilitate connections among learning community members as well as the common course work that they are taking, student cohort initiatives often involve an additional seminar taken only by learning community students. In the second approach, *linked or clustered courses*, learning community students enroll in a series of courses open only to the cohort of learning community students. As a result, greater opportunities are available for faculty to coordinate the curriculum and to integrate material in novel and unique ways (such as using linked syllabi and common assignments). The final approach, *coordinated study*, best approximates Meiklejohn's original conceptualization of a learning community program. Rather taking part in four or five stand-alone courses, students participate in a coordinated program that fully integrates academic content. This approach is marked by the highest levels of coordination among faculty and integration of academic content. In addition, it affords the greatest flexibility in how to schedule students' time and experiences because faculty do not have to follow a fixed semester schedule divided into separate courses that meet at particular times each week.

In sum, many models of learning communities now exist for us to consider. Ultimately, the form a learning community takes depends on the particular constituents involved in creating the initiative, available resources, and the creativity of those involved.

Forming a Psychology Learning Community

One emerging approach in creating a learning community is to move away from its historical roots of having a curricular-based community centered on interdisciplinary or general education themes to a community centered on a particular discipline or major. However, learning communities focused on particular majors are still rare. In a recent review of the popularity of different types of learning communities, Henscheid (2007) found that only 21% focused on a specific academic major. To determine the popularity of psychology-focused learning communities, we conducted an Internet search and identified only a handful of schools currently advertising some form of a psychology learning community (e.g., Temple University, Ohio State University, Loyola Marymount University, Wagner University, UNC Charlotte, and JMU).

However, the notion of creating PLCs should not be so foreign to us. Using Lenning and Ebbers' (1999) typology for learning communities, many psychology departments comprise dedicated faculty who strive to create classroom-based learning communities in any given class being taught. Similarly, many psychology departments facilitate student-based learning communities by sponsoring organizations that regularly bring psychology majors together in Psi Chi and Psychology Club meetings. Lacking are PLCs that adopt the more common definition of learning communities that focus on curricular-based or residence-based approaches.

Below we share our experiences in creating curricular- and residence-based PLCs for first-year psychology majors. We review each of our learning community programs separately to provide two examples of how to approach creating a PLC. Specifically, UNC Charlotte just completed its fifth year of running a curricular-based PLC, and JMU just completed its sixth year of running a combined curricular/residential-based PLC. Additionally, to help showcase key issues that are faced when developing a learning community, we have organized the summary of our programs around the following questions:

1. What are the goals of your learning community?
2. What specific type of learning community do you run, and what key features are incorporated in your learning community?
3. How are students recruited and accepted into your learning community?
4. What resources are needed to develop, deliver, and sustain your learning community?
5. What impact is your learning community having on students?

We encourage you to note the similarities and differences in how we have addressed each of these questions on our respective campuses. We also encourage you to consider how you would answer each of the above questions to design a PLC on your campus.

Case Example: UNC-Charlotte's Psychology Learning Community

What are the goals of UNC-Charlotte's PLC?

The first step in the development of a learning community should be the formulation of goals (Smith et al., 2004). Because our department's PLC was part of a universitywide learning community initiative launched in 2001 to improve retention and academic performance of first-year students, this context clearly influenced the first two goals for us: (a) to improve first-year retention rates and (b) to improve first-year academic performance for participants. We also added a third goal—to increase student involvement in campus and department activities because of its demonstrated effect on retention (Tinto, 2000). Our last goal, to positively impact timely progression toward graduation, emerged from our department's concern that students' progress toward obtaining their degrees was frequently delayed by their failure to move through our sequence of prerequisite courses required for the major. These four goals shaped our rationale for program design and informed all decisions regarding program elements and curriculum (Buch & Spaulding, 2008).

What specific type of PLC do you run at UNC-Charlotte, and what key features are incorporated into your PLC?

Our PLC can be categorized as a discipline-based, curricular learning community, open to first-year students who have declared a psychology major. Our curriculum follows a *student cohort embedded within existing courses* approach. Students enroll in a set of four courses during the first semester and two courses during the second semester. Given our emphasis on first-year retention and related student outcome goals, we designed a program that incorporated the following elements known to contribute to first-year student success: (a) provide a small community of learners within the context of a large department (containing over 1,000 undergraduate majors); (b) facilitate students' transition to and success in college and expose them to opportunities for campus connections; (c) develop basic student success skills in reading texts, taking notes, studying, and time management; and (d) introduce students to the breadth and diversity of their discipline and help them explore its many subdisciplines and corresponding career paths.

To create a small community of learners, our cohort of PLC students are embedded into the same set of courses during the fall semester, which includes General Psychology, General Psychology Lab, and a general education course (e.g., Global Connections). One advantage of having learning community cohorts embedded in courses with non–learning community students is that it ensures the cohort is not too insulated and has opportunities to meet students beyond their community while still providing the cohort opportunities to repeatedly interact. In addition to embedded courses, our PLC students participate in a specially designed course, the Freshman Seminar for psychology majors, open only to our PLC cohort. This course serves as an integrative seminar for their curricular experience. Our Freshman Seminar represents the core of the PLC, both academically and socially, and as a result, it embodies all four of our planning elements. We use a range of activities and assignments in the class to facilitate students' transition to and success in college, and we encourage campus connections and departmental involvement. We assign a team project to introduce students to the breadth and diversity of psychology and its subdisciplines and a service learning project to expose students to practitioner areas of psychology and to contribute to our community-building goals (Buch & Spaulding, 2008).

How are students recruited and accepted into UNC-Charlotte's PLC?

We use two mechanisms to recruit students for our PLC. First, the university manages a campuswide learning community Web site, which is our primary recruiting vehicle. The Web site hosts a central application system where students can apply for the learning community of their choice and where learning community coordinators can review and accept applicants. UNC Charlotte currently offers 17 learning communities to first-year students. The PLC is one of six discipline-based communities focused on a particular major. Others include collegewide communities (e.g., engineering and education) and communities focused on special interest topics such as community service or leadership.

Second, to attract as many entering psychology majors as possible, we conduct additional recruiting strategies through the Psychology Department. We send a letter describing the PLC and its benefits to all entering freshmen accepted to the university who have declared psychology as a major. The letter encourages students to apply for the PLC online and provides contact information on how to meet with PLC coordinators during summer orientation. We have found meeting students face-to-face to "sell" the PLC during summer orientation is our best recruiting tool, and every year we have filled the community well before the end of the summer.

What resources are needed to develop, deliver, and sustain UNC-Charlotte's PLC?

Because our PLC is part of a universitywide initiative, we receive a yearly budget of $6,000 from Academic Affairs, which we use to support extracurricular events and pay an undergraduate teaching assistant (TA). The TA is a psychology major who ideally was a member of the PLC as a first-year student. The TA leads some class discussions, participates in the service learning projects, and is available to answer questions and provide advice to PLC members via e-mail and office hours. We also use our budget to pay for the departmental recruiting activities described above. A universitywide Learning Communities Steering Committee, made up of all learning community coordinators and student affairs staff, supports all of our external recruiting efforts and provides general oversight, organization, and assistance for our learning community programs. Our department supports the PLC through release time for faculty participation. Finally, participation in the learning community requires a strong investment of time and commitment from the faculty, because it promotes the development of more intense and sustained relationships with PLC students than what we normally experience with other first-year students.

What impact is UNC-Charlotte's PLC having on students?

To evaluate our program, we use a matched-control design to compare PLC participants' first-year retention, first-year GPA, and timely progression toward major and graduation requirements to a non-PLC control group. On a yearly basis, we match students in the control group on ethnicity, SAT scores, and predicted GPA scores and select them from the pool of entering psychology majors who are not PLC members. We then conduct *t* tests or chi-square tests to evaluate yearly differences between each cohort of PLC and control group students, and we collapse across all cohorts to evaluate overall differences since we began the program. For the current analyses, we evaluated data over the first 4 years of our program.

On first-year GPA, PLC students performed significantly better than control students in all but 1 year that we have offered the program. Likewise, first-year retention rates have been significantly higher for PLC students than control students in all but one year. When combining data across all years of the program, the average first-year GPA for all PLC students was 2.98 and average retention rate was 91%, which were both significantly higher than the average first-year GPA of 2.48 and retention rate of 84% for the control students.

To determine the impact of the PLC on students' timely progression toward graduation and major requirements, we measured students' overall level of course completion and how quickly students completed their research methods course work in psychology. Comparisons for both of these measures showed that the PLC students made significantly better progression toward graduation and major requirements than non-PLC students. For example, students ideally should complete their research methods during their third or fourth semester because it is an important gateway course for the major; however, departmental data indicate that many students wait and take it much later. When comparing our PLC and non-PLC students, the overall percentage of PLC students completing their research methods course work by the end of their fourth semester was 42%, which was more than twice as high as the 18% of control students.

Finally, to assess the PLC on our last goal of increasing student involvement in campus and departmental activities, we began tracking student enrollment in psychology independent research, practicum courses, and honors theses. Because all three courses are designed for (and in some cases restricted to) upper class students, it is too early to conclusively measure involvement rates except for our first cohort. However, preliminary data suggest that PLC students are getting involved in these activities earlier than our non-PLC students.

Case Example: JMU's Psychology Learning Community
What are the goals of JMU's PLC?

Like our colleagues at UNC-Charlotte, JMU's PLC is part of a broader campus-wide learning community program run in conjunction with the Orientation Office, Office of Residence Life, and the Psychology Department. However, rather than being motivated by a particular university initiative (like increasing student retention), we had flexibility in coming up with the specific goals for our community. Two frameworks to promote student success guided us. First, we adopted the list of 10 learning goals and outcomes recommended by the 2002 APA Task Force on Undergraduate Psychology Major Competencies (Halonen et al., 2002). The 10 learning goals are listed in Table 7-1. Second, based on Astin's (1993) research on college student success, we also wanted to promote the three factors noted above that he found most associated with student success.

What type of PLC do you run at JMU, and what specific features are incorporated into your PLC?

Like UNC Charlotte's PLC, JMU's PLC is a discipline-based, curricular learning community, open to first-year students who have declared a psychology major. However, JMU's program also combines a residential component. In fact, at JMU, learning communities are "officially" defined as small groups of first-year students who take one or more classes together and live in the same residence hall. JMU's PLC is designed for up to 20 first-year students, and our first cohort began in fall 2002.

The curriculum of JMU's PLC is best labeled as a *linked* or *clustered courses* approach. Sudents participate in three courses over their freshman year that are open only to students in the learning community. During the fall semester, students are co-enrolled into two courses. First, students participate in PSYC

Table 7-1

APA's 10 Learning Goals and Outcomes for the Undergraduate Psychology Major

Goal 1. Theory and Content of Psychology—Demonstrating familiarity with the major concepts, theoretical perspectives, empirical findings, and historical trends in psychology.

Goal 2. Research Methods in Psychology—Understanding and applying basic research methods in psychology, including research design, data analysis, and interpretation.

Goal 3. Critical Thinking Skills in Psychology—Respecting and using critical and creative thinking, skeptical inquiry, and, when possible, the scientific approach to solve problems.

Goal 4. Application of Psychology—Understanding and applying psychological principles to personal, social, and organizational issues.

Goal 5. Values in Psychology—Being able to weigh evidence, tolerate ambiguity, act ethically, and reflect other values that are the underpinnings of psychology as a discipline.

Goal 6. Information and Technological Literacy—Demonstrating information competence and the ability to use computers and other technology for many purposes.

Goal 7. Communication Skills—Being able to communicate effectively in a variety of formats.

Goal 8. Sociocultural and International Awareness—Recognizing, understanding, and respecting the complexity of sociocultural and international diversity.

Goal 9. Personal Development—Developing insight into one's own and others' behavior and mental processes and applying effective strategies for self-management and self-improvement.

Goal 10. Career Planning and Development—Emerging with realistic ideas about how to implement one's psychological knowledge, skills, and values in occupational pursuits.

Adapted with permission from Halonen, J. S., Appleby, D. C., Brewer, C. L., Buskist, W., Gillem, A. R., Halpern, D., et al. (Eds.). (2002). *Undergraduate major learning goals and outcomes: A report.* Washington, DC: American Psychological Association.

200 (Orientation to Psychology and the Major). Similar to UNC Charlotte's Freshman Seminar, this is a special course that was developed for the PLC that introduces students to the diversity of areas studied in psychology, to different careers connected to these areas, and to the unique opportunities of being a psychology major at JMU. Second, students take PSYC 212 (Psychological Research Methods and Data Analyses, Part I) to begin important

prerequisite course work for the major and their methodology training. Then in the spring semester, students are enrolled in their third course, PSYC 213 (Psychological Research Methods and Data Analyses, Part II), to complete their methodology training.

The three courses that we selected for our community allow us to promote students' growth and development on both of our guiding frameworks. For example, one benefit of selecting our research methods and statistics course work (PSYC 212 and 213) is that it provides the opportunity to promote students' growth along numerous APA learning goals (most notably Learning Goals 2, 3, 4, 5, 6, and 7; see Table 7-1). Another benefit is that our methods and statistics courses are often regarded as the most challenging courses of our curriculum, and the learning community environment offers a forum to provide additional interventions to help facilitate students' success with the material. For example, because our students live together in the same residence hall, they can easily form study groups and seek each other out for additional assistance (promoting student-student interaction and increased time-on-task), and we hold office hours and exam review sessions in the residence hall.

We created PSYC 200 to promote students' growth along the remaining APA learning goals (specifically Learning Goals 1, 8, 9, and 10; see Table 7-1). Our typical format involves guest speakers leading a discussion on a particular topic area and profession within psychology (e.g., industrial/organizational psychology or social psychology), providing examples of research in that area, and suggesting how students could get more involved in that area. During the course of the semester, students interact with 20 to 25 different faculty guest presenters (promoting student-faculty interaction), and we strongly encourage students to follow up with our presenters to pursue independent research or practicum opportunities. We also use PSYC 200 for community building and engage in numerous ice-breakers and team building activities, especially in the beginning of the semester, to foster student-student interaction.

Interestingly, we chose not to include introductory psychology as one of our core PLC courses. With the increased popularity of Advanced Placement psychology courses in high school, many of our incoming psychology majors already have credit for introductory psychology, and we did not want to exclude this group from participating in the learning community. Instead, we selected our statistics and research methodology courses, which represent the next required courses in our major. As a result, PLC students are able to get a jumpstart in our major and can take advanced course work at the beginning of their sophomore year that the typical psychology major does not begin until the middle of the sophomore year or beginning of the junior year. If PLC students do not have credit for introductory psychology, they are enrolled in the course during the fall semester as well.

A final feature of our community is that PLC faculty are assigned to be the primary academic advisors for PLC students. Thus, in addition to promoting student-faculty interaction, we are able to foster regular advisee–advisor interaction as well.

How are students recruited and accepted into JMU's PLC?

Before students have committed to JMU, our office of admissions sponsors a series of on-campus preview days for prospective students. During these sessions, prospective students are provided general information about JMU's learning community program. The Psychology Department also presents information about our undergraduate program, and we highlight the PLC as an innovative way to begin the major. We also have former PLC students participate in a student panel to share their experiences with prospective students, and applicants regularly mention that it was hearing the student panel talk about the PLC (e.g., hearing statements similar to the opening student quotes that began our chapter) that sold them on wanting to join.

Once students commit to attend JMU, the Office of Residential Life contacts students about housing options and how to apply to JMU's residential learning communities. JMU currently sponsors eight different residential learning communities. Three focus on particular majors (psychology, education, and biology), three focus on specialized topics that are linked to general education course work (community service, multiculturalism, and environmentalism), and two focus on particular JMU programs (health professions and honors). Interested students complete an additional online application on why they want to join a learning community. Initial acceptance decisions are made early in the summer; however, we typically do not fill all of our available spots through the initial housing application process. Like our colleagues at UNC-Charlotte, we continue to recruit additional students through on-campus summer orientation activities when students in psychology spend a day on campus to enroll in fall courses and learn more about JMU. We also send targeted mailings to students who have declared psychology as a major and invite them to apply to the PLC if we are still short on applicants.

What resources are needed to develop, deliver, and sustain JMU's PLC?

Different constituents involved in JMUs learning community program share responsibility in running our PLC. Faculty in psychology organize the primary mission and goals of our PLC program as well as day-to-day course instruction, the Orientation Office oversees general administration of the program, and the Office of Residence Life coordinates the application process as well as providing specialized housing for learning community students. JMU also provides each learning community with a yearly budget of $500. However, JMU made a conscious decision to limit the number of additional resources that would be needed to run the program to help ensure the long-term sustainability of JMU's learning community program. For example, because we face increasing enrollment and class size pressure at JMU, class sizes for PLC courses are no different from the sizes of non–learning community sections of comparable courses, and faculty in our department teach PLC classes as part of their normal teaching load.

What impact is JMU's PLC having on students?

To assess the impact of JMU's PLC, we obtained university records for all psychology majors during the years the PLC has existed and extracted key variables that would allow us to evaluate how similar or different the experiences of our PLC students were from our other psychology majors. Initially, to determine if there were pre-existing differences between PLC and non-PLC students, we examined students' prior performance in high school and SAT scores, but we found no significant differences. Then, we investigated how student participation in the PLC impacted their subsequent academic success and involvement in our major.

Regarding academic performance, we investigated differences in students' initial JMU performance (first year GPA), overall JMU performance (cumulative GPA), and performance in psychology courses (psychology GPA). On all three measures, PLC students outperformed our non-PLC psychology students. Specifically, PLC students' first-year GPA ($M = 3.43$), cumulative GPA ($M = 3.40$), and psychology GPA ($M = 3.55$) were significantly higher than non-PLC students' first-year GPA ($M = 3.11$), cumulative GPA ($M = 3.22$), and psychology GPA ($M = 3.36$). Effects sizes were strongest for first-year GPA (Cohen's $d = .72$), and moderate for cumulative GPA and psychology GPA (Cohen's d of .42 and .40, respectively).

We also evaluated differences in students' participation in higher level research and practicum experiences within our curriculum. At JMU, students can enroll in PSYC 290 (directed study), PSYC 402 (independent study), and PSYC 499 (senior honors thesis). Again we found key differences where PLC students participated in each of these courses at a higher rate than non-PLC students. Specifically, 53% of PLC students enrolled in at least one directed study compared to 17% of non-PLC students; 64% of PLC students enrolled in at least one independent study compared to 35% of non-PLC students; and 13.3% of PLC students participated enrolled in a senior honors thesis compared to 5.8% for non-PLC students. PLC students also began their initial directed study or independent study experiences significantly earlier than non-PLC students, providing support for the jumpstart that the PLC provides. Specifically, PLC students averaged enrolling in their first directed study and independent study experiences a year earlier than non-PLC students (Cohen's d effect sizes were 1.26 and .86, respectively). In addition, PLC students enrolled in a greater overall number of directed study and independent study experiences compared to non-PLC students (Cohen's d effect sizes were .74 and .52, respectively).

In short, JMU's PLC students are thriving academically and fulfilling our goals to get more involved in higher level research and practicum experiences. Interestingly, these differences were documented without any significant preexisting differences in prior high school achievement or SAT scores.

Conclusions

We started our chapter with three questions: Could you define what a learning community is, would you see value in creating a learning community, and would you know how to develop and sustain a learning community given the available resources on your campus? We hope you now are in a better position to answer all three of these questions.

We also shared our experiences in how learning communities can be used in psychology as an innovative beginning to the major. However, learning community initiatives can be created at any point of a student's undergraduate career. For example, in our Internet search on the prevalence of PLCs, we discovered that Wagner University offers a Psychology Senior Learning Community as an innovative capstone experience to end the major.

Finally, even though our universities approached us to initiate our learning communities in psychology, this is not a necessary requirement in creating a learning community. Being a part of a broader university initiative can offer advantages and additional resources, but it can also limit flexibility in creating the type of learning community most appropriate for your students, your faculty, and the mission and goals of your department.

Although learning communities were at one time considered an experiment and on the periphery of higher education, they are now a part of the mainstream of higher education and offer a powerful intervention to consider adopting to promote student success (MacGregor & Smith, 2005). We hope our experiences will encourage you to think creatively about how you can incorporate and adapt different ideas from past learning community initiatives to improve the quality of experiences for your students as well.

Recommended Readings

We would like to conclude by highlighting resources that we have found particularly helpful in educating ourselves about different learning community models and finding a network of colleagues to share and exchange ideas.

Resources about Learning Communities
Key Books/Chapters

Smith, B.L., MacGregor, J., Matthews, R., & Gabelnick, F. (2004). *Learning communities: Reforming undergraduate education.* San Francisco: Jossey-Bass.

Shapiro, N.S., & Levine, J.H. (1999). *Creating learning communities: A practical guide to winning support, organizing for change, and implementing programs.* San Francisco: Jossey-Bass.

Laufgraben, J. L., & Shapiro, N. S. (2004). *Sustaining and improving learning communities.* San Francisco: Jossey-Bass.

Key Web Sites

http://www.evergreen.edu/washcenter/project.asp?pid=73
    Learning Communities National Resource Center sponsored by Evergreen State University.
http://pcc.bgsu.edu/rlcch/index.php#definition
    The Residential Learning Communities International Clearinghouse sponsored by Bowling Green State University.

http://www.temple.edu/vpus/programs_initiatives/lc/documents/
   lcbibliography.pdf
   Web link to bibliography on Learning Communities.

Key Conferences

National Learning Communities Conference
National First-Year Experience Conference
(see http://www.sc.edu/fye/events/annual/index.html for more information).

References

Association of American Colleges and Universities National Panel. (2002). *Greater expectations: A new vision for learning as a nation goes to college.* Washington, D.C: Association of American Colleges and Universities.

Astin, A. W. (1985). *Achieving educational excellence.* San Francisco: Jossey-Bass.

Astin, A. W. (1993). *What matters in college? Four critical years revisited.* San Francisco: Jossey-Bass.

Buch, K., & Spaulding, S. (2008). A longitudinal assessment of an initial cohort in a psychology learning community. *Teaching of Psychology 35,* 1–5.

Chickering, A. W., & Gamson, Z. F. (1987). Seven principles for good practice in undergraduate education. *AAHE Bulletin, 39,* 3–7.

Cross, K. P. (1998). Why learning communities, why now? *About Campus, 3*(3), 4–11.

Halonen, J. S., Appleby, D. C., Brewer, C. L., Buskist, W., Gillem, A. R., Halpern, D., et al. (Eds.). (2002). *Undergraduate major learning goals and outcomes: A report.* Washington, DC: American Psychological Association. Retrieved from http://www.apa.org/ed/pcue/taskforcereport2.pdf.

Henscheid, J. M. (2007). *The myths and magic of learning communities.* Symposium presented at the Annual Conference on the First-Year Experience in Addison, Texas.

Lenning, O. T., & Ebbers, L. H., (1999). *The powerful potential of learning communities.* ASHE-ERIC Higher Education Report, Volume 26, Number 6.

MacGregor, J., & Smith, B. L. (2005). Where are learning communities now? National leaders take stock. *About Campus, 10*(2), 2–8.

Smith, B. L., MacGregor, J., Matthews, R. S., & Gabelnick, F. (2004). *Learning communities: Reforming undergraduate education.* San Francisco: Jossey-Bass.

Tinto, V. (2000). What we have learned about the impact of learning communities on students. *Assessment Update, 12*, 1–12.

Shapiro, N. S., & Levine, J. H. (1999). *Creating learning communities: A practical guide to winning support, organizing for change, and implementing programs*. San Francisco: Jossey-Bass.

Zhao, C. M., & Kuh, G. D. (2004). Adding value: Learning communities and student engagement. *Research in Higher Education, 45*, 115–138.

8 Displacing *Wikipedia*

Information Literacy for First-Year Students

Charles M. Harris and *S. Lynn Cameron*

Enabling students to become liberally educated lifelong learners is a recurring theme among the mission statements of institutions of higher education. In the 1990s, librarians' support of lifelong learning focused on promoting information literacy as a core component of the academic curriculum (Behrens, 1994). Shapiro and Hughes (1996) proposed that information literacy should be viewed as a new liberal art. A report by the American Psychological Association (APA) on learning goals and outcomes for undergraduate psychology majors (Halonen et al., 2002) included the following under Goal 6, Information and Technology Literacy:

> Students will be able to use selected sources after evaluating their
> suitability based on appropriateness, accuracy, quality, and value of
> the source, potential bias of the source, the relative value of primary
> versus secondary sources, empirical versus non-empirical sources,
> and peer-reviewed versus nonpeer-reviewed sources. (p. 14)

As an outcome goal for undergraduate psychology majors at James Madison University, Halonen et al. (2006) reported that faculty expected students to "use evidence to develop and evaluate positions regarding social and behavioral issues" (p. 201). Such use would be exemplified by discriminating between reputable and no reputable sources of information, recognizing the criteria that constitute reputable sources, identifying potential bias in the sources of information, and recognizing the potential for personal bias to influence decision making.

In view of the progressive emphasis on teaching information literacy skills and in concert with Orr, Appleton, and Wallin (2001), we are promoting an across-the-curriculum strategy for first-year students that repeatedly infuses information literacy skills into discipline-based learning experiences. Success in such an endeavor requires collaboration and coordination among librarians, faculty, and administrators committed to the common goal of inculcating information literacy skills. The remainder of this chapter will present the rationale, structure, and content of the online across-the-curriculum model implemented at James Madison University for teaching information literacy to first-year students.

Displacing *Wikipedia*

Effective search strategies and techniques for evaluating information are essential skills for students in the contemporary environment of proliferating sources of information. The Internet, because of worldwide availability and ease of use, has become for many the primary avenue for accessing information. However, the ease of access and use that explains the popularity of the Internet also contributes to its most serious weakness: unfiltered information lacking evidence of authenticity, validity, and reliability. A prime example of an unfiltered source is *Wikipedia*, the free online encyclopedia that anyone can edit. The following is excerpted from the *Wikipedia* (2008, ¶ 2) home page:

> *Wikipedia* is written collaboratively by volunteers from all around the world. Since its creation in 2001, *Wikipedia* has grown rapidly into one of the largest reference Web sites. Every day hundreds of thousands of contributors from around the world make tens of thousands of edits and create thousands of new articles to enhance the knowledge held by the *Wikipedia* encyclopedia. Contributors do not need specialized qualifications, because their primary role is to write articles that cover existing knowledge; this means that people of all ages and cultural and social backgrounds can write *Wikipedia* articles.

By its own report, *Wikipedia* is a source of voluminous, if unfiltered information. Because of its open structure and ease of access, *Wikipedia* can be a problematic source for unsophisticated first-year students.

To assess the frequency and extent to which first-year students at James Madison University use *Wikipedia* as a source of information, we conducted a survey on the following functions: (a) using *Wikipedia* as a source of information, (b) using information from *Wikipedia* for academic assignments, and (c) verifying information from *Wikipedia* by checking other sources. The survey sample included students randomly selected from the five colleges comprising the university. The findings of the survey are presented in Table 8-1.

Table 8-1 documents the extent to which first-year students consider *Wikipedia* to be a reliable source of information. Over 64% of first-year students use information obtained from *Wikipedia*; over 36% use *Wikipedia* information for research papers, presentations, and other course requirements; and 63% never, rarely, or only occasionally attempt to verify information obtained from *Wikipedia* by checking other sources. The findings reinforced our commitment to implementing an online across-the-curriculum model for information literacy. We concluded that in order to supplant students' reliance on popular sources, such as *Wikipedia*, we must inculcate the fundamentals of information literacy.

Table 8-1
Using and Verifying Wikipedia Information

Survey items	Response options			
	Never	Rarely	Occasionally	Frequently
I use *Wikipedia* as a source of information	8	28	51	13
I use information from *Wikipedia* for academic assignments	28	36	31	5
I verify *Wikipedia* information by checking other sources	13	20	30	37

Note: Two hundred and seventy-one first-year students responded to the three survey items. The values represent the percentage of students who selected each response option.

Information Literacy Defined

Historically, the concept of information literacy is rooted in the supportive services offered by librarians since before the Civil War (Salony, 1995). Librarians began using the term *information literacy* in the mid-1970s (Behrens, 1994). The subsequent creation of the Internet and the rapid development of digital technologies enabled proliferation of the amount and sources of information that now necessitate proficiency in information literacy. Accordingly, Grafstein (2002) defines information literacy as the ability to access, understand, evaluate, and appropriately use digital information.

Table 8-2
Association of College and Research Libraries (ACRL) Information Literacy Standards and Selected Performance Outcomes

Standard 1. Determine the nature and extent of information needed

    a. Explore general information sources

    b. Identify key concepts

    c. Identify scholarly vs. popular resources

Standard 2. Access information effectively and efficiently

    a. Identify keywords, synonyms and related terms

    b. Construct and implement a search strategy

    c. Records all pertinent citation information

Standard 3. Critically evaluate information and its sources

    a. Evaluate reliability, validity, accuracy, authority, timeliness, and point of view or bias for information and its sources

    b. Select information that provides evidence for the topic

    c. Investigate differing viewpoints in the literature

Standard 4. Use information effectively to accomplish a purpose

    a. Articulate knowledge and skills from prior experiences to plan and create a product

    b. Integrate new and prior information

    c. Communicate clearly to fulfill the purpose of the assignment

Standard 5. Access and use information ethically

    a. Use approved passwords to access information resources

    b. Understand what constitutes plagiarism

    c. Use appropriate documentation style

The Association of College and Research Libraries (ACRL), a division of the American Library Association (ALA) (ACRL, 2000) constructed an operational framework for teaching and assessing information literacy in higher education. The framework comprises the following five standards for information literacy competency in higher education: (a) identifying needed information, (b) finding needed information, (c) evaluating information, (d) effectively utilizing information, and (e) using information ethically. The five standards are complemented by 22 performance indicators and 87 performance outcomes (the complete text of the standards and performance outcomes is available at http://www.ala.org/acrl/ilcomstan.html). For each of the five ACRL standards, Table 8-2 presents the three performance outcomes selected for implementation within our online information literacy curriculum. Collectively, these 15 performance outcomes are fundamental skills to be learned by first-year students. Proficiency in these basic skills enables students to access and critically evaluate scientific information in support of course work in general education and major programs of study.

Case Example: Information Literacy Curriculum

Our online information literacy curriculum comprises three interrelated, skill-based modules: (a) finding and using a subject encyclopedia, (b) finding peer-reviewed journal articles, and (c) finding association/organization Web sites. Each module incorporates one or more performance outcomes for each of the five ACRL standards. Each module works well as an individual or small-group assignment. By infusing discipline-specific terminology and content, instructors within any discipline may apply the three modules. In this chapter, the terminology and content will be representative of the discipline of psychology.

Subject Encyclopedia

module is to select, from a list of seven topics, one matter when completing the remaining assignment modules. The seven psychology-related topics are tion, euthanasia, false memories, intelligence and single parents. The second assignment is to selected topic in one or more of the following online encyclopedias: *Encyclopedia of Bioethics, Encyclopedia of Human Development, Encyclopedia of Health and Behavior*, and *Encyclopedia of School Psychology*. We conducted a preliminary search to ensure that the selected encyclopedias contained sufficient relevant information. The third assignment is to prepare a report on two aspects of the topic that was selected in the first assignment. For example, a student report might address the similarities and differences between euthanasia and physician-assisted suicide. Instructors set their requirements for student reports and determine whether students work individually or in small groups.

The *Psychology Research Guide* (see Figure 8-1) facilitates direct access to online resources for assignments within each of the three modules comprising our information literacy curriculum. We recommend that librarians at other institutions develop similar research guides in concert with instructors who incorporate information literacy into their courses.

A requirement of the information literacy curriculum within psychology is for all references to conform to specifications in the fifth edition of the *Publication Manual of the American Psychological Association* (APA, 2001). Figure 8-2 displays *CheckCite*, an online resource with examples of citations that conform to APA and three other major styles. As an outcome of following the three steps depicted in Table 8-2, students will see an example of an APA

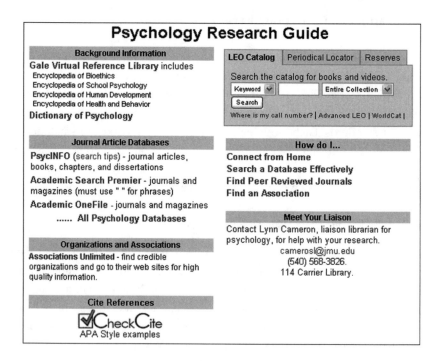

Figure 8-1   The Psychology Research Guide includes links to primary research databases and tools.

Note: Access the Psychology Research Guide at http://www.lib.jmu.edu/psychology/default.aspx

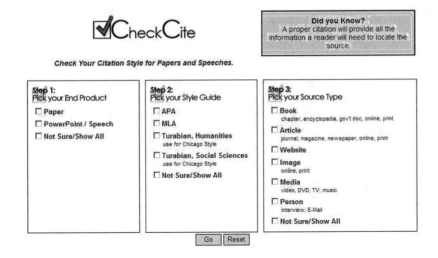

Figure 8-2   CheckCite includes examples of APA style citations for a variety of sources. *Note:* Access CheckCite at http://www.lib.jmu.edu/help/checkcite.

style reference for a specific type of source and an example of how to cite that reference within the text.

Module 2: Finding Peer-Reviewed Journal Articles

The assignments in this module are to find and summarize a peer-reviewed journal article related to each of the two aspects of the topic selected in Module 1, such as euthanasia and physician-assisted suicide. Two online PowerPoint-based instructional guides are available to assist with this assignment. The first instructional guide, *Peer-Reviewed Scholarly Journals*, lists the distinguishing features of scholarly journals versus popular publications, displays appropriate databases, and illustrates how to limit a search. The second instructional guide, *Searching a Database Effectively*, describes and illustrates how to identify and search for main concepts, delimit a search, select an article, check for full text, and request help from the reference desk librarian in person or online. Additionally, this guide illustrates how to expand a search by generating alternative search terms. Students access the instructional guides through the *Psychology Research Guide* (see Figure 8-1) that also includes a hyperlink to PsycINFO, the online database of publications in psychology from 1872 to the present. Also, the guide includes hyperlinks for Academic OneFile and

Academic Search Premier, multidisciplinary databases that index magazines and scholarly journals.

Module 3: Finding Association or Organization Web Sites

The initial assignment in this module is to find two Web sites for professional or advocacy associations. Students find one Web site for each aspect of the topic selected in Module 1, such as euthanasia and physician-assisted suicide. For assistance, with this assignment, instructors direct students to the *Psychology Research Guide* (See Figure 8-1) for a hyperlink to an online PowerPoint-based instructional guide, *How to Find an Association*. The instructional guide includes a hyperlink to the online resource, *Associations Unlimited*, and guidelines for selecting an association. The second assignment is to summarize the mission or goal of each association with content from each association's Web site.

In summary, our three-module curriculum incorporates information literacy skills that are fundamental for first-year students. Successful performance throughout the three modules will be indicative that students can identify key concepts for exploration of general information sources, construct and implement effective search strategies, evaluate the validity and reliability of information and its sources, integrate new and prior information, and use information ethically.

Assessing Information Literacy

We recommend both quantitative and qualitative assessment strategies in conjunction with our information literacy curriculum. By combining quantitative measures of students' knowledge and attitudes with qualitative measures of students' performance, assessment is more likely to be comprehensive and authentic (Halonen et al., 2003).

Quantitative assessment can provide efficient, preliminary measures of the scope and accuracy of students' knowledge and attitudes. Using brief questionnaires, instructors can quickly identify conceptual errors that tend to cause inefficiencies and inaccuracies. For example, a multiple-choice item can quickly and accurately assess a student's knowledge of the best way to find a scholarly journal article on specific topic. A knowledgeable student will select the second or third of the following options: (a) search on the Web browser

Google, (b) search Google Scholar, (c) search a research database (e.g., PsycINFO), (d) search the library catalog, or (e) all of the above. Effectively searching a database is an activity accompanied by an online instructional guide within Module 2. Additional items for quantitative assessment of students' knowledge might include (a) understanding the use of *and* to narrow a search and *or* to expand a search, (b) specifying dates to delimit a search, or (c) using an asterisk to search for all endings of a key word.

To quantitatively assess student attitudes, one might use a 1 to 5, strongly agree to strongly disagree, response scale in pretests and posttests. Pretest attitudinal items could focus on student perceptions of competence in functions, such as (a) finding reliable background information, (b) finding peer-reviewed scholarly journal articles, or (c) finding appropriate Web sites on a topic. Posttest attitudinal items assessing perceived competence for the same three functions might be preceded by a qualifier such as the following: Because of my experience in completing the three information literacy modules . . . Quantitative assessment of students' knowledge and attitudes can complement qualitative assessment of student performance within a comprehensive assessment strategy.

Qualitative or authentic assessment of performance focuses on the extent to which students accurately and consistently apply information literacy skills (Archbald, 1991). Whereas quantitative assessment utilizes multiple choice, true-false, and matching items, qualitative or authentic assessment uses essays, demonstrations, and interpretive exercises that test student ability to apply and transfer prior knowledge in novel situations in order to assess students' collective abilities. The need for performance-based learning for first-year students was a central theme in the Boyer Commission (1998) report, *Reinventing Undergraduate Education*. Important considerations for developing a qualitative or authentic assessment strategy are (a) collaboration among instructors, librarians, and administrators; (b) identification of institutional resources for comprehensively assessing student performance; and (c) constructing rubrics and instruments that are germane for both general and discipline-specific knowledge creation.

An in-depth discussion of authentic assessment is beyond the scope of this chapter; however, we will address some distinguishing features of qualitative or authentic assessment. Archbald (1991) described authentic assessment as any type of assessment that requires students to demonstrate skills and competencies that realistically represent problems and situations likely to be encountered in daily life. Students are assessed according to specific criteria in rubrics that are known to them in advance of an assignment. Rubrics vary in form and level of complexity; however, common features include (a) focusing on measurement of stated objectives, (b) using a scale to rate student performance, and (c) having task-specific levels of performance to assess the extent to which an objective has been accomplished (Pickett & Dodge, 2008). Authentic assessment facilitates both formative assessment, in-process measures as integral components of the learning process, and summative assessment as an end-of-process measure of overall accomplishment of stated objectives. The five ACRL standards and accompanying performance outcomes in Table 8-2 offer a comprehensive frame of reference to be considered when constructing rubrics for qualitative or authentic assessment of information literacy.

Conclusions

The first year of college life is a time of complex social and academic transitions. It is therefore essential that institutions of higher education make the most of those teachable moments by inculcating fundamental skills through performance-based learning. By infusing discipline-specific content into a curriculum similar to the one presented in this chapter, institutions can implement instruction in information literacy across the curriculum within any or all disciplines. An information literacy curriculum with both conceptual and applied outcomes will enable students to learn effective search strategies and techniques for finding, evaluating, and using information. Psychology students will more likely be capable of effectively and consistently applying the skills specified in Goal 6 of the APA report (Halonen et al., 2002) on learning goals and outcomes for undergraduate psychology majors. Students, in general, will tend to be more discriminating users of information from any and all sources and especially from the myriad of open-structure sources such as *Wikipedia*. To that end, the acquisition of applied fundamental information literacy skills will serve first-year students well as requisites for further study as they engage in both general and discipline-specific knowledge creation.

Recommended Readings

Grafstein, A. (2002). A discipline-based approach to information literacy. *Journal of Academic Librarianship, 28*(4), 197–204.

Lampert, L. (2005). Getting psyched about information literacy: A successful faculty-librarian collaboration for educational psychology and counseling. *The Reference Librarian, 89/90,* 5–23.

Larkin, J. E., & Pines, H. A. (2005). Developing information literacy and research skills in introductory psychology: A case study. *Journal of Academic Librarianship, 31*(1), 40–45.

References

American Psychological Association. (2001). *Publication manual of the American Psychological Association* (5th ed.). Washington, DC: Author.

Archbald, D. (1991). *Authentic assessment: What it means and how it can help schools.* Madison: National Center for Effective Schools Research and Development, University of Wisconsin.

Association of College and Research Libraries. (2000). *Information literacy competency standards for higher education.* Chicago: American Library Association.

Behrens, S. (1994). A conceptual analysis and historical overview of information literacy. *College and Research Libraries News, 55,* 309–322.

Boyer Commission on Educating Undergraduates in the Research University. (1998). *Reinventing undergraduate education: A blueprint for America's research universities.* Retrieved April 7, 2008, from http://naples.cc.sunysb.edu/Pres/boyer.nsf/.

Grafstein, A. (2002). A discipline-based approach to information literacy. *Journal of Academic Librarianship, 28,* 197–204.

Halonen, J. S., Appleby, D. C., Brewer, C. L., Buskist, W., Gillem, A. R., Halpern, D., et al. (2002). Undergraduate psychology major learning goals and outcomes: A report. Retrieved April 30, 2008 from http://www.apa.org/ed/pcue/taskforcereport2.pdf.

Halonen, J. S., Bosack, T., Clay, S., & McCarthy, M. (with Dunn, D. S., Hill, G. W., IV, McEntarfer, R., Mchrotra, C., Nesmith, R., Weaver, K., & Whitlock, K.). (2003). A rubric for authentically learning, teaching, and assessing scientific reasoning in psychology. *Teaching of Psychology, 30,* 196–208.

Halonen, J. S., Harris, C. M., Pastor, D. A., Abrahamson, C. E., & Huffman, C. J. (2006). Assessing general education outcomes in introductory psychology. In D. S. Dunn & S. L. Chew (Eds.), *Best practices for teaching introduction to psychology.* Mahwah, NJ: Erlbaum.

Orr, D., Appleton, M., & Wallin, M. (2001). Information literacy and flexible delivery:Creating a conceptual framework and model. *Journal of Academic Librarianship, 27,* 457–463.

Pickett, N. & Dodge, B. *Rubrics for web lessons*. Retrieved April 10, 2008, from http://edweb.sdsu.edu/webquest/rubrics/weblessons.htm.

Salony, M. F. (1995). The history of bibliographic instruction: Changing trends from books to the electronic world. *The Reference Librarian, 51/52*, 31–51.

Shapiro, J. J., & Hughes, S. K. (1996). Information technology as a new liberal art: Enlightenment proposals for a new curriculum, *Educom Review, 31*, 31–35.

Wikipedia, the free encyclopedia. Retrieved March 16, 2008, from http://en.wikipedia.org/wiki/Wikipedia:About.

9 Crafting and Implementing a Career Development Course in Psychology

Eric A. Goedereis and *Stanley H. Cohen*

A quick look around your own campus probably confirms what research suggests: Psychology is a very popular major. Indeed, it is estimated that nearly one million undergraduate degrees in psychology have been awarded in the past decade (Landrum, 2007). Quite often, students pursue psychology for broad reasons (e.g., "I want to help people") whereas others have more concrete aspirations (e.g., "I want to have my own private practice"). However, many students are not aware of the post-baccalaureate training that is required to pursue some of these career paths. In addition, graduate programs, particularly those in clinical psychology, are highly competitive, with as few as 6% of applicants gaining admission (Norcross, Sayette, Mayne, Karg, & Turkson, 1998). Consequently, it becomes increasingly important to introduce psychology students to the depth and the breadth of the discipline so they can make informed decisions about later career choices.

One way to introduce students to psychology is through career development (CD) or orientation to the major (OM) courses. Many institutions offer general, credit-bearing CD courses (Collins, 1998). A recent survey by the American Psychological Association (APA) indicated that such courses have become increasingly popular in psychology, with as many as 16% of departments (APA, 2008) offering major-specific CD courses designed to expose students to the wide variety of career options available within psychology.

Although the emerging prevalence of CD courses within psychology departments is encouraging, only 10% of departments offer orientation to the major courses aimed at introducing students to the psychology major and required curriculum within a given department (APA).

The purpose of this chapter is to present one method of crafting and implementing a course (PSYC 201: Psychology as a Profession) that has proven valuable to students at West Virginia University (WVU), a public institution with approximately 28,000 students. The WVU model serves both a career development and an orientation to the major function consistent with APA's (2007a) *Guidelines for the Undergraduate Psychology Major* by incorporating several key components of successful career interventions that Brown and Krane (2000; Brown et al., 2003) identified in major reviews of the career development literature.

As a point of departure we briefly review APA's Career Planning and Development goal and the "critical ingredients" that Brown and Krane (2000; Brown et al., 2003). identified Next, we provide a brief history of the evolution of the course at WVU, as well as some specific course components. Throughout the chapter, we integrate recent course assessment data (when available) with the APA *Guidelines* (2007a) and relevant findings from Browne and Krane (2000; Brown et al., 2003) on effective career development instruction. We conclude with recommendations for best practices for using such a course to introduce students to the psychology major. Finally, because we recognize that there cannot be a one-size-fits-all application of these recommendations, we encourage readers to liberally select and apply those recommendations that seem most appropriate for their respective institutions and students.

Organizational Framework

The APA offers 10 goals (and several general learning outcomes within each goal) to collectively serve as a set of guidelines for the undergraduate psychology major (APA, 2007a). These goals fall into two broad categories: The first relates to the science and application of psychology, and the second describes how psychology can contribute to a liberal arts education.

The guidelines address career planning and development with Goal 10. Specifically, this goal suggests that students pursuing degrees in psychology should "emerge from the major with realistic ideas about how to implement their psychological knowledge, skills, and values in occupational pursuits in a variety of settings" (APA, 2007a, p. 21). Specific learning outcomes related to this goal include (a) applying psychological knowledge when making career choices; (b) identifying types of experiences that will facilitate entry into graduate or professional school, the workforce, or both; (c) describing career paths; (d) identifying and developing skills related to one's career goals; (e) articulating how the plasticity of societal needs impacts career opportunities; and (f) demonstrating the importance of lifelong learning (APA). Career development and major orientation courses provide a platform for addressing and delivering information with respect to these important learning outcomes.

Career and orientation courses vary across institutions, but successful courses incorporate certain key components. For example, in their original meta-analysis of career choice interventions, Browne and Krane (2000) found that successful courses include one or more of the following elements: (a) written exercises, (b) individualized feedback on potential career decisions, (c) structured opportunities for gathering "world of work" information, (d) modeling, and (e) opportunities that help students develop and reflect upon various career plans. Further, although none of the reviewed studies incorporated more than three of these elements, courses that included various combinations of these components resulted in larger effect sizes on career outcomes than studies that included only one component (Brown et al., 2003). Thus, instructors that include multiple empirically supported elements in their career development and orientation to the major courses are likely to provide a positive impact on their students' experiences. Taken together, the *Guidelines* (APA, 2007a) and Browne and Krane's (2000; Brown et al., 2003) findings provide a useful framework for identifying and assessing the impact of psychology-specific CD and OM courses.

Case Example: The WVU Model
History

The Psychology as a Profession course at WVU addresses the Career Planning and Development goal of the APA *Guidelines* and incorporates several of Browne and Krane's (2000; Brown et al., 2003) components of successful career interventions. Further, we contend that the WVU model integrates the skill acquisition and career planning aspects of CD courses with the academic advising and curriculum planning components of OM courses.

The Department of Psychology at WVU began informally offering the Psychology as a Profession course in the late 1970s (see Lattal, 1980). Originally, instructors designed and offered the course as a means of facilitating advising contact between faculty and students and formally added it as a required course to the department's curriculum in 1984. As the popularity of the psychology major has grown, so too has enrollment in the course, with as many as 280 students taking Psychology as a Profession during the 2007–2008 academic year (compared to 40 students per semester in the late 1970s). The course is taught as a weekly one-credit, single section course. Students now receive standard grades compared to previous versions where performance was on a "Pass/Fail" basis. Student feedback, which suggested that the required workload warranted a letter grade, was directly responsible for this change in grading procedures. We believe that regular and systematic assessment of such a course is imperative, given the dynamically changing needs of the department and students. Specifically, frequent assessment allows the instructor to adjust the structure, content, and delivery of the course in response to student feedback.

In the spirit of a true orientation to the major course, we believe that it is important for students to take such a course early and begin thinking about what they plan to do with their degrees and how to get there. Recently, freshmen and sophomores constituted as many as 80% of students in a given semester which, when compared to previous semesters that limited enrollment to second-semester sophomore and junior psychology majors (Lattal, 1980), signifies a major shift in pedagogy. Thus, Psychology as a Profession now serves as a gateway course that students must pass prior to formally entering the major. This requirement seems warranted, given course assessment data suggesting that as many as 93% of students either changed their career plans or became more confident of their career plans after taking the course (Macera & Cohen, 2006).

Topics

Instructors use specific lecture topics to introduce students to the depth and breadth of psychology. One of the lecture topics, "Choosing a Major," encourages students to think about the advantages and disadvantages of pursuing a degree in psychology versus another discipline. The course then transitions to the various job opportunities available within psychology.

The general "Careers in Psychology" lecture provides information about careers at various degree levels of education as well as training requirements in an effort to expose students to the wide variety of career paths they might pursue with their psychology degrees. One useful method of introducing this topic presents data on employment settings for recent graduates, which provides students with concrete examples of career paths and ultimately serves to stimulate discussion about the career ladder in psychology across different degree levels. Thus, following a general "careers" lecture, instructors can provide specific information about both bachelor's- and graduate-level job opportunities as well as "psychology-related careers," given that many students express broad interests in "people-focused careers" such as special education and social work. Instructors often arrange guest lectures and panel discussions on potential career paths, graduate school, and professional development to coincide with specific lecture topics.

Given that many psychology graduates often pursue advanced education and training in psychology and related fields, instructors often devote a great deal of attention to graduate study. During this section, instructors present different training models for clinical and nonclinical graduate programs. Always important here is drawing a clear distinction among PhD, PsyD, and MD degree requirements and related career opportunities. Further, the instructor presents detailed information about the graduate application process, with a focus on matching a student's interests with specific programs. Structured graduate student panels provide students with potential role models and can serve as dynamic teaching tools within the context of such a course.

In addition to these career development topics, the course serves an advising function by emphasizing orientation to the major. One lecture topic, "The Four-year Plan," often includes guest lectures on pre-psychology advising and registration and an emphasis on professional development. Specifically, students are encouraged to consider potential minors that might complement their psychology major and to plan their elective courses in disciplines that might provide information and experiences relevant to their prospective career paths. In addition, the lectures "Making the Most of Your Undergraduate Years" and "Opportunities at WVU" further emphasize advanced planning and critically encourage students to take advantage of the many available resources and opportunities within the department (e.g., undergraduate research and teaching assistantships) and in the community (e.g., volunteer projects).

The final section of the course emphasizes interviewing skills. Instructors have utilized various local resources, including the University Placement

Service, to provide students with individual feedback and guidance with respect to this important skill.

Activities and Assignments

Instructors offer assignments and exercises that correspond with and supplement the various course topics. Such exercises encourage students to think critically about their choice of major and to consider the costs and benefits associated with pursuing careers in psychology.

A summary of class activities includes open-notes lecture quizzes, closed notes reading quizzes, collaborative topic exercises, and structured discussion questions for guest speakers. Students also submit structured and nonstructured questions for advisors and complete plagiarism exercises. Instructors identify career development and exploration resources, including department- and university-level services as well as faculty and graduate student research interests.

Students complete several required assignments. For example, students might conduct structured personal interviews with potential career role-models. In addition, the completion of a skill inventory, vocational interest test (e.g., Strong Interest Inventory [Donnay, Morris, Schaubhut, & Thompson (2004)]; SIGI Plus [Educational Testing Services (1993)]), and a career-related report is often required. Instructors also assign world-of-work assignments, including finding jobs related to psychology (or prospective graduate programs) and professional interview skills training. In addition to these career exploration exercises, the course provides opportunities for resume and vita preparation.

In terms of department-level options, students have the opportunity to participate in research projects. Students also complete a quiz and an assignment on degree requirements, which includes completing their departmental advising booklets. This assignment allows students the opportunity to tentatively map out their plan to fulfill their degree requirements.

In our most recent revision of the course, students attend the Senior Capstone Poster Conference, held at the end of each semester. The posters summarize each graduating senior's capstone experience, whether the student participated in an organized research lab, served as a teaching assistant, or completed a structured field experience within a setting related to psychology (e.g., probation office, mental health facility).

The requirement that students in the Psychology as a Profession course attend the conference serves several important functions in orientation to the major development. First, attendance provides a structured opportunity for prospective psychology majors to interact with senior students who have successfully navigated the required curriculum. Second, it allows psychology students to see firsthand the diverse capstone options and professional experiences one can pursue within psychology. Third, it provides an opportunity for out-of-classroom learning as well as an opportunity to interact with advanced undergraduate students, graduate students, and faculty members.

Readings and Materials

Originally, the course did not require any specific readings. However, instructors have adopted APA publications focused on career paths for psychology majors (e.g., APA, 2007b; Sternberg, 1997; Woods & Wilkinson, 1987) as well as other career development resources (e.g., Bolles, 1980; DeGalan & Lambert, 2006; Kuther, 2006; Landrum, Harter, & Davis, 2007) as either required or optional readings. Instructors also create required course packets (purchased by the students), which further emphasize the degree requirements and advising aspects of the course.

One specific revision of interest was the advent of student options. Specifically, students had the option of purchasing one of three required textbooks dealing with admission to graduate school (APA, 1993; Keith-Spiegel, 1990) or employment with a psychology major (DeGalan & Lambert, 2006). This shift in course design allowed students to apply relevant information from each topic to their self-selected paths. The year 2000 marked the addition of an ancillary Web site (Cohen, Futoran, Thorn, & Karraker, 2000). Heffner and Cohen (2005) found that students rated the Web site highly and that Web site hits were positively related to performance on course assignments, which suggests that the Web site potentially encourages student involvement with the course.

Evaluation of Program Success
Student Satisfaction

The importance and utility of empirically based course assessment data from a variety of sources suggest that the changing variety of in-class and out-of-class requirements has maintained the high value of the course. For example, nearly

80% of the students from the initial 1979 cohort felt that the course provided information they had not previously known about and that the course offered valuable information about employment and post-graduate educational opportunities (Lattal, 1980). Data from the most recent Senior Survey administered to all students involved in the capstone class indicate that the majority of graduating seniors felt that the course was either "somewhat useful" (46%) or "very useful" (29%) in preparing them for the psychology major at WVU, while a recent cohort comparison suggests that students from both the 2003 cohort and the 2006 cohort rate the course as having "moderately high" value (Goedereis, Cohen, Macera, & Margrett, 2007). Further, students from the 2003 cohort provided the first systematic ratings of specific lecture topics and course assignments (see Table 9-1). Taken together, these results provide empirical support that students value the course.

A recent exploratory follow-up (Goedereis et al., 2007) examined students' perceptions of the course 3 years after having taken it and whether the course helped with educational/career planning or graduate school pursuit. Students' perceptions of both major-related and career-related lectures at Time 1 were positively associated with perceptions of these lectures at Time 2, suggesting some stability in course perceptions over time. In addition, our results suggest that students not only value the course while taking it but also rated it highly 2 years later.

Table 9-1
Students' Overall Ratings of Specific Lecture Topics and Assignments

		M (SD)
Lecture topics		
	Applying to graduate school	3.86 (.89)
	The four-year plan	3.80 (.89)
	MA/PhD-level job opportunities	3.71 (.82)
	How to write a good resume	3.71 (.93)
Assignments		
	Create a four-year plan	3.98 (.89)
	Write a resume	3.69 (.93)
	Career exploration	3.18 (1.10)

Note: All responses on a 5-point Likert scale (1 = very low value, 5 = very high value).

Of the students who eventually applied to graduate school, 93% reported seeking out at least one of the undergraduate experiences recommended during the course (e.g., research assistantship, teaching assistantship, field placement, membership in Psi Chi or Psychology Club), and many of these students actually participated in two or more of these experiences. Thus, it is possible that the Psychology as a Profession course serves an important career development function by introducing students to certain undergraduate experiences early in their college experience that they then seek out during subsequent years.

Career Identity Data

One of the key aspects of these courses is the contribution to students' career identities. Data from a variety of sources suggest that the Psychology as a Profession course does, in fact, provide useful information with respect to career exploration and development. For example, 20% of respondents in a recent sample reported feeling more confident with their plans (Macera & Cohen, 2006). Similarly, the majority of respondents (71%) in our follow-up study felt that the Psychology as a Profession course did affect their career plans and actually made 42% of respondents "more confident" in their career plans (Goedereis et al., 2007).

In general, students value the course and have suggested that the department should continue to require it (Heffner & Cohen, 2005; Lattal, 1980). Data from student evaluations suggested that students prefer the weekly, one-credit in-class format to providing the information in a written booklet or offering optional evening meetings. Although students from various cohorts seem to value the course and its weekly, one-credit in-class format, disagreement exists with respect to the required workload. For example, 70% of students in the 2003 cohort felt that the workload was "just right" (Macera & Cohen, 2006) whereas many of the students in the 2007 cohort suggested there was "too much" work involved. This difference could be attributed to different instructors but more likely reflects differences in the required readings and assignments between the two cohorts. We anticipate yet another revision of the course based on student feedback and changing departmental needs.

Summary and Recommendations for "Best Practices" for Career Development Courses

Based on more than 35 years of experience, we believe that the WVU model integrates both the career development and the major orientation aspects necessary to address the APA's Career Planning and Development *Guidelines* (2007). In general, regular assessment suggests that students value the course and feel that it should continue to be a requirement within the department. Assessment data also indicate that the course might actually promote career development by introducing students to a variety of opportunities within the department and community. Similarly, in terms of serving an orientation to the major function, assessment data suggest that the course provides advising and course planning information.

Credit-Bearing Professionalization Course

First, given the necessary work associated with career exploration and course planning, we feel that psychology-as-a-profession courses should be credit-bearing. However, one credit seems sufficient, given the limits on psychology credits likely imposed by various institutions. Although there probably is no perfect time for such a course, we believe it is important for such a course to be offered (and taken) early enough that students can make informed decisions with respect to potential career paths. We recognize that the timing of such a course largely depends on the local curriculum and circumstances associated with a given institution.

   Our model encourages students to take the course during their second or third semester and actually requires that students take a careers course prior to admission into the major. Thus, a student cannot complete too much of the required curriculum until he or she has been exposed to the variety of career paths within psychology. Offering the course in this manner serves at least four positive functions: (a) It encourages a realistic self-assessment by providing objective information about the various career options and required education for each, (b) it encourages undecided students to consider psychology as a potential major by introducing these students to the variety of career options available to someone with a degree in psychology, (c) it serves to affirm pre-psychology majors' choice of major, and (d) it might cause students to rethink their career plans through self-assessment and educational requirements.

Valid Information About Psychology and Associated Careers

To serve a career development function, we believe that a course should debunk myths about psychology and psychology-related careers. This goal can be accomplished by providing information on a broad series of topics. Given the breadth and depth of psychology, it is important that students receive accurate information about the discipline as well as the skills, education, and training necessary to pursue various careers within psychology. Lectures on the diverse fields within psychology, the variety of job settings, and required education serve a CD function. Practical assignments related to writing resumes/curriculum vitae, finding jobs and potential graduate programs fulfill two of Browne and Krane's (2000) criteria for successful career interventions by providing (a) written exercises and (b) individualized interpretation and feedback (Brown et al., 2003). Introducing a variety of career paths and emphasizing how each career path relates to psychology is informative and serves to provide students with accurate information regarding the field, while practical assignments encourage realistic self-assessment, each of which will ideally encourage students to make informed decisions with respect to their chosen paths.

Details About Requirements for the Major

We believe that a psychology as a profession course should include orientation to a major information. Recently, Dunn and colleagues published a set of recommendations for "quality benchmarks in undergraduate psychology programs" (Dunn, McCarthy, Baker, Halonen, & Hill, 2007). The "Student Development" domain identified various mechanisms by which psychology departments might provide enriching opportunities for their students. Two such opportunities include student advising and advising materials.

At WVU, the department has built advising into the required curriculum via the Psychology as a Profession course. Specifically, students must review the requirements of the college and the department and complete an updated copy of the Advising Booklet as a course assignment. Many times, this assignment has been scheduled to coincide with course preregistration, and in recent semesters, the pre-psychology advising assistant has delivered a guest lecture to the class that serves as an advising workshop. We believe that the Psychology as a Profession course, as well as similar orientation courses at other institutions, can serve as a particularly appropriate opportunity to provide students with a variety of comprehensive and accurate information about the requirements in the major. Given the depth and breadth of career options within psychology, coupled with the large numbers of students who pursue psychology degrees, it is important that students understand the specific prerequisites (e.g., math, statistics) in order to make timely progress toward earning their degrees. Thus, lectures covering degree requirements, advising and registration information, and practical assignments (e.g., completing a 4-year plan) provide information that might encourage students to plan ahead and take an active role in their education.

Web Site

In addition to these recommendations, we feel that a psychology as a profession course could benefit from a supplemental Web site. Research examining the WVU model has suggested that students both use and value the Web site, and Web site use is positively correlated with many aspects of course performance (Heffner & Cohen, 2005). Based on an examination of students' open-ended comments, it might be useful to make the same course resources and materials available to students after they have completed the course on the general departmental Web site.

Guest Speakers as Role Models

Finally, although Norcross (2007) found guest speakers to be one of the lowest rated elements in his career development courses, we believe guest speakers could be included in such a course. In our experience, guest speakers, especially faculty members and graduate students from within the department, program directors from other psychology-related units in the university, and graduates from the department working locally in a variety of fields and at differing degree levels (the latter are always eager to return to the department and relate their life stories) are a valuable resource. Within the WVU model, students rate guest speaker lectures quite positively. We tend to have a fairly focused structure around guest lectures and subsequent discussions. We feel that, if utilized effectively, guest speakers provide yet another useful element to a CD-OM course by providing students with potential models.

Conclusion

We hope that this model will serve as a blueprint for instructors planning to craft and implement a psychology as a profession course. Students' evaluations and systematic assessment data suggest that this type of course successfully meets the Career Planning and Development *Guideline*. Given the important findings by Brown and Krane (2000; Brown et al., 2003) suggesting that successful career interventions contain multiple critical ingredients, we encourage instructors to borrow liberally from our recommendations in crafting and implementing such a course that meets the needs of their students and departments.

Recommended Readings

DeGalan, J., & Lambert, S. (2006). *Great jobs for psychology majors* (3rd ed.). New York: McGraw-Hill.

Kuther, T. L. (2006). *The psychology major's handbook* (2nf ed.). Belmont, CA: Thomson Wadsworth.

Landrum, R. E., Harter, J. H., & Davis, S. F. (2007). *The psychology major: Career options and strategies for success* (3rd ed.). Upper Saddle River, NJ: Prentice-Hall.

References

American Psychological Association. (1993). *Getting in: A step-by-step plan for gaining admission to graduate school in psychology.* Washington, DC: Author.

American Psychological Association. (2007a). *APA guidelines for the undergraduate psychology major.* Washington, DC: Author. Retrieved March 16, 2008, from www.apa.org/ed/resources.html.

American Psychological Association. (2007b). *Graduate study in Psychology: 2008 Edition.* Washington, DC: Author.

American Psychological Association. (2008). *Profiles of undergraduate programs in psychology.* Retrieved March 16, 2008, from http://www.apa.org/ed/pcue/offerings.html.

Bolles, R. N. (1980). *What color is your parachute?* Berkeley, CA: Ten Speed Press.

Brown, S. D., & Ryan Krane, N. E. (2000). Four (or five) sessions and a cloud of dust: Old assumptions and new observations about career counseling. In S. D., Brown & R. W. Lent (Eds.), *Handbook of counseling psychology* (3rd ed., pp. 740–766). New York: Wiley.

Brown, S. D., Ryan Krane, N. E., Brecheisen, J., Castelino, P., Budisin, I., Miller, M., & Edens, L. (2003). Critical ingredients of career choice interventions: More analyses and new hypotheses. *Journal of Vocational Behavior, 62,* 411–428.

Cohen, S. H., Futoran, D. L., Thorn, C. A., & Karraker, K. H. (2000, August). *Integrating the psychology major with a web site.* Poster presented at the meeting of the American Psychological Association, Washington, DC.

Collins, M. (1998). Snapshot of the profession. *Journal of Career Planning and Employment, 58,* 32–36, 51–55.

DeGalan, J., & Lambert, S. (2006). *Great jobs for psychology majors* (3rd ed.). New York: McGrawHill.

Donnay, D. A., Morris, M. L., Schaubhut, N. A., & Thompson, R.C. (2004). *Strong Interest Inventory® manual: Research, development, and strategies for interpretation.* Mountain View, CA: Consulting Psychology Press.

Dunn, D. S., McCarthy, M. A., Baker, S., Halonen, J. S., & Hill, G. W. (2007). Quality benchmarks in undergraduate psychology programs. *American Psychologist, 62,* 650–670.

Educational Testing Service (1993). SIGI Plus (Computer Program). Princeton, NJ: Author.

Goedereis, E. A., Cohen, S. H., Macera, M., & Margrett, J. (2007, October). Psychology as a profession at WVU: Assessment and evaluation. In S. Cohen and E. Goedereis (Chairs), *Psychology as a Profession at WVU: Evolution and Impact.* Symposium conducted at the meeting of Best Practices for Introducing and Bringing Closure to the Undergraduate Psychology Major, Atlanta, GA.

Heffner, M., & Cohen, S. H. (2005). Evaluating student use of Web-based material. *Journal of Instructional Psychology, 32,* 74–81.

Keith-Spiegel, P. (1990). *The complete guide to graduate school admission: Psychology and related fields.* Mahwah, NJ: Erlbaum.

Kuther, T. L. (2006). *The psychology major's handbook* (2nd ed.). Belmont, CA: Thomson Wadsworth.

Landrum, R. E. (2007, October). The big picture: Outside involvement and skills for collegiate success. In R. E. Landrum and B. T. Loher, *Designing a psychology orientation course—Common themes and sample exercises.* Pre-conference workshop conducted at the meeting of Best Practices for

Introducing and Bringing Closure to the Undergraduate Psychology Major, Atlanta, GA.

Landrum, R. E., Harter, J. H., & Davis, S. F. (2007). *The psychology major: Career options and strategies for success* (3rd ed.). Upper Saddle River, NJ: Prentice-Hall.

Lattal, K. A. (1980). "Psychology as a profession": A brief course providing career information for psychology majors. *Teaching of Psychology, 7,* 243–244.

Macera, M., & Cohen, S. H. (2006). Psychology as a profession: An effective career exploration and orientation course for undergraduate psychology majors. *Career Development Quarterly, 54,* 367–371.

Norcross, J. C., Sayette, M. A., Mayne, T. J., Karg, R. S., & Turkson, M. A. (1998). Selecting a doctoral program in professional psychology: Some comparisons among PhD counseling, PhD clinical, and PsyD clinical psychology programs. *Professional Psychology: Research and Practice, 29,* 609–614.

Norcross, J. C. (2007, August). *Let your life speak: Teaching the career development seminar.* G. Stanley Hall/Harry Kirke Wolf Lecture at the 115th annual convention of the American Psychological Association, San Francisco.

Sternberg, R. J. (1997). *Career paths in psychology: Where your degree can take you.* Washington, DC: American Psychological Association.

Woods, P. J., & Wilkinson, C. S. (1987). *Is psychology the major for you? Planning for your undergraduate years.* Washington, DC: Author.

Part II

Endings

10 The Capstone Course in Psychology as Liberal Education Opportunity

Dana S. Dunn and *Maureen A. McCarthy*

A liberal arts education in general, and the study of psychology in particular, is a preparation for lifelong learning, thinking, and action; it emphasizes specialized and general knowledge and skills.

—MCGOVERN, FUROMOTO, HALPERN, KIMBLE, &
MCKEACHIE (1991, P. 600)

A career preparation focus must not eliminate the need for outcomes that are broader than the content of the course and consistent with the ideals of liberal education.

—MCGOVERN & HAWKS (1988, P. 113)

Liberal education is at the heart of the teaching and learning mission of higher education in the United States. In our experiences, liberally educated people write well, reason logically, create connections among diverse elements of information, recognize what they already know and what they need to learn, engage in critical thinking, and use research skills to verify the validity and reliability of their suppositions. In short, liberally educated people engage in all the activities that faculty who teach in the arts and sciences pride themselves in passing on to generations of students.

This chapter is about applying the strengths of liberal education to a particular arena: the capstone course in the psychology major. A capstone course marks a final educational experience in an undergraduate curriculum as well as the beginning of a student's next learning opportunity in the world of work or graduate or professional education. We believe that liberal education should be an integral concern when crafting capstone courses for psychology students. Our belief is founded on two seemingly incompatible goals. First, relatively few psychology majors will have careers in the discipline; thus, we believe they should graduate with skills grounded in liberal education that will help them make their way in the world beyond campus. Second, we believe that psychology majors should have a final, in-depth educational experience that allows them to think, act, and communicate like academic psychologists. We believe these goals are easily reconciled with one another because quality capstone courses represent the goals of truly liberal learning—to evaluate, integrate, and apply knowledge to some challenge, problem, or question. Naturally, the knowledge here pertains to psychology.

Although it may be the end of the psychology major, a capstone is not the end of one's liberal education; rather, it can represent a broad beginning, an opportunity to demonstrate how intellectual skills and disciplinary knowledge can be brought to bear in a culminating academic experience and beyond. To that end, we discuss the rationale for the capstone courses in psychology, the four established capstone courses often found in psychology curricula, how to design liberally educating capstone courses, and the importance of assessing liberal learning outcomes at the end of undergraduate education in psychology.

Why a Capstone Course in Psychology?
Mastery Experiences

Academic programs elect to add capstone courses to their curricula for a variety of reasons, including the idea that students should complete their undergraduate education by having some mastery experience (Davis, 1993). Mastery experiences bring a sense of closure to undergraduate education in a major area of study. As Wagenaar (1993) and other educators argue, such mastery experiences entail activities aimed at

- Integrating and synthesizing disciplinary topics and issues
- Critiquing and broadening a discipline's scope
- Examining main theories in a discipline
- Applying disciplinary concepts to particular problems or situations
- Exploring issues originally raised in the introductory course but at an advanced level
- Connecting disciplinary issues with general education (and vice versa)
- Comparing and contrasting a discipline with other disciplines
- Examining values and views of life through a disciplinary lens

Such mastery experiences also benefit the sponsoring department or program by providing an opportunity for students to apply what they have learned.

Assessment Concerns

Given the assessment fervor gripping higher education generally (e.g., Allen, 2004; Bergquist & Armstrong, 1986) and lately, the discipline of psychology (Dunn, Mehrotra, & Halonen, 2004; Halpern et al., 1993), one would assume a sizable literature examining the virtues of the capstone course. Not so. There are few, if any, works dealing with capstone experiences in traditional undergraduate majors. For whatever reason, too, psychologists have been slow to write about capstone experiences (but see Ault & Multhaup, 2003; Durso, 1997; Weiss, 2004; Zechmeister & Reich, 1994).

What makes capstone courses desirable for a psychology curriculum? A simple answer is that a capstone course is an ideal (perhaps the ideal) place to assess summative student learning outcomes in psychology (Graham, 1998; Halonen et al., 2002a, 2002b; Halonen et al., 2003). Have psychology majors learned what their instructors intended? Is a psychology department's educational mission being fulfilled? Are the department's academic goals being met? These sorts of questions represent a good starting point for psychology faculty when they are considering developing a capstone experience for their majors. We revisit these issues later in this chapter in the context of assessing learning outcomes in capstone courses.

Aligning the End of the Curriculum With Department Mission

In fact, when deciding to develop a capstone course, one of the first steps a psychology department or program should take is to review its existing mission statement. Although some mission statements can be too broad, even grandiose, many do a fine job of specifying a department's perceived strengths, shared interests, and philosophy of educating undergraduate students. A good mission statement is a public declaration about a program's orientations toward the discipline and its expectations and goals for student learning (Pusateri, Poe, Addison, & Goedel, 2004). In turn, the departmental mission statement should reflect the mission statement espoused by the larger institution (Nichols & Nichols, 2000)—that is, the two should complement, not contradict, one another. Substituting the latter in the absence of the former is probably not an organizationally sound approach. In the absence of a department or program mission statement, then one should be created before seeking to develop an effective capstone course. Guidelines for writing a program mission statement can be found in *Strategic Leadership: Integrating Strategy and Leadership in Colleges and Universities* (Morrill, 2007).

Established Capstone Experiences in Psychology

Many psychology departments already offer some type of capstone experience for students; however, it may not be billed as such, or even required of all students. In lieu of creating a common capstone experience from scratch, some departments may simply wish to reevaluate a course they already offer. Naturally, these existing courses can be revised and tightened where connections to valued learning outcome issues are concerned. The more common capstone courses already in many departmental curricula are courses in history and systems, honors or independent study opportunities, internships, and senior seminars or other integrative experiences. Even when a department makes all of these course options available, the majority of psychology majors are likely to enroll in only one of them.

History and Systems

History and systems is often touted as the ideal capstone course because it identifies the origins of psychological questions and, through the lens of history, ties many of them to contemporary trends in the discipline. Simply offering a traditional history and systems course does not ensure a capstone experience. However, psychology majors (and their teachers) may benefit greatly from learning that certain questions regarding mind and body have not changed a great deal over the millennia—what has changed is how they are answered. Most history of psychology courses and representative textbooks review the history of psychological ideas from ancient Greek philosophy through the birth of experimental psychology in the mid to late 19th century. After a bit of Freud and James, and then the reign of American behaviorism, the focus is on how to best represent the cognitive revolution from the 1950s to the present (soon enough, perhaps, this discussion will shift to the best way to present the increasing hegemony of the neurosciences). Students, too, appreciate learning about the source of theories and research questions, especially after having studied several main content or core areas in the psychology major. Although history and systems is an ideal capstone course, having it serve as an intellectual gateway to the major is not a bad idea, either (see Benjamin, this volume).

Honors or Independent Studies

Honors and independent studies courses allow very talented students an opportunity to study some psychological topic in greater depth than can usually be accomplished in a traditional course. Students, too, are expected to be more self-motivated and self-directed than is the case with other courses. In ideal circumstances, an honors or independent study opportunity allows students to conduct actual independent research, preferably some empirical venture.

When designated a capstone experience, many honors courses are year-long ventures wherein students conceive a research project, often an experimental or quasi-experimental work, under the supervision of a faculty member. Capable students benefit from this capstone experience by selecting a research topic, reading the relevant psychological literature, formulating a testable hypothesis, recruiting participants, running an experiment, analyzing the data, and writing up the results (typically using APA style) as a formal research report or honors thesis. Thus, all of the tools of research design, methodology, and writing taught in prior courses are brought to bear on a problem chosen by the student. As part of the honors requirement, there is often an opportunity for a student to defend his or her thesis in a public venue. The real virtue of the defense option is that students can demonstrate their public speaking skills.

In practice, independent study courses probably operate like mini-honors projects: Students pick a topic, collect and read articles from the literature, and then discuss them with a faculty member. Empirical research is less likely to be part of an independent study, but it is certainly not precluded. Many independent studies begin when a student develops a particular interest in an issue raised in another class or wants to learn in depth about a topic not currently represented in a department's curriculum. Although the capstone nature of independent studies is less obvious, instructors can impose activities (e.g., writing assignments, research papers, leading discussion) that ensure skills learned earlier in major courses are applied to the independent study topic.

Both honors and independent study opportunities serve as excellent preparation for the rigors of graduate school, especially because they help hone students' organization skills and their ability to work independently, so they finish a project within some specified period of time. Independent research experience, too, can help students gain admission to more competitive graduate programs in psychology.

Internships

Also known as field study opportunities, internships or practicum courses allow students to apply what they have learned in the psychology major to actual social problems or to challenges in the workplace. Although internships can take place on campus in administrative or service-related offices, most placements are found in the local community in not-for-profit, healthcare-related (e.g., hospital, nursing home, hospice), or industry settings. Occasionally, students may be placed in a day care or senior center, or in a primary or secondary educational setting.

Thus, the primary capstone element for internships is the application of acquired knowledge and skills to a real-world setting. Students who select an internship effectively provide volunteer services to businesses, public or private agencies, or other organizations. Their work in a field setting should represent meaningful engagement (albeit supervised) with the routine demands of the site (i.e., menial tasks should be kept to a minimum level). In general, student performance is monitored by both a faculty member (often an internship coordinator) and an on-site supervisor. Often, student interns in various placements will meet on campus, as a class, to discuss their experiences with one another. Many internships will conclude with some final paper assignment and possibly an oral presentation.

Not surprisingly, students are drawn to internship experiences because of their practical nature and their particular promise for future employment. In other words, a good placement may give them an advantage when entering the job market and interviewing for work in the future. Many faculty members realize that internships can help students truly determine what they do or, perhaps more important, what they do *not* want to pursue as a future career.

Senior Seminars or Integrative Experiences

Writing about curriculum matters following the 1991 St. Mary's Conference, Brewer and colleagues (1993) noted that the breadth of the typical psychology major curriculum demands at least one integrative experience (see also Dunn et al., 2010). Thus far, we reviewed three possibilities that can serve as an integrative experience. A fourth, suggested by Brewer et al. is to have students take a more depth-oriented course, such as an advanced general psychology course or a great ideas in psychology course. Both are intriguing possibilities since most students will have completed a basic introductory level course as well as one or more of several intermediate core offerings (e.g., social, personality, cognitive, developmental, experimental). Yet another possibility is to create a capstone experience around some special topic (e.g., emotion, nonverbal communication) that is examined from several different perspectives (i.e., evolutionary, developmental, social, psychobiological).

In some ways, senior seminars offer departments the most flexibility where capstone experiences are concerned. If more than one seminar is available, students can usually enroll in the seminar that is topically appealing to them. Different faculty members can offer different topical seminars once learning goals, outcome measures, general assignments, and the like are agreed upon. Successful seminar topics can be offered more than once, perhaps within some planned rotation of seminar topics.

Designing Liberally Educating Capstone Courses

What if a department decides to create a capstone course from scratch or to strengthen one or more of the four established capstone experiences? What criteria should be used? We believe that psychology faculty should attend carefully to those aspects of the course that reinforce the values of liberal education. We say this not to downplay the importance of psychology as a discipline but to complement it. Further, we believe that psychology teachers must recall the aforementioned truth as they teach the capstone and prepare students for the world beyond campus: Few will go to graduate school and fewer still will do so in psychology. Thus, we are responsible for helping students learn to use the best that psychology has to offer in terms of knowledge, research, and communication skills with an eye to applying them in other worthy domains beyond the discipline's boundaries.

McGovern, Furumoto, Halpern, Kimble, and McKeachie (1991) identified eight common goals for psychology majors that are grounded in the goals of liberal education. Now, as then, the advantage of these goals is their fit to a variety of institution types and educational settings. Like McGovern and colleagues, we believe these goals can be adjusted as needed in the course of crafting a department-specific capstone course. We review each in turn with an eye to the role they play in crafting capstone experiences.

Frameworks for Knowledge

Students learn best when they have a frame of reference to draw upon and to use when evaluating new ideas. Thus, a capstone course should be designed to intentionally draw upon the disciplinary knowledge acquired during the undergraduate years. The knowledge base of psychology is grounded in the scientific method and reliance on empirical techniques for determining cause and effect. The discipline's adherence to the scientific method and empiricism lead to the generation of data and the development of theory. Hand in hand, data and theory allow researchers to add to the corpus of psychological knowledge which, while increasingly specialized, nonetheless deals, at its base, with brain, mind, and behavior. Different core areas approach psychological questions somewhat differently, but all contribute to "one psychology" (Matarazzo, 1987).

Critical Thinking

Doing work in a capstone course requires that students be capable and comfortable with critical thinking. Critical thinking is not displayed by one intellectual activity but instead by many, including skills advancing focus on, motivation for, and engagement with new ideas (Halonen & Gray, 2000). Critical thinkers search for and recognize patterns; perform problem solving in practical, creative, or scientific ways; think like psychologists; and consider multiple points of view or perspectives when evaluating ideas or issues. Encouraging students to think critically in a capstone course prompts them to observe, infer, question, decide, develop new ideas, and analyze arguments concerning some topic or question of interest. A chief goal of teaching critical thinking in a psychology capstone course is to refine students' abilities to describe, predict, explain, and control behavior (see also Dunn, Halonen, & Smith, 2008).

Scientific Writing and Disciplinary Discourse

Students in a capstone course must be able to speak and read the discipline's vernacular. We are not referring exclusively to reading and writing APA style

(American Psychological Association, 2001), important as that is (see Beins, Smith, & Dunn, this volume). Writing in psychology is certainly a form of critical thinking (Dunn & Smith, 2008), as is writing about psychological issues and speculating about cause and effect where human or animal behavior is concerned. McGovern et al. (1991) make an obvious, if often forgotten, point about writing in psychology: Learning to do so is a way to "comprehend the discourse of the discipline used in textbooks and scientific journal articles" (p. 601). A quality capstone course should require students to both read and produce scientific writing in psychology.

Information Literacy

Good writing is supported by persuasive, compelling evidence. Today's students need to be able to find whatever kind of information they need for their education in psychology. All undergraduate students, including psychology majors, should be able to search for research evidence in libraries and databases. The good news is that current students are highly facile with computers and online searching. Nevertheless, we should ensure the information literacy of our students (McCarthy & Pusateri, 2006). As teachers of psychology, our task is to direct our students to—perhaps even require them to use—our disciplinary databases. In fact, their search skills can help to shape the capstone course. For example, in course syllabi, not all reading material should be provided by capstone course teachers; rather, students should have an opportunity to find appropriate readings relevant to class topics.

Research Methods and Data Analysis

Methodological (qualitative as well as quantitative) and statistical skills are rightly touted as essential for students to learn. Unfortunately, these tend to be the skills that are quickly forgotten if they are not used. Too few undergraduate students get the opportunity to conceive a research project, execute it, and then analyze the data to learn whether their hypotheses were supported. A quality capstone course should have some sort of empirical requirement that encourages students to manipulate and measure variables (or alternatively, to explore the utility of a qualitative method of inquiry). If nothing else, the experience of designing a study of some sort will allow students to consider various methods for answering their research question, weighing the strengths and weaknesses of each in the process. In turn, students should be able to select and plan the data analysis using the appropriate test statistic in advance of actual data collection (this prevents gathering information that can not be analyzed). We also believe that one of the unsung virtues of the marriage of method with analysis is learning to interpret results and to present them to others in prose form. Thus, this liberal education goal supports the earlier goal devoted to enhancing scientific communication skills.

Interpersonal Skills and Diversity

The hope for expanded self-knowledge is often what draws students to psychology in the first place. True self-knowledge not only promotes self-reflection but also connection to others. An appreciation of and for other people should be fostered in a capstone experience precisely because it is virtually impossible for college graduates to remain isolated from human diversity. A mark of a liberal learning is awareness of and sensitivity toward differences and similarities where race, gender, religion, disability, sexual orientation, ethnicity, culture, social class, and education are concerned. A quality capstone experience in psychology should afford students the chance to learn about as well as from differences displayed by individuals or groups.

History of Psychology as Context

Although we have already touted the importance of understanding psychology's contributions to intellectual history, we reiterate that whether established or novel, any quality capstone experience must trace the development of key ideas. Students should "appreciate the evolution of the methods of psychology, its theoretical conflicts, its sociopolitical uses, and its place in the broader intellectual traditions of the humanities, sciences, and social sciences" (McGovern et al., 1991, p. 602). The design of a capstone experience should consciously link the genesis of ideas and issues to the ways in which they are currently manifested in disciplinary discourse.

Ethics and Values

No inquiry occurs in a vacuum; informed inquiry relies on ethical principles learned through disciplinary trial and error. Most psychology students are well acquainted with *The Ethical Principles of Psychologists and the Code of Conduct* (APA, 2002) where deception, debriefing, voluntary research participation, and the ethical treatment of animals are concerned. What many students do not realize, however, is that the reach of the discipline's ethics and values is much broader than the lab or even the field. Psychologists and students of psychology have a duty to use the skills acquired in the course of their educations to better human welfare by resolving conflicts, applying knowledge, and defending the integrity of science and academic inquiry. Capstone experience steeped in the values of liberal education will afford students the opportunity to think about and perhaps act on issues pertaining to social and ethical responsibilities. As McGovern et al. (1991) suggest, opportunities to do so can involve matters of race, gender, class, culture, and ethnicity where theory, research, and the practice of psychology are concerned.

The Importance of Assessing Liberal Learning Outcomes in Capstone Experiences

We have discussed the purpose for a capstone course and the types of psychology courses that allow us to fully integrate the liberal arts experience. A capstone course can also serve as the culminating setting for assessing the goals of psychology as a liberal arts degree.

The following are examples of intended student learning outcomes that can be addressed in a capstone experience (Murphy, 2008).

1. Write in a clear, organized, effective manner.
2. Speak effectively and intelligently.
3. Work constructively in groups, on teams.
4. Make reasoned decisions.
5. Use the library effectively for research.
6. Evaluate critically what is read and heard.
7. Understand theories and perspectives of the discipline.
8. Demonstrate higher order thinking (critical thinking).
9. Use research skills.

Although these are examples, they are not an all-inclusive listing of possibilities. Minimally, within the context of a liberal arts degree, the capstone course provides an opportunity to assess expression of ideas in writing and as presented by students, content and the ability to integrate ideas.

Assessment of the goals associated with an undergraduate degree in psychology is difficult and measuring writing skills can be particularly cumbersome. For example, some would suggest that an accurate measure of writing requires a portfolio of examples that must be evaluated by several faculty. Yet, any one of the capstone courses identified above provides an opportunity to assess writing skills that have been acquired throughout the educational experience. Rather than create a portfolio of materials, it may be sufficient to evaluate the culminating product from the capstone experience.

A well designed history and systems course provides students with the opportunity to consider the origins of the discipline relative to contemporary issues facing psychologists today. Assessment of writing, and students' abilities to synthesize historical and contemporary issues using psychological language can take the form of a standardized assignment. Evaluation of student products may necessarily include synthesis of ideas, critical examination of theory, and general writing skills. As such, this culminating activity would provide a useful evaluation of several learning goals consistent with the capstone course (i.e., research, writing, critical thinking).

The independent study or honor's course is a unique opportunity for both the student and the professor. Creation of new ideas, theories, or research is the ultimate goal for the science of psychology. From an assessment perspective this type of capstone can be used to measure writing skills, and it provides an opportunity to measure presentation skills. Many independent study courses result in a product that is disseminated in a local, regional, or national venue; this type of course and peer review is frequently an inherent part of the process. Therefore, submission and acceptance of the student's work at a conference offers an evaluative measure of communication and presentation skills. Opportunities for student research awards offer an additional measure of outstanding levels of success.

Internships not only provide students with valuable practical experiences and potential post-graduate employment opportunities but can also be used as a measure of student learning outcomes. A final paper that fully integrates the concepts of psychology into the practical setting provides a compelling demonstration of fully meeting the goals of a liberal arts degree in psychology. For example, a student working at an internship in a community mental health setting may assist a chronically mentally ill client with maintaining a cognitive behavioral treatment plan. The student's culminating paper may require an explanation of psychological constructs from his or her undergraduate courses relative to the work the student is performing at the internship site. Assessment of the number of linkages between psychological constructs and practical applications would constitute an effective measure of knowledge of the discipline.

A specific integrative or capstone course offers the richest opportunity for assessing writing skills. Murphy (2008) suggests that students should be able to use reference materials to write a well-informed, critically reasoned, integrated thesis or research paper that brings the depth of the discipline in one final experience. This type of assignment may be required in all sections of the course. A standardized rubric could also be used to grade each of the capstone papers and a copy of these rubrics could be retained for the purpose of documenting the outcomes of the major. Instead of creating the more cumbersome portfolios (but see, Keller, Craig, Launius, Loher, & Cooledge, 2004), documentation of proficiency in writing could be demonstrated through an analysis of the rubrics used to grade the papers.

Local Concerns

Virtually every educational institution has a set of learning outcomes that reflect its core concerns. For example, an institution might value students' abilities to work well in groups, an activity commensurate with the team-based efforts commonly found in corporate settings. Similarly, an institution might emphasize service learning because it is critical to its mission. Assessment practices should be campus specific and carefully linked to the respective mission of the department.

Liberal Learning in the Capstone as Looking Ahead

In this chapter we offer a review of the variety of capstone experiences that are offered in undergraduate programs. As originally conceptualized (Brewer et al., 1993) and reaffirmed by the *Guidelines for the Undergraduate Psychology Major* (APA, 2006), the capstone experience is central to the liberal arts degree in psychology. Not only does it provide students with an opportunity to realize their depth of knowledge but it provides an opportunity for faculty to assess student development.

Despite the relative importance of the capstone experience, we believe it is threatened. An intensive writing experience is at the heart of the capstone experience. Assessment of writing can also be a time-intensive activity for faculty. As the whole of higher education experiences reductions in faculty lines and pressure to increase class size, capstone experiences will become increasingly challenging.

References

Allen, M. J. (2004). *Assessing academic programs in higher education.* Bolton, MA: Anker.

American Psychological Association. (2001). *Publication manual of the American Psychological Association* (5th ed.). Washington, DC: Author.

American Psychological Association. (2002). Ethical principles of psychologists and code of conduct. *American Psychologist, 57,* 1060–1073.

American Psychological Association. (2006). *Guidelines for the Undergraduate Psychology Major.* Washington, DC: Author.

Ault, R. L., & Multhaup, K. S. (2003). An issues-oriented capstone course. *Teaching of Psychology, 30,* 46–48.

Bergquist, W. H., & Armstrong, J. L. (1986). *Planning effectively for educational quality: An outcomes-based approach for colleges committed to excellence.* San Francisco: Jossey-Bass.

Brewer, C. L., Hopkins, R., Kimble, G. A., Matlin, M. A., McCann, L. I., McNeil, O. V., Nodine, B. F., Quinn, V. N., & Saundra. (1993). Curriculum. In T. V. McGovern (Ed.), *Handbook for enhancing undergraduate education in psychology* (pp. 161–182). Washington, DC: American Psychological Association.

Davis, N. J. (1993). Bringing it all together: The sociological imagination. *Teaching Sociology, 21,* 233–238.

Dunn, D. S., Brewer, C. L., Cautin, R. L., Gurung, R. A., Keith, K. D., McGregor, L. N., Nida, S. A., Puccio, P., & Voight, M. J. (2010). The undergraduate psychology curriculum: A call for a core. In D. Halpern et al. (Eds.), *Undergraduate education in psychology: A blueprint for the future of the discipline* (pp. 47–51). Washington, DC: American Psychological Association.

Dunn, D. S., Mehrotra, C. M., & Halonen, J. S. (Eds.). (2004). *Measuring up: Educational assessment challenges and practices for psychology.* Washington, DC: American Psychological Association.

Dunn, D. S., & Smith, R. A. (2008). Writing as critical thinking. appear In D. S. Dunn, J. S. Halonen, & R. A. Smith (Eds.), *Teaching critical thinking in psychology: A handbook of best practices* (pp. 163–173). Malden, MA: Wiley-Blackwell.

Dunn, D. S., Halonen, J. S., & Smith, R. A. (Eds.). (2008). *Teaching critical thinking in psychology: A handbook of best practices.* Malden, MA: Wiley-Blackwell.

Durso, F. T. (1997). Corporate-sponsored undergraduate research as a capstone experience. *Teaching of Psychology, 24,* 54–56.

Graham, S. E. (1998). Developing student outcomes for the psychology major: An assessment-as-learning framework. *Current Directions in Psychological Science, 7,* 165–170.

Halpern, D. F., Appleby, D. C., Beers, S. E., Cowan, C. L., Furedy, J. J., Halonen, J. S., Horton, C. P., Peden, B. F., & Pittenger, D. J. (1993). Targeting outcomes: Covering your assessment needs and concerns. In T. V. McGovern (Ed.), *Handbook for enhancing undergraduate education in psychology* (pp. 23–46). Washington, DC: American Psychological Association.

Halonen, J. S., Appleby, D. C., Brewer, C. L., Buskist, W., Gillem, A. R., Halpern, D. F., Hill, G. W., IV, Lloyd, M. A., Rudmann, J. L., & Whitlow, V. M. (APA Task Force on Undergraduate Major Competencies). (2002a). *Undergraduate major learning goals and outcomes: A report.* Washington, DC: American Psychological Association. Retrieved July, 8, 2005, from http://www.apa.org/ed/pcue/reports.html.

Halonen, J. S., Appleby, D. C., Brewer, C. L., Buskist, W., Gillem, A. R., Halpern, D. F., Hill, G. W., IV, Lloyd, M. A., Rudmann, J. L., & Whitlow, V. M. (APA Task Force on Undergraduate Major Competencies, Eds.). (2002b). *The Assessment CyberGuide for learning goals and outcomes.* Retrieved August 11, 2009, http://www.apa.org/ed/guidehomepage.html.

Halonen, J., Bosack, T., Clay, S., & McCarthy, M. (with Dunn, D. S., Hill, G. W., IV, McEntarffer, R., Mehrotra, C., Nesmith, R., Weaver, K. A., & Whitlock, K.) (2003). A rubric for learning, teaching, and assessing scientific inquiry in psychology. *Teaching of Psychology, 30,* 196–208.

Halonen, J., & Gray, C. (2000). *The critical thinking companion for introductory psychology* (2nd ed.). New York: Worth.

Keller, P. A., Craig, F. W., Launius, M. H., Loher, B. T., & Cooledge, N. (2004). In D. S. Dunn, C. M. Mehrotra, & J. S. Halonen (Eds.), *Measuring up: Educational assessment challenges and practices for psychology* (pp. 197–207). Washington, DC: American Psychological Association.

Matarazzo, J. D. (1987). There is only one psychology, no specialties, but many applications. *American Psychologist, 42,* 893–903.

McCarthy, M. A., & Pusateri, T. P. (2006). Teaching students to use electronic databases. In W. Buskist & S. F. Davis (Eds.), *Handbook of the teaching of psychology* (pp.107–111). Malden, MA: Blackwell.

McGovern, T. V., Furumoto, L., Halpern, D. F., Kimble, G. A., & McKeachie, W. J. (1991). Liberal education, study in depth, and the arts and science major—psychology. *American Psychologist, 46,* 598–605.

McGovern, T. V., & Hawks, B. K. (1988). The liberating science and art of undergraduate psychology. *American Psychologist, 43,* 108–114.

Morrill, R. L. (2007). *Strategic leadership: Integrating strategy and leadership in colleges and universities.* Washington, DC: American Council on Higher Education.

Murphy, P. D. (2008). Capstone experience. Retrieved March 4, 2008, from http:www.ndsu.edu/ndsu/accreditation/assessment/capstone_experience.htm.

Nichols, J. O., & Nichols, K. W. (2000). *The departmental guide and record book for student outcomes assessment and institutional effectiveness* (3rd ed.). New York: Agathon Press.

Pusateri, T. P., Poe, R. E., Addison, W. E., & Goedel, G. D. (2004). Designing and implementing psychology program reviews. In D. S. Dunn. C. M. Mehrotra, & J. S. Halonen (Eds.), *Measuring up: Educational assessment challenges and practices for psychology* (pp. 65–89). Washington, DC: American Psychological Association.

Wagenaar, T. C. (1993). The capstone course. *Teaching Sociology , 21,* 209–214.

Weiss, R. (2004). Using an undergraduate human-service practicum to promote unified psychology. *Teaching of Psychology, 31,* 43–46.

Zechmeister, E. B., & Reich, J. N. (1994). Teaching undergraduates about teaching undergraduates: A capstone course. *Teaching of Psychology, 21,* 24–28.

11 History of Psychology as a Capstone Course

Ludy T. Benjamin, Jr.

Schools have offered history of psychology courses in the United States since the 1920s, at least as early as 1922. They may have existed a decade earlier as evidenced by the existence of several books that would have been appropriate as textbooks for such a class. For example, two books appeared in 1912. One was G. Stanley Hall's *Founders of Modern Psychology*, which featured chapters on the work of six individuals including Gustav Fechner, Herman Helmholtz, and Wilhelm Wundt. The second was the first volume of George S. Brett's three-volume work entitled *History of Psychology*.

The first textbooks to cover the history of modern scientific psychology appeared in 1929, perhaps inspired by the 50th anniversary of the founding of Wundt's Leipzig laboratory. Three appeared that year. One was by Walter Pillsbury (1929) of the University of Michigan. It was not very successful and did not make it into a second printing. A second text was by Columbia University's Gardner Murphy (1929), a book that went through four editions, the last of those published in the 1970s. But it was the third of that trio that would become the standard-bearer for the history of psychology, the bible for students and teachers of the history of psychology. Its title was *A History of Experimental Psychology* (1929) and the author was Harvard University's Edwin G. Boring. He revised the book only once in 1950, and it was still on recommended graduate school reading lists in the 1970s.

It is a sad happenstance that the name that is synonymous with the history of psychology is Boring. Students typically find that amusing. For me, I think that the humor of that juxtaposition disappeared a long time ago. I say that because too often I hear people say or I read that history is boring. I even have a very good friend who once published an article in the journal *Teaching of Psychology* entitled "Teaching and Learning the History of Psychology Need Not Be Boring." I still speak to him despite the deplorable title of his article (Davis, Janzen, & Davis, 1982).

History Is Not Boring

Let me make a significant declaration at this point: History is not boring! Some historians are boring. Some history books are boring. But history is not boring. History is the story of fascinating lives in fascinating times. If it were not interesting, why would anyone take the time to remember it? History recounts the drama of our past. It allows us to connect our lives to that past. It helps us make sense of the present. It gives us some basis on which to speculate intelligently about our future. It helps us integrate our knowledge in a framework of more meaningful understanding. It gives meaning to events and information that might otherwise be meaningless. It teaches us some humility for our own views and, we hope, some tolerance and understanding of the views of others. Like any good story, history alternately fills us with joy or sadness, hope or despair. It is the stuff of intrigue, of romance, of ambition, of betrayal, of sacrifice. It is the story of the best and the worst of humanity. Jacques Barzun (1954) has written that "Whoever wants to know the heart and mind of America had better learn baseball" (p. 159). I would add that whoever wants to understand the human condition had better learn the history of psychology.

I have been doing research and writing in the history of psychology for more than 30 years now. In observing my colleagues in other areas of psychology it is clear to me that I have much more fun in my vocation than they do in theirs. I don't have to get the approval of Internal Review Boards (IRBs). None of my subjects bite me. I don't need expensive equipment. And I don't even have to know how to use structural equation modeling. Instead I get to engage in what amounts to detective work. I travel to interesting places to work in archives that hold great secrets, waiting for me to discover them. I spend some of my research time talking with the most interesting senior citizens in the field, none of whom ever interrupt our conversation to answer their cell phones. And I get to use a writing style that is worthy of the label "writing." When I retire in about 5 years I will go on permanent sabbatical. Unlike my colleagues in neuroscience who can't work in the absence of their expensive labs, or my social psychology colleagues who will be out of work without access to large groups of subjects, I will be able to pursue my research full time. I even plan to write some baseball history.

Why Are There History of Psychology Courses?

As a field, psychology has a long-standing interest in its history. History of psychology courses are commonly part of the undergraduate and graduate curricula in most colleges and universities today. Indeed, departments often require such courses for our majors or for some doctoral specialties, particularly the programs in clinical, counseling, and school psychology because of recommendations in the accreditation criteria of the American Psychological Association (APA). So why are psychologists so interested in their own history? Such interest does not appear in the other sciences. It is rare to find courses on the history of biology or chemistry or sociology or economics. So why psychology?

In trying to answer this question, consider the following quotations from two eminent British historians: Robin Collingwood, writing in the 1940s and Edward Carr, writing in the 1960s. Carr (1961) is the author of a profound little book entitled *What Is History?* I have a friend in the history department at Texas A&M who says he rereads that book every year. I confess I have read it cover to cover only once but I understand why it could be read again and again.

Collingwood (1946) wrote that the "proper object of historical study . . . is the human mind, or more properly the activities of the human mind" (p. 215). Carr (1961) added that "the historian is not really interested in the unique, but what is general in the unique" and that "the study of history is a study of causes . . . the historian . . . continually asks the question 'why?'" (pp. 80, 113). Thus, according to these historians, to study history is to study the human mind, to be able to generalize beyond the characteristics of a single individual or single event to other individuals and other events, and to be able to answer the "why" of human behavior in terms of motivation, personality, experience, expectations, and so forth.

Collingwood (1946) has gone even further in defining history as "the science of human nature" (p. 206). In doing so he has allowed history to usurp psychology's definition for itself. I would argue that Collingwood is wrong in his labeling of history as science. Science is largely experimental, and history, although fervently empirical, is not. I should add that I think that good historians follow some of the rules and practices of science. Historical research often begins with a question or questions. These questions serve as hypotheses and guide the search for evidence that would confirm or disconfirm them. Like scientists, historians should not be allowed to pick and choose their evidence. They follow their questions wherever the evidence trail leads, and the story evolves from the evidence collected. Thus the intellectual pursuits of the historian and psychologist are not very different. As psychologists, we are not moving very far from our own field of interest when we study the history of psychology.

The History of Psychology Course as Introduction

In the undergraduate curriculum, the history of psychology course is almost always an upper level course with multiple prerequisites (Fuchs & Viney, 2002; Raphelson, 1982). This chapter is about the history of psychology course as a capstone course, but I want to mention, briefly, that history of psychology can also be taught as a course that introduces students to the discipline of psychology. As such it is a very different course from what is typically offered. Such an introductory course would draw students from all majors, thus allowing students of all interests and talents to benefit from the lessons learned in such a history course. I would love to see that model catch on. It would mean that the course could become an offering at community colleges where it is largely absent today. Over the years I have had many students tell me, both graduate and undergraduate students, that they wish they had taken the course at the beginning of their course of study in psychology. I think it is easy to make a case for the benefits of such an introductory history class.

What Is a Capstone Course?

In looking up capstone in my dictionary, the second definition is "the crowning achievement or final stroke, the culmination or acme" (Soukhanov, 1992,

p. 286). That is an interesting mix of labels. I don't think I like "final stroke." It sounds too much like a fatal illness. "Acme" might be okay, but then it is associated with one of the world's great losers, namely Wile E. Coyote. "Culmination" could be good, but often it is taken to mean completion, and completion by itself isn't necessarily good. So I think I am left with "crowning achievement." I cannot speak for you, but I would like to teach the class that was to be regarded as the crowning achievement for students. I could even envision myself dressed in some elaborate costume, far more impressive than the best of academic regalia, placing crowns on the enlightened heads of my students at the end of the course. So what should a course be if it is to qualify as the crowning achievement?

I used the Web to look at capstone courses at various colleges. I wasn't so much interested in what courses were offered as capstones as I was in learning what criteria a course had to meet to be considered a capstone. Although there was considerable variability in these requirements, there was also much agreement. Part of the consensus is that a capstone course should allow students to demonstrate what they have learned, especially by invoking higher cognitive domains such as application, analysis, and evaluation. According to my reading, four avenues are suggested as critical in that regard. First, proponents of these courses argue that they should emphasize competence in communication skills. Students should be able to write and speak well, communicating their ideas effectively. As part of communication competence, they should also be able to listen. Second, capstone courses should allow students to demonstrate their ability to think critically. Third, capstone courses should emphasize context, embedding disciplinary material in a broader social, cultural, and historic framework, helping students understand their subject as it affects and is affected by an increasingly interconnected world. Finally, capstone courses should help motivate students toward lifelong learning, understanding the critical importance of continued learning for personal, professional, and civic life. I will argue that history of psychology courses can do all of those things and more.

Communication Skills

Giving students the opportunity to speak and write in class is not exclusively the domain of a history of psychology course. Such activities ideally would be part of any psychology course. Classes must be small to ensure ample opportunities with sufficient feedback. Those seem to be getting rare at many colleges and universities, especially the large doctoral granting research universities. There are people who will tell you that they can hold discussions in their class of 250 introductory students. I have colleagues and graduate students tell me that all the time. They are deluded. They simply don't know what a real discussion is about. There is a rich literature on discussion techniques, and ideal discussion groups are small, for example, around 8–12 students. Rarely do we have such a luxury in academe except at some of the elite liberal arts colleges that offer students such class sizes for the common first-year seminar and/or a capstone course. It is also difficult, if not impossible, to have any significant writing experiences in large classes. You can use ungraded 1- or 2-minute papers, and they have value. Or you can jump on the bandwagon of the latest fad for teaching writing in large classes, such as calibrated peer review (Robinson, 2001). The bottom line is that if you want students to have opportunities to speak, to write, and to receive feedback about their outputs, then history of psychology is one of many courses that can accomplish this goal. But it will work only if the classes are small and the instructor is dedicated to the extra work required. Writing is greatly important, but learning to write will work only if students engage in rewriting. Students must get critical feedback on their writing and then be asked to rework their writing to evidence their understanding of the feedback (Nodine, 1990).

Critical Thinking

Critical thinking is surely among the most prominent of catch phrases in modern higher education. It is intended to be one of those lifelong benefits of a college education, educating a citizenry to be better thinkers. Teachers of psychology are fortunate because as a science, critical thinking is part and parcel of the scientific method. So, like communication skills, there are many courses in psychology that address the topic of critical thinking. But history is a discipline that also embraces critical thinking as part of its methodology.

Although there are many models of critical thinking, I use one slightly modified from a version described by Doug Bernstein (personal communication) because it is the one I teach in my introductory psychology courses and in my history courses. There are four stages to this model: (a) What claim are you being asked to believe? (b) What evidence are you given to support that claim? (c) What alternative explanations might you give for the claim? (d) What kinds of evidence could you gather to support or refute the various explanations?

The history of psychology, because it is the history of a science, is replete with examples of critical thinking. The rejection of phrenology, facial vision, the variability hypothesis, paranormal phenomena, racial inferiority, and much of Hullian learning theory are a few of the many examples of changing beliefs in psychology because of critical thinking approaches (see Henderson, 1995). Indeed, we have several early systems of psychology that touted their way as the one right path to psychological truths. Philosophical systems such as structuralism, behaviorism, and psychoanalysis all claimed exclusivity with regard to providing the secrets of psychology. Ultimately, all were found wanting.

As an example, take the origins of intelligence testing in America. If there is any activity that defines the profession of psychology for much of the 20th century in the United States, it is psychological testing, and it began with the work of James McKeen Cattell in the 1890s. Cattell had returned to the States in 1889 after contact with Francis Galton at Cambridge University. Galton was involved in what he called anthropometric testing, using sensory, motor, physical, and cognitive measures to develop measures of intelligence. Cranial dimensions purportedly measured brain size. Measures of sensory acuity were judged to be important because of the critical role of the senses in acquiring all information, a belief grounded in the beginnings of British empiricism. Reaction time measures were important because psychologists believed them to be a measure of the speed of information processing within the nervous system. Galton believed that all of these measures were indicative of intelligence and thus had important eugenic implications.

Cattell, a eugenicist and disciple of Galton, coined the term *mental test* in an 1890 article promoting the value of such tests, arguing that they were especially useful in identifying individuals with exceptional aptitudes. For nearly a decade Cattell collected data on the incoming first-year students at Columbia University, hoping to discover some relationships between his measures and academic performance. Even without such data, he believed in the face validity of his tests. When around 1900 Galton and Pearson developed a statistical measure of relationship called correlation, Cattell was obligated to put his measures to the test. He encouraged one of his graduate students, Clark Wissler, to use this measure to test for relationships among his anthropometric measures and academic performance in college. Wissler applied this method and found largely zero correlations. It marked the end of anthropometric testing in America, essentially the end of Cattell's research career, and, oh yes, Clark Wissler became an anthropologist (Sokal, 1982).

In fact, the subject of intelligence testing is not only an excellent topic for exploring critical thinking but is especially useful for discussing the third of the consensual capstone qualities: context.

Emphasizing Context

Let me define context again. Earlier I said that capstone courses should emphasize context, embedding disciplinary material in a broader social, cultural, and historic framework, helping students understand their subject as it affects and is affected by an increasingly interconnected world. Whereas the first two dimensions I mentioned—communication skills and critical thinking—can be part of most psychology courses, I cannot think of another course in our curriculum that can serve the needs of context in the same way as a history course.

History is about context. Historians talk about the differences between internal histories and external histories. The latter are much preferred. You could teach the history of intelligence testing by staying largely within the discipline of psychology, thus covering the birth and death of anthropometric testing, the subsequent move to Binet-type tests, the standardization issues, the concept of the IQ, the notion of general intelligence or g, performance IQs, crystallized versus fluid intelligence, cultural bias issues, social and emotional intelligence, and so forth. You could describe that epoch by detailing the changing views of intelligence within psychology, describing the changing methods of measuring intelligence, and describing the multiple uses of intelligence tests and how that usage changed over time. That would be an internal history, and a very incomplete and misinformed history at that. Historians would point out that intelligence testing developed in a social-political-historical context, influenced tremendously by factors outside of psychology, and to provide an adequate account of that history would mean embedding the story of intelligence testing in this broader context, thus producing an external history. Here is an example from the work of Franz Samelson.

In the 1910s virtually all American psychologists writing on intelligence differences among the races interpreted the differences as supporting the superiority of the White race. A mere 20 years later a survey of 100 psychologists showed that 25% still espoused such a belief, 11% believed in the intellectual equality of Blacks and Whites, and 64% believed the data were inconclusive. What brought about this rather remarkable change by 1930? Samelson (1978) wrote:

> This . . . looks like a beautiful example of the progress of empirical
> science; objective data triumph over prejudices and speculation and
> overcome, in self-corrective fashion, even the misconceptions and
> biases of the first generation of researchers. (p. 270)

Samelson notes, however, that it didn't happen that way. He states, "empirical data certainly did not settle the issue one way or the other" (p. 270). In fact Samelson argues that most psychologists who formed opinions on this subject either early on, or 20 years later, did so without even seeing the data. Instead, this change in the interpretation of IQ differences from one of indicating racial inferiority to one of indicating the effects of racial prejudice occurred because of the changing nature of the psychological field by the 1930s. Samelson argues convincingly that the reason for the change was that the field of psychology began to be differently populated in the 1930s with names such as Klineberg, Herskovits, Feingold, Hirsch, Viteles, Lasker, Katz, Lehman, and Horowitz. Samelson notes that these were not the only voices making a cultural bias argument. But he adds, "It seems likely . . . that personal experiences sensitized individuals to different aspects of the problem and led some to question the assumptions taken as self-evident by others lacking such experiences" (p. 273). It was this cultural shift in America and in the cultural and ethnic makeup of psychologists that brought about a radical change in how obtained IQ differences were viewed. That context is key to making sense of this important historical change.

Another example is the work of R. M. Bache, a graduate student of Lightner Witmer. Bache (1895) tested three racial groups (i.e., Native Americans, African Americans, and Whites) on auditory and visual reaction time tests. Recall that psychologists were especially interested in reaction time because it was believed to measure an individual's speed of mental processing with faster processing speeds assumed to be indicative of greater intelligence. Bache found that Native Americans had the fastest reaction times followed by African Americans followed by Whites. Oops! Not to be deterred, he explained that these simple reaction time tasks were largely spinally mediated reactions and not the product of cerebral activity. Thus it could be expected that more "primitive races" would excel at this more primitive task. These post hoc revisionist explanations on the topic of racial inferiority have not gone away in more than a century since Bache's interpretation of his data. One of the reasons I mention this study is that a similar explanation for racial differences was offered by Arthur Jensen (2006) in his most recent book. In that work he emphasized his ongoing research on reaction time because he believes it to be the purest measure of general intelligence, unbiased, of course, by culture and experience (see Nisbett, 2005).

With ease, I could give you hundreds of examples of the importance of context in the history of psychology. SPSSI, the Society for the Psychological Study of Social Issues, was founded in 1936. It would not have been founded in the 1920s or the 1940s. During the Great Depression of the 1930s with high unemployment, race riots, labor disputes, poverty, and an impending war in Europe, the time had come for psychologists to take action in applying their science to the social ills of the world. You cannot explain the history of SPSSI without embedding that organization in the context of the American and world history of its time. The American popular psychology magazines enjoyed enormous popularity in the 1920s, a popularity brought on by an American euphoria that embraced the science of psychology as the new path to health, happiness, and success. Studies of the psychology of sex differences became especially important in the 1910s in the decade leading up to the passage of the Nineteenth Amendment giving American women the right to vote. E. C. Tolman, B. F. Skinner, and Clark Hull all published their ideas on learning in the 1930s. For decades the debate focused on Tolman and Hull, mostly on the latter. Skinner's work was largely ignored until the 1960s when developments in education and psychopathology made his ideas seem suddenly relevant. Organizational psychology began in the 1930s, coincident with the growth of influence of labor unions, with these new psychologists emphasizing such topics as job satisfaction. Clinical psychologists, and later counseling psychologists, got to play major roles in psychotherapy delivery in the 1940s because the U.S. government desperately needed mental health professionals beyond psychiatrists to meet veteran needs at the end of World War II. Psychologists became the major providers of psychotherapy services in the 1970s by factors outside the profession rather than any developments within (Benjamin & Baker, 2004).

There are many other examples, but I hope you get the idea. Psychology does not exist in a vacuum. We work in a field that is greatly influenced by all that goes on around us. Geography, politics, art, religion, culture, literature, and so on are among the many forces that shape our discipline. To understand psychology means that you are able to see it as part of its context. It is the context that gives richness to interpretation and understanding.

In psychology we understand that behavior is complex, that cause and effect relationships are almost never, if ever, one-to-one, that multiple independent variables and multiple dependent variables are the order of the day. It is important to help students recognize this complexity in thinking about history and current events. Things are never as simple as they seem. The history of psychology course as a capstone course is best suited to play this critically important role in intellectual maturation.

Lifelong Learning

Finally, we come to the topic of lifelong learning, again, like critical thinking, one of those buzz words of higher education. Most of us are in academia because long ago we fell in love with learning. I remember as a college student being enamored with the college environment. I wanted to stay on a college campus and reasoned that being a college professor was the way to do that. I was interested in so many fields: anthropology—probably my first love—zoology, history, literature, and psychology. I think I could have been happy being a professor in any of those fields. I continue to read in most of those areas, although my job keeps me focused on psychology and its history.

Sadly, our students do not always share our love of learning, lifelong or otherwise. But for students in a capstone course, about to leave the university and thus likely their last formal learning experience, it seems especially crucial that we help them understand the need to read, to read well, to think critically, to think about context and the way its shapes the world in which they live. Our world depends on our educated citizenry making better decisions, even making better decisions about their own lives. I think of, as one example, the importance of being able to consult on medical decisions that affect you or your family, something that has been especially salient to me in the last few years, and that means using your intelligence to read in the medical literature and not to assume that your physician will know all that is needed. I tell my students that they are educated and that one of the skills of an educated person is the knowledge of how to get first-rate information. They will need to know that as parents of children in school. They will need to know that in addressing potential job changes. The lessons of history can provide thousands of examples of how lifelong learning can lead to better outcomes.

Assessment Concerns

To review, I have argued that the history of psychology course as a capstone experience should improve communication skills, enhance critical thinking, help students understand the critical importance of knowledge in context, and promote an attitude of lifelong learning. I confess to being uncertain about how to assess the last of those four; however, the first three can be evaluated in any number of ways—for example, student research projects, departmental histories, critical thinking exercises, debates, quiz-show games, role-playing and live in-class theater projects, writing newspapers embedding psychology in its times, giving mock convention papers in decades past, constructing cognitive maps, using letters from archival collections, replicating pioneering experiments, oral history projects, jigsaw classroom approaches, case study methods, and use of art and music to understand psychology's history. In addition to standard pencil-and-paper examinations, students can write, act, orate, debate, interview, research, and experiment. You do not need to invent these methods on your own. Creative teachers of the history of psychology have done so for you and they have published their best teaching and assessment ideas (see, for example, Carroll, 2006; Cole, 1983; Goodwin, Dingus, & Petterson, 2002). You will find more than 100 of these articles listed in a bibliography on my Web site (see http://people.tamu.edu/~l-benjamin/historybooks.htm).

Conclusions

I want to reiterate that history allows us to connect our lives to the past. It helps us make sense of the present. It gives us some basis on which to speculate intelligently about our future. It helps us integrate our knowledge in a framework of more meaningful understanding. It gives meaning to events and information that might otherwise be meaningless. It teaches us some humility for our own views and, we hope, some tolerance and understanding of the views of others.

Having taught history of psychology for 38 years and read student evaluations from all of those classes, I can tell you that the most frequent comment I read is that the course helped students to integrate their knowledge of psychology and other subjects in a meaningful framework where no such meaning existed before. Students tell me that all of their psychology courses existed as pieces of a puzzle and that the history course made them fit together. They often exult in this newfound sense of understanding of their major. If you have taught this course my guess is that you have heard similar expressions. It is exactly the outcome that Dana Dunn and his colleagues (2007) have argued is part of a *distinguished* undergraduate program in psychology. Such distinguished programs "attempt to unify the major in a capstone experience designed to integrate the variety of course offerings" (p. 654).

Psychology today is an ever-fragmenting discipline of greater and greater specialization. Sigmund Koch (1969) told us that psychology was not a single, coherent discipline but a number of different disciplines. Perhaps he was right. Today, in our PhD-granting departments, faculty and graduate students exist in separate fiefdoms. The clinical students don't interact with the neuroscience students who, in turn, have no contact with the cognitive students who don't mix with the social students and so forth. The same is largely true of the faculty. When one of the areas brings in a prominent researcher in their field, the colloquium is mostly attended by faculty and graduate students from that area with little attendance from others.

Bill Bevan (1991) raised concerns about this phenomenon:

> My concern is . . . that the character of psychology is increasingly manifest in the rapid proliferation of narrowly focused and compulsively insular camps, a proliferation that seemingly knows no limits. We persevere in looking at small questions instead of large ones and our view of the forest is forever obscured by the trees. (p. 475)

Bevan (1991) described one of the outcomes of this approach: "Yet specialized knowledge derives its meaning . . . from the context of larger perspectives and questions. When it loses touch with that larger context, it loses its coherence and meaning" (p. 475).

It is this sad reality of an ever-specializing contemporary psychology that makes the history of psychology course more important than it perhaps has ever been. As psychologists we share a connection, and that connection, however tenuous, is found in our history. It is arguably our one last hope for fostering a sense of community in our discipline. It can remind us of the large questions that once guided our field. We owe it to our students to help them connect to their past. We owe it to them to help them make sense of their present. We owe it to them to help them create a better future.

Recommended Readings

Benjamin, L. T., Jr. (2007). *A brief history of modern psychology.* Malden, MA: Wiley-Blackwell.

Danziger, K. (1990). *Constructing the subject: Historical origins of psychological research*. New York: Cambridge University Press.

Finger, S. (2000). *Minds behind the brain: A history of the pioneers and their discoveries*. New York: Oxford University Press.

Guthrie, R. V. (1998). *Even the rat was white: A historical view of psychology* (2nd ed.). Boston: Allyn & Bacon.

Scarborough, E., & Furumoto, L. (1987). *Untold lives: The first generation of American women psychologists*. New York: Columbia University Press.

References

Bache, R. M. (1895). Reaction time with reference to race. *Psychological Review, 2,* 475–486.

Barzun, J. (1954). *God's country and mine: A declaration of love spiced with a few harsh words*. Boston: Little, Brown.

Benjamin, L. T., Jr., & Baker, D. B. (2004). *From séance to science: A history of the profession of psychology in America*. Belmont, CA: Wadsworth.

Bevan, W. (1991). Contemporary psychology: A tour inside the onion. *American Psychologist, 46,* 475–483.

Boring, E. G. (1929). *A history of experimental psychology*. New York: Century.

Brett, G. S. (1912). *A history of psychology: Ancient and patristic*. London: George Allen.

Carr, E. H. (1961). *What is history?* New York: Random House.

Carroll, D. W. (2006). Thinking about historical issues: Debates in the history and systems class. *Teaching of Psychology, 33,* 137–140.

Cattell, J. McKeen. (1890). Mental tests and measurements. *Mind, 15,* 373–381.

Cole, D. L. (1983). The way we were: Teaching history of psychology through mock APA conventions. *Teaching of Psychology, 10,* 234–236.

Collingwood, R. G. (1946). *The idea of history*. London: Oxford University Press.

Davis, S. F., Janzen, W. V., & Davis, R. L. (1982). Teaching and learning the history of psychology need not be boring. *Teaching of Psychology, 9,* 183–184.

Dunn, D. S., McCarthy, M. A., Baker, S., Halonen, J. S., & Hill, G. W., IV. (2007). Quality benchmarks in undergraduate psychology programs. *American Psychologist, 62,* 650–670.

Fuchs, A. H., & Viney, W. (2002). The course in the history of psychology: Present status and future concerns. *History of Psychology, 5,* 3–15.

Goodwin, C. J., Dingus, M., & Petterson, S. (2002). The genealogy project: Tracing academic roots within the history and systems course. *Teaching of Psychology, 29,* 61–63.

Hall, G. S. (1912). *Founders of modern psychology.* New York: D. Appleton.

Henderson, B. B. (1995). Critical-thinking exercises for the history of psychology course. *Teaching of Psychology, 22,* 60–63.

Jensen, A. R. (2006). *Clocking the mind: Mental chronometry and individual differences.* Amsterdam: Elsevier.

Koch, S. (1969, March). Psychology cannot be a coherent science. *Psychology Today, 3,* 14, 64, 66–68.

Murphy, G. (1929). *An historical introduction to modern psychology.* New York: Harcourt Brace.

Nisbett, R. E. (2005). Heredity, environment, and race difference in IQ: A commentary on Rushton and Jensen (2005). *Psychology, Public Policy, and Law, 11,* 302–310.

Nodine, B. F. (Ed.). (1990). Psychologists teach writing. *Teaching of Psychology* (special issue), *17,* 5–66.

Pillsbury, W. B. (1929). *The history of psychology.* New York: W. W. Norton.

Raphelson, A. C. (1982). The history course as the capstone of the psychology curriculum. *Journal of the History of the Behavioral Sciences, 18,* 279–285.

Robinson, R. (2001). An application to increase student reading and writing skills. *American Biology Teacher, 63,* 474–480.

Samelson, F. (1978). From "race psychology" to "studies in prejudice": Some observations on the thematic reversal in social psychology. *Journal of the History of the Behavioral Sciences, 14,* 265–278.

Sokal, M. M. (1982). James McKeen Cattell and the failure of anthropometric mental testing, 1890–1901. In W. R. Woodward & M. G. Ash (Eds.), *The problematic science: Psychology in nineteenth-century thought* (pp. 322–345). New York: Praeger.

Soukhanov, A. H. (Ed.) (1992). *The American Heritage dictionary of the English language* (3rd ed.). Boston: Houghton Mifflin.

12 Research Teams

Developing a Capstone Experience With Programmatic

Research

Bernard C. Beins and *Phil D. Wann*

Without laboratories, psychology is simply philosophy (Wolfe, 1895). Harry Kirke Wolfe systematically included laboratory work in the undergraduate curriculum at the University of Nebraska in the 19th century (Benjamin, 1991) and many psychologists ever since have worked to foster enthusiasm for research in their students. As desirable as it is for students to gain research experience, it is not universal. Furthermore, at many institutions, students' first exposure to conducting research does not come until their junior or senior year (Perlman & McCann, 2005).

One of the barriers to offering research opportunities to large numbers of students is the additional work that faculty must devote to discretionary (i.e., nonrequired) student projects that is typically not a standard component of the faculty member's teaching load. This fact leads to a two-dimensional problem: There is little motivation for faculty to attract large numbers of students, and low levels of student interest may not make the research experience attractive to many students.

In spite of the barriers to creating universal research experiences for psychology students, two institutions have adopted a strategy to provide such exposure. Ithaca College and Missouri Western State University have created research teams that generate original research. Faculty who lead these teams direct research in their areas of expertise; students on the teams help create the projects and learn the process of generating research. At both institutions this course, known as Research Team, is a standard part of the teaching load and is intended to take students beyond the level of knowledge typically gained in the research methods or experimental psychology course.

Benefits and Importance of Student Experience With Research

There is general agreement among psychologists that research experience is a critical component of a good undergraduate psychology education. The report of the St. Mary's Conference on Enhancing the Quality of Undergraduate Education in Psychology emphasized that the basic aim of education in psychology should be to teach students to think like scientists about behavior (Brewer et al., 1993; McGovern, 1993). More recently, the reports of the APA Task Force on Learning Goals and Outcomes (Halonen et al., 2002, available online at www.apa.org/ed/pcue/taskforcereport2.pdf) and "Measuring Up: Best Practices in Assessment of Psychology Education Conference" (Halonen et al., 2003) have reaffirmed the importance of teaching and assessing scientific reasoning skills across the psychology curriculum.

The emphasis on increasing undergraduate research opportunities for psychology students is part of a multidisciplinary "research-across-the-curriculum movement" (Malachowski, 2003) that has taken place over the past two decades. A recent publication by the Council on Undergraduate Research (Karukstis & Elgren, 2007) describes the efforts to achieve this goal at a variety of different types of institutions. At doctorate-granting universities, the Boyer Commission Report was a wake-up call to include more inquiry-based learning in the curricula (Katkin, 2003). At larger schools, undergraduate student-faculty research partnerships appear to improve student retention (Nagda, Gregerman, Jonides, von Hippel, & Lerner, 1998). Another key factor driving the movement is that many predominantly undergraduate institutions (PUIs) are in a state of flux because of expectations that faculty become more engaged in scholarship that leads to publishable results (Malachowski, 2003).

Unfortunately, many psychology programs still do not provide adequate research opportunities for students. After studying the curriculum of 500 psychology departments, Perlman and McCann (2005) concluded that there is an inconsistency between what psychologists say about the importance of undergraduate research experiences and the typical psychology program. Many schools offer their students little or no opportunity to gain research experience. Based on their survey results, Perlman and McCann argued that undergraduate curricula need to incorporate more active learning of science for psychology majors; Berthold, Hakala, and Goff (2003) recommended that it start with the introductory psychology course.

According to the recently published benchmarks for undergraduate psychology programs, one characteristic of "distinguished" programs is that they require students to *demonstrate* the skills and behaviors of scientists (Dunn, McCarthy, Baker, Halonen, & Hill, 2007). We believe that a research team course is one of the best ways to achieve this objective. Unlike traditional laboratory courses, students engage in original, significant research. Unlike independent research, which typically can be offered to only a few of the best students in a program, research teams that are a regular part of faculty workload allow many more students to have a meaningful active learning experience. At Ithaca and Missouri Western, *all* psychology majors are required to participate on a research team.

Incorporating research opportunities in the curriculum clearly has benefits for both faculty and students. Gentile (2007) argued that "engaging undergraduate students in research is indeed the purest form of student learning, an exceptional model of faculty teaching, and a key ingredient of faculty scholarly development" (p. 271). We agree. Faculty at PUIs benefit because scholarship informs and motivates quality teaching. Moreover, the increased opportunities for professional presentations and publication also enhance professional development and career advancement.

For students, participating in research has myriad tangible and intangible benefits. Lorig (1996) noted that undergraduate research experiences help build useful job-related skills. These include analytical and problem-solving skills, oral and written communication skills, quantitative and computer skills, and interpersonal and teamwork skills. Many of these same skills were among those most valued by the employers surveyed by Landrum and Harrold (2003). Most especially, employers are seeking to hire persons with demonstrated ability to get along with others (interpersonal skills, teamwork) and work ethic (ability and willingness to learn).

Involvement in research that leads to presentation or publication is very important for students planning to pursue graduate studies in psychology. Numerous studies (e.g., Collins, 2001; Landrum & Nelson, 2002) have found that only grades and GRE scores outweigh research experience in graduate school selection criteria. Research experience and commitment to research is especially important for admission to experimental psychology or clinical psychology programs. Muñoz-Dunbar and Stanton (1999) found that directors of APA programs in clinical psychology reported that it was the most important factor. For pre-medicine students, research experience not only helps prepare psychology majors for medical school but also may help them to attain entrance (Schwebel & Tzanetos, 2005). Students who participate in research are also more likely to receive strong letters of recommendation either for jobs or for professional or graduate schools (Appleby, 1997, 2001; Morgan & Korschgen, 2006).

Varieties of Research Experience

As we noted above, most academic psychologists stress the importance of the empirical nature of psychology, but at many schools, students may not have the opportunity for research experience until late in their undergraduate careers and, in some instances, the research is not original (Perlman & McCann, 2005). Labs accompany the introductory course at perhaps a quarter of schools, a substantial minority, but still a minority. The first contact with empirical or quantitative psychology typically occurs in the statistics class or in a combined statistics-research methods course. At some schools, there is a general research methods course; at others, there is a more narrowly defined experimental psychology class. These courses often have an allied laboratory component, but not always. Most baccalaureate, master's, and doctoral programs offer independent research opportunities for advanced students (Perlman & McCann, 2005). A different approach to providing students with research opportunities while allowing faculty members to generate research ideas in their specialty areas is the concept of the research team course. This idea originated at Ithaca College in the 1970s (Graf & Williams, 1975) and has since become the linchpin of its psychology curriculum. Students engage in original research with the same professor for three semesters. At Missouri Western, the single-semester team concept is new, which means that its evolution has had to comply with the current environment of fiscal constraint.

Obstacles to Student Research

There are numerous obstacles to creating a research team course. These must be overcome in order to persuade faculty, administrators, and students of the value and viability of the course. Although most faculty readily appreciate the potential of research team to enhance their scholarship, many will have concerns about time and workload. At PUIs, typical faculty workloads of three or four courses each semester leave little time for research or mentoring research students. To overcome this problem, at Ithaca and Missouri Western, Research Team is a regular part of faculty workload. At Missouri Western, it is a two-credit course that actually reduces the normal workload by one credit hour. In addition, the faculty/student ratio is reduced for the semester, with four to six students on the research team as compared to 20–75 for a lecture class.

At many institutions, lack of laboratory space and equipment may be an impediment to creating the course. However, this problem can be overcome by limiting studies to those that can realistically be done with the available space and equipment. At Missouri Western during the past academic year, none of the research teams required more than the use of computers, a video projector, and the Internet for their projects. At Ithaca College, the neuroscience research team requires technical equipment, but the other teams generally need only the type of apparatus used by the Missouri Western teams. As such, neither of the authors, who chair their departments, must worry about the threat of being fired for exceeding the equipment budget by $75, which happened to Harry Kirke Wolfe (Benjamin, 1991).

Administrators will focus on different issues, primarily those related to budget. It is important for the department to show that research teams will not add greatly to the cost of the program. At Missouri Western, we accomplished this by reducing the frequency of offering of other courses in the psychology curriculum. We did this without eliminating courses or reducing frequency of offerings so drastically that it would inconvenience either our majors or those of other disciplines in our service classes. Primarily, we reduced offerings of relatively small elective classes; this resulted in somewhat larger but still manageable class sizes in those courses.

One of the best ways to convince administrators to support the department's efforts at curriculum revision is to tie the changes to the institution's strategic plan. At Missouri Western, the state-designated mission is to focus on applied learning, which is defined very broadly as any experiential learning outside of the traditional classroom setting. We submitted the Research Team proposal to the university curriculum committee and administration as a course in applied learning because students apply the skills that they learn in their methodology and content classes to conducting an original research project. The committee, dean, and provost were enthusiastic about the idea once they saw how it fit with the university mission. In fact, the course is listed in the university catalog not as a laboratory, seminar, or practicum, but as an "applied learning experience," a unique designation.

Another obstacle to incorporating additional research into the curriculum is that many undergraduate psychology students have little interest in research and do not perceive it as relevant to their career plans (Vittengl et al., 2004). For this reason, at both Ithaca and Missouri Western we take time in introductory classes to explain why research and critical thinking skills are important, and, as mentioned above, talk about how these skills are highly valued by employers and graduate school selection committees. At Missouri Western, the instructors for the statistics and psychology research methods classes that are prerequisites for Research Team reiterate and elaborate on this connection. Thus, most students enter the research team course not only with the statistical and methodological background to be successful in pursuing an original research study but also with an awareness of the relevance of the experience, and they are motivated to perform well.

Case Examples
Establishing Research Teams
Student Prerequisites

The course is for upper level students who have completed basic statistics and research methods. At both institutions, they will have learned the basics of descriptive statistics, SPSS, and the writing style set forth in the publication manual of the American Psychological Association (APA, 2001) formatting of research papers. Because the nature of the course is to generate original research, students will need to have had experience finding, reading, and interpreting relevant journal articles.

Method of Selecting Students for Teams

Students at Ithaca rank the Research Teams that are accepting students for the subsequent semester. In some cases, faculty who will be taking sabbatical leave or who have committed all available spaces may not be accepting new students. For instance, in one particular semester, Beins had three students who temporarily left the team to study abroad for a semester; they all returned the following academic term, limiting the new students I could accommodate.

Most of the students eventually end up on their first or second choice, although occasionally a student may end up on the third choice. Often students will be able to join a highly desired team by deferring joining a team for a semester. This plan does not always work because students must complete three semesters of team, so if they have entered the major late (e.g., as a junior) or transferred from another institution, they will not have the luxury of postponing entry onto a team. In such a case, they may have to join a less preferred team. In addition, students may discover that their team is not what they thought it would be and want to change teams. This is relatively rare, but faculty who supervise teams are generally willing to accommodate student wishes.

Table 12-1 shows the research teams at Ithaca College and at Missouri Western State University. In the Ithaca College model, because there are 10 active teams, students have little problem finding one or two very desirable teams and perhaps one or two somewhat desirable teams. Students typically enjoy their required three-semester commitment and can be taken aback to learn that students at other institutions do not have the same opportunity.

Another model for developing teams is used at Missouri Western. In this case, there are fewer options for a given student, with three research teams

Table 12-1

Research Teams at Ithaca College and at Missouri Western State University

Ithaca College	Missouri Western State University
Human Motivation	Cognitive Neuropsychology
Cognitive Development	Psycholinguistics and Cognitive
Psychology of Humor	Psychology
Psychology of Television and Other Media	Human Motivation
Neuroscience	Group Dynamics and Social Psychology
Adult Development	Developmental Psychology
Social Judgment	Health Psychology
Clinical and Mental Health Research	
Developmental and Educational Psychology	
Autism Research Team	

offered each semester. Students submit a research team application while they are taking psychology research methods, the course prerequisite. On the application, students rank their choices of teams and indicate why they want to be on a particular team. The final decisions are made by the faculty, balancing them out so that each team has four to six students. We are able to anticipate how many students will need research team each semester because Missouri Western has an admissions process for the psychology program, even though the institution is open enrollment. Students apply for the program after completing introductory psychology and the general studies math and English courses. Admission to the psychology program is limited to 18 students each semester, and those students typically move through the program as a cohort. Thus, we know that three research teams each semester will meet the student demand.

Required Participation

Both models described in this chapter include Research Team as a required component of the major. The major difference between the two programs we are describing involves the length of student participation. At Missouri Western, students complete one semester of the research team course, although they can participate on a team for additional semesters by doing independent research projects. At Ithaca, students are on the same team for three semesters. At one point, one faculty member suggested reducing the commitment to two semesters. Most faculty were opposed to this idea, and when they broached the subject with students, the students were also opposed. Students generally said that they valued the length of the commitment and, as noted above, from the perspective of alumni, viewed their research experience as highly valuable. The implication here is that students can become highly invested in the research enterprise when they are a vital link in the process, from developing an idea, to testing participants, to data analysis, to drawing conclusions, and finally, to presenting their results.

Selecting Faculty Who Will Have Teams

Both at Missouri Western and at Ithaca College, the research team course counts as one of the faculty member's preparations for the semester. At Ithaca, students received two credits per semester, for a total of six credits of Research Team. (Incidentally, it is not unusual for Ithaca students to complete one or two additional semesters of independent research, sometimes in conjunction with research team activities. Thus, these students can graduate with four or five semesters of original research experience. They are also likely to have had multiple opportunities to present their research at undergraduate and at professional research conferences.) At Missouri Western, the course is also two credits, but it can only be taken once. However, a student who has taken research team can enroll in a follow-up independent research course and remain affiliated with the team.

The advantage of creating permanent teams is offset to some degree by the restrictions it places on course offerings by the department. Research teams at both schools are costly. With about 10 to 12 students on a typical team at Ithaca College and the need to offer spots to about 90 students each semester, the program draws heavily on faculty resources. Without the team structure, we could offer two or three courses of 30 to 45 and free up seven faculty to teach specialty courses or to reduce the size of classes we currently offer. However, there is sufficient recognition of the importance of the research experience that there has been no discussion of changing the curriculum to reduce or remove this emphasis on research. At Missouri Western, as noted above, the addition of Research Team has necessitated a reduction in the frequency with which the department offers some courses.

Given that one benefit of having research teams is the opportunity for faculty to remain current in their fields of expertise, there could be competition among faculty members for such teams. In general, every faculty member who has requested a team has been able to offer it. Those who have not developed a team have been reluctant to relinquish some of the other courses that they teach. The general rule in the department is that those who do not teach research team have first choice in offering our Senior Seminar, a coveted course to teach that constitutes a second capstone experience. Not having a team also permits a faculty member to participate in the college's honors program, another desirable addition to teaching responsibilities.

At Missouri Western, all of the full-time faculty have chosen to lead a research team, with the exception of our practicum coordinator, a counseling psychologist. Each faculty member has a team one semester of the academic year, and it is our intention to keep each line of research active with one or two independent research students in the alternate semesters.

Course Requirements

At Missouri Western, teams consist of four to six students, with three active teams in a given semester. Students work on a project for one semester, paving the way for follow-up research by other students in the next. At Ithaca, teams are somewhat larger, varying between half a dozen or so and around 15. Students develop team-based projects that they complete and are themselves able to follow up in the next semester.

At Missouri Western, students are required to present their final project at the campus Multidisciplinary Research Day, and their work is posted on the National Undergraduate Research Clearinghouse Web site (http://clearinghouse.missouriwestern.edu). In addition, the students are encouraged to submit their work either to an undergraduate research conference, usually the Great Plains Students' Psychology Convention, or to a professional research conference such as the Midwestern Psychological Association or the Association for Psychological Science.

At Ithaca, there is no requirement to present or publish a final project, but many students do so. Ithaca students have recently presented or co-authored their work at professional conferences like the conventions of the Eastern Psychological Association, the New England Psychological Association, the Society for Research in Child Development, the Society for Experimental Social Psychology, the Society for Personality and Social Psychology, and the Association for Psychological Science. Students also regularly present their work at undergraduate venues like the University of Scranton Psychology Conference, the Eastern Colleges Science Conference, and the Northeast Undergraduate and Graduate Student Sigma Xi Poster Conference.

Advantages of Research Teams
Comparison With Traditional Labs

In many undergraduate research courses, students are exposed to pre-existing or canned research projects. For example, a significant number of classes at schools around the country use the Online Psychology Laboratory (OPL; http://opl.apa.org). This site provides exposure to research protocols of published research; students engage as participants and provide data. In the end, the students combine their own class data with that of others at different institutions. OPL exposes students to the way that research actually proceeds. However, although the studies are original from the perspective of students, it constitutes replication of published research. Furthermore, traditional psychology laboratories often developed fairly simple projects that students can appreciate and complete.

In contrast, research teams produce original research that relates to the faculty member's expertise. The ongoing nature of the teams provides the opportunity for students to build on their own (or their fellow students') research ideas. As such, students get a sense that new ideas develop from previous research and that their research, ultimately, leads to new ideas.

Advantages for Students, Faculty, and Department

Students benefit greatly from the team experience because they engage in active and interactive learning. They have to help generate the research ideas, including developing stimuli, creating the methodology, managing recruitment of participants, testing the participants, engaging in data analysis, and drawing conclusions. Each of these steps in developing the methodology requires making decisions that invariably include compromises relative to what would be ideal. When students replicate the work of earlier psychologists, many of the decisions about the study have already been made.

Another positive aspect of the team is that students learn by modeling the professor. That is, in generating a project, it is important to know what has come before. The best way to do this is to examine the research literature. The faculty member will have a good sense of what other researchers have done and can induce students to increase their knowledge of the topic. Students also see that it is useful to adopt the methodologies of previous researchers rather than recreating the research method *ab initio*. When students each have to find and read a small number of journal articles, they can present them to the rest of the team so that, in the end, they have compiled a significant amount of information on the topic.

In the Ithaca program, advanced students can also mentor new students, providing role models. At Missouri Western, if students remain on a team by enrolling in an independent research class, the new students also have exposure to successful students.

A further advantage to students is that, because they work with faculty members very closely, the students can ultimately benefit from strong letters of recommendation because the faculty member has had the chance to see the student assume responsibility for important work, cooperate with team members, generate ideas, and write research papers. With detailed knowledge of students' strengths (and weaknesses), the faculty member can write a detailed letter that is tailored to that student.

Faculty members benefit from the research team approach, too. They get to work with emerging junior colleagues. Some strong students will, predictably, flourish; other students, surprising the faculty member, will rise to the occasion and show strengths that were not previously apparent. Another distinct advantage in departments with heavy teaching loads is that the course becomes part of the faculty member's teaching load. Thus, the individual can keep current in his or her area of expertise, generate research ideas, and give students experience with actual research.

Assessment

When the research team course was initiated at Missouri Western during the 2007–08 academic year, department faculty decided to assess students' perceptions of the experience with the Applied Learning Assessment Tool (ALAT; Kempf, Wilson, & Henry, 2008). The ALAT has three subscales—Reflection, Application, and Diversity—useful in determining the quality of different types of applied learning experiences. We were particularly interested in how students would rate the course on application, the degree to which academic and disciplinary content was applied in the research team project, and on reflection, the extent to which students integrated their research experience with academic content through discussion and writing. On a scale of 1 (*strongly agree*) to 5 (*strongly disagree*), the students ($N = 15$) in the first semester in which a full complement of three teams was offered gave ratings on the Application ($M = 1.96$) and Reflection ($M = 1.67$) subscales that indicated they agreed that these course objectives had been accomplished.

Because the program at Ithaca has been in existence for three decades, it is possible to monitor the degree of success of the Research Team program. Recently, the department surveyed graduates about their team experiences, which provided data for assessment.

Outcomes of Research Teams
Outcomes: Alumni Evaluations

In a recent survey of Ithaca College graduates, about 80% said that Research Team was somewhat (20%) or very beneficial (60%). This figure is the second highest of all courses required for the major. The mean value for all courses was 73%, with Research Team a full standard deviation above the mean. Further, when the graduates rated the various majors courses regarding how well the courses had prepared them for their careers, Research Team had the most favorable rating. On a scale of 1 (*very beneficial*) to 20 (*least beneficial*), the average for this course was 6.0, over 1.5 standard deviations from the mean, indicating that the graduates believe that Research Team was the most beneficial course in terms of preparation for their careers.

Outcomes: Presentations

Student presentations at Ithaca College constitute one of the consistently notable outcomes of Research Team activity. For most teams, students present at conferences every year, although sometimes studies do not yield expected outcomes or circumstances conspire to prevent completion of a project, and a team may skip a year occasionally. The college provides funding for student presentation at conferences; the psychology department is one of the greatest beneficiaries of the college's support. The large number of students who present or co-author presentations is due in part to the size of the major; but it is also due to a great degree to the opportunities for research afforded by the teams.

During the 2006–2007 academic year, Ithaca's psychology students were named as authors on 24 off-campus presentations. This is not an atypical number of presentations in an academic year. The median number of student co-authors on each presentation was four, reinforcing the idea that the research was a team effort. The various faculty members have different approaches to authorship. Some list as authors or co-authors only those presenting the research at the conference, whereas others list everybody on the team as a co-author. Ithaca students have regularly received awards for research they have presented at various conferences, including the Eastern Psychological Association convention, the New England Psychology Association convention, and the Eastern Colleges Science Conference. Such awards provide external validation regarding the quality of research that the Research Teams generate.

Outcomes: Publications

In addition to presentations, students' names occasionally appear as co-authors on published papers. This occurrence is much less frequent than student presentations, but it is a possibility for the most capable students. Table 12-2 lists the recent publications, with student names appearing in bold.

Outcomes: Graduate School Admissions

Finally with respect to outcomes, student acceptances to graduate programs provide one measure of success of the psychology program. At Ithaca College, students regularly receive acceptances to master's and doctoral programs.

Table 12-2
Publications Arising from Ithaca College Research Teams with Student Co-Authors

Rich, D., & Rader, N. (under review, 2006). Human plant interactions: Cognition, creativity, and well-being. *Journal of Environmental Psychology.*

Stephenson, H., Pena-Shaff, J., & **Quirk, P.** (2006). Predictors of college student suicidal ideation: Gender differences. *College Student Journal, 40,* 109–117.

Vaughn, L. A., **Malik, J., Schwartz, S., Petkova, Z., & Trudeau, L.** (2006). Regulatory fit as input for stop rules. *Journal of Personality and Social Psychology, 91,* 601–611.

Wimer, D. J., & Beins, B. C. (in press). Expectations and perceived humor. *Humor: International Journal of Humor Studies.*

Note: Student names appear in bold.

Although one cannot attribute the level of success solely to the Research Team program, it is likely that the combination of significant research experience and strong letters from faculty who know students very well are instrumental in those acceptances.

Over the past several years, Ithaca students have entered programs such as industrial/organizational psychology, clinical psychology, counseling, social work, developmental psychology, forensic psychology, sport psychology, drama therapy, health administration, social work, human-environment relations, law school, criminal justice, and nursing. Students have been competitive in a number of top programs, including those at Yale, Harvard, University of Pennsylvania, Columbia, Cornell, University of Akron, Miami University, Syracuse University, University of Maryland, and many others.

Conclusion

Research Teams serve several different purposes. First, they are pedagogically sound approaches to including students in the research process. Second, they help the departments move to the goal of universal research experience for students. Third, these teams allow faculty to maintain contact with their areas of specialization when teaching responsibilities might otherwise interfere with the development of programmatic research.

The teams also have a cost. In terms of departmental resources, faculty who teach a research team course with a relatively small enrollment are not available to staff other courses. So a small number of students on a given team consume a relatively large amount of faculty teaching time.

Fortunately, the outcomes of a research team program are quite positive. Students and faculty are well served with respect to skill development, achievement of curricular goals, and useful pedagogy that Harry Kirke Wolfe would have appreciated.

Recommended Readings

Collins, L. H. (2001, Winter). Does research experience make a significant difference in graduate admissions? *Eye on Psi Chi,* 26–28.

Gentile, J. (2007). Undergraduate research programs: Is there a magic bullet for success? In K. K. Karukstis & T. E. Elgren (Eds.), *Developing and sustaining a research-supportive curriculum: A compendium of successful practices* (pp. 271–284). Washington, DC: Council on Undergraduate Research.

Karukstis, K. K., & Elgren, T. E. (Eds.). (2007). *Designing and sustaining a research-supportive undergraduate curriculum: A compendium of successful practices.* Washington, DC: Council on Undergraduate Research.

Vittengl, J. R., Bosley, C. Y., Brescia, S. A., Eckardt, E. A., Neidig, J. M., Shelver, K. S., & Sapenoff, L. A. (2004). Why are some undergraduates more (and others less) interested in psychological research? *Teaching of Psychology, 31,* 91–97.

References

Appleby, D. C. (1997). *The handbook of psychology.* New York: Longman.

Appleby, D. C. (2001, May). *A data-based strategy to receive strong letters of recommendation for jobs and graduate school.* Paper presented at the annual meeting of the Midwestern Psychological Association, Chicago, IL.

American Psychological Association (2001). *Publication manual of the American Psychological Association* (5th ed.). Washington, DC American Psychological Association.

Benjamin, L. T., Jr., (1991). *Harry Kirke Wolfe: Pioneer in psychology.* Lincoln: University of Nebraska Press.

Berthold, H. C., Hakala, C. M., & Goff, D. (2003). An argument for a laboratory in introductory psychology. *Teaching of Psychology, 30,* 55–58.

Brewer, C. L., Hopkins, J. R., Kimble, G. A., Matlin, M. W., McCann, L. I., McNeil, O. V., et al. (1993). Curriculum. In T. V. McGovern (Ed.), *Handbook for enhancing undergraduate education in psychology* (pp. 161–182). Washington, DC: American Psychological Association.

Collins, L. H. (2001, Winter). Does research experience make a significant difference in graduate admissions? *Eye on Psi Chi, 26*–28.

Dunn, D. S., McCarthy, M. A., Baker, S. C., Halonen, J .S., & Hill, G. W., IV. (2007). Quality benchmarks in undergraduate psychology programs. *American Psychologist, 62,* 650–670.

Gentile, J. (2007). Undergraduate research programs: Is there a magic bullet for success? In K. K. Karukstis & T. E. Elgren (Eds.), *Developing and sustaining a research-supportive curriculum: A compendium of successful practices* (pp. 271–284). Washington, DC: Council on Undergraduate Research.

Graf, E., & Williams, D. V. (1975). The educational laboratory: Output or input. *Teaching of Psychology, 2,* 122–124.

Halonen, J. S., Appleby, D. C., Brewer, C. L., Buskist, W., Gillem, A. R., Halpern, D., et al. (2002). Undergraduate psychology major learning goals and outcomes: A report. Retrieved April 30, 2008, from http://www.apa.org/ed/pcue/taskforcereport2.pdf.

Halonen, J. S., Bosack, T., Clay, S., McCarthy, M., Dunn, D. S., Hill, G. W., IV, et al. (2003). A rubric for learning, teaching, and assessing scientific inquiry in psychology. *Teaching of Psychology, 30,* 196–202.

Karukstis, K. K., & T. E. Elgren, T. E. (Eds.). (2007). *Designing and sustaining a research-supportive undergraduate curriculum: A compendium of successful practices.* Washington, DC: Council on Undergraduate Research.

Katkin, W. (2003). The Boyer Commission report and its impact on undergraduate research. *New directions for teaching and learning, 93,* 19–38. San Francisco: Jossey Bass.

Kempf, E. J., Wilson, E., & Henry, K. B. (2008). *Beyond counting: An assessment tool for measuring the quality of applied learning.* Manuscript submitted for publication.

Landrum, R. E., & Harrold, R. (2003). What employers want from psychology graduates. *Teaching of Psychology, 30,* 131–133.

Landrum, R. E., & Nelsen, L. R. (2002). The undergraduate research assistantship: An analysis of the benefits. *Teaching of Psychology, 29,* 15–19.

Lorig, B. T. (1996). Undergraduate research in psychology: Skills to take to work. *Council on Undergraduate Research Quarterly, 16,* 145–149.

Malachowski, M. R. (2003). A research-across-the-curriculum movement. *New Directions for Teaching and Learning, 93,* 55–68.

McGovern, T. V. (1993). Introduction. In T. V. McGovern (Ed.), *Handbook for enhancing undergraduate education in psychology* (pp. 3–15). Washington, DC: American Psychological Association.

Morgan, B. L., & Korschgen, A. J. (2006). Majoring in psych? Career options for psychology undergraduates (3rd ed.). Boston, MA: Pearson Education.

Muñoz-Dunbar, R., & Stanton, A. L. (1999). Ethnic diversity in clinical psychology: Recruitment and admission practices among doctoral programs. *Teaching of Psychology, 26,* 259–263.

Nagda, B. A., Gregerman, S. R., Jonides, J., von Hippel, W., & Lerner, J. S. (1998). Undergraduate student-faculty research partnerships affect student retention. *Review of Higher Education, 22,* 55–72.

Perlman, B., & McCann, L. I. (2005). Undergraduate research experiences in psychology: A national study of courses and curricula. *Teaching of Psychology, 32,* 5–14.

Schwebel, D.C., & Tzanetos, D.B. (2005). Premedical psychology majors in the laboratory. *Teaching of Psychology, 32,* 118–120.

Vittengl, J. R., Bosley, C. Y., Brescia, S. A., Eckardt, E. A., Neidig, J. M., Shelver, K. S., & Sapenoff, L. A. (2004). Why are some undergraduates more (and others less) interested in psychological research. *Teaching of Psychology, 31,* 91–97.

Wolfe, H. K. (1895). The new psychology in undergraduate work. *Psychological Review, 2,* 382–387.

13 Honors Thesis as a Capstone

A Possible Perfect Ending

Sherry L. Serdikoff

Capstone courses are intensive experiences that provide an opportunity for integration of specialized knowledge, theories, research methods, and technical skills (Wagenaar, 1993). The capstone course should be a culminating educational experience for students as it is an opportunity for them to demonstrate that they have achieved the goals established by their institution and program (Davis, 1993).

Although capstone courses can be challenging, they provide a truly unique learning experience and provide an ideal way to ensure that graduates are prepared for life after graduation (Moore, n.d.). These important courses give students the opportunity to collaborate with others, practice their presentation and organizational skills, use their knowledge, and highlight what they have learned and achieved during their college experience (Moore, n.d.; Murphy, n.d.). Although capstone experiences are not in and of themselves a means of assessment, they do offer access to a representative body of a student's work. As a result, capstone courses provide an ideal setting for conducting authentic assessments (Rowles, Koch, Hundley, & Hamilton, 2004). Many types of capstone options exist both within and across disciplines. Among them is senior thesis, one of the most widely used capstone course formats because it provides an excellent opportunity for authentic assessment of students' knowledge, skills, and abilities (Boyer, 1987).

Psychologists have recognized the importance and utility of the senior capstone in the various assessments of the undergraduate curriculum for over half a century (e.g., Brewer & Halonen, 2003; Dunn et al., 2010; McGovern, 1992, 1993). The first conference addressing such issues took place in 1950 (Buxton et al., 1952), and a second occurred in 1960 (McKeachie & Milholland, 1961). The Kulik report (Kulik, Brown, Vestewig, & Wright, 1973) and the Association of American Colleges Report (McGovern, Furumoto, Halpern, Kimble, & McKeachie, 1991) followed. At the APA's National Conference on Enhancing the Quality of Undergraduate Education in Psychology held at St. Mary's College in Maryland during June 1991, participants reaffirmed the study of psychology as a scientific discipline in the liberal arts tradition. Although they concluded that no single curriculum is best for every school and every student, they did advocate certain common characteristics that should be reflected in all programs, including an integrative capstone experience for seniors. As a testament to these two positions, two groups charged with examining the undergraduate psychology curriculum listed completing a research project with faculty, collaboratively from beginning to end, as a defensible capstone experience for the psychology major (Brewer et al., 1993; see also Dunn et al., 2010).

Terry (1996) reported that 27% of surveyed psychology departments offering research experiences to undergraduates required an undergraduate thesis, although he did not indicate whether this work served as a capstone experience. Perlman and McCann (1999) reported that 15% of the bacca-laureate colleges they surveyed allowed students to choose from a variety of capstone experiences but that only 5% included a senior research project among the options. More recently, Perlman and McCann (2005) noted that 26% of departments at four-year colleges and universities responding to their survey included a "large" project as part of the capstone experience. Of these, 80% of four-year institutions, 82% of master's institutions, and 100% of doctoral institutions required research with data collection and analysis. Stoloff et al. (2010) surveyed 374 schools and reported that 44% of the responding schools offer an honors thesis course, with 4% requiring it for the major. A capstone experience is required at 40% of the schools that responded, and the honors thesis or an equivalent experience is an acceptable course for meeting this requirement at 7% of those schools. Despite the fact that relatively few schools include the honors thesis as a psychology capstone option, the extent to which it is an acceptable option merits further examination. The remainder of the chapter describes an effort to accomplish this end.

Case Example

Honors Thesis in Psychology

At James Madison University (JMU), the Senior Honors Project serves as the capstone experience for the Honors Program and as a capstone experience for the psychology major. The JMU Honors Program specifies that honors projects be comparable to a graduate thesis in the chosen discipline. Students complete the project in their major discipline under the supervision of an advisor with expertise in that discipline (typically a faculty member with an appointment in the major department). In completing the project, students must demonstrate that they are familiar with and understand the relevant literature, and they must make original insights or contributions. In the JMU Department of Psychology, the senior honors project must be an empirical research study that makes a scholarly contribution to the current body of psychological knowledge. Completing the project provides the student with an opportunity to integrate knowledge and experience acquired through the recommended core curriculum in psychology (Dunn et al., 2010) while exploring a topic in depth.

Students prepare for a senior thesis early in their academic career. By the second semester of the junior year, each student secures the agreement of one faculty member to serve as the project advisor and two additional faculty readers to serve as members of the project committee. Students write a research proposal under the supervision of the advisor. The expectation is that the thesis proposal will result from an iterative process where, in order to develop a high-quality document, the advisor edits drafts of the proposal that the student prepares. Minimally, the proposal must include (a) an Introduction that reviews relevant literature and presents the rationale for the proposed research questions; (b) a Method section that describes the proposed subjects/participants, apparatus and/or materials, and procedures; (c) a Data Analysis and Interpretation section that describes how the student will analyze and interpret the data in light of the proposed research questions; (d) a Reference section; and (e) any supporting materials including a copy of the institutional review board (IRB) or institutional animal care and use committee (IACUC) protocol.

Once the proposal is approved by the advisor, the student distributes the completed proposal to all committee members for review and schedules a proposal meeting. During the proposal meeting, the student makes a brief presentation and answers any questions posed by committee members. The committee decides whether the proposal is approved, approved with specified revisions discussed in the meeting, or rejected. In all cases, the committee members provide formative feedback regarding the quality of the written document and oral presentation to aid the student in preparing the written thesis and completing the oral defense. The target date for proposal approval is the middle of the second semester of work (i.e., first semester of the senior year).

Once the student collects and analyzes the data, he or she writes the thesis under the supervision of the advisor. Like the proposal, the thesis manuscript results from an iterative process in which the advisor edits drafts that the student prepares; once the advisor approves the document the student distributes the completed written thesis to all committee members for review and schedules an oral defense meeting. During the oral defense, the student makes a brief presentation during which he or she demonstrates foundational knowledge, skills, and abilities relevant to the project and fields questions about the project and the written document. Members of the committee discuss the thesis and the student's performance during the oral defense and decide whether they approve the thesis, approve the thesis pending revisions, or reject the thesis.

Although the JMU Psychology Department has a multifaceted assessment program (see, for example, Apple, Serdikoff, Reis-Bergan, & Barron, 2008; Stoloff, Apple, Barron, Reis-Bergan, & Sundre, 2004; Stoloff & Feeney, 2002), to date it has not included any measures specific to the capstone requirement (aside from the grades that students earn in the courses). All psychology capstone classes that JMU offers, including the Senior Honors Project, require students to (a) actively seek information through libraries and other information retrieval systems; (b) analyze, synthesize, and evaluate information from primary sources to address psychologically relevant issues; (c) demonstrate effective written communication skills using APA style; and (d) demonstrate effective oral communication skills *at the individual level*, using one or more professional formats (e.g., individual paper/proposal presentation, participate as a member of a symposium). The effort described in this chapter is a step toward developing a specific component for our assessment program to document how the honors thesis is meeting the capstone requirements (Dunn, McCarthy, Baker, Halonen, & Hill, 2007). In addition to examining specific capstone requirements, I was interested in the extent to which the Senior Honors Project encourages a wide range of activities that involve skills associated with scientific psychology (Dunn et al., 2010) and has potential for facilitating transition from the role of undergraduate to that of graduate student and lifelong learner (Rowles et al., 2004). For these reasons, I assessed the students using a modified version of an instrument we developed to assess the first-year apprenticeship experience of students enrolled in our Psychological Sciences Master of Arts program (Serdikoff, 2007).

In addition to demographic information, the Research Activities Inventory prompted students to report the frequency with which they engaged in specific activities. The specific questionnaire items appear in Table 13-1. For items 1 to 5 and 6 to 9, which cover activities associated with the research process and technology skills, respectively, students indicated how often they engaged in each activity during the project (*not at all, rarely, sometimes,* or *frequently*). For items 10 to 13 and 14 to 22, which covered professional development activities and communication skills, students indicated how many times they engaged in each activity as a part of the project (0, 1, 2, 3, 4 or more). Item 23 asked students to indicate their overall perception of how much the experience prepared them to successfully complete work at the next level (i.e., graduate school or a job).

The sampling frame included 44 JMU students who completed the honors thesis course sequence during any semester of the 2006–2007 and 2007–2008

Table 13-1
Research Activities Inventory

The research process

1. Research Idea Development (e.g., brainstorming, generating hypotheses, theory development, research design)
2. Literature Review (e.g., information gathering with PsycINFO, MEDLINE, or ERIC, reading, discussing, summarizing, integrating, and/or synthesizing literature)
3. Technical Activities (e.g., setting up research materials/equipment, maintaining research materials/equipment, design/development/fabrication of research materials/equipment)
4. Data Collection (e.g., instrument identification & development, recruitment & scheduling subjects, administer tests/interviews/protocols)
5. Working with Data (e.g., data entry, data coding, data verification, data analysis, reliability analysis, interpreting results)

Technology skills

6. Develop computer programs to control/present research conditions and/or collect data (e.g., Visual Basic, .NET Framework, Medstate Notation, MEDS)
7. Use specialized software to control/present research conditions and/or collect data (e.g., WebSurveyor, MedPC, Praat)
8. Use data analysis software (e.g., SPSS, SAS, LISREL, BMDP)
9. Use organizational (spreadsheet/database) software (e.g., Excel, Access)

(continued)

Table 13-1 (*continued*)

Professional development
10. Attend a conference
11. Attend a workshop
12. Attend a colloquium
13. Attend lab/research team meetings

Communication skills
14. Write text for a research protocol
15. Write text for an IACUC /IRB proposal
16. Write text for a conference submission (e.g., abstract)
17. Write text for a poster presentation
18. Write text for an oral presentation
19. Write text for a grant/scholarship proposal
20. Write text for a manuscript/paper/book/chapter intended for publication
21. Present a poster at a professional conference
22. Present a paper at a professional conference

Overall
23. Please provide an overall rating of how working on this research project contributed to your preparation for successfully completing work at the next level (e.g., graduate school, a job, etc.). This experience _____ for successfully completing work at the next level.

   a. did not contribute to my preparation
   b. contributed only minimally to my preparation
   c. satisfactorily prepared me
   d. contributed a great deal to my preparation

academic years. The students received an e-mail from the psychology department head asking them to complete an online questionnaire as a part of the department's ongoing assessment efforts. Five men and 15 women, all between the ages of 18 and 22, completed the questionnaire. Eighteen students indicated their ethnic origin as White or Caucasian, one indicated Multi-ethnic, and one indicated Other. Seven students indicated that they intended to get a job after graduation but attend graduate school within the next 5 years, 11 indicated they had been admitted to graduate school, and 2 indicated they intended to go straight to graduate school but had not been admitted at the time they responded to the questionnaire.

The top panel of Figure 13-1 shows the percentage of students who engaged in each of the research process activities as a function of how often they did so, and the bottom panel of the figure presents the data for the technology skills items in the same format. Almost all students reported that they frequently engaged in the five categories of activities associated with the research process, with the fewest reporting that they frequently engaged in technical activities like setting up equipment or fabricating research materials. Close to 75% of the students reported using data analysis software often and using organizational software sometimes or often. In contrast, only 30% reported using specialized software often, and the overwhelming majority reported that they never engaged in computer programming, which is not surprising given that these activities are not necessary in many areas of psychological research.

The top panel of Figure 13-2 shows the percentage of students who engaged in each of the professional development activities as a function of how often they did so, and the bottom panel of the figure presents the data for the communication skills items in the same format. Seventy-five percent of the students had attended one or more professional conferences and regularly attended lab or research team meetings. Only a few had attended a workshop or colloquium, but this may have been because there were not any project-relevant workshops or colloquia available. Most of the students had contributed to writing a research protocol, an IACUC/IRB proposal, a conference submission, or conference poster. Approximately half of the students had contributed to writing a grant proposal or manuscript intended for publication. Regarding presentations, approximately half had presented a poster at a professional conference but only 20% had delivered a presentation as part of a paper session or symposium, which is not surprising given that many professional organizations prohibit students from delivering oral presentations. Additionally, this finding is consistent with the growing use of posters as an alternative means of presentation over oral presentations at professional conferences (Matthews, 1990).

In response to the last questionnaire item, all but one student indicated that they felt that the honors project experience contributed a great deal to their preparation for successfully completing work at the next level. Although these data do not assess the extent to which students *are* prepared for future work, to the extent the self-reports of their activities are accurate, the data confirm that these students engaged in a wide range of activities that involve skills associated with scientific psychology, thus meeting a primary objective of the psychology capstone course (Dunn et al., 2010). In addition, to the extent

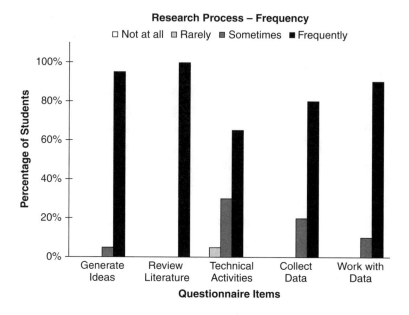

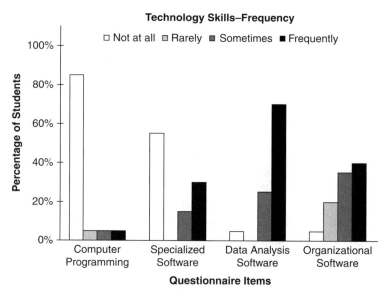

Figure 13-1   The percentage of honors students who engaged in each of the research process activities (top) and technology skills (bottom) as a function of how often they did so.

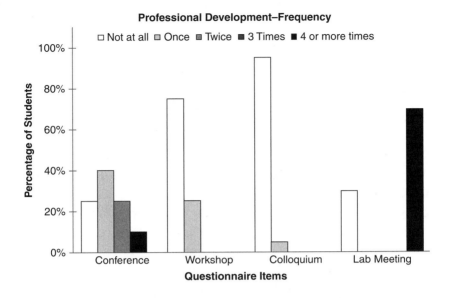

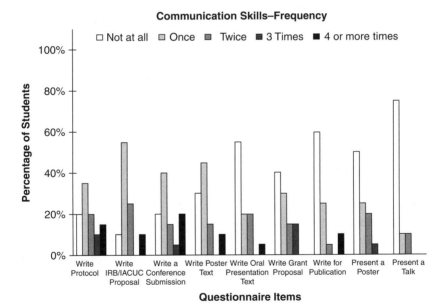

Figure 13-2   The percentage of honors students who engaged in each of the professional development activities (top) and communication skills (bottom) as a function of how often they did so.

that these activities are required and valued in graduate school and beyond, it is reasonable to infer that engaging in them as part of the honors thesis experience will facilitate students' transition from the role of undergraduate to that of graduate student and lifelong learner (Rowles et al., 2004).

Conclusion

Although a relatively small number of undergraduate psychology programs offer senior thesis as a capstone option (Stoloff et al., 2010), the data presented in this chapter suggest it is a reasonable option for meeting capstone goals. JMU psychology majors who complete the Senior Honors Project capstone option develop a research idea, conduct a literature review, collect and analyze data, summarize and interpret results, and present the findings in a presentation and written thesis. This process builds upon key curricular components in that it necessarily involves knowledge of research methods and data analysis techniques, theories and findings in relevant substantive content areas, and ethical considerations. Although the honors thesis is but one of many ways to provide psychology students a culminating educational experience at the baccalaureate level, I would advocate it is a possible perfect ending in that it integrates knowledge and experience acquired throughout the psychology major curriculum as well as promotes a range of professional activities associated with the discipline of scientific psychology.

Suggested Readings

Dunn, D. S., Brewer, C. L., Cautin, R. L., Gurung, R. A., Keith, K. D., McGregor, L. N., Nida, S. A., Puccio, P., & Voight, M. J. (2010). The undergraduate psychology curriculum: A call for a core. In D. Halpern et al. (Eds.), *Undergraduate education in psychology: A blueprint for the future of the discipline* (pp. 47–51). Washington, DC: American Psychological Association.

Wagenaar, T. C. (1993). The capstone course. *Teaching Sociology, 21,* 209–214.

References

Apple, K. J., Serdikoff, S. L., Reis-Bergan, M., & Barron, K. E. (2008). Programmatic assessment of critical thinking. In D. S. Dunn, J. S. Halonen,

& R. A. Smith (Eds.), *Teaching critical thinking in psychology: A handbook of best practices* (pp. 77–88). Malden, MA: Blackwell.

Boyer, E. L. (1987). *College: The undergraduate experience in America.* New York: Harper & Row.

Brewer, C. L., & Halonen, J. S. (2003). A recent history of curriculum and assessment in undergraduate programs in psychology. Retrieved March 9, 2008, from http://www.pkal.org/documents/HistoryOfCurriculumAssessmentInUndergraduatePsychology.cfm.

Brewer, C. L., Hopkins, J. R., Kimble, G. A., Matlin, M. W., McCann, L. I., McNeil, O. V., et al. (1993). Curriculum. In T. V. McGovern (Ed.), *Handbook for enhancing undergraduate education in psychology* (pp. 161–182).

Buxton, C. E., Cofer, C. N., Gustad, J. W., MacLeod, R. B., McKeachie, W. J., & Wolfle, D. (1952). *Improving undergraduate instruction in psychology.* New York: Macmillan.

Davis, N. J. (1993). Bringing it all together: The sociological imagination. *Teaching Sociology, 21,* 233–238.

Dunn, D. S., Brewer, C. L., Cautin, R. L., Gurung, R. A., Keith, K. D., McGregor, L. N., Nida, S. A., Puccio, P., & Voight, M. J. (2010). The undergraduate psychology curriculum: A call for a core. In D. Halpern et al. (Eds.), *Undergraduate education in psychology: A blueprint for the future of the discipline* (pp. 47–51). Washington, DC: American Psychological Association. Dunn, D. S., McCarthy, M., Baker, S., Halonen, J. S., & Hill, G. W., IV. (2007). Quality benchmarks in undergraduate psychology programs. *American Psychologist, 62,* 650–670.

Kulik, J., Brown, D. R., Vestewig, R. E., & Wright, J. (1973). *Undergraduate education in psychology.* Washington, DC: American Psychological Association.

Mathews, D. L. (1990). The scientific poster: Guidelines for effective visual communication. *Technical Communication, 3,* 225–232.

McGovern, T., Furumoto, L., Halpern, D., Kimble, G., & McKeachie, W. (1991). Liberal learning, study-in-depth, and the arts and sciences major: Psychology. *American Psychologist, 46,* 568–605.

McGovern, T. V. (1992). Evolution of undergraduate curricula in psychology, 1892–1992. In A. E. Puente, J. R. Matthews, & C. L. Brewer (Eds.), *Teaching psychology in America: A history* (pp. 13–38). Washington, DC: American Psychological Association.

McGovern, T. V. (Ed.). (1993). *Handbook for enhancing undergraduate education in psychology.* Washington, DC: American Psychological Association.

McGovern, T. V., & Brewer, C. L. (2003). Undergraduate education. In D. K. Freedheim (Ed.), *Handbook of psychology* (Vol. 1, pp. 465–481). Hoboken, NJ: Wiley.

McGovern, T. V., & Reich, J. N. (1996). A comment on the Quality Principles. *American Psychologist, 51*, 252–255.

McKeachie, W. J., & Milholland, J. E. (1961). *Undergraduate curricula in psychology.* Chicago: Scott, Foresman.

Moore, R. C. (n. d.). Capstone courses. Retrieved March 9, 2008, from http://users.etown.edu/m/moorerc/capstone.html.

Murphy, P. D. (n.d.). Capstone experience. Retrieved March 9, 2008, from http://www.ndsu.nodak.edu/ndsu/marmcdon/assessment/assessment_techniques/capstone_experience.htm.

Perlman, B., & McCann, L. I. (1999). The most frequently listed courses in the undergraduate psychology curriculum. *Teaching of Psychology, 26*, 177–182

Perlman, B., & McCann, L. I. (2005). Undergraduate research experiences in psychology: A national study of courses and curricula. *Teaching of Psychology, 32*, 5–14.

Rowles, C. J., Koch, D. C., Hundley, S. P., Hamilton, S. J. (2004). *Toward a model for capstone experiences: mountaintops, magnets, and mandates. Assessment update: Progress, trends, and practices in higher education, 16*, 1–2, 13–15.

Serdikoff, S. L. (2007, October). *Honors thesis as a capstone experience: A possible perfect ending.* Address delivered at the annual Best Practices in the Teaching of Psychology: Beginnings and Endings conference, Atlanta, GA.

Stoloff, M., Keller, L., Lynch, J., Makara, K., Simmons, S., Smiley, W., & Varfolomeeva, V. (2010). The undergraduate psychology major: An examination of structure and sequence. *Teaching of Psychology.*

Stoloff, M. L., Apple, K. J., Barron, K. E., Reis-Bergan, M., & Sundre, D. (2004). Seven goals for effective program assessment. In D. S. Dunn, C. M. Mehrotra, & J. S. Halonen (Eds.), *Measuring up: Educational assessment challenges and practices for psychology* (pp. 29–46). Washington, DC: American Psychological Association.

Stoloff, M. L., & Feeney, K. J. (2002). The Major Field Test as an assessment tool for an undergraduate psychology program. *Teaching of Psychology, 29,* pp. 92–98.

Terry, R. L. (1996, December). Characteristics of psychology departments at primarily undergraduate institutions. *Council on Undergraduate Research Quarterly,* 86–90.

Wagenaar, T. C. (1993). The capstone course. *Teaching Sociology, 21*, 209–214.

14 The Capstone Research Course

A Case Study in the Evolution of Educational Efficacy

Wayne S. Messer and *David B. Porter*

When undergraduates engage in research, they benefit in a number of significant ways. Continuing calls for the integration of research experiences into all undergraduate programs (e.g., Boyer, 1998; Council on Undergraduate Research and National Council for Undergraduate Research, 2005; Hu, Scheuch, Schwartz, Gayles, & Li; 2008; National Science Foundation Committee for the Review of Undergraduate Education, 1996) and growing expectations for faculty research (Malachowski, 2004) have contributed to an increase in the numbers of natural and social science departments that are offering or requiring research experiences in the undergraduate curriculum (Cooney & Griffith, 1994; Katkin, 2008; Kierniesky, 2005; Messer, Griggs, & Jackson, 1999; Perlman & McCann, 2005; Russell et al., 2007; Strassburger, 1995). Although we acknowledge the many desirable student outcomes, we also know the challenges of developing a departmental capstone course that includes completion of a research project. Over the last decade, we have found that an incremental, evolutionary approach has facilitated our development of an increasingly effective course. In this chapter, we offer a candid account of our experiences to benefit others who may find themselves in the position of developing and teaching such a course.

Case Example: What We Do at Berea College and Why We Do It

Berea College, founded in 1855, is a four-year, private, liberal arts college of approximately 1,500 students. The mission of the college is to educate and inspire economically disadvantaged yet academically capable students. Currently the Psychology Department of 4.5 faculty graduates approximately 20 majors each year.

Our Senior Research capstone course culminates a three-course sequence: Statistics, Research Methods, and Senior Research. Our curriculum also requires two additional laboratory-based content courses. Thus, in a major requiring 10, four-semester-hour courses, half the courses directly involve hands-on methodological empiricism. In our Senior Research course, students are responsible for a start-to-finish project that includes all the typical elements of the research process: developing a hypothesis, reviewing the literature, designing and conducting an experiment, analyzing the results using SPSS, and presenting the results in three media: a 15-minute talk during a campus symposium, a standard research poster, and a 10-page APA-style manuscript. In addition, students often present their work at state and regional conferences. A single assigned instructor has sole responsibility for the course. Class size has ranged from 4 to 14, with the typical size of 10.

We support continuing the requirement that all departmental majors complete this course for several reasons. First, our alumni surveys indicate that around 72% of our graduates pursue graduate and professional school, for which we feel this course provides excellent preparation. Second, we believe the course provides general benefits for students regardless of whether they attend graduate school. Finally, we endorse the APA's learning goals for undergraduate psychology programs (APA, 2007), believing that the course provides a unique opportunity for students to acquire new skills as well as to restructure their somewhat tacit understanding of the science of psychology.

We will briefly review goals and the benefits gained when they are met. Then, we turn to challenges faced in teaching the course and offer some possible solutions.

Learning Goals

The *APA Guidelines for the Undergraduate Psychology Major* (APA, 2007) provides a set of 10 optimal expectations (i.e., learning goals) for the acquisition of knowledge, skills, and values for students majoring in psychology. A rigorous undergraduate research experience is well suited for contributing to the attainment of these goals. Our independent considerations generated a set of goals concerning students' knowledge, skills, and values that was quite similar to the APA's 10 learning outcomes.

We developed our research capstone within the context of a traditional course and, within this structure, identified and prioritized the learning outcomes we most wanted students to achieve. Our analysis involved three different questions: What did we want students to know or to more fully understand? What did we want students to be able to do? And how did we want them to feel about what they learned after completing the course? Our answers to these three questions framed the knowledge, skill, and affective outcomes for the course. Porter (1991) has suggested that overall learning is the product of these three distinctly different outcomes. Each of these component questions warrants further examination and explanation.

Declarative knowledge is the outcome most commonly associated with the first learning outcome. Definitions of general terms and theories and the contributions of various schools of psychology (viz., Goals 1 and 2 of the APA *Guidelines*) made up much of the general knowledge goals for courses in the psychology major, and thus were adopted as learning outcomes for our research capstone course. We emphasized the importance of students' recognizing the conceptual boundaries that separate true experiments from other approaches, such as quasi–experimental, correlational, and case studies, and understanding the advantages and disadvantages of each approach. Experimentation is the most potent means of establishing causation and thus became the primary focus of our course.

We drew the skills outcomes that we identified from our understanding of the scientific method and the component activities it requires. We identified five types of skills we wanted students to acquire:

1. Logical skills—understanding arguments (finding conceptual coherence in theoretical claims and being sensitive to common reasoning errors)
2. Design skills—translating or "operationalizing" theories into realistic plans for experiments; learning how to disassemble situations to reduce complexity and eliminate confounds using a variety of controls

3. Observation skills—learning how to look and record; recognizing the value of multiple perspectives and a diversity of ways of measuring human thought and behavior reliably
4. Analytic skills—being able to use an array of descriptive and inferential statistics appropriately to collect observations and discern patterns unlikely to have occurred solely by chance
5. Media skills—learning how to focus and prioritize relevant information and experimental data to communicate with a professional audience in an oral presentation, poster, and paper

There were also several important affective outcomes. Our hope was that through their experiences, students might increase their intellectual curiosity, open-mindedness, and a commitment to integrity and high ethical standards. It also became apparent that students needed support in overcoming some of the anxiety and fears they brought with them to the capstone course. We sought to create opportunities for students to develop an aesthetic appreciation for quality research and an eagerness to get involved. That these goals can be met by an appropriately structured undergraduate research experience is seen in the student benefits discussed and documented in the literature. It is to these benefits that we now turn.

Benefits of Undergraduate Research Experiences

Kardash (2000), Kardash, Wallace, and Blockus (2008), Landrum and Nelsen (2002), Lapatto (2004), Russell, Hancock, and McCullough (2006), Serdikoff (2007), and Seymour, Hunter, Laursen, and Deantoni (2004), among others, have written about the positive outcomes of the undergraduate research experience. Table 14-1 presents a list of outcomes for which a general consensus appears to have developed from the sources cited.

Serdikoff (2007) sorted research benefits into four broad clusters: (a) those concerned with the research process itself, (b) technology skills, (c) professional development, and (d) improved writing in the discipline. On the other hand, Landrum and Nelsen (2002) used factor analysis to reduce 40 benefits to just two factors: (a) technical skills and (b) interpersonal skills. Seymour et al. (2004) discussed seven categories of benefits including (a) thinking/working like a scientist, (b) clarification of career/educational path, and (c) enhanced career/educational preparation. Analyses such as those above suggest that potential benefits of undergraduate research are real, exist in

Table 14-1

Potential and Expected Benefits from an Undergraduate Research Experience

1. Improved acceptance rates by graduate and professional programs.
2. Increased competitiveness in the job market.
3. Improved everyday reasoning, troubleshooting, and problem-solving skills.
4. Improved numerical literacy ("numeracy").
5. Better oral, visual, and written communication skills.
6. Increased self-directedness and independence of thought.
7. Increased self-confidence.
8. An expanded sense of what can be accomplished.
9. Improved data analysis and interpretation skills.
10. Improved time-management skills.
11. Improved library research skills.
12. Better letters of recommendation from faculty.
13. Deeper understanding of topics.
14. An improved tolerance for obstacles and ambiguity.
15. Networking benefits (from off-campus presentations)
16. Improved confidence to engage in scientific work.
17. Improved technical, laboratory, and/or field skills.
18. An integration of previous course work in psychology.
19. Preparation for more demanding and advanced research.
20. Improved collaboration and leadership skills.
21. Clarified ethical standards.
22. An increased (or decreased) interest in going to graduate school.
23. A better understanding of career demands.
24. An improved understanding of the research process and of how knowledge is gained.
25. Becoming a more informed consumer of media information.

numerous domains, and overlap with the learning goals of quality under-graduate programs (APA, 2007).

Are there common features that characterize successful undergraduate research? Lapatto (2003) found that faculty considered reading scientific litera-ture, working independently or with a team of peers (with faculty mentorship), feeling ownership and an increasing sense of independence, attaining mastery of the relevant research techniques, and opportunities for both oral and written communication as the most relevant features of undergraduate research. Other features, such as having an opportunity to attend a professional meeting, were seen as less critical.

Are there common and widely encountered challenges or problems as well? Our own experiences, our reading of the literature, and our discussions with colleagues at teaching conferences, have led us to believe there are. Here, we outline some of these challenges and indicate our attempts and those of others to resolve them.

Initial course development often reflects best guesses about which policies and processes are likely to achieve the most important outcomes. It is important that courses include mechanisms that provide informative feedback to students and the instructor during the course as well as aggregate data that can be used to effect larger adjustments to the course between offerings. We use our experiences and our data to guide our search for principles that drive the relationships between course characteristics and student learning. Although principles may be universal, "best practices" need to evolve locally, within the context of the particular institution. The effectiveness of any particular practice is influenced by characteristics of the students, the teacher, and the academic context. Any curricular strategy, no matter how well it may have worked in one context, will have to be *adapted* (rather than *adopted*) to a new context (Angelo & Cross, 1993; Angelo, 1995). Thus the particular best practices may differ significantly from one program, and even from one course, to the next. For this reason, the following discussion reflects our efforts to provide a candid account of our particular experiences that might influence or inform the development of general prescriptions for course design.

Although we believe that the best solutions must be local, we also recognize that many of the problems we confront are likely to be quite general. In developing our course, and in pursuing our stated outcomes, we encountered challenges met by many who teach similar courses and who have shared their experiences with us at teaching conferences. We outline a few of these common challenges and indicate some approaches—some our own, some suggested by others—to meet them.

Common Challenges and Suggested Solutions

In our capstone course, students are still in the process of developing their knowledge, skills, and values but have already completed a statistics and a research methods course, and possibly one or more of the lab-based content courses. Although our students have had these preparatory courses, they still come to us relatively unprepared to conduct independent research. If senior research were not a requirement of our program, a few of the least well prepared students would select not to take it. In general, it is these few students who often require the greatest amount of faculty support. The time demands of the capstone course often exceed those of more traditional lecture courses, and projects must fit, from conception to finished product, within a single semester.

Review of Content

Another common challenge is how to balance individual preparation in the necessary background knowledge with the development of a supportive classroom community necessary for project development. We've found one particular collaborative learning technique referred to as "quiz-first" (Porter 1989; Johnson, Johnson, & Smith, 1991; Michaelsen, 1992) to be very useful in achieving this balance. Using this technique, students review assigned material before each of the classes during the first third of the semester. The initial readings are chapters from an experimental psychology text (Kantowitz, Roediger, & Elmes, 2005) that students use in a prerequisite course. Later, chapters are assigned from Slater's (2004) provocative book, *Opening Skinner's Box*. At the beginning of each class, students are offered opportunities to ask questions before a 10-item multiple choice quiz is administered.

Once all students individually complete the quiz, they are randomly assigned to groups of three or four students and re-take the quiz collaboratively. Their overall score comprises the average of their scores on the individual and group quiz. After all groups reach consensus, the instructor leads a class conversation about each item. Collectively the best answer is identified; students are challenged to support their responses and to explain the relevance of each question and consider how the information covered might apply to their own research project.

Students have reported considerable support for this approach. Many students realize that although the material had been covered in previous courses, they may not have really learned it sufficiently well to use it. Many students also come to realize how "academic" concepts might actually impact the decisions they will need to make about their individual experiments. Beyond refreshing their knowledge of the material, this activity also provides an opportunity for community building within the class. Students learn the give and take of negotiating with one another as professional colleagues. They also learn that the best way to earn the respect of one's peers is to be prepared consistently and to admit when one does not know the answer. Establishing this collaborative classroom culture provides a useful foundation as students set forth on their individual experimental adventures in the second half of the course.

Course Structure and Instructor Feedback

Structure, feedback, and freedom must be balanced so that students do not feel "adrift" during the research process nor feel over-evaluated or too narrowly constrained. When too much emphasis is placed on performance, especially during the early stages of development, learning may be diminished. Students need to be encouraged to take risks, and they also need objective feedback on their performance. Heylings and Tariq (2001) described a useful strategy for delivering the right amount of feedback at the right time. Many of the activities during the first half of the semester, such as taking quizzes, writing and rewriting a research proposal, and constructing and analyzing a dummy data set, were designed to help students develop necessary skills and acquire essential knowledge. Student performance is evaluated and the scores are used to provide substantive feedback and as a mid-term grade. However, because the emphasis throughout the first half of the course is on learning, grades reflecting the quality or relative "success" of these preliminary products do not directly affect students' grades at the end of the course. Students understand that they will be held accountable for the quality of their final research project, not for their performance during preparatory activities.

Identifying a Research Question

Guiding students through the process of selecting a topic, refining a good research question, and designing a viable experiment is also a common challenge. We experimented with imposing topic constraints for several semesters—students did independent projects, but each one had to be related to an umbrella topic specifically chosen for that semester. This approach reduced the need for the instructor to review the literature on a dozen different topics and appeared to help weaker or perhaps less motivated students, but some students balked at a perceived loss of academic freedom.

During other semesters, we allowed students who seemed to be experiencing extreme difficulty in settling on a suitable topic or design to choose from among four or five "topic packets." Each of these topic packets contained three or four "core" articles surrounding a particular area (e.g., body image, alcohol expectancies, effects of nature) and provided examples of several different experimental variables that could be manipulated in the examination of that topic. Students could almost use a "mix-and-match" approach to variables from the articles to design a relevant and feasible experiment.

Regardless of the general area of inquiry, the scope of the research question is critical. Smith (2007) suggested that faulty research questions typically fall into three categories: "the non-causal project, the breakthrough [i.e., wildly speculative] project, and the so-what project." Smith defined each of these types of projects, discussed the specific student misconceptions that induce them, and offered cogent suggestions for addressing these misconceptions and steering students toward more appropriate designs.

Gradually we have learned that a process of negotiation is sufficient to guide most students toward viable research questions without stunting their intellectual curiosity or ownership of the project outcome. We now allow students relatively free rein in selecting their topics (albeit with the constraints of feasibility, ethics, and time considerations) but provide extensive feedback.

Writing an Integrated Literature Review

Students often need help in evaluating and integrating ideas from their background literature review into a coherent written narrative for their experiment. Froese, Gantz, and Henry (1998) presented a strategy for writing based on a meta-analytic model; they instructed students to systematically search for linked variables and to use coding sheets not only to keep track of the information in their selected articles but also to evaluate connections and develop a common means of describing outcomes. Clearly, learning to produce a comprehensive literature review is a complex skill and a time-consuming activity. Recognizing this, some programs use the literature review as the focus of their entire capstone course. However, our decision to provide students with a comprehensive research experience has necessarily meant that this important activity receives somewhat less emphasis than others might deem appropriate. One of the key goals for the program is to allow students the opportunity to reconcile their own data with theoretical perspectives and previous research. Our hope is that our course is not just about students collecting the dots but actually doing the difficult conceptual work of connecting them as well.

Presentation Anxiety

Our capstone necessarily involves multiple presentations as well as the demonstration of research skills and abilities. Much of the anxiety students experience is often focused on the oral presentation rather than the research itself (Wood & Palm, 2000). Recognizing this, our initial approach was to attempt to habituate students to the presentation process: students developed and delivered practice portions of each talk (i.e., Introduction, Method), and later in the term, we videotaped and critiqued the entire 15-minute practice presentations. Students, reviewers from our Learning Center, and the instructor provided oral and written feedback on presentation style as well as on content, clarity, and organization. Students watched their video clips, filled out evaluation forms on themselves and considered adjustments for their next presentation. The instructor videotaped each student's final presentation at our Senior Symposium and, before the end of the semester, required them to reflect on the experience. Students with public-presentation anxiety acknowledged the benefits of practice and they seemed to develop tighter, better organized presentations. We had hoped that students would apply comments on the organizational, methodological, statistical, and other elements of the presentations to their papers and posters. However, criticisms of the oral presentations appeared to have been compartmentalized; students often reverted to previous errors when writing their paper or preparing their poster. Ironically, the emphasis on the particulars of presentation rather than the research itself may have led some students to conclude that what mattered most was appearance and impression rather than substance of the experiment. Eventually, we decided to refocus the course on the experiment itself while encouraging those students with high presentation anxiety to use our Learning Center and providing extra credit for those who availed themselves of this opportunity.

In its most basic form, research is about simplifying circumstances and observing behaviors. Research includes the adventure of discovery and the construction of an objective and coherent account of that process. Once students recognize this, they seem to have less difficulty finding a way to convey their research story.

Assessment: Using Evidence to Assess and Refine Course Structure and Policies

Assessment and learning are continual processes. Assessing learning is complex and multifaceted. No single measure, including a meticulous evaluation of any particular work product, adequately captures student learning. Although one can grade a paper, a poster, or an oral presentation directly (but imperfectly), the learning that underlies that performance is more difficult to judge (Bjork, 2001). Discerning the patterns of learning across groups of students poses an even greater challenge. As Rueckert (2008) suggested, the assessment challenge is even greater for courses designed to promote learning through the research process rather than by more traditional methods.

This challenge may explain the dearth of empirically based studies that support the actual attainment of the touted potential benefits of undergraduate research. When, for example, Seymour, Hunter, Laursen, and DeAntoni (2004) reviewed 54 articles, only nine provided any empirical evidence of benefit attainment. Nearly all of the research on benefits involves students who individually seek out and choose research participation. In contrast, we require all of our students to participate in research to complete the psychology major. In general, research reports rely more heavily on student perceptions of the benefits of research participation than other, more objective, measures of outcomes. Assessment methods for demonstrating attainment of benefits in an empirically convincing way are still evolving and are yet to be widely used.

Our own search for evidence that might help us assess and improve student learning within our capstone course has included the collection and analysis of a wide variety of data from several sources including students, faculty, and external evaluators. We offer data from four different types of assessments and implications for their use.

Grade Distribution

Grades, as commonly used in higher education, can be poor measures of student learning (Walvoord & Anderson, 1998). Standards often differ among faculty within particular departments and even more widely across different departments, schools, or colleges. However, as Walvoord and Anderson (1998) showed, by establishing clear criteria and standards for grading through a process referred to as Primary Trait Analysis (PTA), grades can provide useful and relevant information about student learning and performance. Although many psychology faculty do not use PTA systematically, they often employ it implicitly through the rubrics they use to assess students' performance and provide feedback. Thus, an examination of the grades given in this course over the last 10 semesters provides a potentially relevant source of data and generally confirms our faculty's positive impressions of the quality of student research.

The distribution shows that the grades for this course are significantly higher than for other courses in the psychology department; it is particularly notable that nearly half the students enrolled in the course earned A's. This result could simply be bias on the part of faculty members teaching the course. However, other evidence supports the conclusion that many students have performed well in the course. Students' self report of the amount of time they invested in this course shows that they spent more time in this course than in most other academic courses. For example, only 36% of students reported spending fewer than 10 hours per week in this course compared to 65% who reported spending less than 10 hours per week in other courses on campus. Also, students' presentations are public, and the posters of the best projects are posted prominently in the psychology laboratory area. The general impression of student work across departmental faculty is that about half the projects over recent years have been top quality work, worthy of A grades.

As Figure 14-1 shows, at the other end of the distribution, about 15% of the students do not produce credible research and received grades of C or lower. Even a well-designed experiment may not yield significant results; and there is no grade penalty based on the experimental results per se. However, even those students who failed to make use of the feedback provided during the course are given the opportunity to pass the course by articulating their mistakes and demonstrating what they have learned from the experience.

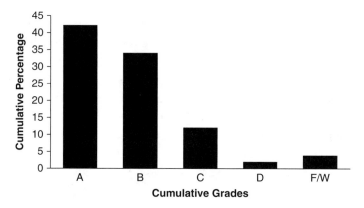

Figure 14-1 Cumulative frequency distribution of final grades given in Senior Research Course over the last 10 semesters (n = 94).

The Knowledge Survey

A knowledge survey is a systematic self-reported inventory of what students know and what they do not know about a body of knowledge (Nuhfer & Knipp, 2003). Although students' perceptions of their learning are not the same as learning itself, this same criticism might be applied to any other particular measure of student learning. Individual student scores on the knowledge survey correlate only moderately with measures of subsequent individual performance. However, when data are aggregated across groups of students, survey results provide useful approximations of students' general knowledge and understanding. We have also found that responses to this survey can be helpful in identifying individual students who may lack prerequisite skills or confidence at the beginning of the course and provide them with additional feedback and support.

The process for constructing and conducting a knowledge survey is relatively simple. For each of about 50 discrete items, students rate their own comprehension on a 3-point scale. A "3" represents the respondent's confidence that she or he could answer this question fully without reference to other material. A "2" reflects a subject's familiarity with the particular concept or idea and expectation that the student could develop a complete answer within about 15 minutes. A rating of "1" reflected the student's admission that the concept is unfamiliar. The items for the knowledge survey used in this course were drawn from the concepts covered in the first five chapters of *Experimental Psychology* by Kantowitz et al. (2005). For the last several years, student responses before and after the Research Methods and Senior Research course have been collected. The dotted line on Figure 14-2 reflects the average ratings of students entering the Research Methods after having completed the Psychology Statistics course. The dashed line in the middle shows the combined average of students at the completion of the Research Methods course and at the beginning of the Senior Research course. The solid line at the top of the graph reflects the ratings of students at the completion of the Senior Research course. Response rate has been nearly 100%.

Results of this survey provide a representation of students' perception of their learning across our three-course sequence. Some concepts or ideas such as those relating to theories and variables and familiarity with the library were rated above 2 from the start of the sequence, but other ideas like interactions and the notions of parsimony or falsifiability were rated near 1 (i.e., no familiarity) initially. By the end of the three-course sequence the self-reported

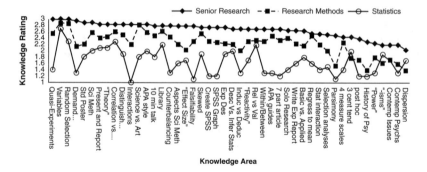

Figure 14-2 Cumulative average self-ratings for students enrolled over 3 semesters in research courses across 46 knowledge areas relevant to experimental psychology. Knowledge areas are arranged from highest to lowest ratings at the completion of senior research. Average ratings reflect inputs from approximately 50 students with most students accomplishing the survey multiple times. Ratings collected from students at the completion of the statistics course are the lowest whereas those taken at the completion of the senior research course are the highest. Ratings provided at the conclusion of the research methods and/or the beginning of the senior research course are at an intermediate level. The relative size of gaps between the lines indicates learning in the research methods and senior research courses, respectively.

average understanding of students was above 2 in all categories and above 2.5 for over 75% of the items.

Student Ratings of Course Effectiveness

Students in every course at Berea College provide subjective ratings of their experience in each course at the end of the semester. The final item asks respondents to rate the overall effectiveness of the course using a scale that ranges from *excellent* (5) to *very poor* (1) (see Figure 14-3). The overall average for the psychology department and the college on this general indicator of student satisfaction has been about 4.0 consistently. Average ratings of overall course effectiveness for the last 10 semesters appear below. These results show some variation in students' perception of the effectiveness of the course across the past 5 years. Carefully assessing the potential course and systemic factors associated with unusually low average ratings provided a great deal of useful information relevant to improving student experiences and learning within the course. The apparent divot in generally positive ratings occurred due to the administrative exigency of using a sabbatical replacement for a year. It provides clear evidence that simply adopting a previously successful syllabus is not sufficient to ensure

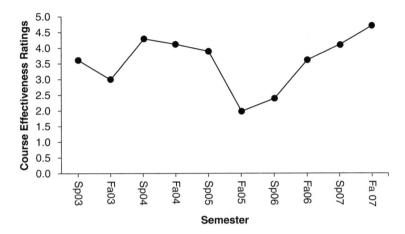

Figure 14-3   Students' average ratings of course effectiveness over 10 semesters on a 5 point scale ranging from Excellent (5) to Very Poor (1) (n = 89). The relatively high rating for effectiveness of some earlier offerings as well as the recent improvement in ratings is apparent.

continued course success. No pedagogical practices are so powerful that they assure success when faculty do not understand the underlying philosophy or share the general educational approach. Recent improvements in ratings reflect the value of this approach. It is also noteworthy that results of the senior survey conducted just prior to graduation also reflect the recent rise in student ratings of their experiences within the psychology major.

Student reflections (mid-term). Students also provide written reflections of their own learning both at mid-term and at the end of the course. Although anecdotal in nature and ubiquitously positive in tone, common themes provide useful insights into the student learning experience. Nearly all students claim that they had to work much harder than they anticipated but most express pride in their accomplishment. Many students report being surprised by how different knowledge is when it is put into a personal and practical context (e.g., learning the formal definition of an "interaction" and discovering one for yourself within your own data). Students report that knowing they would be required to present their findings to faculty and peers is especially motivating. Similarly, preparing a poster that may be displayed for other students to observe (and admire) was cited as a source of motivation. Most students expressed appreciation for the support provided by their classmates and the discovery that mistakes identified by others can be an invaluable opportunity for new learning and improvement. Students' final reflections invariably mention the increase in self-confidence at having overcome what they had considered to be a significant challenge. One of the most common conclusions is expressed directly in the following student reflection:

> As my experiment came together, I felt as if I finally understood what we had been talking about in all the psychology courses leading up to this course. We have information on terms, major contributions to the field, important people, and overviews of lots of pieces of the puzzle. This course is helping me to fit all those pieces together and actually makes me more excited to go on with school and to become a professional in the field of psychology. Senior Research has allowed me to take the knowledge I have gained over the past three years and pull it together to see it as a whole.

Conclusion

Education, like politics, is a local phenomenon. Although principles of best practice can provide a useful framework for designing a course, faculty must work out the particular structures and policies of each course within particular academic contexts. A commitment to pursuing multiple sources of evidence provided by embedding assessment mechanisms (such as the knowledge survey, quizzes, student reflections, and public presentation of work) is essential to the evolution of effective courses. This commitment is especially relevant to a capstone research course such as the one at Berea College. We realize that many opportunities for improvement in this course remain; however, this evolutionary approach has already provided evidence of its value in increasing and sustaining the overall educational effectiveness of our program.

Suggested Readings

Miller, R. L., Rycek R. F., Balcetis, E., Barney, S. T., Beins, B. C., Burns, S. R., Smith, R., & Ware, M. E. (2008). *Developing, promoting, and sustaining the undergraduate research experience in psychology*. Available from the Society for the Teaching of Psychology Web site: http://teachpsych.org/resources/e-books/ur2008/ur2008.php.

Walvoord, B. E., & Anderson, V. J. (1998). *Effective grading: A tool for learning and assessment*. San Francisco, CA: Jossey-Bass.

References

American Psychological Association. (2007). *APA guidelines for the undergraduate psychology major.* Washington, DC: Author. Retrieved from www.apa.org/ed/resources.html

Angelo, T. A. (1995). Improving classroom assessment to improve learning: Guidelines from research and practice. *Assessment Update, 7*(6), 1–2, 12–13.

Angelo, T.A., & Cross, K. P. (1993) *Classroom assessment techniques: A handbook for college teachers* (2nd ed.). San Francisco, CA: Jossey-Bass.

Bauer, K. W., & Bennett, J. S. (2003). Alumni perceptions used to assess undergraduate research experience. *Journal of Higher Education, 74,* 210–230.

Bjork, R. A. (2001, March). How to succeed in college: Learn how to learn. *American Psychological Society Observer, 14,* 9.

Boyer Commission on Educating Undergraduates in the Research University. (1998). *Reinventing undergraduate education: A blueprint for America's research universities.* Stony Brook, NY: Carnegie Foundation for the Advancement of Teaching.

Cooney, B. R., & Griffith, D. M. (1994). The 1992-1993 undergraduate department survey. Washington, DC: American Psychological Association.

Council on Undergraduate Research and National Conference for Undergraduate Research. (2005). *Joint statement of principles in support of undergraduate research, scholarship, and creative activities.* Retrieved September 11, 2008, from http://www.cur.org/SummitPosition.html.

Froese, A. D., Gantz, B. S., & Henry, A. L. (1998). Teaching students to write literature reviews: A meta-analytic model. *Teaching of Psychology, 25,* 102–105.

Heylings, D. J. A., & Tariq, V. N. (2001). Reflection and feedback on learning: A strategy for undergraduate research project work. *Assessment and Evaluation in Higher Education, 26,* 153–164.

Hu, S., Scheuch, K., Schwartz, R., Gaston Gayles, J., & Li, S. (2008). *Reinventing undergraduate education: Engaging college students in research and creative activities.* ASHE Higher Education Report, Vol. 33, No. 4. Hoboken, NJ: Wiley Periodicals.

Johnson, D. W., Johnson, R. T., & Smith, K. (1991). *Cooperative learning: Increasing college faculty instructional productivity.* ASHE-ERIC Higher Education Report No. 4. Washington, DC: George Washington University.

Kantowitz, B. H., Roediger, H. L., III, & Elmes, D. G. (2005). *Experimental psychology; Understanding psychological research* (8th ed.). Belmont, CA: Wadsworth Thomson Learning.

Kardash, C. M. (2000). Evaluation of an undergraduate research experience: Perceptions of undergraduate interns and their faculty mentors. *Journal of Educational Psychology, 92,* 191–201.

Kardash, C. M., Wallace, M., & Blockus, L. (2008). Science undergraduates' perceptions of learning from undergraduate research experiences. In R. L. Miller, R. F. Rycek, E. Balcetis, S. T. Barney, B. C. Beins, S. R. Burns, R. Smith, & M. E. Ware (Eds.), *Developing, promoting, and sustaining the undergraduate research experience in psychology* (pp. 258–263). Available from the Society for the Teaching of Psychology Web site: http://teachpsych.org/resources/e-books/ur2008/ur2008.php.

Katkin, W. (2008). The Boyer Commission Report and its impact on undergraduate research. *New Directions for Teaching and Learning, 93,* 19–38.

Kierniesky, N. C. (2005). Undergraduate research in small psychology departments: Two decades later. *Teaching of Psychology, 32,* 84–90.

Landrum, R. E., & Nelsen, L. R. (2002). The undergraduate research assistantship: An analysis of the benefits. *Teaching of Psychology, 29,* 15–19.

Lapatto, D. (2003). The essential features of undergraduate research. *Council on Undergraduate Research Quarterly, 20,* 139–142.

Lapatto, D. (2004). Survey of undergraduate research experiences (SURE): First findings. *Cell Biology Education, 3,* 270–277.

Malachowski, M. R. (2004, March). The importance of placing students first in designing research programs at predominantly undergraduate institutions. *Council on Undergraduate Research Quarterly, 24,* 106–108.

Messer, W. S., Jackson, S. L., & Griggs, R. A. (1999). A national survey of undergraduate degree options and major requirements. *Teaching of Psychology, 26,* 164–171.

Michaelsen, L. K. (1992). Team learning: A comprehensive approach for harnessing the power of small groups in higher education. *To Improve the Academy, 11,* 107–122.

National Science Foundation Committee for the Review of Undergraduate Education. (1996). *Shaping the future: New expectations for undergraduate education in science, mathematics, engineering, and technology.* (NSF Publication No. 96-139). Arlington, VA: Author.

Nuhfer, E. B., & Knipp, D. (2003). The knowledge survey: A tool for all reasons. *To Improve the Academy, 21,* 50–78.

Perlman, B., & McCann, L. (2005). Undergraduate research experiences in psychology: A national study of courses and curricula. *Teaching of Psychology, 32,* 5–14.

Porter, D. B. (1989). Educating from a group perspective; What, why, and how. Invited address. *Proceedings of the Human Factors Society 33rd Annual Meeting*. Santa Monica, CA: HFS, 507–512.

Porter, D. B. (1991). A perspective on college learning. *Journal of College Reading and Learning, 24*, 1–15

Rueckert, L. (2008). Tools for the assessment of undergraduate research outcomes. In R. L. Miller, R. F. Rycek, E. Balcetis, S. T. Barney, B. C. Beins, S. R. Burns, R. Smith, & M. E. Ware (Eds.), *Developing, promoting, and sustaining the undergraduate research experience in psychology* (pp. 272–275). Retrieved from the Society for the Teaching of Psychology Web site: http://teachpsych.org/resources/e-books/ur2008/ur2008.php.

Russell, S. H., Hancock, M. P., & McCullough, J. (2006). *Evaluation of NSF support for undergraduate research opportunities*. Arlington, VA: National Science Foundation.

Russell, S.H., Hancock, M.P., McCullough, J. (2007). Benefits of undergraduate research experiences. *Science, 316*, 548–549.

Serdikoff, S. L. (2007, October). *Honors thesis as capstone experience: A possible perfect ending*. Paper presented at the conference, Beginnings & Endings: Best Practices for Introducing and Bringing Closure to the Undergraduate Psychology Major, Atlanta, GA.

Seymour, E., Hunter, A-B, Laursen, S. L., & Deantoni, T. (2004). Establishing the benefits of research experiences for undergraduates in the sciences: First findings from a three-year study. *Science Education, 88*, 493–594.

Slater, L. (2004). *Opening Skinner's box; Great psychological experiments of the twentieth century*. New York: W.W. Norton.

Smith, P. C. (2007). Assessing students' research ideas. In D. Dunn, R. A. Smith, & B. C. Beins (Eds.), *Best practices for teaching statistics and research methods in the behavioral sciences* (pp. 59–70). Mahwah, NJ: Erlbaum.

Strassburger, J. (1995). Embracing undergraduate research. *American Association for Higher Education Bulletin, 47*, 3–5.

Walvoord, B. E., & Anderson, V. J. (1998). *Effective grading; A tool for learning and assessment*. San Francisco, CA: Jossey-Bass.

Wood, M. R., & Palm, L. J. (2000). Students' anxiety in a senior thesis course. *Psychological Reports, 86*, 935–936.

15 Ten Things I Hate About My Capstone Course—And a Few Ways to Fix Them

Tracy E. Zinn, Monica J. Reis-Bergan, and *Suzanne C. Baker*

The capstone seminar, in which faculty teach advanced topics in their specialty areas, has the potential to be an ideal teaching situation. What could be better than sharing our favorite topic with students at the pinnacle of their undergraduate experiences? These students have had the experience of taking many psychology courses before the capstone (at James Madison University [JMU], that means approximately 12 courses), and the teacher is an expert in the topic area (e.g., animal behavior, industrial organizational, health psychology). However, we find that sometimes what should be an ideal teaching situation can end up anything but ideal. In this chapter, we discuss the seminar capstone experience, three categories of problems we have had with our capstone courses, and ways teachers can address these problems.

Case Example: Seminar Capstone

At the 1991 St. Mary's conference, educators recommended that curricula should include four different types of courses, culminating in an integrative course experience (Brewer et al., 1993). These "integrative experiences for seniors may take several forms, including internships; research projects supervised by faculty members; or capstone courses, such as History of

Psychology, Advanced General Psychology, or Great Ideas in Psychology" (Brewer, 1997, p. 439; see Dunn & McCarthy, this volume). There are several different types of integrative capstone experiences offered by JMU: (a) field placements or service practica; (b) advanced independent research experiences, often in the form of an honor's thesis; and (c) integrative course experiences, or seminar capstone. Here, we discuss the seminar capstone, which is the most common type of capstone experience offered (Perlman & McCann, 1999).

As per the recommendations of the St. Mary's conference, the primary objectives of the capstone experience at JMU focus on integrating information from other courses and experiences into the content of that particular capstone. In particular, we ask students to (a) analyze, synthesize, and evaluate information from primary sources; (b) demonstrate effective written communication skills, which could include preparing empirically based reports, literature reviews, theoretical papers, or program evaluations; and (c) demonstrate effective oral communication skills at the individual level (i.e., not only group presentations), in the form of individual paper presentations or as a member of a symposium, or in some comparable forum. In order to accomplish these objectives we require that courses remain small (approximately 12 students), include an APA writing component, involve students in active information seeking through libraries and other information retrieval systems, and include an oral presentation.

Ideal Teaching Situation

On the face of things, teaching a seminar capstone appears to be an ideal teaching situation. We have small, manageable class sizes that allow for abundant discussion. The seminar format allows for meaningful participation, in-depth activities, and student ownership of the course. Because the course is at the end of the major and students likely have several choices about the capstone experience for which they sign up, we expect motivated students who are interested in the course topic to enroll. Furthermore, students have already gained the fundamental knowledge base that allows them to discuss topics at a more advanced level. Finally, students can bring skills (e.g., statistical proficiency) from prior course work. Nonetheless, too often these courses end up being much less than ideal teaching experiences. Often, the capstone does not live up to our expectations or those of our students.

Ten Things We Hate About Our Capstone Classes

Several factors can contribute to capstone classes being a less than ideal experience for students and faculty. We conceptualize these into three categories: (a) issues related to student skill level, (b) issues related to student expectations and behavior, and (c) issues related to faculty expectations and behavior. A mismatch between our expectations and reality can make teaching a capstone class an unexpectedly negative experience. Here, we list our "Top Ten" frustrations with our capstone experiences along with our "internal monologues" about those frustrations. The issues on our list are not mutually exclusive; many of these factors clearly interact with and influence one another.

Student Skill Level

The first category is related to our expectations of students' skill levels when they enroll in our capstone courses. Because students enrolled in capstone courses are nearing the end of their psychology matriculation, we expect that our curriculum has provided them with a certain set of skills and a significant knowledge base in psychology. However, this is not always the case.

1. Lack of integration/synthesis skills: "Have they taken any psychology classes at all?" Faculty often approach a capstone class as an opportunity to engage students in an advanced level of thinking about issues in the discipline. We often believe that because students have completed many hours of course work in psychology, they should be able to discuss and write about psychological concepts in a way that incorporates material from their previous courses. Furthermore, students should be able to apply psychological concepts learned in other courses to issues we discuss in the capstone course. In reality, students may not be functioning at this advanced level or have the skills to integrate material from the diverse set of courses they have taken as psychology majors. We may need to explicitly teach integration and synthesis skills, like any others. We might assume that students come to the end of their academic careers with these advanced skills, which might not be the case.

2. Poor professional communication skills: "I can't believe I'm reading this!" We may erroneously assume that by the time our students are seniors, they have engaged in extensive writing. Students may need more practice before they can write a polished paper. Even toward the end of the major, professors comment that students' writing skills are lacking (Fallahi, Wood,

& Austad, 2006). Besides having students with poor writing skills, we are often confronted with students who have had a dearth of oral communication experience. Many students may not have led a class discussion or attended to how their professors have led class discussion.

3. *Poor critical thinking skills: "What are they thinking? Are they thinking?"* In a similar vein, we may expect that senior capstone students will be well versed in the critical thinking skills we have attempted to impart during the course of their major (e.g., see Dunn, Halonen, & Smith, in press). Because many psychology professors emphasize the importance of developing critical thinking skills and because it is the focus of many curriculum decisions (Halpern, 2002), we may assume that these skills are polished by the time students enter our capstone courses. However, many students may not have had adequate practice in developing these skills (Edman, 2007). Their performance may not live up to our expectations.

Student Expectations and Behaviors

A second set of issues involves misaligned student expectations about the capstone course, often leading to troublesome behaviors from students. Students may not expect the advanced demands of a capstone class, and the strategies they have used in previous classes may not be successful.

4. *The teacher should "teach" the students: "Why do I have to do all the work? I'm paying to be taught."* The activities typical of a capstone experience, in which students may lead class discussion, design their own integrative projects, or write original research, may differ in important ways from what students have experienced in their other classes. Some students view the instructor's role as one of an active "teacher" and the student as a passive consumer of information that is imparted by the instructor. In fact, students tend to remark that they are customers buying products and services from the university (Zinn, 2007). Therefore, if professors ask students to take an active role in class, some students may feel that they are not "getting their money's worth"

5. *Workload expectations: "This class is too hard/too much work/too much* ____.*"* Depending on how it is designed, the intellectual or workload demands of a capstone class may be greater than students have experienced in other classes. These are often the most labor-intensive courses in the major and students may balk at the requirements. We also know that, in general, professor and student expectations of how much time should be devoted to course

work are not in agreement (Zinn et al., in press). In fact, students report that "outstanding effort" would require only two-thirds of the study time that faculty expect.

6. Senioritis: "I'm graduating—who cares?" "I shouldn't have to work this hard my senior year. I already got into grad school." Although "senioritis," or a drop-off in student motivation late in the senior year, is an acknowledged phenomenon among high school seniors (e.g., Hoover, 2003), similar factors may be operating among college seniors, as well. For example, a significant motivator for many students is the prospect of getting into graduate school. By the second semester of senior year, this one-time motivator is usually no longer relevant, with students already having been accepted to graduate schools. Many other students have already secured jobs, and getting one letter grade higher in a course is not a strong motivator. Finally, students may have many competing activities during their senior year (e.g., farewell events and time spent with friends).

Faculty Expectations and Behaviors

Finally, we may have a problem with our own expectations of advanced students. Their skills may not be at the level we hope. In addition, we may not recognize the different set of teaching skills required for a capstone seminar course. Much of our training may have been in how to teach introductory courses; thus, our skills may not be as proficient for capstone courses.

7. All the students are ready to be "capped off": "These students are graduating???" Faculty may expect that, as seniors, all students will be "ready" for graduation and will have developed the requisite academic and intellectual skills. We may lose sight of the fact that students in our capstone classes, although they may be at the same place in their academic histories, may not have homogeneous motivation or skill levels. Faculty need to recognize that there is more variability in students' skills than we might expect.

8. Expectations for student interest in a faculty member's specialty area: "Everyone should love my favorite topic." Faculty who teach capstone seminars in specialty areas may be surprised and disappointed if students do not share their excitement about and engagement in the course. For example, we teach capstone courses in Addictive Behaviors (MJR), in Performance Management (TEZ), and in Primate Behavior (SCB). The specialized topics that we have spent years studying may not automatically engender the same level of excitement in our students.

9. I should "impart my wisdom": "Everyone needs to know what I think about this topic." This is closely related to the previous point. Faculty who have spent years immersed in a research area may have insights or strong opinions about it. Therefore it is tempting to use our capstone course as an opportunity to lecture about our favorite topics. However, this may not be the best practice for a capstone course.

10. Faculty expectations about teaching demands: "This is too much work. This was supposed my easy/fun class." We may have the expectation that teaching a course in one's specialty area to a small group of advanced students will be easier or will carry a lighter workload than other types of courses. If (or when) it turns out that the course is more work than expected, faculty frustration can result.

Moving From Hating to Loving Your Capstone

How can you have that "peak" capstone experience without feeling like Sisyphus having to push that giant rock up a mountain over and over again? The keys to ensuring a "peak" capstone experience include setting appropriate expectations for both you and your students, and good course design that will augment the skills that are often lacking in capstone students. In this section we offer suggestions for meeting the challenges that can occur when teaching a capstone course. We believe it is essential to create a course that integrates the students' previous experiences with different areas of psychology, engages them in analysis of information, and further develops written and oral communication skills.

Techniques to Help You Love Your Capstone Course

Course planning: Make the implicit explicit. Organization is often the key to success in a capstone course, in part because students often have diverse expectations about the course. Creating clear guidelines for discussion and writing assignments can improve the experience for students and faculty. Because students' writing and discussion skills are frequently not where we thought they would be, and because faculty expectations about the homogeneity of student skill are often incorrect, we might not provide the appropriate level of structure in a capstone course. One way to create awareness of skill levels is to require students to engage in a self-assessment at the beginning of the course. In this way they can reflect on their current level of professional development and their strengths and weaknesses (Sasser, 2005). Faculty can then use these reflections to discuss the expectations for the course and provide guidance tailored to the needs and interests of the students.

Faculty can also use the first class meetings to discuss workload requirements for the course. Using this approach, faculty can provide students with a rationale for why they have chosen specific assignments. By walking students through the goals of each assignment, students will be less likely to think of the course requirements as "busywork," and more likely to see the assignments as fair assessments of their skills (Tata, 1999). Students might also be willing to work harder in a class if they understand the rationale behind the assignments. Another technique is to provide the class with the course objectives and allow them to design assignments and activities that will help them meet the objectives.

Simply setting goals for the course is not enough. Instructors need to be explicit in describing how students will achieve these goals, as well as outlining specific contingencies. For example, if one of the goals is improving writing ability, teachers could set contingencies for completing multiple drafts of a paper. Teachers could award points not only for the final draft but also for improvements in the paper throughout the course. In addition, grading rubrics should reflect the goals instructors have set for the course, assigning "the highest point values to those aspects of the assignment the instructor deems most important" (Morgan & Morgan, 2006, p. 55).

Encouraging "good" discussion. Active class discussion can improve student learning (McKeachie, 2002). However, our impression is that some students believe merely talking equals good discussion. Even at the senior level many students respond to the prompt to discuss the readings with "I found X interesting." Although we are pleased that students found something interesting, this is not the type of discussion that encourages critical thinking about the topic. One way of improving class discussion is to provide students with resources on how to lead a class discussion (see Zinn & Saville, 2006). Authors suggest several key techniques for having a good class discussion, including the importance of preparation, ideas for facilitating discussion, ways to ask questions that encourage discussion, and evaluating the discussion at the end of the class period.

One technique for improving student discussion uses Questions, Quotations, and Talking Points (QQTPs), and involves students constructing discussion-oriented questions, quotations from the reading material, and talking points that students can bring up in class (Connor-Greene, 2005). Connor-Greene (2005) suggests asking students to construct questions that are at the higher levels of Bloom's taxonomy—analysis, synthesis, and evaluation (Anderson et al., 2001) and that cannot be answered simply by extracting factual information from the text. These types of questions encourage students to integrate and apply material to novel contexts. Encouraging students to identify quotations that are particularly compelling or controversial often excites class discussion as well. Finally, "talking points encourage students to construct, organize, and focus their ideas prior to class discussion" (Connor-Greene, 2005, p. 173), which can be especially beneficial for students who are hesitant to speak. By using talking points, all students will have points to bring up in class and should not feel as though they have been put on the spot during discussion.

We have had some success in using QQTPs in our capstone courses. Specifically, during end-of-semester formal evaluations students have typically responded well to the question "How valuable were the QQTPs to your learning experience?" (i.e., receiving an average of 4.27/5.00). In addition, students often provide positive open-ended statements about the QQTPs (e.g., "I *definitely* think you should continue with the QQTPs; they were very thought-provoking" and "This course was set up in such a way that it facilitated great discussions and learning. We were able to present topics to each other and engage in very in-depth talk about the material at hand"). These comments mirror results presented by Connor-Greene (2005).

Pre-class questions (PCQs) can help set the context of meaningful discussion in class (Benedict & Anderton, 2004). PCQs, a component of Just-in-Time Teaching (JiTT), typically include short-answer essay questions as well as one difficult multiple-choice question that students answer before class. It is also possible to use application-oriented questions, whereby students have to complete an assignment before coming to class. Teachers can then review these answers or assignments before class. By using the answers provided by students, teachers can tailor material in class to focus on the more difficult material. For example, in a health behavior capstone, one PCQ required students to estimate the cost of healthy food versus unhealthy food for a family of four for a week. Students submitted this information before class, and then the discussion leader (either the instructor or another student in class) used this information to structure that day's class. Other PCQs can directly model the discussion questions in class. For example, "Compare and contrast the Health Belief Model approach to flu vaccinations and exercise behavior."

The instructor can start out with this question knowing that all students have answered the question prior to coming to class, and also knowing what typical misinterpretations there are about the concept. Because of the likely diversity of responses, interesting class discussions often result.

Another strategy to improve discussion involves increasing ownership in the discussion. For example, in a capstone course on addictive behaviors, each student selects an addictive behavior to study for the duration of the semester. Students are responsible for relating the readings to their specific addictive behavior and sharing it with the class. This process makes the student responsible for the learning of their peers. Each of these methods capitalizes on perhaps the most important part of having a good class discussion—preparation. Furthermore, these methods impose contingencies for being prepared to participate in the class discussion (see above). For example, QQTPs and participation in class discussion contribute to the students' grades. To use each of these methods effectively it helps to clarify with students the purpose of having a class discussion, rather than simply lecturing. It would also be beneficial if teachers used some class time at the beginning of the course to explain the purpose of each of these techniques as well as how to complete these assignments effectively (Zinn & Saville, 2006).

Improving writing skills. In the capstone course, students are wrapping up their psychology major experiences. Therefore, one important task of the course is to make sure the students' writing skills are up to par. One strategy to motivate students to turn in their best work is to make writing expectations clear in the syllabus. In order for writing assignments to be successful, instructors need to explain both the purpose of the assignment and the expectations for that assignment (Morgan & Morgan, 2006). We may assume that students know that writing is important and take for granted that they would understand the purpose of the writing we assign in the capstone. Based on our top 10 list, this would be a big mistake.

One way instructors can design their capstone courses to address writing skills is to use a portfolio, "a systematic collection of a student's work over time" (Eagan, McCabe, Semenchuk, & Butler, 2003, p. 234). Portfolios can include rough drafts of assignments, related class questions or QQTPs (see above), or other material relevant to the writing assignments in class. By using a student portfolio, the focus is not on one draft of a paper but on the process of constructing and formulating ideas, editing, and continual improvement. Because there is a focus on presenting their best work, students often show increased motivation to complete a good product.

Another way to focus on improving writing skills in the capstone course is to use peer reviews or collaborative writing assignments. In some capstones it makes sense to create teams in order to simulate the work environments in the real world. On the job after college, students will be required to research, write, and present material in a collaborative format. In fact, two of the top five most important skills that employers value are the ability to get along with others and the ability to work with people as a team (Landrum & Harrold, 2003). Peer review of writing products can be effective in improving writing as peers will often address errors and attend to details that students might miss in rereading their own work (Dunn, 1999). Students have also reported that writing peer reviews is even more beneficial than receiving peer reviews, and that they better understood the professional peer review process by participating (White & Kirby, 2005). Some researchers have used a double-blind peer review process, more akin to professional journal reviews (White & Kirby, 2005). Other assignments can use open reviews, depending on the purpose. For example, in one of our capstone writing assignments, students wrote an article about a particular issue and the name of the writer was known to the "editor" (i.e., it was not blind review). The editor's job was to suggest changes and provide the feedback needed to make the article worthy of publication. Thus, the student serving as the "editor" took partial responsibility for the quality of the work. Some instructors prefer peer review in a situation where both the reviewer and the original author have ownership in the final product and final grade.

Including diverse writing assignments mirrors the types of writing our students will do in the workforce. Nontraditional writing assignments, such as newsletters, letters to individuals involved in public policy, budget rationales, book chapters, grant proposals, and letters to parents can highlight strengths and weaknesses of writing ability and critical thinking. By incorporating different types of writing assignments into the capstone course, we can accomplish two primary objectives. First, we will likely help students improve their writing skills, especially for the writing that they are most likely to engage in after graduation. Second, we can (hopefully) increase motivation for completing quality assignments by addressing issues that appear to be more relevant to our students' lives.

For any type of writing assignment, instructors should be explicit about the purpose of the assignment and how they will grade the assignment (i.e., a grading rubric). Students often have difficulty with assignments because their expectations do not match those of their professors. One way for instructors to clarify the expectations is to use an analogy that college students can understand and apply to their own lives. The work involved in a capstone course is similar to the work involved in owning a dog. You need to constantly take care of your dog and you cannot do the work all in one night. For example, you need to buy dog food, feed the dog, take the dog out after the dog eats, and repeat the cycle. This analogy reminds students that they need to nurture their papers over time, continuing to refine the product throughout the semester. Faculty need to assess the paper as it progresses rather than just grading the final product. Research shows that requiring multiple drafts of papers both improves writing and reduces the anxiety students feel about the writing process (Morgan & Morgan, 2006).

Improving information literacy. Undergraduate students primarily receive information in the forms of textbooks and easily understood review articles. Like good mother birds, textbook writers chew up the existing literature and regurgitate it into a content that is digestible for the students. The capstone class often involves reading primary literature, including material that the instructor assigns and often material that is the product of students' own primary literature search. This search can be a problem for students. Although faculty may be able to quickly identify the quality from the name of the source, students struggle more in the evaluation process. In one of our capstone classes, we collected responses from students about their abilities to identify good primary sources. Student comments about the process of evaluating sources include two opposite problems. "I'm not good at evaluating sources. I pretty much believe everything I read," and "My weakness is evaluation. I don't know what to believe." When asked about their weakest skills as researchers, four students out of eight students enrolled in an addictive behaviors capstone mentioned evaluation of sources. It is important to set up a course structure that helps students evaluate the quality and timeliness of different sources. One possibility is to include evaluation of sources as an additional component of the reference section. This practice will open discussion of explicit criteria to help students in the process.

Connecting the island to the mainland. The specific capstone topic is important, but typically our students do not become specialists after only one semester. The in-depth capstone experience is like an appetizer—hopefully tasty but increasing the anticipation of the main course to follow. Therefore the capstone instructor is well advised to keep the specific course content integrated to the field of psychology as a whole. It is tempting to think that senior-level students can see the "big picture" of how the multiple strands of psychology fit together. In reality, our experience is that many students will not make these connections on their own. Explicit exercises that require students to connect their learning in the capstone with material from other courses may be necessary. For example, students might be required to discuss how theories from the capstone course relate to topics covered in a different course. Having students construct diagrams or maps showing the interrelationships among different domains can also be useful.

"Instructing" a capstone course. The role of instructor can vary widely among capstones. A similarity that we share is our desire to encourage students to shape their own learning experiences. We engage in intentional behaviors to distance ourselves as the only source of information. We may sit in the corner of the seminar room (even through seemingly unbearable silence during discussion). One of the most difficult tasks is to remain silent and "let the students do the talking" (Finkel, 2000, p. 31). Our approach is to scaffold the class but let the students create the masterpiece. Providing limited guidance in class requires constant monitoring and cheerleading combined with occasionally sharp prodding from the instructor. It can be exhausting and exhilarating all at the same time. When it works, it results in student comments that reflect the process. "The semester-long research project was put together in such a way that it pushed me to move beyond the things I've done the past four years, and on to the level of scholarship that I hope to find in future programs."

Reflection. The ending of the semester-long capstone experience is educationally momentous. Reflection on the accomplishments of the course can include integration of the college experience as a whole. As one student stated, "When I first looked at the syllabus for this course, I almost ran away.... I enjoyed the final project and it was a great assignment to end my senior year because I was able to apply everything that I have learned up to that point. It was this assignment where I put everything to use, even things that I learned in my psychology 200 and 201 course. I had to pull out some of my old notes just to refresh my memory on statistical tools and the overall research setup."

Capstone courses are often smaller than other classes and may require more in-depth discussion and writing. This type of interaction enables faculty to get to know students better and to appreciate the growth of individual students. Formal written reflection or informal discussion of reflection can provide closure to the semester for the instructor as well as the students. As one of our students stated, "This class was an eye-opening experience. After completing the work for the class, I look back in amazement. I would have never thought that I could write a paper over 20 pages on such an extensive topic. With all the work that we had to do throughout the semester, I really felt like I was completing the necessary steps to become an expert on a given topic." Comments like these can motivate the exhausted instructor to consider engaging in the process again the next semester.

Conclusion

In fact, we do not hate our capstone courses. However, teaching these courses requires certain considerations and a heavy dose of reality. We have to teach the students from where they are, not from where we want them to be. And even though we love teaching, we might not be where we want to be in terms of our proficiency at teaching these types of courses. As always, classes will have different personalities, skill sets, and motivations. It is up to us to reach into our pedagogical toolbox to address these differences each time we take on the challenge of teaching a capstone class. Despite the challenges (for both instructors and students) that are inherent in the capstone course, the results of a well-designed capstone experience are more than worth the work. Although we may spend time bemoaning all the "things we hate" about our capstones, in the end, there is one big "thing we love"—graduating psychology majors who are ready to take their skills with them to the next phase of their lives.

Recommended Readings

Brewer, C. L. (1997). Undergraduate education in psychology: Will the mermaids sing? *American Psychologist, 52*, 434–441.

Perlman, B., & McCann, L. I. (1999). The structure of the psychology undergraduate curriculum. *Teaching of Psychology, 26*, 171–176.

Sasser, J. R. (2005). Designing and implementing a gerontology capstone seminar: Synthesis and action. *Educational Gerontology, 31*, 89–101.

References

Anderson, L.W., Krathwohl, D. R., Airasian, P.W., Cruikshank, K.A., Mayer, R.E., Pintrich, P.R., Raths, J., & Wittrock, M. C. (Eds.). (2001). *A taxonomy for learning, teaching, and assessing: A revision of Bloom's taxonomy of educational objectives*. New York: Longman.

Benedict, J. O., & Anderton, J. B. (2004). Applying the just-in-time teaching approach to teaching statistics. *Teaching of Psychology, 31,* 197–199.

Brewer, C. L., Hopkins, J. R., Kimble, G.A., Matlin, M.W., McCann, L.I., NcNeil, O.V. et al. (1993). Curriculum. In T. V. McGovern (Ed.), *Handbook for enhancing undergraduate education in psychology* (pp. 161–182). Washington, DC: American Psychological Association.

Brewer, C. L. (1997). Undergraduate education in psychology: Will the mermaids sing? *American Psychologist, 52,* 434–441.

Connor-Greene, P. A. (2005). Fostering meaningful classroom discussion: Student generated questions, quotations, and talking-points. *Teaching of Psychology, 32,* 173–175.

Dunn, D. S. (1999). Collaborative writing in a statistics and research methods course. *Teaching of Psychology, 23,* 38–40.

Dunn, D. S., Halonen, J. S., & Smith, R. A. (Eds.). (in press). *Teaching critical thinking in psychology: A handbook of best practices.* Malden, MA: Wiley-Blackwell.

Eagan, P. J., McCabe, P., Semenchuk, D., & Butler, J. (2003). Using portfolios to teach test-scoring skills: A preliminary analysis. *Teaching of Psychology, 30,* 233–253.

Edman, L. (2007). Are they ready yet? Epistemological development and critical thinking. In B. K. Saville, T. E. Zinn, S. A. Meyers, & J. R. Stowell (Eds.), *Essays from e-xcellence in teaching, 2006* (chap. 1). Retrieved September 15, 2008, from the Society for the Teaching of Psychology Web site: http://teachpsych.org/resources/e-books/eit2006/eit2006.php.

Fallahi, C. R., Wood, R. M., & Austad, C. S. (2006). A program for improving undergraduate psychology students' basic writing skills. *Teaching of Psychology, 33,* 171–175.

Finkel, D. (2000). *Teaching with your mouth shut.* Portsmouth, NH: Heinemann.

Halpern, D. F. (2002). Teaching for critical thinking: A four-part model to enhance thinking skills. In S. F. Davis & W. Buskist (Eds.), *The teaching of psychology: Essays in honor of Wilbert J. McKeachie and Charles L. Brewer* (pp. 91–105). Mahwah, NJ: Erlbaum.

Hoover, E. (2003, June). Fighting "senioritis." *Chronicle of Higher Education, 49*(42), A30–A31.

Landrum, R. E., & Harrold, R. (2003). What employers want from psychology graduates. *Teaching of Psychology, 30,* 131–133.

McKeachie, W. J. (2002). *Teaching tips: Strategies, research, and theory for college and university teachers.* Boston, MA: Houghton Mifflin.

Morgan, R. K., & Morgan, D. L. (2006). Writing in psychology. In W. Buskist & S. F. Davis (Eds.), *Handbook of the teaching of psychology* (pp. 54–58). Malden, MA: Blackwell.

Perlman, B., & McCann, L. I. (1999). The structure of the psychology undergraduate curriculum. *Teaching of Psychology, 26*, 171–176.

Sasser, J. R. (2005). Designing and implementing a gerontology capstone seminar: Synthesis and action. *Educational Gerontology, 31*, 89–101.

Tata, J. (1999). Grade distributions, grading procedures, and students' evaluations of instructors: A justice perspective. *Journal of Psychology, 133*, 263–271.

White, T. L., & Kirby, B. J. (2005). 'Tis better to give than to receive: An undergraduate peer review project. *Teaching of Psychology, 32*, 259–261.

Zinn, T. E. (2007, May) *Students as customers: Are we selling our wares?* Invited presentation given at the Teaching Institute for the Association for Psychological Science. Washington, DC.

Zinn, T., Magnotti, J., Marchuk, K., Schultz, B., Luther, A., & Varfolomeeva, V. (in press). Performance vs. effort: More about what makes the grade. *Teaching of Psychology*.

Zinn, T. E., & Saville, B.K. (2006). Leading discussions. In W. Buskist & S.F. Davis (Eds.), *Handbook of the teaching of psychology* (pp. 85–89). Malden, MA: Blackwell.

16 Writing for Psychology Majors as a Developmental Process

Bernard C. Beins, Randolph A. Smith, and *Dana S. Dunn*

Scientific writing need not be—though it often is—dull. This I believe in spite of much evidence to the contrary.

—BRUNER, 1942, P. 52

Katherine Bruner, an editorial assistant at the American Psychological Association (APA), provided some sage and humorous comments about manuscripts she processed for one of APA's journals. She was not the first to imply or state that at least some psychologists were deficient in writing. In the first APA style guide of 1929, the authors suggested that "the writer who is incompetent in spelling, grammar, or syntax should seek help" ("Instructions in Regard," 1929, p. 38). Psychology teachers today recognize that students need at least as much guidance in developing their writing skills as would-be authors did in Bruner's era.

> Why are writing skills important for psychology students? Educators have argued that, at a deeply practical level, writing sustains American life and popular culture in many ways that are clear and in some that are rarely noticed. Most people understand that somebody has to write a book or a short story. But there is not a movie, advertising jingle, magazine, political campaign, newspaper, theatrical production, hit record, comic book, or instructional manual that does not begin with writers and rest on writing. (*The Neglected "R,"* 2003, p. 10)

Perhaps a more obvious practical reason for developing sound writing skills is that job applicants who cannot write well are at a disadvantage relative to good writers for many attractive jobs, and if they do land one of those jobs, they are less likely to get raises and promotions (*Writing: A Ticket to Work,* 2004).

Furthermore, for the betterment of the discipline, competence in writing is of paramount importance. If psychologists are interested in reaching the general public, active and energetic prose will always engage the audience more than dull and turgid prose will. This fact was not lost on prominent figures in the history of psychology, like William James and Joseph Jastrow, both of whom wrote with a facility that many people would like to have (Sommer, 2006). In part, writers need to find a balance between lively prose that is relatively devoid of important content and dense prose that is relatively devoid of interest. Neither accomplishes the mission intended by the author (Beins & Beins, 2008). It is probably a good idea to keep in mind Holland's (2002, ¶ 4) suggestion that "science writing is not so much about science, but about people—human problems and their solutions, curiosity and discovery." That is, in many respects, what psychology is all about.

Psychology teachers also spend a great deal of time instructing students in APA style, which according to Madigan, Johnson, and Linton (1995), is a model for the way we think about psychological phenomena. This idea alone provides the impetus for teachers to emphasize writing skills—because the way we write says something about the psychologists that we are. Unfortunately, many students (and some psychologists) regard APA style as something of an impediment to their writing predispositions (e.g., Roediger, 2004). And the little humor that once existed in the APA publication guidelines seems to have disappeared. For instance, Anderson and Valentine (1944) noted with some wit that writers should take care in using hyphens: "It is only in the English language that a gentleman can take unto himself a gentle-woman and beget a generation of gentle children" (p. 352). APA style has, for many, become the style we love to hate (Beins, 2006b).

Fortunately, psychology teachers have recognized the importance of writing and have documented strategies that promote the development of this valuable skill. Between 1975 and 2007, the journal *Teaching of Psychology* published 123 articles whose keywords included *writing*. Obviously, not all articles focused on the improvement of writing specifically, but they all pointed to the utility that psychology teachers associate with writing.

One point that teachers and authors recognize is that writing is an arduous task at times. (Reading the writing of students just developing their skills may be even more so.) Students (and writers of all stripes) have difficulty penning interesting and informative prose if they have little interest in what they write. The first trick is to generate that interest. Once the interest shows itself, the next trick is to convey the complex ideas clearly, simply, and cogently. This ability is a major source of the problem: It is terribly difficult to write both simply and cogently, but those characteristics are imperative if one is to engage a reader.

As hard as it may be to write well, it is just as difficult to teach students to do so. This difficulty may be why writing receives so little attention in the educational system. According to *Writing and School Reform* (2006), writing tends to take a back seat to other parts of the curriculum associated with high-stakes testing: "Both the teaching and practice of writing are increasingly short-changed throughout the school and college years" (p. 3). Instruction in writing is time- and labor-intensive, and teachers outside of English often receive little or no instruction in how to teach writing and may not have developed a high level of proficiency themselves. At the same time, teachers would do well to keep in mind Bruner's (1942) admonition about producing deadly prose: "It is neither good science nor good common sense to put one's reader to sleep and then expect him to grasp the highlights of an experiment, the significance of which one has assiduously buried" (p. 53).

In this chapter, we will discuss important issues in teaching students to write well and bring their ideas to life. This process must take into account the level of the student, the nature of the writing, the process of revision and peer review, the effectiveness of collaborative writing projects, and the development of skill in using APA style. Because good writing is not easy, it should come as no surprise that teaching good writing is very difficult. We hope to identify elements of best practices that lead to student successes.

Pitched Perfectly: Appropriate Levels for Writing Assignments

To be effective where learning and desired learning outcomes are concerned, writing assignments should reflect the level of the relevant course. Most undergraduate psychology programs probably have three distinct course levels. Although the labels attached to these levels may vary from school to school, we will use the familiar beginner, intermediate, and advanced, making note of the requirements and suggesting sample writing assignments within each. These levels are consistent with the APA's document, *Teaching, Learning, and Assessing in a Developmentally Coherent Curriculum* (American Psychological Association, 2008). The approach to writing that we describe here provides a process that complements those outlined in that document.

Beginner-Level Courses

Beginning- or introductory-level courses generally provide a broad overview of the discipline. Introductory psychology or general psychology is the paradigmatic example of the beginner course, although courses such as the psychology of adjustment and life-span development may also fit in this lower level category. As a beginning course in the psychology major, introductory psychology or its equivalent introduces students to the discipline's vocabulary and basic concepts, its variety of methodologies (perhaps with a primary focus on experimentation), and how students can apply main ideas toward understanding everyday experiences. Given the survey nature of introductory-level courses, they usually have no prerequisites and serve to prepare students for the more demanding work offered in intermediate and advanced courses.

What sorts of writing assignments are best suited to beginner-level courses? The most appropriate assignments are those that involve some degree of self-exploration in which students can write about how course concepts help to inform their experiences. Such assignments could include writing a paper relating some course concept (e.g., short-term memory, cognitive dissonance) to a personal experience, writing and sending a letter to friends or family members about what students are learning in the class (e.g., Abramson & Hershey, 1999; Dunn, 1996; Keith, 1999), or simply describing a psychological topic in the student's own words (e.g., describing how children behave in each of Piaget or Kohlberg's respective developmental stages).

Faculty members, like their students, often worry about the requirements for beginning-level course assignments. We believe that several shorter writing assignments are a better idea in beginning courses than only one or two longer papers (the goal early in their academic careers should be to help students learn to generate prose with a reasonable amount of effort—more focused, in-depth assignments are best saved for later in their psychology education). Descriptions of brief assignments suggest that the norm is somewhere between two and five double-spaced pages. Instructors should mark grammar and punctuation, however time-consuming the exercise may be. (Having students exchange, read, and edit the work of peers during class is one way to decrease the time spent on correcting the papers' mechanics; see, e.g., Dunn, 2008; Elbow & Belanoff, 2002). Students can, but do not necessarily need to, cite specific works from the psychological literature unless a particular reading (e.g., a journal article, a textbook chapter) is the focus of the assignment. Dunn (2007) also provided a variety of relevant writing assignments.

The one main question faculty ask about lower level writing assignments is whether students should have to learn or know American Psychological Association or APA style (APA, 2010) in order to complete the assignments. Although learning APA format early may be desirable, we need to point out that most of the students who enroll in beginning-level psychology courses are there out of interest or to satisfy some general education requirement; few will go on to major in psychology. Thus, although learning APA style writing could arguably help anyone think more clearly or critically (Dunn, 2008; Madigan et al., 1995), we are not sure the time and effort to do so—not to mention the necessary grading and feedback on formatted papers—is worth the effort at this basic level. Instructors, of course, must decide this matter for themselves.

As an alternative, we recommend saving the teaching and learning of APA format for intermediate-level courses, notably research methods and statistics. Thus, instructors of lower level courses may allow students to submit their work completed in the style they already know, which is usually MLA but can sometimes be APA or another approach (in practice, perhaps, the main issue for student learning here is how to cite works correctly in the text as well as to reference them properly at its end). A final alternative in the introductory course is for instructors to specify their own style for the papers. We believe there is one exception to this suggestion that formatting issues are of secondary importance: when students take a lab course that accompanies the introductory course.

Case Example

When students begin their careers as psychology majors, they may be unfamiliar with highly structured writing that relies on evidence or data. As such, an early start in an introductory psychology laboratory can foster the rudiments of disciplined writing. At Ithaca College, all psychology majors and minors must complete the General Psychology Laboratory. The course is set up so that the faculty member supervising the course creates the labs and the scoring rubrics associated with each writing assignment. About 150 students complete the lab each academic year.

It would obviously be impossible for a single faculty member to read and score five or six lab papers for each student. Consequently, the department identifies undergraduate lab assistants (LAs) who conduct the lab and score the

APA-style reports according to a rubric that the professor generates. Each semester there are usually seven to nine lab sections that can each accommodate a maximum of nine students. The undergraduate LAs score the papers, with the professor doing a reliability check on a subset of the papers. (The LAs must enroll in a Laboratory Techniques course that introduces them to the laboratory exercises and exposes them to the use of scoring rubrics.)

This setup allows the Psychology Department to offer a lab course for the introductory course that (a) exposes students to varied research methodologies that psychologists use, (b) provides an introduction to descriptive statistics and to the use of SPSS, and (c) ensures frequent and consistent writing of APA-style research reports. Ithaca College students entering as first-year students are considered above average, at least as reflected in their mean SAT scores and high school rank. So their writing is reasonably proficient as such things go. As upper level students, many can communicate quite cogently and in relatively error-free APA style format (Beins, 2006a). Because the students take several psychology courses that involve writing, along with other writing-intensive courses, it is impossible to document the introductory lab experience as a singular cause of proficient writing; however, it seems reasonable to attribute the orientation toward good writing as partially attributable to the early writing experience.

Intermediate-Level Courses

Intermediate-level courses should build on basic principles presented in the beginning courses; indeed, introductory psychology tends to be a prerequisite for later courses. The chief purpose of intermediate courses in psychology is to expand students' knowledge and familiarity with research methodologies and designs. The middle courses may also be the entry point for the major, so that students usually must enroll in a course in research methods and one in statistics or, with increasing frequency, two sequenced courses covering these topics. Other intermediate-level courses can include subarea surveys that provide depth in the core areas of the discipline (e.g., cognitive psychology, biopsychology, social psychology, personality, developmental psychology). Whether focused on method or topical content, intermediate courses should provide students with a language for describing behavior (e.g., the predictors for the presence or absence of helping or prosocial behavior associated with social psychology). Finally, intermediate courses should trigger significant personal engagement in students both in and outside of the classroom.

In contrast to writing assignments in beginning-level courses, such assignments in intermediate-level classes should require use and mastery of APA style (e.g., Dunn & Smith, 2008; Schmidt & Dunn, 2007). The ideal way to learn APA style is by conducting some piece of empirical research from start to finish, including writing a formal research report based on the APA's standard journal article format. At Moravian College, for example, students individually conceive and conduct an original piece of research during a required two-semester statistics and research methods course that they typically complete during the sophomore year.

As noted elsewhere in this chapter, there are many books available that can help students learn to craft APA style papers. Nonempirical papers, such as research summaries or brief literature reviews, can also follow APA style, although style issues here often involve only references and perhaps levels of headings. For example, a student might write a literature review of recent studies on the physiology of sleep and dreaming for a course in psychobiology.

Whether an empirically based paper or an integrative review, assignments should be lengthy enough that students need to create a thesis, produce an argument to support the thesis, identify relevant research and theory, and generate a compelling conclusion, a task that probably requires at least 10 to 15 pages. Naturally, instructors can craft and assign other less traditional writing exercises; however, requiring use of APA style tends to be a touchstone for courses represented in this level. At Ithaca College, the Research Team experience provides further writing experience. Psychology majors complete three semesters of research with a single professor in a team setting (see Beins, 2008). During this time, they engage in original research and write APA-style research reports based on the research. It is also common for students, in conjunction with faculty researchers, to create posters that they present at various research venues (e.g., APA convention, Eastern Psychological Association convention, Association for Psychological Science convention, Society for Personality and Social Psychology convention, National Conference on Undergraduate Research, Eastern Conferences Science Conference, University of Scranton Psychology Conference). Students at other schools may also have the chance to present their research projects at such conferences and at on-campus research festivals.

The combination of experience in the introductory laboratory course and the three semesters on Research Team provides students with significant exposure to engaging in scientific writing. At the introductory level, undergraduate LAs review their papers for content and style (including APA style) based on a scoring rubric. At the Research Team level, faculty evaluate the work. At Ithaca College, the students often show considerable understanding of APA style, with fewer errors than some manuscripts written by PhD-level psychologists. As one might expect, the content of the papers is that of a new researcher who does not have the breadth of knowledge that one expects from a researcher who has completed graduate work.

Reaction papers. Teachers have used extended writing assignments to enhance learning (Beins, 1993; Bryant & Benjamin, 1999), but even simple exercises can improve student writing. For example, Keith's (1999) students wrote letters to friends, relatives, or parents about psychological topics. Such tasks facilitate the learning of psychological content and help students with their writing. Another approach to writing is reaction papers (Procidano, 1991). Reaction papers associated with topics in content areas like mental illness undoubtedly have intrinsic interest, but research-related writing can also spark student interest. One of this chapter's authors (BCB) uses research-related scenarios as the basis for reaction papers. Such assignments give students practice both in writing and in critical thinking about research.

One example of a reaction paper relates to beliefs by students (and many others) that their driving abilities do not deteriorate if they drive while talking on a cell phone. After a brief class discussion on this issue, students read what others have written on the topic, including a summary of a research report, an editorial written by a student for a college newspaper, and a news report about laws prohibiting cell phone use during driving. Based on the readings, students evaluate the credibility of various arguments and viewpoints, then present their views on the statement, with supporting statements. The details of the assignment appear in Table 16.1. This kind of assignment relies on students' abilities to evaluate research reports in the popular media and news/opinion related to it. As the students generate their arguments, they develop their writing skills.

This type of assignment illustrates to students that people can raise different arguments in support or in refutation of some position but that not all of those arguments are equally credible. The assignment also encourages students to evaluate the messages that people proffer to see which of them are

Table 16-1
A Sample Reaction Paper

Reaction Paper: Some states have laws against driving while talking on cell phones. *Some people don't like the laws.* Other people seem to *ignore the laws.* A number of different studies have reached the same result, including research showing *deficits similar to that while driving drunk* and *slower driving.*

How credible are the different points of view given here? Do you believe the research that is cited here (which appeared in scientific journals and was done by credible researchers) is relevant to real life? Should there be laws against cell phone use and driving? Are the research results likely to change your behaviors about driving and talking? Please explain your responses.

Note: Underlined material indicates hyperlinked sources that students use to create their reaction papers. The Web site with the links is http://www.ithaca.edu/beins/methods/methsyl.htm. (c) 2006 Bernard C. Beins.

most valid. As students develop their critical thinking skills, they are also practicing writing skills. When they encounter arguments and counterarguments, the students have to reconcile the different perspectives and generate a conclusion based on the strengths of the arguments. There are several useful questions to which students should attend in writing a reaction paper (How to Write a Response Paper, n.d.; Response/Reaction Paper, n.d.):

1. What are the important issues or questions that the writer(s) have raised? Are there contradictory viewpoints?
2. Does the author have a viewpoint or perspective that is driving the discussion?
3. What evidence does the author bring to the discussion, and how credible is that evidence? Does some evidence support an argument whereas other evidence refutes it?
4. Do the authors oversimplify their arguments or fail to present important evidence so they omit discussion of issues that are important to the topic?
5. What is your reaction to the arguments? Can you develop a logical argument to reconcile different viewpoints, or is one viewpoint superior to another?

The reaction papers can rely on varied sources of information and different types of arguments, such as evaluation of the ethics of a research project, the adequacy of a project's research design, and why people in a certain circumstance (e.g., supposedly witnessing the murder of Kitty Genovese) acted as they did. Thus, the writing practice is the center around which various topics circle, and the goal is that students learn to evaluate evidence and draw conclusions that they can logically support.

Literature reviews. Lamar University has two required research courses in its curriculum, the first of which (Methods in Psychology) serves as an intermediate-level course. Students complete research projects in the second course (Experimental Psychology), so the first course's writing assignment serves as a bridge between the introductory course and the advanced courses. Students compile a literature review on a specific, narrow topic (proposed by the student and approved by the instructor [RAS]). Because Methods in Psychology serves as students' introduction to research methods in the discipline (other than a chapter in General Psychology), the focus of the review is somewhat different from the focus of a typical literature review that serves as the introduction in an empirical research report. In this assignment, students not only conduct a review of literature but also focus their attention on the research process. For each article in the literature review, students must include information about the purpose of the study, the researchers' hypothesis, the research participants, the researchers' methods, the results obtained, how the results contributed to the existing knowledge, and a scientific evaluation of the merits and limitations of the study.

Because this literature review assignment is a bridge assignment to the department's upper level courses, the grading follows suit—it focuses on both grammar and APA style. Although the course uses the APA *Publication Manual* (2010) as one of its required texts, getting students to read it is a difficult task. Thus, one of the guidelines provided to students is a brief APA-style checklist (Dunn et al., 2001). This checklist is much shorter than the APA manual but serves to alert students to some of the many formatting requirements of APA style. The second guideline given to students is one devised by the instructor (RAS), which he uses to simplify making comments on students' first drafts of the paper (see Table 16.2). Rather than making marks throughout the entire paper, Smith marks two to three instances of a particular error and highlights that error on the guideline sheet. The intent is to show students their errors, have them learn about the error through the explanation on the sheet, and then find other instances of their errors to correct before completing their final papers. The combination of these two guidelines shows students that both grammar and APA format are important in their writing, which seems appropriate for intermediate-level writing assignments.

Table 16-2
Handout for Intermediate-Level Writing Assignment Stressing Grammar and APA Style

RESEARCH METHODS
Common Writing Problems, Explanations, and Solutions

My mark(s) on paper	Explanation/solution
Awk	Awkward prose, wording, or construction
Cf	Cross-reference; compare to another page—usually when you spelled a name one way in text and another in reference
✓	In Reference list: In left column: You did cite this reference in the paper.
font size	Do not change font size anywhere in the paper
font style	Do not change font style (i.e., font appearance or type) anywhere in the paper.
informal *or* colloq	Informal writing/word or colloquial wording—paper should be written more formally
INC *or* inc.	Incomplete sentence—no subject or verb, or is introduced with a word to make it incomplete
indef *or* circled word	According to APA style, "this, that, these, those" are indefinite and need a noun to specify the referent
Itals	The marked word(s) should be italicized.
lc *or* ℬ	Change a capital letter to a lowercase letter
male/female	In APA style, are used as adjectives, not nouns (unless the age range includes children and adults). Thus, it is OK to say "female participants," but not "females."
# *or* # mis.	There is a number mismatch—you have used a singular and plural referent for the same person/people (e.g., "the *participant* wrote *their* answers on a sheet of paper"). Often, you are trying to avoid using an awkward construction such as he/she. You may be able to use plural referents such as "they."
# *or* in|the ∧	Insert a space, usually between words or initials
opinion *or* editorializing	You have written something that does not appear to be based on any evidence—it seems to be only your opinion or you are drawing a conclusion that does not seem warranted.

(continued)

Table 16-2 (*continued*)

RESEARCH METHODS
Common Writing Problems, Explanations, and Solutions

My mark(s) on paper	Explanation/solution
p.? *or* p.#	What is the page number? All quotes must have page citations.
p. 406 (in purple)	Consult this page of the chapter posted at the class my.Lamar site. Most typically, this refers you to the distinction between "that" and "which" or to words with temporal meaning ("since," "while").
PV	APA says to avoid passive voice. You use passive voice whenever you use a form of the "be" verb as a helping verb. Example: The participants *were given* a recall test. WHO gave them the test? You can remove PV by specifying the actor (The experimenters had the participants recall the words.) or by making the subject of the sentence do something (The participants completed a recall test.). For further information and more examples, consult the chapter posted at the class my.Lamar site (pp. 405–406).
Proved	Remember that drawing a sample never allows us to prove anything—we may "demonstrate" or "show" or other similar words, but we can't remove all uncertainty.
Ref?	You have made a statement that needs a reference. This is a clue to help you avoid plagiarism—sometimes I wrote it beside a sentence/phrase that does not sound like your writing style.
Ν	Transpose—reverse the order (words or letters)
?	Something is unclear—reread and rewrite to clarify.
wd *or* wd choice	The word you used does not seem to fit or seems inappropriate.

Other Important Points

Use past tense to refer to all aspects of the previous research that you cited. It was done in the past, so that is the tense you should use.

For any test or questionnaire you mention (by name) that some researchers have used, you must provide a reference for that instrument. If you refer to it generically (e.g., an intelligence test) rather than by name (e.g., WAIS), then you do not need a reference.

Use the word "relationships" to refer to a connection between people. Use the word "relations" to refer to associations between or among variables.

Table 16-2 (*continued*)

You should provide an in-text citation for every reference, and you should provide a reference for every study/article you mention in the text. The citations and references should match—the order of authors is very important!

Writing in a literature review should be informative, not flowery or dramatic. You are simply trying to communicate basic information to the reader. Strive for conciseness and felicity of expression. In other words, be as specific and direct and brief as you can in your writing. One particular example occurred frequently in many papers:

> "In a study by Smith and Jones (1984), the researchers found . . . " *indirect, more wordy than necessary* "Smith and Jones (1984) found . . . " *much more direct and less wordy*

Avoid redundancy: whether (or not); their (own) *parenthetical words are typically redundant*

AFFECT vs. EFFECT

These words are frequently used words but are often confusing—probably because both can be a noun and both can be a verb. However, in the vast majority of cases, you will probably use "affect" as a verb (The IV affected the DV.) and use "effect" as a noun (The IV had a large effect on the DV).

In case you are interested, when you use "affect" as a noun, it is pretty much synonymous with emotion ("The patient showed flat affect").

When you use "effect" as a verb, it means to bring about ("The presidential candidates hope to effect a change in U.S. policy").

Advanced and Capstone Courses

Advanced, especially capstone, courses bring closure to the major by encouraging students to apply the skills they acquired in previous courses to some challenging topic (see Chapter 10, this volume). The topics of such courses may be emerging, popular, or controversial (e.g., terrorism and terror-management theory, stereotype threat, repressed memory, trauma and war service) and taught in a seminar format in which critical discussion of readings and research findings is key. On the other hand, the courses may be more traditional, such as honors, independent study courses, and internship experiences.

The writing required in advanced course should be more rigorous still than that found in the intermediate courses. Students should use APA style in any and all papers, save for very brief reaction papers. In general, paper assignments should be longer and more involved. Thus, 20 or more pages may well be the norm; longer papers are likely typical for honors theses and some independent study efforts. Because APA style should be familiar to students, the more pressing issue about writing concerns its overall quality and how well students are able to convey their findings and to summarize the published work of others. Clarity in expression and economy of presentation should matter. To achieve these desired ends, it is important to encourage students to generate drafts, seek feedback from the instructor and class peers, and to recognize—and use—revision as an essential part of the writing process.

Useful steps in generating a coherent paper include three kinds of library research. First, preresearch involves brainstorming, reading popular and scholarly writing, and gradually arriving at the focal topic. Second, preliminary research deals with developing and focusing the main idea of the paper. In this stage of the writing process, the student discards material deemed to be less relevant to the selected topic and concentrates on information that will eventually help generate a coherent thesis with supporting material. Third, the student engages in focused research that results in a body of information that provides varied perspectives on the thesis; at this point, the student takes notes that will help develop arguments regarding the thesis (Beins & Beins, 2008).

Table 16.3 summarizes the qualities of the three levels of courses and their respective writing assignments. If professors craft writing assignments to fit course levels, then students should have the opportunity to excel by improving their writing skills incrementally, both across time in the major and across

Table 16-3

Scope of Writing Assignments by Course Level

Introductory

   Introduces basic vocabulary, concepts, research methods, and applications of psychology

   Assignments tend to be short (2–3 pages) and reflective, often self-reflective or personal; grammar and punctuation matter

   Explores the study of behavior in broad terms (e.g., survey of psychology embodied in introductory psychology)

   Encourages critical thinking about behavior and different ways of knowing

   Provides students with knowledge base and disciplinary skills (i.e., disciplinary language) relevant to intermediate and advanced courses

   May introduce APA style; introduction to and use of databases (e.g., PsycINFO) is desirable

Table 16-3 (*continued*)

Intermediate

Builds on writing assignments and skills learned in introductory courses; writing is less personal or self-focused

Assignments tend to be longer (5 or more pages) and grounded in published research; grammar and punctuation matter

Multiple drafts, peer editing, and ongoing revision are encouraged

APA style and database searching (e.g., PsycINFO) are usually required

Assignments describe, explore, and speculate about specific research findings

Encourages personal engagement with material in and beyond the classroom (e.g.,conducting and describing observational research, running a "canned" experiment)

Begin to use psychological concepts to express original ideas about behavior

May involve collaborative writing between or among students (research teams)

Advanced

Builds on writing assignments and skills learned in introductory and intermediate courses; writing is not personal but aimed at drawing general conclusions about behavior

Writing should give students the opportunity to define a research question, review relevant literature, and speculate about complex relations among variables

Writing assignments are often empirically based, involving design and execution of method, as well as data collection and analysis

APA style and database searching (e.g., PsycINFO) are required; grammar and punctuation matter

Quality of writing should demonstrate use of higher order thinking skills, such as analysis, synthesis, and evaluation of published research as well as student's own effort

Papers are longer (20 or more pages); multiple drafts, peer editing, and ongoing revision are strongly encouraged, if not required

May involve collaborative writing between or among students (research teams)

specific courses. We note that these goals for writing are also important parts of the available rubric for scientific reasoning in psychology (see Chapter 21 this volume; Halonen et al., 2003) as well as the quality benchmarks for undergraduate education (Dunn, McCarthy, Baker, Halonen, & Hill, 2007).

Collaborative Writing Strategies

Collaborative Writing

The creation of student groups to collaborate on research or writing projects is not a novel idea. However, the potential for a new dynamic of collaboration has arisen with the advent of such tools as Google Docs (http://docs.google.com) and wikis. In the past, collaboration may have meant that students stood near a person who is typing and offered suggestions. In the era of typewriters and even with contemporary word processing, the first draft may have been the final draft because revisions required retyping much or nearly all of the paper. Thus, true collaboration was more an ideal and less a reality.

With tools like Google Docs, though, students (or any set of collaborators) can actively join in the process of creating and revising. This approach will rely on very different modes of work, one with which students at this point are probably not familiar. In the student academic world, the current situation is more likely to involve variations on the tradition of a single person doing much of the work, with other students in the group attempting to edit as a manuscript is passed from one person to the next in a serial fashion via e-mail.

The experience of one of the authors (BCB) with Google Docs in a class is instructive; the same issues are pertinent to collaboration with any wiki. Overall, there are few technical issues on Google Docs to overcome. The instructor can create (and "own") the document; once students receive permission to access the document, they can write and edit a manuscript on their own schedules. Throughout the process, the instructor can monitor the progress that the students are making. Anyone with access to the file can view it, but the owner can designate people merely as viewers or as editors who can make changes and leave notes for other collaborators. Students are not used to this type of collaboration, so initially they seem skeptical or reluctant. Part of this response is undoubtedly due to individual differences—some students prefer to work alone. But part of the response involves the fact that the students are entering a new technological realm. In spite of the fact that they are so-called technological natives, they do not speak this language very fluently. They are developing a new type of skill that requires active participation and learning.

When individual students take responsibility for specific tasks in an APA-style paper, the paper requires active participation of all members of the group, and the group must function as a team. As one might expect, some students are more fastidious than others; furthermore, even when a given student works meticulously, if the student's skill or knowledge level is not at the level needed for success on the task, the preliminary product will be substandard.

This collaborative process provides several notable advantages: Each student can potentially provide a remedy for the deficiencies of others.

Optimally, the weaker students will learn from the responses of the others in the group, and the stronger students will sharpen their editing and critical thinking skills as they tailor the document to meet the group's needs. It is also likely that different students will show different strengths, so the collaborative effort will involve each student reinforcing the work of others as they all contribute from their strengths.

Students (and the instructor) have to work out the details of this type of collaborative process, but one aspect on which students have commented is that face-to-face meetings facilitate the group work. Even in this era of remote, asynchronous teamwork, students have commented on the need to meet in person and establish the parameters of group operation. Those meetings enhance the likelihood that students have a shared vision of the work, so when they develop their own ideas, it is within the context of the overall group sentiment. Face-to-face meetings may also create the kinds of bonds that facilitate commitment to the project and increase motivation in the students.

Not surprisingly, some of the same issues arise in this type of collaboration as with traditional group work. Students have noted that the final product did not take the shape they had envisioned for it; they have commented that it was different, not necessarily inferior or undesirable. Further, some students are unprepared to contribute to their segment of the paper, some are disorganized, and some are merely uninterested. Those characteristics differentiate the outstanding students from their ordinary or low-functioning colleagues (Credé & Kuncel, 2008).

Collaborative Peer Review

Instructors have become more focused on the development of student writing skills for approximately the past two decades. It is clear that students can become better writers. For example, Goddard (2003) documented student progress in a class specifically devoted to writing. She noted that their abilities regarding grammar and the use of APA style improved in a semester-long, three-credit course. Unfortunately, not many departments or programs may have the luxury of being able to offer courses devoted specifically to writing. So some compromise is needed in which students engage in writing and then receive feedback from an instructor who should not be inundated with students' papers to critique.

Traditionally, each student writes a paper in which the writing is a solitary process. But collaborative writing and editing may make this solitary process a team affair. However, if each person on the team writes an intact section of a paper, the final product will only be as strong as the weakest writer. For example, the 1931 mystery novel, *The Floating Admiral* (Christie, 1931/1990), written by Agatha Christie, G. K. Chesterton, and others serially and one chapter at a time, resulted in a book that was reasonably interesting but clearly uneven. (Perhaps none of the group was permitted to edit the others' work.)

In considering student writing, a paper written in independent segments is also likely to be uneven. One might remedy this problem by asking students to edit and comment on the work of others. This approach, too, has its problems, most notably that students who are learning to be proficient, or merely competent, writers do not always have the ability to see weaknesses in the writing of others. This problem is compounded when a student reviewer does not have sufficient content knowledge to critically assess another student's writing.

A second issue related to peer reviewing is that students may not know how to provide constructive feedback on others' writing. Students have commented that they feel uncomfortable revising the writing of others, with the suggestion that to do so would show disrespect. A third important issue is that instructors may have to spend a considerable amount of time overseeing the peer review process (Cho & Schunn, 2007).

Nonetheless, a number of instructors have advocated reviews by fellow students and have reported the benefits of peer review. Students have rated the peer review process positively and have claimed that they learned from the feedback of other students (e.g., Cathey, 2007; Dunn, 1996, 2008). One of us [DSD] routinely sets aside one or two class periods in his intermediate- and advanced-level courses where students read and comment (verbally and in writing) on the rough drafts of their peers' papers. Furthermore, Fallahi, Wood, Austad, and Fallahi (2006) noted improvement in student writing after those students received instruction in class in the basics of writing and received feedback on their writing from the instructor and from fellow students. With Fallahi et al.'s methodology, though, one cannot identify the specific benefit of peer review because the instructor also commented on student writing.

Fortunately, there is also support for improved writing abilities with peer review (Cho & Schunn, 2007). These authors used a peer-review system called scaffolded writing and rewriting in the discipline (SWoRD). Their approach used an online reviewing process. The model resembles the publication process in professional journals in which the student (i.e., the author) writes on a topic, submits it for review, and responds in revision to comments by multiple reviewers. In the review process, each student evaluates the writing of another student based on the three criteria of flow, logic, and insight on a Likert-type scale that ranges from 1 (*Disastrous*) to 7 (*Excellent*). The process also involves providing feedback on the reviewers' feedback. In the end, students receive grades based on their papers, and reviewers receive grades based on the adequacy of their feedback.

In an empirical test of SWoRD, Cho and Schunn (2007) provided feedback to students from a single expert, a single peer, or from multiple peers. The results of their research are either very positive or very negative, depending on one's perspective. When students received feedback from a single expert, the change in their writing was negative; that is, the writing as judged by a blind reader was worse than at baseline. When the feedback came from multiple, fellow students, the writing was significantly improved. (When comments came from a single, fellow student, the writing was better than when the expert provided the feedback, although not significantly so.)

Various authors have hypothesized about the reason that an expert's comments might have no positive effect on the student. For instance, Sperling and Freedman (1987) speculated that "the student holds values that, even if well-intended, can be enough out of line with the teacher's as to interfere with the student's and the teacher's matching their definitions of writing problems and solutions" (p. 17). Thus, if an expert (i.e., the instructor) has a perspective that the student cannot adopt, feedback might be irrelevant at best. Students might also misinterpret comments and revise in ways that detract from their writing. The concept here clearly relates to the suggestion of Madigan et al. (1995) that psychological writing reflects the perspectives of the writer.

Instructors might consider this result a negative because it suggests that providing copious feedback to students on their writing has a deleterious effect; thus, the considerable time involved in commenting on student writing may be wasted. At the same time, one could see a positive outcome from this result. If expert feedback does not lead to improved student writing, then one could justify refraining from making extended comments on the basis of pedagogical efficacy.

A further question involves whether students progress better with constant collaboration rather than writing individually with subsequent peer review. Zammuner (1995) reported that the improvement in young children aged 9 or 10 occurs when students write alone, receive subsequent feedback, and revise collaboratively. Zammuner suggested that the presence of a different perspective after the individual writing led to some of the improvement. So a system like SWoRD might be more efficacious than collaborative writing in that SWoRD builds in solitary writing followed by feedback. One caveat regarding this suggestion is that Zammuner's research involved elementary school children who were learning only how to generate complex prose. College-level students may undergo a different dynamic.

The process of collaborative activity involving peer review appears to be effective in improving a final product for students. As of now, it is still not clear whether the effect is permanent. That is, will students generate better writing in the absence of peer review than they did before having engaged in this process? One hopes that students will incorporate the helpful ideas of the reviewers, but that is itself an empirical question.

Ethical Writing

Plagiarism is one of the banes of instructors' existence. Students sometimes simply cut and paste sources without attribution, the most blatant form of plagiarism. At the college level, this type of unethical writing is probably entirely intentional; the students simply use the words and ideas of others to avoid having to generate original ideas. The Internet makes such plagiarism entirely too easy. Unfortunately for students, the writing style of plagiarized material often does not match the students', so fortunately for instructors, they may be able to identify instances of plagiarism relatively easily. And with search engines, it is often fairly easy to find the source of the plagiarized material.

Less problematic ethically are those situations in which students are not aware that they are plagiarizing. Even though the ethical issues are less troubling, the pedagogical issue is still critical. Students need to learn what they can and cannot do in their professional writing. Even though students may not use words identical to those in an original source, they are plagiarizing if they present others' ideas as their own. Students need to know four main rules associated with ethical writing. First, if they use the exact words of other authors, they need to use quotations marks, cite the authors, and provide appropriate referencing (e.g., page numbers). Second, if students adapt the ideas of other writers in indirect quotation, the students still need to cite the original source. Third, if students rely on a secondary source, they should not cite the primary source as the reference; rather, they should cite the secondary source. Fourth, students cannot merely rearrange the order of ideas presented in their sources; they need to use their own words to capture those ideas (e.g., Beins & Beins, 2008; Dunn, 2008).

Technology is evolving to help instructors deal with plagiarism. Turnitin (http://turnitin.com/static/index.html) is a program to which universities (or individual instructors) can subscribe. In Turnitin, an instructor can submit a student paper and have it analyzed against an incredibly large number of documents (including other student papers). Turnitin produces a printout in which suspicious passages are highlighted and matched to their possible sources. In addition, the printout provides the instructor with an overall plagiarism index. As with any such tool, the instructor must inspect this printout carefully to avoid accusing an innocent student of plagiarism. One of the authors (RAS) has used Turnitin to teach students how to avoid plagiarism in their writing. Rather than using the program simply to catch students who have plagiarized (whether intentionally or unintentionally), this approach uses Turnitin as part of the educational process. After writing their papers, students upload them to Turnitin for analysis. Rather than restricting the analysis to the instructor, an option allows students to see the analysis. Another option allows the students to revise and resubmit their papers for another analysis. In this manner, students can learn to determine what is considered plagiarism and what is not. It seems that one of the difficult aspects of teaching students about plagiarism is that there is no black-and-white rule about what kind of paraphrasing is acceptable and what is not. Working with Turnitin can help students with that difficult distinction.

One issue that can be troublesome and about which teachers need to instruct students is the use of common knowledge. Scholars typically believe that common knowledge does not need a citation. The problem is determining what *common* means. Depending on the audience, *common* means different things. If the audience is the scholarly community in one's discipline, some technical and professional information is truly commonly known. If the audience is the general public or scholars in another discipline, there is less communal knowledge, so citations should be more prevalent. Students are less likely to be aware of subtle differences between common and uncommon knowledge, so they may be on safer ground by overreliance on citations compared to the extent of citing that a scholar might use. Finally, students will be less likely to engage in unintentional plagiarism if they take copious notes on what they read and keep close track of the citations they use. It will be easier for them at a later time to find where they came across the ideas they incorporate in their writing.

Resources

Fortunately for students, there are multiple resources that they can use to help them learn to write well and to learn APA style. Some sources are in traditional book format (e.g., American Psychological Association, 2010; Beins & Beins, 2008; Dunn, 2008). Other sources are accessible online. For instance, Long Island University offers reference citation help (http://www.liu.edu/cwis/cwp/library/workshop/citapa.htm), and Purdue University offers help at its Online Writing Laboratory (OWL; http://owl.english.purdue.edu/owl/resource/560/01/). The OWL site includes help with both APA style and with general writing. Use of a search engine for "APA Style" yields well over a million hits; unlike many searches whose hits rapidly become unrelated to the topic, hits for APA style are relevant for many pages.

When students (or any writers) refer to a style guide for help, they should remember that the guidelines for writers are merely that. Instructors hope that the voice of the student will emerge within the structure of professional writing. The writing should exhibit clarity, conciseness, and felicity of expression, but it should also be interesting. Most people find psychological topics engaging. There is no need for students to hide what excites people within prose devoid of humanity.

Conclusion

Writing is neither an easy skill for students to learn nor for instructors to teach. However, writing is a vital skill for psychology majors to master both for their writing in psychology and for their more general communication. Rather than attempting to develop in students all of the various skills required for good writing in a single course or assignment, we propose that approaching writing as a developmental skill throughout the major will make the process less frustrating for both students and faculty. Conceptualizing writing assignments as at beginning, intermediate, and advanced levels allows students and faculty to focus on different skills at each level, thus dividing the learning-to-write process into a set of concrete steps that students can climb one at a time.

References

Abramson, C. I., & Hershey, D. A. (1999). The use of correspondence in the classroom. In L. T. Benjamin, B. F. Nodine, R. M. Ernst, & C. Blair-Broeker (Eds.), *Activities handbook for the teaching of psychology* (Vol. 4, pp. 33–37). Washington, DC: American Psychological Association.

American Psychological Association. (2010). *Publication manual of the American Psychological Association* (6th ed.). Washington, DC: Author.

American Psychological Association. (2008). *Teaching, learning, and assessing in a developmentally coherent curriculum.* Washington, DC: American Psychological Association, Board of Educational Affairs. Retrieved from www.apa.org/ed/resources.html.

Anderson, J. E., & Valentine, W. L. (1944). The preparation of articles for publication in the journals of the American Psychological Association. *Psychological Bulletin, 41*, 345–376.

Beins, B. C. (1993). Writing assignments in statistics classes encourage students to learn interpretation. *Teaching of Psychology, 20*, 161–164.

Beins, B. C. (2006a, January). *Writing in APA style: An exercise with common errors.* Poster presentation at the National Institute on the Teaching of Psychology. St. Petersburg Beach, FL.

Beins, B. C. (2006b). Writing in APA style: The style we love to hate. *The General Psychologist, 41*(2), 33–35.

Beins, B. C. (2008). Creating research groups in an undergraduate psychology curriculum. In R. L. Miller, R. F. Rycek, E. Balcetis, S. Barney, B. Beins, S. Burns, R. Smith, & M. E. Ware (Eds.), *Developing, promoting, and sustaining the undergraduate research experience in psychology* (pp. 111–115). Society for the Teaching of Psychology. Retrieved from http://www.teachpsych.org/resources/e-books/e-books.php.

Beins, B. C., & Beins, A. M. (2008). *Effective writing in psychology: Papers, posters, and presentations.* Boston: Blackwell.

Bruner, K. F. (1942). Of psychological writing: Being some valedictory remarks on style. *Journal of Abnormal and Social Psychology, 37*, 52–70.

Bryant, W. H. M., & Benjamin, L. T., Jr. (1999). Read all about it! Wundt opens psychology lab: A newspaper assignment for history of psychology. In L. T. Benjamin, B. F. Nodine, R. M. Ernst, & C. Blair-Broeker (Eds.),

Activities handbook for the teaching of psychology (Vol. 4, pp. 47–49). Washington, DC: American Psychological Association.

Cathey, C. (2007). Power of peer review: An online collaborative learning assignment in social psychology. *Teaching of Psychology, 34*, 97–99.

Cho, K., & Schunn, C. D. (2007). Scaffolded writing and rewriting in the discipline: A Web-based reciprocal *peer review* system. *Computers and Education, 48*, 409–426. Retrieved from http://www.sciencedirect.com.

Christie, A. (1931/1990). *The floating admiral.* New York: Jove Books.

Credé, M., & Kuncel, N. R. (2008). Study habits, skills, and attitudes: The third pillar supporting collegiate academic performance. *Perspectives on Psychological Science, 3*, 425–453.

Dunn, D. S. (1996). Collaborative writing in a statistics and research methods course. *Teaching of Psychology, 23*, 38–40.

Dunn, D. S. (2007). Introducing writing in introductory psychology: Practical matters, teaching resources, and activities. In R. A. Smith, *Instructor's resource manual for Weiten's Psychology: Themes and variations* (7th ed., pp. 885–902). Belmont, CA: Thompson.

Dunn, D. S. (2008). *A short guide to writing about psychology* (2nd ed.). New York: Longman.

Dunn, D. S., McCarthy, M. A., Baker, S., Halonen, J. S., & Hill, G. W., IV. (2007). Quality benchmarks in undergraduate psychology programs. *American Psychologist, 62,* 650–670.

Dunn, D. S., & Smith, R. A. (2008). Writing as critical thinking. In D. S. Dunn, J. S. Halonen, & R. A. Smith (Eds.), *Teaching critical thinking in psychology: A handbook of best practices* (pp. 163–173). Malden, MA: Wiley-Blackwell.

Dunn, J., Ford, K., Rewey, K. L., Juve, J. A., Weiser, A., & Davis, S. F. (2001). A modified presubmission checklist. *Psi Chi Journal of Undergraduate Research, 6,* 142–144.

Elbow, P., & Belanoff, P. (2002). *Being a writer: A community of writers revisited.* New York: McGraw-Hill.

Fallahi, C. R., Wood, R. M., Austad, C. S., & Fallahi, H. (2006). A program for improving undergraduate psychology students' basic writing skills. *Teaching of Psychology, 33,* 171–175.

Goddard, P. (2003). Implementing and evaluating a writing course for psychology majors. *Teaching of Psychology, 30,* 25–29.

Halonen, J. S., Bosack, T., Clay, S., & McCarthy, M. (with Dunn, D. S., Hill, G. W., IV, McEntarffer, R., Mehrotra, C., Nesmith, R., Weaver, K. A., & Whitlock, K.).

(2003). A rubric for learning, teaching, and assessing scientific inquiry in psychology. *Teaching of Psychology, 30,* 196–208.

How to write a response paper. (n.d.). Retrieved from http://www.usd.edu/fye/sjwriteresp.html#_ftnref1.

Holland, A. (2002). *Eureka! The importance of good science writing.* Retrieved March 14, 2007, from http://www.writersblock.ca/winter2002/essay.htm.

Instructions in regard to preparation of manuscripts. (1929). *Psychological Bulletin, 26,* 57–63.

Keith, K. D. (1999). Letters home: Writing for understanding in introductory psychology. In L. T. Benjamin, B. F. Nodine, R. M. Ernst, & C. Blair-Broeker (Eds.), *Activities handbook for the teaching of psychology* (Vol. 4, pp. 30–32). Washington, DC: American Psychological Association.

Madigan, R., Johnson, S., & Linton, P. (1995). The language of psychology: APA style as epistemology. *American Psychologist, 50,* 428–436.

The neglected "R": The need for a writing revolution. (2003). Report from the National Commission on Writing. Retrieved from http://www.writingcommission.org/prod_downloads/writingcom/neglectedr.pdf.

Procidano, M. E. (1991). Students' evaluation of writing assignments in an abnormal psychology course. *Teaching of Psychology, 18,* 164–167.

Response/reaction paper. (n.d.). Retrieved from http://uwp.duke.edu/wstudio/resources/documents/response.pdf.

Roediger, H. L., III. (2004, April). What should they be called? *APS Observer, 17*(4). Retrieved December 18, 2008, from http://www.psychologicalscience.org/observer/getArticle.cfm?id=1549.

Schmidt, M. E., & Dunn, D. S. (2007). Teaching research methods and statistics as a writing intensive course. In D. S. Dunn, R. A. Smith, & B. Beins (Eds.), *Best practices for teaching statistics and research methods in the behavioral sciences* (pp. 257–273). Mahwah, NJ: Erlbaum.

Sommer, R. (2006). Dual dissemination: Writing for colleagues and the public. *American Psychologist, 61,* 955–958.

Sperling, M., & Freedman, S. W. (1987). *A good girl writes like a good girl: Written response and clues to the teaching/learning process.* Technical Report No. 3, National Center for the Study of Writing. Retrieved from http://www.nwp.org/cs/public/download/nwp_file/131/TR03.pdf?x-r=pcfile_d.

Writing: A ticket to work . . . Or a ticket out: A survey of business leaders. (2004). Report from the National Commission on Writing. Retrieved from http://www.writingcommission.org/prod_downloads/writingcom/writing-ticket-to-work.pdf.

Writing and school reform. (2006). Retrieved from http://www.writing-commission.org/prod_downloads/writingcom/writing-school-reform-natl-comm-writing.pdf.

Zammuner, V. L. (1995). Individual and cooperative computer-writing and revising: Who gets the best results? *Learning and Instruction,* 5(2), 101–124. Retrieved from http://www.sciencedirect.com.

17 Capping the Undergraduate Experience

Making Learning Come Alive Through Fieldwork

Joann H. Grayson

Fieldwork is a powerful teaching strategy that continues to gain support and acceptance in higher education (Birge, 2005; Ehrlich, 2007; Exley, 2004). According to the National Service Learning Clearinghouse (2008), 12% of college faculty members currently offer service learning courses. However, a senior capstone field placement course is a challenging endeavor. Butin (2005) suggests that offering a service learning capstone requires organization, foresight, time, creativity, networking, and tolerance for ambiguity. It can even be a risky undertaking that could fail in a very public way.

Why Offer Fieldwork?

McGovern and Reich (1996) identified five common elements of quality undergraduate psychology programs: (a) multiple opportunities for students to be active and collaborative learners, (b) research projects to help students learn the science of psychology, (c) fieldwork and community service to help students learn the application of psychology, (d) an emphasis on ethical issues and values, and (e) experiences that heighten students' understanding of diversity. Fieldwork can encompass all of these essential elements. There are multiple opportunities for students to be "active and collaborative" learners through the application of psychological principles, ethical issues such as confidentiality, and values such as decisions about which populations to serve. There is the potential to interact with diverse populations. For example, many students have not had close associations with people who live in poverty, are disabled, struggle with persistent mental illness, or are impaired in basic functioning. Although a service learning experience is less likely than other possible capstone experiences to involve basic research, some sites, especially those in industry or agencies that require program evaluation, may provide valuable applied research opportunities.

Fieldwork can offer many benefits to students including the opportunity for students to leave their comfort zones and venture into unknown socio-emotional territory (Jones, Gilbride-Brown, & Gasiorski, 2005). For example, reading about a psychosis is not the same as meeting and relating to a person who has sought hospitalization because of psychotic symptoms. Classroom learning about homelessness and its causes is not the same challenge as being the person assisting a homeless family with changes that will help them acquire their own place to live.

Service learning, academic work that engages the student in the community, and fieldwork offer opportunities for students to apply classroom knowledge and to contribute to others (Osbourne, Weadick, & Penticuff, 2006). Students bring enthusiasm, energy, and a new perspective; and they can make significant contributions to sites when supervisors craft challenging assignments that require developing and practicing new skills but at the same time allow students to work within their range of competence. Experienced supervisors may encourage students to actively deliver services, even if the student is initially uncomfortable; yet supervisors should also be careful to avoid situations in which the student experiences major failures or discouragement.

Case Example

Students in my capstone field placement (a 400-level course) have designed curricula for groups (e.g., self-esteem groups, preventing relapse with addictions, or managing delusions and hallucinations) and have presented parts of the curricula during groups; designed Web sites for guidance counselors at high schools and assisted high school students in navigation of the sites; compiled resources for high school students seeking summer jobs and assisted students in applying; and been academic case managers for struggling college peers. Undergraduate students have created guidebooks for agency volunteers, have designed and implemented training for foster parents on specific topics, and have researched selected topics for supervisors seeking the most up-to-date clinical information.

Another benefit to fieldwork is enhancing student self-confidence (Osborne et al., 2006). Through serving others, students have the opportunity to watch someone grow and change. Students experience their power to make a positive difference in the lives of others. They learn to believe in themselves because they witness the positive effects of their actions on the individuals they serve.

Furthermore, through field experience, students can clarify career directions. Students may have preconceptions about careers and work sites. Being able to shadow a professional and assist in an agency can help a student to determine whether that setting is one where he or she will be comfortable and feel fulfilled. Many students are affirmed in their career direction by their field experiences. Others elect to withdraw employment or graduate school applications and rethink their future, either because their site experience exposed them to new opportunities or because they realized that the work they completed did not match their interests. Career planning is also enhanced by the development of mentoring relationships with supervisors who can serve as references for jobs and graduate school.

Students engaged in service learning show positive changes including enhanced critical thinking and reflection skills as well as greater commitment to helping others (Cress, 2006). Eyler, Root, and Giles (2006) maintained that students exposed to service learning show improved problem-solving skills and may be better able to transfer learning from one setting to another. They discuss studies showing that students with fieldwork experience, compared to students who had only classroom experience, showed more complex and realistic understandings; improved in their complexity of problem analysis; showed greater increases in moral reasoning; and demonstrated greater determination to act in the face of uncertainty.

Making Service Learning an Academic Experience

Service learning that is offered for academic credit is different from volunteer work. Duffy and Bringle (2006) suggested that students should not receive academic credit for community service because of an important distinction between service learning and community service. The focus in community service activity is the need of the agency whereas the focus of academic service learning or fieldwork is the growth and development of the student.

There are several ways to distinguish between volunteer work and academic service learning. In an academic experience, the goal is to reinforce classroom learning and have students develop or refine skills. Thus, the agency needs to designate supervisors who have knowledge, skills, abilities, and training to move the student forward on the learning curve (as opposed to simply assigning the student tasks that can be completed with little supervision).

There should be few, if any, expectations that the student will be productive in the sense of doing routine work for the agency. Students are placed at the agency to learn from, not to replace, staff members. Thus, undergraduate students generally should not expect payment for their time at the agency. In fact, if the student can perform at the level that merits pay for the work assigned, then it is less likely that the agency will focus on providing supervision and teaching new skills or allowing the student to spend considerable time simply observing professionals.

Furco (1996) noted that service learning can meet both agency and student needs by placing an equal focus on the service provided and the learning obtained. Duffy and Bringle (2006) stated that in high-quality service learning no one is exploited and reciprocity exists; therefore, students and agencies both give and receive. Thus, the goal is to find tasks for the student that are challenging and that develop new skills while at the same time make a meaningful contribution to the site (Elyer et al., 2006). For example, a student in a day hospital program might assist patients with low reading abilities. The student can develop skills relating to clients one-on-one while staff members are freed for other duties.

Planning a Capstone Field Placement

Instructors who wish to create a capstone field placement course face numerous decisions and considerations. Table 17-1 provides a capstone field planning checklist. Instructors can rely on this checklist from conceiving field

Table 17-1
A Checklist for Planning a Capstone Field Placement

Objectives

   __Apply classroom principles and knowledge to practical situations
   __Active and collaborative learning
   __Apply ethical principles
   __Understanding of diversity
   __Participate in research
   __Help students make career decisions
   __Enhance self-confidence and leadership
   __Develop critical thinking skills
   __Enhance social responsibility

Meeting agency needs while promoting student learning

   __Student has opportunities to observe professionals
   __Students are offered opportunities to learn and practice new tasks/skills
   __Students are able to contribute to the site

Academic components

   __Students read and learn about best practice guidelines related to their site
   __Writing assignments

      __Literature reviews/book reviews
      __Journaling/reflection
      __Formal paper

   __Presentation skills
   __Class time (decide on topics)
   __Decide on time required at site

University policies

   __Check with Office of Risk Management

Establishing sites

   __Site is accessible
   __Clear expectations about supervision
   __Contracts specify responsibilities
   __Obtaining site-specific information (opportunities/requirements)
   __Check mission/goals/training opportunities

Selecting students

   __Determine prerequisites
   __Application Packet (specify what to include)
   __Screening interview
   __References
   __Extending Invitations

(continued)

Table 17-1 (continued)

Matching students to placements

___Consider student's background
___Arrange interviews or match

Helping students be successful

___Dress codes
___Documentation
___Goal-setting
___Mid-term evaluation
___Individual meetings
___Ongoing contact with sites

Guiding students through stages
Stage One

___Help students identify training opportunities
___Have students talk with prior students

Stage Two

___Help students orient
___Individual meeting
___Contact with site supervisors

Stage Three

___Reconcile student's expectations

Stage Four

___Reinforce student productivity

Stage Five

___Help students successfully terminate

Evaluating students

Onsite evaluation ___% of grade

___Rating scale
___Instructions for supervision
___Rating items

Class work ___% of grade

Attendance at class ___% of grade or deduction

Teaching best practices

___Lecture
___Observation
___Readings
___Writings (critiques/paper)

placements (i.e., developing course objectives) through evaluation (i.e., both of students and any "best practices" used in the classroom portions of the experience).

Service learning for academic credit needs to incorporate reading, research, and critical thinking. Students should learn to relate academic content to their site. Students need to think about, discuss, react to, present, and write about their experiences (Dunlap, 1998). Class discussion can examine the issues that students are encountering. Class time can also be spent training students on specific skills such as reflective listening or conflict resolution or in discussion of ethical issues (Kitzrow, 2006).

Case Example

Consistent with recommendations for service learning (Duffy & Bringle, 2006; Dunlap, 1998; Kronick, 2007), at James Madison University (JMU), students write weekly reflection logs that are graded on critical thinking skills. Students are expected to offer critical thinking on topics such as how the agency's policy reflects the American Psychological Association's (APA) ethics code, how the site handles diversity issues, how decisions are made about what services to offer, how the agency encourages staff training and continuing education, and how a positive working environment is maintained. Students also examine their preconceptions about service delivery and clinical populations. Reflections are crucial and allow students to express emotions, record what they are learning and what they observe, and examine questions and values. The instructor can offer list of potential questions or journal topics (Dunlap, 1998) and provide journals from previous students, all of which can enhance student reflection.

Students are required to write an APA-style paper as a culminating experience. The assignment is to examine best practices of a focused aspect of service delivery and compare these guidelines to agency practices. Each student chooses a specific, narrow topic such as "Best Practices for Involving Parents in Preschool Education" or "Best Practices for Use of Seclusion and Restraint in Psychiatric Units" or "Best Practices for Conducting a Home Visit." We also require students to demonstrate presentation and public speaking skills. Students meet this requirement through class discussion and an hour-long presentation about the site and its mission, history, structure, funding, and services.

Establishing Sites: Negotiating With Agencies for Placements

Not every community agency is able to offer exceptional training. The university supervisor will need to identify community partners that can provide the desired experiences and supervision. One way to establish the best learning climate for students is to offer clear expectations for participating agencies. Written guidelines for agencies clarify the respective roles of the university supervisor, the agency, and the student. For example, the guidelines might specify policies for placing and removal of students. General policies, expectations, and the supervisor's role in evaluating the student should be clear.

Promising sites share common characteristics. Exley (2004) maintained that the partnership between the university or college and the community agency must be based on a shared commitment to the student's education. University instructors should seek agencies that have training as part of their mission and should examine the agency's current model of training. The amount of supervision time the agency is prepared to offer the student is important. Larger agencies may have multiple staff who can offer supervision, and student learning can be enhanced when several mentors are available.

Service learning sites may have additional requirements and application procedures for accepting students. For example, some sites prefer full-time interns. Some sites require criminal records checks (and some require the student to pay for this), additional references, and health status documentation. Some agencies will not accept students who have had alcohol-related arrests or other criminal offenses. Students should be aware that to be placed, they must meet not only the college or university's standards but also the agency's standards. New programs might want to experiment with procedures, but arriving at a model with uniform expectations will assist both students and agencies in honoring requirements.

In addition to the clarification of agency and university expectations, it is essential to consult with campus legal counsel to identify risk management and liability issues. It needs to be clear to students that the "contract" is between the academic unit and the agency, not between the student and the agency. For example, it may be necessary to specify that agencies have the freedom to dismiss students from their site if the student is not functioning well.

Selecting Students

Some authors (Clary, Snyder, & Stukas, 2006) have concerns about requiring or guaranteeing every student a field experience. The practice of offering service learning to all psychology majors creates opportunities for students to become better citizens and to contribute to the larger community. In addition to the practical difficulties of maintaining a large number of placements, supervising larger numbers of students, and legal liability for substandard work by unmotivated students, there is a possibility of an undermining effect if service learning is required rather than optional. Requiring students to engage in service learning can decrease the student's desire to be involved in community service once the requirement is fulfilled (Clary et al., 2006). Finally, serving a smaller number of students can allow more flexibility in matching the student to a compatible site.

Sites may depend upon the instructor to choose students who will perform well and be an asset to the agency. Werner (2006) noted that positive student qualities are essential to maintaining working relationships with community agencies. Mismatched students or students who perform poorly can mean that a site will no longer accept students in future years. Unless sites are paid for participating in the field placement program, the only motivation is to help students and to benefit from the students' involvement. Therefore, it is imperative that students consistently perform and relate well to site supervisors. Not every senior student is adequately prepared or suited for fieldwork. Therefore, university supervisors need to select students carefully for a capstone experience and to identify alternative capstones that do not require fieldwork.

An application packet can facilitate the placement of students. A cover sheet can include contact information and a release of information allowing the instructor to discuss the student with all other faculty and with listed references. An accompanying photograph can help faculty identify and remember student applicants. Because the student is representing the institution's psychology department, the university supervisor may want to require the student to identify at least some faculty references. Students write a statement that explains what experience and training they seek as well as the background that has prepared and qualified them for fieldwork.

The university supervisor can use a copy of the student's transcript or degree progress report to determine whether course work matches agency preferences. Some sites have preferences for students with specific academic preparation. For example, substance abuse treatment providers may require that students have courses in abnormal psychology and substance abuse. Elementary or secondary schools stress a background in child development whereas legal sites may give preference to students with courses in criminal justice. The goal is to find a match between the student's academic preparation and the site expectations.

Once the instructor has identified students with strong course backgrounds, perhaps the next most important attribute is work ethic. The university supervisor can ask references and professors about the applicant's attendance and punctuality, two behaviors that are essential to strong performance in the field. Students who routinely skip class, submit assignments late, or have time management problems can repeat these patterns at a site and compromise their performance or even be asked to terminate the placement.

A written application and reference check constitutes the first step in creating a viable match for the student and the agency. A screening interview will allow the university supervisor and the student applicant to clarify the expectations of the course. Sites appreciate students who are eager to contribute and who can work independently. A student who can "see the work that needs to be done" and who offers to assume tasks or responsibilities will likely perform well. Those who need encouragement to become involved or who require repeated instruction on tasks will be more difficult to supervise. (However, a field placement capstone can be a growth experience for shy students who are willing to push themselves and become more outgoing. Students who are weak in attributes such as assertiveness and independence can benefit greatly from the field training and experience and should not be eliminated solely on these personality attributes.)

The interview of applicants can be instrumental in matching students to appropriate sites. During the interview, the instructor should determine each student's interests and direct the student to potential sites that might be a good match. One way to facilitate the matching process is for the university instructor to create a Web page containing information about the participating service learning sites, a description of the training offered, and student comments about the site. Prospective students are then able to begin the matching process by choosing some placements that are attractive. Additional Web-based information may include a classification of placements (e.g., children, forensic), university procedures, and the application.

A formal invitation to join the capstone service learning course and a formal acceptance can help set the tone for a professional experience. The invitation can reiterate the course requirements and grading, the benefits of fieldwork, and potential challenges.

Setting Expectations for Student Success

Student success will depend on multiple factors. The first, and the most important, is a good work ethic. Attendance and punctuality should be part of the evaluation criteria. Students are also expected to dress professionally. It is important for students to consider how clothing intersects with tasks and with client perception.

Documentation is an important expectation. Students learn to document in order to meet legal requirements of agencies, as a way of processing their experiences, and to provide a record of their work. Students learn what to document and how to write to suit the particular style required by the agency. Class time can be devoted to this topic early in the course with the instructor providing samples of writing from past students in each site.

Students set individual learning goals to guide their experience. For example, one student at a psychiatric hospital wants to observe neurological testing and intakes while another student at the same site wants to learn about multidisciplinary teams and discharge planning with the community mental health center. Students can develop personal goals such as being able to decide between career options, becoming more outgoing and contributing to meetings, or being able to calmly handle difficult clients. Although students will not achieve every goal, instructors can encourage students to be specific about what they seek to learn and what experiences they desire. These goals can be incorporated into the student's evaluation and can also guide the site supervisor in crafting a rewarding and growth-producing experience.

Stages of Fieldwork

Once students are selected and matched with agency sites, the instructor begins the task of successfully guiding students through the stages of a capstone field experience. Grayson and Reedy (2002) identified several stages in fieldwork and discussed the changes in students as they progress through the experience. Instructors can use these stages to guide classroom discussion and assignments and to anticipate student reactions and growth.

Stage One: Arranging and Anticipating the Field Experience

During the first stage, students are often excited, idealistic, motivated, and anxious; they may have unrealistic expectations. It is helpful for students in this stage to talk to prior students from their site or for the instructor to invite prior students to lead classroom discussions. Instructors can help students identify both the training opportunities and the limitations of the site.

Stage Two: Orientation and Establishing Identity

The second stage described by Grayson and Reedy (2002) is orientation and establishing identity. As students begin work at the site, they must find a balance between observation/training and contribution. Some students are overwhelmed and overly reliant upon supervisors. Others err on the side of being heedless and fail to seek sufficient direction before making mistakes. After the student has been on site for 2 to 3 weeks, instructors may want to schedule a private, individual meeting with each student to determine whether the student needs help integrating into the site and to assist the student with course assignments. If students are submitting weekly reflections, these are helpful in determining whether any adjustments are required.

Stage Three: Reconciling Expectations With Reality

Reconciling expectations is the third stage (Grayson & Reedy, 2002). As students progress through the experience, most will thrive and enjoy their placement. It will reaffirm their career objectives and these students will remain excited. Other students may be disillusioned with their sites and some may even change career goals. The instructor can guide the student to become more realistic about what is possible within the placement and help the student find ways to integrate into the work group of the agency.

The students selected for fieldwork are likely to be bright, energetic leaders who are accustomed to success. Furthermore, students of this generation are likely to expect quick results and fast resolutions. Their history of success may not have prepared them well for the realities of delivering psychological services. Instructors will likely be sending students into arenas where progress can be slow, and disappointments may seem as frequent as rewards. The student working with guidance counselors realizes sooner or later that encouragement and enthusiasm will not erase poverty, quickly teach a new immigrant English, or compensate for years of deprivation or abuse. The student in the psychiatric unit will come to understand that major mental illness is something that can be managed but not usually cured. Those working in substance abuse treatment learn that the relapse rates of even the very best programs mean that half or more of clients won't remain sober. A student at the homeless shelter may be disappointed when a family makes poor spending decisions and can't afford to move into their own apartment.

The work psychologists do is difficult. Students may be unprepared for disappointments. Instructors can assist students by teaching them how to measure client progress and what to consider when predicting outcome. Instructors can model a positive attitude and can help students remain realistic, learn to accept setbacks, and still move forward.

The university supervisor can help assure a positive training experience by maintaining contact with the site supervisor. In my experience, at minimum, the university supervisor should initiate contact at the start of the placement, at the mid-term review, and at the end of the training experience. On-site supervisors are encouraged to report problems immediately, and the university supervisor can also spot problems through the weekly writings and the class meetings with students. The university instructor can be instrumental in resolving conflicts between the student and the site and can assist by helping the on-site supervisors identify productive ways to relate to and structure the student.

Stage Four: Productivity, Independence, and Closure

By mid-term, if not before, the student should have progressed to the point of being a contributor to the site rather than simply observing staff (Stage Four). The student should be developing skills and enhancing his or her knowledge base. Markers of student growth for this stage are increased confidence, initiation of new ideas, acknowledgment of strengths and weaknesses, and understanding of some of the challenges of service delivery for the site (Grayson & Reedy, 2002).

An individual mid-term review is another positive mechanism to assist the student and offer formal feedback. Instructors may choose to ask on-site supervisors to submit a student evaluation and assign a grade at both mid-term and the end of the placement. On-site supervisors may also choose to hold a mid-term meeting with the student to review goals and their evaluation and grading.

Students can benefit from being an active part of the evaluation process. Rather than using a "preset" evaluation that is exactly the same for all, instructors can consider incorporating each student's learning goals into the site evaluation instrument. The process can begin by asking students what characteristics, skills, and abilities are important in performance at their site. Students may soon be in a position that they will be evaluating others; therefore, discussion about evaluation criteria is useful. The process of considering the elements of evaluation and how they relate to job tasks can be a valuable exercise for the student. Students may want to discuss with their supervisors how their sites evaluate staff and it may be helpful for students to examine the evaluation tools used by sites to evaluate staff performance.

The instructor may want to offer some structure to the evaluation. For example, items might fit under headings such as personal qualities; work habits; interpersonal skills; and knowledge, skills, and abilities. The instructor might also want to have several required items. Examples of possible evaluation items that might be required for all students are attendance, punctuality, adherence to agency policy, proper dress, or professional appearance and demeanor.

Students are likely to have similar items under work skills. Habits such as finishing projects on time or traits such as good organization are welcome in most any setting. Likewise, personal qualities that are desirable may be similar. Interpersonal skills that are appreciated in most any site include regular communication with supervisors, willingness to contribute to discussions, showing respect to staff and clients, and conveying interest and enthusiasm.

In contrast, knowledge, skills, and abilities will differ greatly at different sites. Students working with children often desire feedback on their knowledge of child development and skills in relating to children whereas those in the court system might include items rating their understanding of legal issues and their ability to answer clients' questions. Students placed in a psychiatric unit should show increased knowledge of abnormal psychology and the diagnostic system. Those placed in sites in industry will be rated on their knowledge of industrial/organizational psychology whereas those in social work settings might be expected to learn child abuse reporting requirements. Thus, students should set site-specific learning goals and evaluation items to rate their progress in learning information and acquiring skills.

The instructor will need to develop rating scales for supervisors to use in grading the student. It is also important to give the site supervisors criteria for assigning a global (overall) letter grade, regardless of the student's progress on any particular goal or sub-item. Usually, exceptional performance on sub-items will correlate with exceptional performance overall. However, there are exceptions. For example, a student who sets modest goals may have high ratings on some specific items but show only average performance compared to others at the site. In this case, the overall grade should reflect the overall average performance rather than the outstanding rating on some sub-items. It may be that an exceptional student has set extremely high goals and made only partial progress, with average ratings on some items. In this case, the overall grade should reflect the student's overall exceptional performance compared to other students who have interned at the site.

Active participation in creating the evaluation tool is also helpful when students are not performing as well as they had hoped to perform. It is easier for students to accept a lower evaluation and grade when the evaluation tool is one they have had a large part in creating.

Stage Five: Re-entry and Practical Applications

Successful students might find it difficult to leave their site. The last stage of fieldwork is learning how to terminate and find closure (Grayson & Reedy, 2002). Students should feel a sense of accomplishment. It is also a time of looking forward and reflecting on how the student can best use the field experience in future endeavors. Instructors may develop "ending transitions" such as an exit interview or a social event to bring closure to the experience.

The Importance of Teaching Best Practices to Students

Different sites have different standards and regulations as well as different services. Instructors can use classroom teaching time to have students discuss examples from the guidelines that are utilized at their particular site. For example, industrial sites may need to meet Occupational Safety and Health Administration (OSHA) standards whereas a hospital may need to meet standards of the Joint Commission on Hospital Accreditation. State governments may have written protocols for probation officers or for use of seclusion and restraint in a hospital setting. Guidelines for patient rights and clinician responsibilities are governed by both law and ethical standards of various professions.

Some sites have orientation sessions and training that may include information on guidelines and mandates. Students should attend those trainings and the hours spent in training can be credited toward the hour requirement for on-site work. However, in-house on-site training is unlikely to be sufficient to meet the goal of teaching best practices.

There are a number of ways to meet the goal of exposing students to best practices. One method discussed already is careful selection of sites so that students are placed only in agencies that meet high criteria. The students will then observe the best practices as they work in the agency. A second method is to assign readings and research so that students become aware of the standards and guidelines for clinicians and service delivery.

An APA-style paper, can be another mechanism for student examination of best methods in the field. For the capstone paper, students choose an in-depth topic related to services at their site. Examples might be best practices for managing suicidal patients, best practices for enhancing group cohesion, the best methods for assessment of sexual offending or substance abuse, or the best methods to prevent pregnancy in teenagers. Whatever the topic, the student then locates, with help from the instructor, guidelines and research that examine effective approaches and methods for evidence-based practice at their site.

Students summarize the methods and clearly state how services can be effectively delivered. The student then compares the methods shown to be best practices in the literature with the methods used at the site. The student discusses the fit between optimal service delivery and the realities faced by local agencies. For example, model programs funded by grants likely have a different resource base from those at local agencies. The local population may be different from samples of studies in the research, and local placement sites may have made adjustments for the particular population served.

This assignment is difficult for most students because students have primarily learned theoretical perspectives. Critically applying theory to a practical setting allows students to integrate the information from many of their courses in psychology.

The Rewards of a Successful Field Placement Program

Fieldwork changes students. The inexperienced and naïve student can emerge as a confident, capable staff member who knows how to work as part of a team. Fieldwork allows students to develop skills and demonstrate talents. They forge professional contacts that may last a lifetime. It is not unusual for a successful student to accept a job at the field site or use the supervisor's contacts to find a similar position in another community. Supervisors and university instructors often provide key letters of recommendation for graduate school or jobs.

A fieldwork course also enriches the university. The positive ties between the larger community and the university are strengthened. Opportunities for collaboration on research, grant writing, or community service often evolve from service learning contacts.

Ehrlich (2007) proffered three major future directions for service learning in undergraduate education. First is the development of experiences that enhance academic learning and develop the inquiring mind. His second direction is to use fieldwork to promote skills and knowledge needed for leadership. The third direction is to promote civic engagement. Regardless of the particular focus of a capstone service learning course, research by Ehrlich and others has shown significant positive impact of service learning on many aspects of students' understandings, skills, and motivation. Service learning is becoming a component of many undergraduate programs. It is a powerful pedagogy. It is the ultimate capstone for a student's academic career.

Recommended Readings

Bringle, R. G., & Duffy, D. K. (Eds.). (2006). *With service in mind: Concepts and models for service learning in psychology*. Sterling, VA: Stylus Publishing, LLC.

Butin, D.W. (Ed.). (2005). *Service learning in higher education: Critical issues and directions*. New York: Palgrave Macmillan.

Speck, B. W., & Hoppe, S. L. (2004). *Service learning: History, theory, and issues*. Westpoint, CT: Praeger.

References

Birge, J. (2005). The aesthetical basis for service learning practice. In D. W. Butin (Ed.), *Service learning in higher education: Critical issues and directions* (pp. 195–204). New York: Palgrave Macmillan.

Butin, D. W. (2005). Preface: Disturbing normalizations of service learning. In D. W. Butin (Ed.), *Service learning in higher education: Critical issues and directions* (pp. vii–xx). New York: Palgrave Macmillan.

Clary, E. G., Snyder, M., & Stukas, A. (2006). Service learning and psychology: Lessons from the psychology of volunteers' motivations. In R. G. Bringle & D. K. Duffy (Eds.), *With service in mind: Concepts and models for service learning in psychology* (pp. 35–50). Sterling, VA: Stylus.

Cress, C. M. (2006). Defining a service learning pedagogy of access and success. *Campus Compact.* Retrieved on June 29, 2008, from http://www.compact.org/20th/read/defining_a_service learning_pedagogy.

Duffy, D. K., & Bringle, R. G. (2006). Collaborating with the community: Psychology and service learning. In R. G. Bringle & D. K. Duffy (Eds.), *With service in mind: Concepts and models for service learning in psychology* (pp. 1–17). Sterling, VA: Stylus.

Dunlap, M. R. (1998). Methods of supporting students' critical reflection in courses incorporating service learning. *Teaching of Psychology*, 25, 208–209.

Ehrlich, T. (2007). *Service learning in undergraduate education: Where is it going?* Stanford, CA: Carnegie Foundation for the Advancement of Teaching.

Elyer, J., Root, S., & Giles, D. E., Jr. (2006) Service learning and the development of expert citizens: Service learning and cognitive science. In R. G. Bringle & D. K. Duffy (Eds.), *With service in mind: Concepts and models for service learning in psychology* (pp. 85–100). Sterling, VA: Stylus.

Exley, R. J. (2004). A critique of the civic engagement model. In B. W. Speck & S. L. Hoppe (Eds.), *Service learning: History, theory, and issues* (pp. 85–97). Westpoint, CT: Praeger.

Furco, A. (1996). Service learning: A balanced approach to experiential education. In Corporation for National Service (Ed.), *Expanding boundaries: Serving and learning* (pp. 2–6). Columbia, MD: Cooperative Education Association.

Grayson, J., & Reedy, M. (2002, Winter). Success in fieldwork. *Eye on Psi Chi*, 19–20.

Jones, S., Gilbride-Brown, J., & Gasiorski, A. (2005). Getting inside the "underside" of service learning: Student resistance and possibilities. In D. W. Butin (Ed.), *Service learning in higher education: Critical issues and directions* (pp. 3–24). New York: Palgrave Macmillan.

Kitzrow, M. A. (2006). An overview of current psychological theory and research on altruism and prosocial behavior. In R. G. Bringle & D. K. Duffy (Eds.), *With service in mind: Concepts and models for service learning in psychology* (pp. 19–34). Sterling, VA: Stylus.

Kronick, R. F. (2007). Service learning and the university student. *College Student Journal, 41*, 296–304.

McGovern, T. V., & Reich, J. N. (1996). A comment on the quality principles. *American Psychologist, 51*, 252–255.

National Service Learning Clearinghouse. (2008). *Defining service learning.* Retrieved December 4, 2008, from http://www.servicelearning.org/what-is-service learning/servicelearning-is/index.php.

Osborne, R. E., Weadick, K., & Penticuff, J. (2006) Service learning: From process to impact. In R. G. Bringle & D. K. Duffy (Eds.), *With service in mind: Concepts and models for service learning in psychology* (pp. 128–141). Sterling, VA: Stylus.

Werner, C. M. (2006). Strategies for service learning: Internalization and empowerment. In R. G. Bringle & D. K. Duffy (Eds.), *With service in mind: Concepts and models for service learning in psychology* (pp. 119–127). Sterling, VA: Stylus.

18 Helping Undergraduates Transition to the Workplace

Four Discussion Starters

Paul Hettich

Of the 88,000 psychology majors who graduated during 2005–2006 (NCES, 2007), an estimated 25% continued their studies in graduate programs. Undergraduate programs emphasize planning for graduate study and they offer several helpful resources including American Psychological Association (APA) publications, conference presentations, department career events, faculty advisors, and university career planning services. Of the estimated 66,000 graduates who entered the workforce, however, chances are that many did not participate in career planning activities. Yet, the Conference Board report on workplace readiness (Casner-Lotto & Barrington, 2006) and diverse other sources (e.g., Borden & Rajecki, 2000; Gardner, 1998; Holton, 1998; Robbins & Wilner, 2001) indicate many bachelor's level graduates are unprepared for work.

The purpose of this chapter is to introduce four specific dimensions of workplace transition: (a) youth-to-adult transitions, (b) organizational differences between college and workplace, (c) skills employers seek, and (d) characteristics of new employees that lead to promotion, discipline, or termination. The term *workplace* is used in its general context to include most types of paid employment; specific situations may exist where some remarks do not apply.

Why Should We Care What Happens to Students After Graduation?

Students expect that a B.A. in psychology will enable them to obtain employment that leads to a satisfying career. The expectations are reasonable, given students' intense investment of time, money, effort, and trust in their teachers; but course work alone may be insufficient to fulfill their hopes for a satisfying, entry-level, full-time job. Furthermore, most students are more concerned about using their degree to obtain a good job and less interested in learning for the sake of learning. Many psychology departments sponsor events or courses that focus on jobs and careers for B.A. graduates. Landrum and Davis (2007) and Morgan and Korschgen (2009) are excellent resources for addressing these issues. Workplace transition, however, is a multifaceted experience that includes consideration of youth-to-adult transitions, college versus workplace organization/culture differences, skills, social and cognitive development issues, and changing relationships (Hettich & Helkowski, 2005).

Second, the median student debt load among 2003–04 B.A. graduates was $19,300 (College Board, 2008). Thirty-four percent of the graduates from public schools and 49% from private institutions entered the workforce with $20,000 or more loan debt; many carried debts in excess of $40,000 (College Board, 2008). Debt and loan defaults are becoming an increasingly serious problem for new graduates (Pierson, 2007). Debt, new living arrangements, and money management in general are major challenges for most new graduates. To the extent that graduates enter the workforce adequately prepared for a full-time job, they can avoid situations (e.g., excessive job changes, poor adjustment, and inability to advance) that generate undue financial and personal costs (Robbins & Wilner, 2001).

Third, bachelor's level graduates are developmental "works in progress" seeking to establish identity and independence and reach maturity as they maneuver through the minefields of contemporary society. The stresses of transition often lead to crises of confidence, self-doubt, and depression at a time when most graduates begin to live outside the safety net that home and school once provided (Robbins & Wilner, 2001). Marcia's research on identity status (see McAdams, 2001) and Arnett's study (Arnett & Tanner, 2006) of emerging adults (ages 18–25) are worthy frameworks for examining important developmental issues that graduates encounter.

Fourth, graduates with little or no significant work experience are unaware of the dramatic differences between academic and corporate environments.

Many enter the workplace with inadequate skills and inappropriate attitudes (e.g., an "entitlement mentality" characterized by unrealistic expectations of high pay, challenging assignments, and rapid advancement), factors that lead to serious mistakes and early career setbacks. Often new graduates must accept boring entry-level jobs well below their expectations and ability level, jobs that generate frustration, demoralization, and anger because they are the only jobs available. They do not understand such situations are viewed by supervisors and co-workers as the norm for "paying your dues."

Fifth, many graduates are first-generation college-educated persons who never shared dinner table conversations with college-educated parents who could coach them on the fine points of interviewing, corporate acculturation, and office politics. In short, they may not have had mentors.

Finally, and perhaps most important, we care what happens to our students because they are our students and we want them to succeed.

Youth-to-Adult Transitions

The Merriam-Webster dictionary (2005) defines transition as "a passage from one state, place, stage, or subject to another" (p. 521). As life passages (e.g., from single to married, dependent to independent, or unemployed to employed full time) are usually quite complicated, readers who wish to learn about models of transition are referred to Goodman, Schlossberg, and Anderson (2006). In addition to their expectations (realistic or unrealistic) about the school-to-work passage, graduates may also feel pressure from family and society as a whole. Appendix 18A is a discussion starter constructed around the results of a General Social Survey (www.norc.org/Gss+website/) of the importance of seven youth-to-adult transitions (Smith, 2003). "The General Social Survey conducts basic scientific research on the structure and development of American society with a data-collection program designed to both monitor social change in the United States and to compare the United States to other nations." (General Social Survey, 2009, p. 1). I typically ask students to respond to questions about the survey and then we discuss the transitions. At least two salient points are likely to emerge from a discussion. First, students may question the representativeness of the GSS sample (i.e., they are unaware of its broad constituency) and argue that survey respondents are not tuned into contemporary society and young adults. Second, most survey respondents believe all seven transitions should be completed within a 5-year span and by age 26; yet some young adults have not completed any transition by that age, suggesting that there is a shift in the "social clocks" of the current generation of students. In short, if the GSS survey respondents truly represent the population, most college graduates enter the world of work with experiences and attitudes at considerable variance (as measured by this survey) with societal, workplace, and, often, family expectations.

What Makes the Workplace Different From College?

Many graduates are surprised by the differences between college and workplace environments. They may be grateful for their education but many, including high achievers, also feel unprepared for work and have encountered significant adjustment problems. Holton (1998) refers to this phenomenon as the "paradox of preparation."

One way of helping students understand this paradox is to examine the results of a survey in which Holton (1998) asked graduates to compare the differences between college and workplace. Appendix 18B presents highly revealing comparisons that are associated primarily with differences in organizational procedures, culture, and behaviors required for success. A discussion of the 16 comparisons can easily fill a class hour; I will comment on a few key comparisons.

Concrete Feedback

A hypothetical full-time student enrolled in four courses is likely to receive at least 20 to 25 specific measures of performance during a single semester. In contrast, employees in typical full-time jobs may receive a formal performance evaluation once or twice annually. The inability to receive concrete feedback (an expectation fueled and conditioned by many years of formal education) combined with the ambiguities of the workplace will frustrate many new graduates.

Initiative

Unfortunately, most students can complete college successfully without significant participation in class discussions or other activities. However, supervisors expect employees to express themselves clearly and contribute to discussions and problem-solving situations. Students who may not have developed the necessary collaboration skills will be at a disadvantage when asked to participate in staff meetings. Students who are merely shy should consult references such as Carducci (2000).

Individual Versus Team Effort

Few college courses devote all or most of the final grade to teamwork. In many organizations, however, teamwork is an essential skill (NACE, 2008) that is factored into individual performance reviews. In some organizations compensation is based on the knowledge and skills of employee teams (Greenberg, 2005). Being an ineffective team member is a common reason for disciplining new employees (Gardner, 2007).

Structure

Most college courses are highly structured and a detailed course syllabus is appreciated by students, teachers, department chairs, and deans. In the workplace, however, there is no syllabus, and ambiguous tasks are often assigned by supervisors with minimal instructions or advance notice. It is important to note that "structure" and "concrete feedback" are examples of differing processes of succeeding that Holton speaks of in his concept paradox of preparation: Certain processes that are highly valued in the academic world can sometimes be counterproductive to success in the work world (Holton, 1998; Holton & Naquin, 2001). Students should become aware of such distinctions in organizational practices before they begin their first full-time job.

Challenge

Course work is intellectually challenging, but people and productivity most often are the major challenges of the workplace. Students gain theoretical knowledge acquired from books and teachers; employees learn mostly by acquiring new knowledge and applying information and skills acquired in the workplace and college.

Each comparison contained in Holton's survey (see Appendix 18B) represents a major general distinction in practice, procedures, processes (Holton & Naquin, 2001), or organizational cultures. Students are conditioned to expect, and have learned to master, the processes and practices that produce success in college. If they hold the same expectations of supervisors they had of teachers, these new employees will experience frustration and make costly mistakes (Holton, 1998). Similarly, if they begin their first job with a weak work record (e.g., "McJobs") and an education that was restricted to classroom learning only, they are likely to encounter reality shock. The more unrealistic their expectations, the more difficult it is to reduce the discrepancy between these expectations and reality (Ashforth, 2001). I have heard some graduates describe their entry experience as "shocking," "a slap in the face," "hitting a wall," and similar expressions. We must inform students about the differences between college and corporate cultures long before graduation and encourage them to pursue strategies that can, collectively, reduce entry shock.

What Skills Do Employers Seek?

Students have learned to view the products of their efforts primarily as scores or letter grades, but the work world emphasizes skill sets. A recruiter is less interested in knowing an applicant's grades and more concerned with the person's ability to translate such achievements into skills that are potentially useful to the company. Individuals interested in learning about specific workplace skills for psychology majors are encouraged to consult Appleby (2005), Kruger and Zechmeister (2001), Landrum and Davis (2007), and Landrum and Harrold (2003).

Each year the National Association of Colleges and Employers (NACE) surveys its employer members (i.e., service sector, manufacturing, and government/nonprofit) regarding their hiring plans and related issues including desired skills. Appendix 18C, which contains a list of skills and qualities employers seek, reproduces employers' ratings of the most important qualities and skills and contains discussion questions directed to the ratings, categories of skills deficiencies, and other criteria employers consider.

Students may acknowledge that the vast majority of the NACE list of qualities (see Appendix 18C) are "taught" in college; applying these skills to workplace settings, however, will pose a major challenge. In 2008, for the ninth consecutive year, communication skills ranked highest; yet employers maintain that college graduates are most deficient in communication skills, including interviewing, face-to-face, presentation, phone, and overall interpersonal skills (NACE, 2008). Workplace conduct was ranked as the second highest area of skill deficiency. This category includes the lack of a good work ethic, analytical and problem-solving skills, business acumen, initiative, particular computer skills, flexibility, and professionalism.

The NACE survey also reports that an employer will consider the following additional criteria in the hiring process (in descending order of importance): leadership position, academic major, GPA of 3.0 or higher, involvement in extracurricular activities, volunteer work, and the school attended. In addition, 76% of the employers prefer candidates with relevant work experience whereas 18% prefer candidates with any type of work experience. Only 5% of the respondents indicated that work experience does not factor into the hiring decision. Instructors can readily lead a lively discussion of the NACE survey results contained in Appendix 18C and the statistical information above; if a university career counselor is invited to participate, additional insights are likely to emerge. Discussion questions 1 to 3 in Appendix 18C address the NACE skills list; question 4, the two deficiency categories; and question 5 the additional criteria employers consider.

From Preparedness to Promotion (or Termination)

How do graduates' prior experiences, skills, attitudes, and habits relate to success in the workplace? Among the many questions contained in his annual survey of employers, Gardner (2007) asked why new hires were disciplined, terminated, or promoted. Appendix 18D summarizes the employers' responses to these questions. The top 10 reasons (with corresponding percentage of occurrence) new employees are disciplined include lack of work ethic/commitment (52%), unethical behavior (46%), failure to follow instructions (41%), ineffectiveness in teams (41%), failure to take initiative (26%), missing assignments/deadlines (33%), inability to communicate effectively verbally (32%), inappropriate use of technology (34%), being late for work (28%), and inability to communicate effectively in writing (28%). Six of the reasons for discipline were also reasons for terminating new hires (in order of frequency): unethical behavior, lack of motivation/work ethic, inappropriate use of technology, failure to follow instructions, late for work, and missing assignments/deadlines (Gardner, 2007).

What characteristics influence the promotion and new assignments of new hires? From a list of 1,500 characteristics Gardner (2007) compiled a cluster of the seven most frequently mentioned qualities: taking initiative (16%), self-management (13%), personal attributes (9%), commitment (9%), leadership (8%), show and tell (conducting presentations) (7%), and technical competence (7%). How can teachers use the Gardner (2007) survey data? Question 1 in Appendix 18D asks students to compare the Gardner (2007) findings with the Holton (1998) survey of college graduates (see Appendix 18B), the NACE (2008) list of skills (see Appendix 18C), and instructors' performance expectations (which are sometimes listed in syllabi). The repetition of common points from these diverse sources should strengthen their credibility to students. The discussion could connect the college and corporate cultures with the role and application of qualities/skills, and the similarities and differences between instructor and supervisor demands. Perhaps students will recognize that college really is the real world, at least on the dimension of skills and qualities they must acquire.

In addition, teachers can facilitate students' connecting of college to career by explaining course expectations on the first day of class in terms of desired behaviors (e.g., commitment/work ethic, following instructions, on-time assignments, tardiness, and student initiative) and their relation to the workplace. Also, course assignments could be accompanied with a description of the major skills the assignments strengthen, such as written or oral communication, team/group work, analytical thinking, technical skills, or problem solving and their relevance to the workplace using the NACE (2008) survey results. Finally, teachers can use workplace practices as a context for responding to student concerns. For example, when students seek additional time on an assignment or a "makeup" assignment, the instructor could ask if such a request would likely be honored if they held a full-time job. To students who seek excessively specific instructions, a teacher might encourage the student to think more critically about how to find a solution independently (Hettich, 2008).

Although there are no magic bullets that guarantee a successful transition for even the best prepared graduates, students may pursue various strategies to improve their workplace readiness. Appendix 18E, the Transition Strategy Checklist, represents an action plan or blueprint of recommended strategies and activities for students that are derived from these discussion starters. Faculty who teach an "orientation to the major" course (e.g., see chapter 5 in this volume) may wish to address these issues. Providing students with information early in their academic careers can promote development of skills that will help students to transition more comfortably to the workplace.

Conclusions

Of the dimensions that influence a graduate's ability to navigate the transition between college and work, I addressed four specific topics: youth-to-adult transitions, differences between college and workplace, skills and qualities employers seek, and factors that contribute to disciplining, termination, or promotion of new hires. These topics may be introduced in courses (e.g., organizational behavior, small group behavior, interpersonal communications, senior seminar, capstone, career planning, orientation to psychology, and life span), internships, advising sessions, Psi Chi meetings, and career events.

Student knowledge of the information contained in this chapter may be assessed using essay questions, in journal writing (e.g., in courses or internships), or through observing student participation in class discussion. Also, Kruger and Zechmeister (2001) created a skills-experience inventory for psychology majors that may be adapted to one's goals and needs. To assess student initiative for implementing activities that promote preparedness, instructors may use the Transition Strategy Checklist (see Appendix 18E) while requiring students to maintain a log or journal of their activities. The checklist may also be integrated into the advising process when students declare a psychology major. Finally, it is important to point out the strong concurrence of the NACE (2008) qualities/skills with the performance benchmarks recommended for undergraduate psychology programs by Dunn, McCarthy, Baker, Halonen, and Hill (2007). All five student-related benchmarks (i.e., writing skills, speaking skills, research skills, collaborative skills, and information literacy and technology skills) are clearly represented in the NACE (2008) list. All benchmarks except research skills are directly reflected (and research skills are implied) in Gardner's (2007) survey of behaviors.

The transition from college to workplace is one of the most anticipated, exciting, and critical events in our students' lives, but it generates high levels of stress as well as eustress. When we enable students to begin preparing for transition well before their senior year, we offer them, as architects of their own future, a blueprint for building a strong bridge to a new world of living, learning, and relating.

Recommended Resources

Fisher, S. Y., & Shelly, S. (2005). *The complete idiot's guide to personal finance in your 20's and 30's* (3rd ed). New York: Penguin Group.
Holton, E. F., III, & Naquin, S. S. (2001). *How to succeed in your first job: Tips for new college graduates.* San Francisco, CA: Berrett-Koehler.

Landrum, R. E., (2009). *Finding jobs with a psychology bachelor's degree: Expert advice for launching your career.* Washington, DC: American Psychological Association.

Levit, A. (2009). *They don't teach corporate in college: A twenty-something's guide to the business world (2nd ed).* Franklin Lakes, NJ: Career Press.

Wilner, A., & Stocker, C. (2005). *The quarterlifer's companion: How to get on the right career path, control your finances, and find the support network you need to thrive.* New York: McGraw Hill.

References

Appleby, D. C. (2005, August). *Career-related skills that can be developed by Psi Chi officers.* Paper presented at the annual meeting of Psi Chi at the meeting of the American Psychological Association, Washington, DC.

Arnett, J. J., & Tanner, J. L. (Eds.). (2006). *Emerging adults in America: Coming of age in the 21st century.* Washington, DC: American Psychological Association.

Ashforth, B. E. (2001). *Role transitions in organizational life: An identity-based perspective.* Mahwah, NJ: Erlbaum.

Borden, V. M. H., & Rajecki, D. W. (2000). First year employment outcomes of psychology baccalaureates: Relatedness, preparedness, and prospects. *Teaching of Psychology, 27,* 164–168.

Carducci, B. J. (2000). *Shyness: A bold new approach.* New York: HarperCollins.

Casner-Lotto, J., & Barrington, L. (2006, October). *Are they really ready to work? Employers' perspectives on the basic knowledge and applied skills of new entrants to the 21st century U.S. workforce* (The Conference Board, Partnership for 21st Century Skills, Corporate Voices for Working Families, Society for Human Resource Management). Retrieved August 15, 2009, from http://www.conference-board.org/pdf_free/BED-06- Workforce.pdf.

College Board. (2008). *Students relying more heavily on private lenders.* Retrieved August 15, 2009, from http://www.collegeboard.com/prod_downloads/press/cost06/student_debt_06.pdf.

Dunn, D. S., McCarthy, M. A., Baker, S., Halonen, J. S., & Hill, G. W., IV. (2007). Quality benchmarks in undergraduate programs. *American Psychologist, 62,* 650–670.

Gardner, P. (2007). *Moving up or moving out of the company? Factors that influence the promoting or firing of new college hires.* Research Brief 1-2007. Michigan State University Collegiate Employment Research Institute. Retrieved August 15, 2009, from www.ceri.msu.edu/publications/publications.html.

Gardner, P. D. (1998). Are college students prepared to work? In J. N. Gardner, G. Van der Veer, & Associates (Eds.), *The senior year experience: Facilitating integration, reflection, closure, and transition* (pp. 60–78). San Francisco, CA: Jossey Bass.

General Social Survey. Retrieved August 15, 2009, from www.norc.org/GSS+Website.

Goodman, J., Scholssberg, N. K., & Anderson, M. L. (2006). *Counseling adults in transition: Linking practice with theory* (3rd ed.). New York: Springer.

Greenberg, J. (2005). *Managing behavior in organizations* (4th ed). Upper Saddle River, NJ: Pearson/Prentice Hall.

Hettich, P. (March, 2008). Improving students' workplace readiness. *Higher Education Academy Psychology Network Newsletter, 47*, 2–3.

Hettich, P. I., & Helkowski, C. (2005). *Connect college to career: A student's guide to work and life transitions.* Belmont, CA: Thomson/Wadsworth.

Holton, E. F., III. (1998). Preparing students for life beyond the classroom. In J. N. Gardner, G. Van der Veer, & Associates (Eds.), *The senior year experience: Facilitating integration, reflection, closure, and transition* (pp. 95–115). San Francisco, CA: Jossey-Bass.

Holton, E. F., III, & Naquin, S. S. (2001). *How to succeed in your first job: Tips for new college graduates.* San Francisco, CA: Berrett-Koehler.

Kruger, D. J., & Zechmeister, E. B. (2001). A skills-experience inventory for the undergraduate psychology major. *Teaching of Psychology, 28,* 249–253.

Landrum, R. E., & Davis, S. F. (2007). *Psychology major: Career options and strategies for success* (3rd ed). Upper Saddle River, NJ: Pearson/Prentice Hall.

Landrum, R. E., & Harrold, R. (2003). What employers want from psychology graduates. *Teaching of Psychology, 30,* 131–133.

McAdams, D. P. (2001). *The person: An integrated introduction to personality psychology.* Orlando, FL: Harcourt College.

Merriam-Webster Dictionary. (2005). Springfield, MA: Merriam-Webster.

Morgan, B. L, & Korschgen, A. J. (2009). *Majoring in psychology? Career options for psychology undergraduates* (4th ed). Needham Heights, MA: Allyn & Bacon.

National Association of Colleges and Employers (NACE). (2008). *Job outlook 2008.* Bethlehem, PA.

National Center for Educational Statistics. (2007). *Digest of educational statistics,* Ch.3, Postsecondary Education, Degree Granting Institutions, Table 261. Retrieved August 15, 2009, from http://www.nces.ed.gov/pubs2008/2008022_3b.pdf.

Pierson, J. (2007, November). *Student loan default: It's about success.* Paper presented at the 14th National Conference on Students in Transition, Cincinnati, OH.

Robbins, A., & Wilner, A. (2001). *Quarterlife crisis.* New York: Penguin Press.

Smith, T. W. (2003). *Coming of age in 21st century America: Public attitudes towards the importance and timing of transitions to adulthood.* (GSS Topical Report No. 35). Chicago: University of Chicago, National Opinion Research Center.

Appendix 18A   Youth-to-Adult Transitions

In his 2003 study, Tom Smith surveyed approximately 1,400 American adults sampled from the 2002 General Social Survey (GSS) to determine the importance of seven youth-to-adult transitions. The types of transitions, respondents' combined ratings of importance ("extremely," "quite," or "somewhat,"), and the mean age by which the transitions should occur are presented below.

Table A1
Importance and Mean Age of Seven Youth-to-Adult Transitions

Transition:	Importance	Mean age
Completing education	97%	22
Achieving financial independence	97%	21
Obtaining full-time employment	95%	21
Supporting a family	94%	25
Not living with parents	82%	21
Getting married	55%	26
Having a child	52%	26

Discussion Questions

1. What observations or conclusions can you describe from this data?
2. To what extent would your family, friends, and employer, separately, agree with these findings?
3. What are the implications of these data for juniors, seniors, and recent graduates?

Note: Reference: Smith, T. W. (2003). *Coming of Age in 21st Century America: Public Attitudes toward the Importance and Timing of Transitions to Adulthood* (GSS Topical Report No. 35). Chicago: University of Chicago. National Opinion Research Center. Adapted with permission.

Appendix 18B   Graduates' Perceived Differences Between College and Workplace

Table B1
Graduates' Perceived Differences Between College and Workplace

College	Workplace
1. Frequent and concrete feedback	Feedback infrequent and not specific
2. Highly structured curriculum	Highly unstructured; fewer directions
3. Personal supportive environment	Less personal support
4. Few significant changes	Frequent and unexpected changes
5. Flexible schedule	Structured schedule
6. Frequent breaks and time off	Limited time off
7. Personal control over time	Responding to others' directions and interests
8. Intellectual challenge	Organizational and people challenge
9. Choice of your performance level	A-level work required at all times
10. Focus on development/growth	Focus on getting results for organization
11. Create and explore knowledge	Get results with your knowledge
12. Individual effort	Team effort
13. "Right" answers	Few "right" answers
14. Independence of thinking	Do it the organization's way
15. Professors	Bosses
16. Less initiative required	Lots of initiative required

Discussion Questions

1. Based on your work experience, what particular differences in the Holton table between college and the workplace do you anticipate will be or are difficult for you to adjust to? Why?
2. How do perceptions between working and nonworking students in your class differ?
3. What additional dimensions not listed in Table B1 would distinguish college from workplace?

4. Some people argue that teachers should implement workplace-like practices that might better prepare students for real-life jobs. What could teachers do? For example, to *reduce structure,* how would students react if teachers eliminated or sharply reduced information contained in the course syllabus or in written assignments? Or, how would students react if the only *feedback* they receive during the academic term was a final grade with a half- page of teacher comments?

5. What opportunities exist on your campus that could make you aware of the differences between college and workplace?

Note: The table of 16 items is from *The Senior Year Experience* by J. N. Gardner, G. Van der Veer and Associates, Chapter 7 by E. F. Holton, III (p. 102), 1998. San Francisco, CA: Jossey-Bass. Adapted with permission of John Wiley.

Appendix 18C   Skills and Qualities

Employers Seek

According to *Job Outlook 2008* published by the National Association of Colleges and Employers (NACE), the most important qualities/skills employers seek are rated in descending order of importance in Table C1.

Table C1
Skills and Qualities Employers Seek

Skill or quality	Rating*
Communication skills	4.6
Strong work ethic	4.6
Teamwork skills (works well with others)	4.5
Initiative	4.4
Interpersonal skills (relates well to others)	4.4
Problem-solving skills	4.4
Analytic skills	4.3
Flexibility/adaptability	4.2
Computer skills	4.1
Technical skills	4.1
Detail-oriented	4.0
Organizational skills	4.0
Leadership skills	3.9
Self-confidence	3.9
Friendly/outgoing personality	3.8
Tactfulness	3.8
Creativity	3.6
Strategic planning skills	3.3
Entrepreneurial skills/risk-taker	3.2
Sense of humor	3.1

* 5-point scale, where 1 = not at all important and 5 = extremely important.

Discussion Questions

1. Which qualities and skills contained in the NACE list are taught *directly* and which are taught *indirectly* in your current courses? (Suggestion: review course syllabi and assignments.)

2. What can teachers and students do to highlight the importance of workplace skills and qualities in the day-to-day activities of their coursework? Which skills and qualities can be strengthened in co-curricular activities?

3. What qualities and skills on the NACE list are most and least important in your current job?

4. The NACE survey also reported that new hires enter the workplace deficient in communication skills (i.e., interviewing, face-to-face, presentation, phone, and interpersonal), workplace conduct (i.e., lack of work ethic, analytical and problem-solving skills, business acumen, initiative, flexibility, and professionalism), and workplace experience (lack of work experience and internship experience). In which particular academic and nonacademic activities can you strengthen these qualities?

5. The NACE survey identified the following additional criteria employers consider if applicants have equal attributes: leadership position, GPA of 3.0 or higher, involvement in extracurricular activities, and volunteer work. In which of these criteria do you excel and in which do you need to improve? Name activities you can perform that will advance you to the next level.

Note: The NACE qualities/skills and ratings data are reprinted from *Job Outlook 2008*, with permission of the National Association of Colleges and Employers, copyright holder www.jobweb.com/studentarticles.aspx?id=2121.

Appendix 18D   Factors That Influence the Disciplining, Firing, and Promoting of New College Hires

Table D1
Factors That Influence the Disciplining and Firing of New College Hires

Reasons for Discipline	Occurrence: Fairly – Very Often (%)*	Mean (5-point scale)
Lack of work ethic/commitment**	52	3.46
Unethical behavior**	46	3.22
Failure to follow instructions**	41	3.21
Ineffective in teams	41	3.19
Failure to take initiative	26	3.10
Missing assignments/deadlines**	33	2.98
Unable to communicate effectively – verbally	32	2.97
Inappropriate use of technology**	34	2.90
Being late for work**	28	2.83
Unable to communicate effectively – writing	28	2.81

* Percentage of occurrence at the high end (Fairly – Very Often) of the scale

** Reasons given for firing new hires

Table D2
Characteristics That Lead to Promotions and New Assignments

Characteristics	Frequency as listed by employer (%)
Taking initiative	16
Self-management	13
Personal attributes	9
Commitment	9
Leadership	8
"Show and tell" (presentations)	7
Technical competence	7
Organizational savvy	5
Learning	5
Critical thinking	5

Discussion Questions

1. Compare the findings in this survey (Tables D1 and D2) with the NACE list of skills (see Appendix C), and with your instructor's expectations of student performance (review the syllabus and course assignments). What are the similarities and differences among these sources?
2. Using the same information identified in the previous question, explain the ways in which college is different from "the real world." Be sure to include your academic and nonacademic activities.

Note: *From Moving Up or Moving Out of the Company? Factors That Influence the Promoting or Firing of New College Hires.* Research Brief 1-2007.
Michigan State University Collegiate Employment Research Institute. Retrieved August 15, 2009 from
www.ceri.msu.edu/publications/publications.html. Adapted with permission.

Appendix 18E   Transition Strategy Checklist

The activities below represent strategies you can pursue for a successful transition to the workplace. The sophomore year or beginning of the junior year is a good time to assess your experiences to date, identify areas for further exploration, and establish a plan of action to gather and synthesize personal and professional information into flexible goals for your future. Keep a journal that includes names and contact information of people/organizations/activities, a description of the experiences, your personal reactions, and how the experiences serve you now and/or in the future.

- Monitor employment experiences, emphasizing transferable skills, attitudes, and relationships.
- Complete internships to gain experience in workplace settings and enhance skills.
- Complete workplace-related courses such as OB, management, and communications.
- Develop leadership skills in campus organizations, peer programs, sports, and community service.
- Meet regularly with a career counselor beginning the junior year if possible.
- Seek training in team building, stress and time management, and conflict resolution.
- Establish mentoring relationships with faculty, staff, alumni, and employer.
- Seek involvement in faculty research projects.
- Acquire integrative experiences through career planning and senior capstone courses.

I find the great thing in this world is not so much where we stand, as in what direction we are moving: To reach the port of heaven, we must sail sometimes with the wind and sometimes against it—But we must sail, and not drift, nor lie at anchor.

> Oliver Wendell Holmes, Sr. (1809–1894) poet, novelist, physician

Note: Created by P. Hettich and C. Helkowski, 2007.

19 Helping Undergraduates Make the Transition to Graduate School

Brennan D. Cox, Kristin L. Cullen, William Buskist, and *Victor A. Benassi*

Each year thousands of undergraduate psychology majors apply to graduate school, but only exceptional students receive an acceptance letter (American Psychological Association [APA], 2007). For the majority of students who do not gain acceptance into a program, the time between their rejection notice and graduation is likely spent preparing for life after college. Instead of continuing their education, they must begin taking steps toward getting a job and starting their professional careers, though probably not as practicing psychologists. Although students who gain admittance into a graduate program may not be aware of it, they will experience a similar change, and they may benefit from preparing for graduate school as they would for a new career. After all, to get into graduate school, they likely had to

- Apply for a position by submitting an application, letters of recommendation, and other relevant materials, such as a statement of purpose and cover letter.
- Undergo a rigorous selection process during which the admissions committee quickly removed the majority of candidates from consideration and then evaluated the top few choices individually for their potential fit with the program.
- Visit prospective programs and interview with potential mentors and advisors.

- Make an acceptance decision based on the number of offers received and other criteria.
- Relocate to a new town, state, region, or even country to begin their new "careers."

Graduate schools are training programs that prepare students to become professionals in their area of study. In this sense, being a graduate student is a full-time job. No longer are course grades the chief criterion for achievement (e.g., Buskist & Burke, 2007; Goldsmith, Komlos, & Gold, 2001). Students must now begin to acquire vast amounts of new knowledge, apply it in novel ways in an effort to solve particular problems or generate new knowledge, and otherwise contribute to their field in meaningful ways. To maximize their chances for success, prospective graduate students should prepare for the changes and challenges they will experience as they leave the comforts of their bachelor programs and transition into the graduate student way of life.

Although there are numerous books and articles designed to prepare undergraduates for the graduate admissions process (e.g., Buskist, 2001; Buskist & Burke, 2007; Keith-Spiegel & Wiederman, 2000; Kuther, 2003; Kuther & Morgan, 2004), relatively few focus on preparing students for the transition into graduate school. Many successful undergraduate students enter graduate school ill-prepared for the differences between their former and future programs of study. Indeed, a common misconception among first-year graduate students is that graduate school will simply be an extension of their undergraduate experiences (Cox, Cullen, & Buskist, 2008). As we learned in a recent survey of 31 Auburn University psychology graduate students representing clinical, experimental, and industrial-organizational programs, members of each incoming class bring with them certain expectations of what graduate students, faculty, classes, research, teaching, and other components of the graduate school experience will be like. These expectations, however, are often inaccurate and can lead to a turbulent transition.

In this chapter, we highlight several key changes that faculty can help students prepare for as they leave their undergraduate institutions to begin graduate work. We also provide data about common preconceptions and misconceptions of graduate school, including advice from experienced graduate students about how first-year students can successfully negotiate the undergraduate-to-graduate transition. Although this chapter applies mainly to preparing students for PhD programs in psychology, we believe our suggestions will help faculty to prepare their undergraduates for any type of graduate degree in psychology.

Graduate School Raises the Bar: The Curve Shifts

One of the first things new graduate students will discover is that other students are just as smart and hardworking as they are. This realization should not come as too great a surprise, given the significant weight placed on academic success (e.g., GPA and Graduate Record Exam [GRE] scores) during the admissions process. Still, the results of our survey indicate that many students have difficulty adjusting to the idea that simply being smart is no longer sufficient to do well in school. As one respondent commented, "It was difficult to transition from a program where I was the top student without fail to a program where I was not yet the top student and may not ever become the top student." Another graduate student noted that "in graduate school, what was considered going above and beyond as an undergradaduate is instead the norm." Because graduate admission committees select students with very strong academic records from their pool of applicants, incoming students should prepare for the revelation that many of them will be academically average compared to their new peers.

Although bright, many first-year graduate students struggle with the increased reading requirements of their graduate courses. In addition to text-book assignments, most graduate courses will likely require readings from psychological journals and other outside resources. Reading journal articles requires a very different strategy from that required for reading textbook chapters (e.g., new graduate students must adapt to reading materials that do not have bold-faced words). These skills can best be learned through practice. Graduate students will need to spend time reading every day, which may be a different experience for them relative to their undergraduate days. Graduate students can also expect much of their time to be spent in endeavors outside of the classroom. To be sure, in graduate school the focus is no longer strictly on course work—graduate students spend the bulk of their time working on basic research and applied projects that extend well beyond the classroom.

Of course, most undergraduates probably anticipate that the academic and other performance standards are going to be higher in graduate school. Graduate students know that they will have to work harder and study longer, but it may come as a surprise to some that in many graduate programs a grade of a "C" is considered failing and a "B" is not much better (Buskist & Burke, 2007). Suffice it to say, there are few second chances for graduate students who struggle with their course work. The primary assumption in graduate school is that *all* students will excel in *all* of their classes. As a result, students who cannot maintain consistently high marks may stand out for their inability to keep up with their classmates. These sorts of red flags often influence faculty to pass these students over for important research, writing, and teaching opportunities, causing these students to fall even further behind their peers in scholarly achievement. Although rare, in some cases students may even be terminated from their programs for failing to excel scholastically.

Undergraduate faculty can help their students better prepare for the rigors of graduate school by sharing realistic examples of requirements for successful graduate work. It may benefit students, for instance, to learn in advance the key differences between undergraduate and graduate program policies, such as rules on attendance, workload, grading, and deadlines (Terre, 2001). Although these policies likely differ from school to school, many programs list their graduate rules and regulations on their departmental Web sites. Often, these sites also contain information on the program's plan of study, so students can preview the specific courses and research criteria they will be required to complete for a graduate degree. A comparison of the core curriculum requirements for undergraduate and graduate programs will reveal that in graduate school, it truly is all about psychology, all of the time. In addition, many graduate programs' Web sites also provide access to course syllabi. By sampling specific course requirements, undergraduates can gain a realistic impression of what is expected of a successful graduate student.

A Graduate Student Wears Many Hats

One of the biggest changes for which faculty can prepare students is the increased role requirements beyond being "just a student." As one of our survey respondents put it, "I believed graduate school would be a lot of work, but that it would be qualitatively the same as my undergraduate experience. Instead, I have found that taking classes has been only a minor portion of my education." Undoubtedly, course work is only one of many responsibilities that graduate students must undertake. Other common activities include conducting research, providing teaching assistance, working as a clinician or intern, serving as a student representative at departmental and schoolwide functions, and mentoring undergraduate students. Each of these roles demands a unique set of skills that first-year graduate students must develop quickly to succeed. As one of our survey respondents confessed, "Juggling different tasks was the most difficult part of my first year." To ease the transition process, faculty can alert undergraduates of the unforeseen requirements of graduate training programs.

Consider, for instance, the transformation students must undergo the first time they serve as graduate teaching assistants (GTAs). A few months ago, most of these students were undergraduates sitting in a classroom, taking notes, and perhaps hoping their professor would let them out early. Now they find themselves on the other side of the podium, playing the role of teacher, and correcting students for calling them "Doctor" a few years too soon. Graduate programs charge many first-time GTAs with learning how to prepare lesson plans and lead class discussions as well as create, proctor, and grade quizzes and exams, often with little or no training prior to the first day of class. These novice instructors may even find themselves in the unique position of offering advice to undergraduates on how they, too, can prepare for graduate study in psychology.

Undergraduates would be wise to begin developing the skills they need to lead a class prior to the first day of graduate school. To this end, we encourage undergraduate faculty to assign oral presentation projects in their upper level psychology courses. These sorts of presentation experiences provide students with opportunities to be in front of a classroom and talk about an area of psychology that they only recently learned about themselves. We also recommend that senior-level students enroll in seminar-based courses if available in their department. Unlike most lecture-based courses, which often feature one-way communication from the instructor to the students, seminars encourage each individual to contribute to the day's learning objectives. The seminar format is beneficial for prospective graduate students because it provides opportunities for them to engage in meaningful exchanges of ideas, which may require them to explain or defend their position publicly. The more practice undergraduates have in public oral communication, the better prepared they will be for teaching at the college and university level. Additionally, some undergraduate programs permit students to serve as teaching assistants based on their prior course performance. Faculty should encourage prospective graduate students to take advantage of these opportunities whenever available, as firsthand teaching experiences will surely prove invaluable during their transition into graduate school.

To prepare students for the additional responsibilities required in graduate school, faculty should support their undergraduates' involvement in learning activities that take place outside of the classroom. Undergraduates will benefit from joining the psychology club or Psi Chi as well as nationally recognized organizations, such as the APA or the Association for Psychological Science (APS). These organizations provide members the opportunity to discuss psychology in a variety of off-campus contexts. They also are advantageous for enabling undergraduates to attend and present at conferences and to begin establishing their professional networks, all of which contribute to expanding and deepening the graduate school experience.

Graduate advisors generally require their students to conduct independent research, which may even extend beyond the minimum requirements of a master's thesis and doctoral dissertation. Therefore, the more research experience undergraduates acquire, the better. Getting involved in research provides undergraduates an opportunity to shadow experienced psychologists in the long and detail-intensive research process. There are many "behind the scenes" activities involved in getting a research project off the ground and carrying it through to publication. Prospective graduate students would do well to participate in this process from beginning to end to gain a better understanding of the requirements for the research side of graduate study. Because most research projects take a long time to come to fruition, undergraduates should become involved in research labs as early as possible in their undergraduate career. By doing so, they are more likely to complete an entire project with their faculty supervisor and may even have the opportunity to present this research at a conference.

Of course, there is no substitute for learning about research firsthand. Thus, we believe that faculty should involve undergraduates in independent research projects and, when possible, honors theses. These supervised, self-directed projects provide undergraduates with hands-on experience in developing research questions, designing research, collecting and analyzing data, creating an institutional review board protocol, and learning to write in APA style. Conducting their own research allows undergraduates to experience the rigors of research personally but under ample faculty and graduate student supervision. Undergraduates with a demonstrated ability to conduct their own research are not only more attractive to graduate admission committees but are also ahead of the game as new graduate students because they are more likely to know which direction to take for their master's thesis and other research projects (Buskist & Burke, 2007; Keith-Spiegel & Wiederman, 2000). Indeed, for undergraduates interested in pursuing graduate school, the benefits of conducting an undergraduate research project are abundant.

Graduate School Is No Time to Be Shy

Another change that students encounter as they begin graduate school is the increased amount of personal contact they have with their new peers, faculty, and advisors. New students will learn quickly that graduate school is truly a place where everyone knows their names. Because many programs accept only a handful of applicants each year, members of each incoming class get to know each other quite well. Similar to the undergraduate experience, it is normal for first-year graduate students to form exclusive social groups within their cohort, particularly among students with similar research interests. These students should be mindful, however, that they are not only developing friendships at this time but also a professional network that they will likely call upon for years to come. Networks are advantageous for providing social support, stimulating research ideas, and answering any questions students may have throughout graduate school and beyond (DuVernet et al., 2008). Plus, networking is invaluable for generating future professional and job opportunities (e.g., Goldsmith et al., 2001). Thus, it is a good idea for students to avoid burning bridges in graduate school.

In developing a network, it is important for students to demonstrate an understanding and appreciation for differing points of view. After all, most graduate programs consist of students and faculty from a variety of cultural and academic backgrounds. Such diversity of experience leads to differences in opinion, and of course, no one theory is always correct. Faculty can help undergraduates develop an open, yet critical mind by creating opportunities for them to interact with fellow students and faculty from diverse theoretical backgrounds. These conversations will provide students with a broad perspective on psychological theories and avenues of research and may present a new perspective on the students' own orientation. Faculty can also demonstrate through their teaching that there are numerous approaches to explaining any psychological phenomenon and should likewise encourage their students to ask questions and seek alternative solutions to any problem.

In graduate classes, students commonly engage in critical thinking over established theories while exploring unconventional explanations for the *why* of matters. Although many undergraduates have the opportunity to take part in low enrollment, discussion-based courses prior to entering graduate school (e.g., seminars), it may be helpful to remember that nearly all graduate classes are small and driven by student contributions. In fact, many graduate courses are essentially taught by the graduate students, with faculty members serving more as course facilitators than instructors per se. This new responsibility requires much more than just skimming the material ahead of time. Graduate students have to read, reread, and study the material; prepare summary reports; and be able to integrate this information along with their own thoughts about the material while discussing it with their classmates. For first-year students who shied away from participating in class as undergraduates, this aspect of graduate school may require significant adjustment.

Faculty can prepare their undergraduates for this sort of learning environment by providing them with increased exposure to and practice with student-led instruction and theoretical debates. We recommend that faculty hold advanced undergraduates in upper division courses to the same or similar standards they might have for graduate-level courses and require these students to participate in intellectually rigorous class discussions. Although not all students who enroll in these courses will be graduate school–bound, the entire class should benefit from having the opportunity to share and examine one another's unique perspective on the course material. As an alternative, faculty could provide separate course requirements for their undergraduates based on their post-bachelor program plans (e.g., research papers and presentations for those interested in graduate school versus tests and quizzes for the rest of the class) or simply allow prospective graduate students to lead class discussions voluntarily from time to time. Faculty should also encourage their undergraduates to enroll in cross-listed courses that enroll both undergraduate and master's-level students, if available at their institution. Through exposure to participatory classroom settings, undergraduates will likely gain a better understanding of what graduate classes are like, including the fact that some students still come to class unprepared despite these higher expectations.

The more opportunities undergraduates have for discussing their understanding of psychology, the better prepared they will be for entering graduate school with a deeper understanding of the discipline. Faculty should encourage their undergraduates to interact with them not only in the classroom but also during office hours, departmental colloquia, club meetings, and conferences. During these conversations, faculty can help undergraduates clarify their research and professional interests, which may help them when selecting a major advisor in graduate school. (Indeed, one positive outcome of such interactions for faculty is that they may discover undergraduates who would be wonderful junior colleagues in their laboratories.) These meetings also offer opportunities for students to gain experience interacting with faculty in less formal settings, which will prepare them well for the close working relationships they will have with their professors as graduate students. Indeed, at the graduate level it is normal for students to become genuine collaborators with their major professors through research, teaching, and professional development.

We further recommend that faculty alert their undergraduates to the importance of finding mentors early in their graduate careers. In this vein, faculty should stress the importance of identifying and seeking out graduate faculty with whom students can have honest discussions about their professional goals and how to bring these aspirations to fruition. If possible, faculty should put undergraduates in touch with graduate students, so that they might learn firsthand about the intricacies of the mentor-mentee relationship. Current graduate students will also be able to provide prospective graduate students other insights about graduate school, such as those we have already discussed.

Conclusions

In the end, an undergraduate's teachers, mentors, and advisors can provide only so much guidance, training, and support. One final way through which faculty may ease the transition of their students into graduate school is by emphasizing the need for them to take responsibility for their own education. Graduate school offers students a great deal of autonomy, and personal accountability is the cornerstone for graduate school success.

In this chapter, we have discussed a range of issues that confront students as they make the transition from undergraduate to graduate school. These issues include

- No longer being the "smartest" person in class
- Very high academic standards
- Increased reading workload
- Balancing class work with research, teaching, and writing responsibilities
- Increased personal contact with faculty, staff, and peers

- Heavy emphasis on developing public speaking skills in professional venues
- Increased pressure to develop highly refined time-management skills
- Increased need for mentoring relative to professional development

Faculty can help their students prepare for the transition to graduate school not only by informing them of the many changes that they can expect but also by holding these students to academic and professional standards similar to those found in graduate school. More specifically, undergraduate faculty can

- Communicate to students the rigors and realities of graduate study both in class and during office hours
- Direct students to appropriate materials that will help to inform their choices, such as graduate school reference books and program Web sites
- Encourage students to become professionally active in organizations such as Psi Chi, APA, and APS
- Involve students in research-based activities
- Set high standards of academic performance while holding students personally accountable
- Assign students written and oral projects
- Expose students to opposing points of view on psychological phenomena and encourage them to think critically about alternative explanations for events
- Encourage students to enroll in cross-listed upper division seminars (seminars open to both advanced undergraduates and graduate students)
- Partner students with graduate students or faculty with whom they share similar interests
- Reinforce students' efforts and interest in actively preparing for the transition process

Preparing for and starting graduate school is a time-consuming, anxiety-provoking, and incredibly challenging task for even the most talented under-graduates. Any helping hand that faculty extend their graduate school–bound students may go a long way toward saving their students' time, reducing uncertainty and anxiety, and making the challenge a bit more manageable.

Our work with helping undergraduates prepare for graduate study and our experiences working with first-year graduate students has provided us with a clear realization of the obstacles facing new graduate students as well as effective methods for helping these students overcome the challenges. We hope that you will find our ideas and suggestions helpful as you work diligently to prepare the next generation of academic and professional psychologists.

References and Recommended Readings

American Psychological Association. (2007). *Getting in: A step-by-step plan for gaining admission to graduate school in psychology* (2nd ed.). Washington, DC: Author.

Buskist, W. (2001, Spring). Seven tips for preparing a successful application to graduate school in psychology. *Eye on Psi Chi, 5,* 32–34.

Buskist, W., & Burke, C. (2007). *Preparing for graduate study in psychology: 101 questions and answers* (2nd ed.). Malden, MA: Blackwell.

Cox, B. D., Cullen, K., & Buskist, W. (2008). Making the transition from undergraduate to graduate student: Insights from successful graduate students. *Eye on Psi Chi, 12,* 28–30.

DuVernet, A., Behrend, T., Hess, C., McGinnis, J., Poncheri, R., & Vignovic, J. (2008, April). TIP-TOPics for students. *Industrial-Organizational Psychologist, 45*(4), 85–89.

Goldsmith, J. A., Komlos, J., & Gold, P. S. (2001). *The Chicago guide to your academic career: A portable mentor for scholars from graduate school through tenure.* Chicago, IL: University of Chicago Press.

Keith-Spiegel, P., & Wiederman, M. W. (2000). *The complete guide to graduate school admission: Psychology, counseling, and related professions* (2nd ed.). Mahwah, NJ: Erlbaum.

Kuther, T. L. (2003). *The psychology major's handbook.* Belmont, CA: Wadsworth.

Kuther, T. L., & Morgan, R. D. (2004). *Careers in psychology: Opportunities in a changing world.* Belmont, CA: Wadsworth.

Terre, L. (2001). Making the transition to graduate school. *Eye on Psi Chi, 6,* 25–27.

20 Teaching Psychology's Endings

The Simple Gifts of a Reflective Close

Neil Lutsky

This chapter is worth reading. Convincing you of this assertion is the primary end of the beginning you are now reading. So how might I capture your attention? How might I lead you to believe in this chapter, especially given all the other chapters, professional tasks, and attractions and necessities of life clamoring for your time?

Did you notice how short my first paragraph is? One way I can try to successfully begin is to make it easy for you to start reading the chapter and, by opening in this way, to suggest that you can efficiently traverse the territory that lies between this beginning and soon to be promised ends. But ease of action will only get you so far. To keep you reading, I need, implicitly and/or explicitly, to inform you about the goals and character of this chapter and, most importantly, to persuade you that the ends of the piece will be useful. In other words, *my beginning must be magnetic*; it must pull your attention forward by virtue of the value it promises.

Did I mention that this chapter reviews beginning and ending strategies designed to improve the teaching of psychology courses? Can you see that beginnings embody what the literary critic Edward Said (1975, p. 48) called "genetic optimism"? Beginnings and endings focus attention on attractive overarching goals; they offer value and purpose; they promise ease of accomplishment. If successful, the strategies immerse potential beginners in the initial currents of an activity—here, reading a chapter—so that they, including you, may be swept forward to its end.

What might drive your continued attention to this chapter? I've already pledged to identify techniques to enhance your teaching and, in fact, will begin to do so upon completing this introduction. I will briefly address beginning a psychology course and ending that same course. Beginnings and endings are tightly intertwined. The induction into a new activity is also related to what has recently past, so it might be said that a successful beginning is the true ending of what has occurred previously.

In this chapter I will show that endings are grounded in psychological science and that endings—of conversations, relationships, therapy, and lives—are not only significant phenomena in their own right, but when studied scientifically, they have much to suggest about endings in teaching. In other words, I intend to argue that there is a generalized psychology of endings that provides us with insights and guides for pedagogical endings. Generalizing the concept of endings further implies that a prototypic teaching topic—the construction of courses—can be applied to other pedagogical challenges, such as crafting individual class sessions or structuring an entire psychology curriculum. Finally—although that's a dangerous word to use in a discussion of endings—I have a third goal for this chapter: to address teaching as the responsible conveyance of purpose and meaning. Nowhere is that opportunity more in play than when we begin and end.

Beginning a Course

This course is worth taking. Isn't the value of the course the central message we want to send to students as they enter the first class session? To be sure, we want to inform students about the nature of the course, the topics to be covered, the assignments they must complete, the rules they must follow, and the books they must purchase. But beginnings elicit keen attention, and we would be remiss to solely address orienting information. We need to inspire students' interest and commitment, especially if we seek, throughout a course, to engage students' thinking rather than short-term memories (see Gray, 1993). As Friedrich and Douglass (1998) noted, "teaching is at a fundamental level a process of persuasion" (p. 553), and we need to convince students at the outset that *this* course deserves and will reward their attention, efforts, and thinking.

How might we convince students that a course is important? Alas, the ancient Greek technique of shouting "I command you to listen" (Dunn, 1996) is unlikely to succeed, at least for more than a few shocking seconds, so we must look elsewhere. I've already hinted at one alternative: *It's by sharing with students a conviction that a course is important and offering concrete arguments in support of that conviction.* The exact way an instructor chooses to achieve these ends may vary as a function of course content and level, students' characteristics, a teacher's preferred style, and other factors, but here is one method that works for me and my students.

My example is taken from introductory psychology, where I begin the first class by identifying four themes as overarching the course:

1. We experience and navigate the world psychologically.
2. Psychology can be studied scientifically.
3. We have much to gain from psychological science.
4. Carleton is a great school.

The last claim, I must quickly add, is neither as self-centered nor as self-congratulatory as it might first appear. Bear with me until I elaborate each of these points.

The hypothesis, that experience is not directly given to us by the external world, is central to psychology. Psychology rests on the claim that we organize and shape perceptions, understandings, memories, judgments, and self-assessments, and that these constructions, with or without awareness, guide behavior. The discipline exists to make sense of the mediation of external experience, to weigh how significant such constructive activity is, and to develop means of altering these behavioral determinants when that appears desirable. I draw attention to psychological construction with a slide and a song. The slide presents a perceptual stimulus, Lincoln's stovepipe hat illusion (e.g., SandlotScience, 2005) in which the height of the hat appears erroneously to far exceed the breadth of the brim. The song, "It's All in Your Mind" (LaVere, 1941, performed by Jay Ungar and Molly Mason), presents the extreme notion that it's *all* in your mind, which allows me to raise a question for the class's consideration over the term: Just how much of "it" is "all in [our] minds" as opposed to being dictated by the highs and lows of the events of life we experience?

I then build on this first claim by suggesting that it is possible to study constructive psychological phenomena and processes *scientifically* (Friedrich & Douglass, 1998). I promise my students (and my reader) to present an example shortly. My third claim trumpets the potential value of psychological science. Here I cite a story in the *New York Times* (Wald, 2004) summarizing a World Health Organization prediction that by 2020 road accidents will be the third largest cause of death and disability worldwide, behind heart disease and deaths linked to mental illness. The point I develop is that the study of psychology might inform our understanding of all three causes of death, and in certain cases, has led to interventions designed to prevent these tragedies. In sum, I try to tell and show my students that psychology matters.

To reinforce students' appreciation for the potential value of psychological insight, I present slides from an unpublished experiment. In the experiment, conducted by me and a former student, Janet Balanoff, research participants encountered a student leaning against a tree, clutching his abdomen, and moaning loudly. Participants were asked how likely they would be to stop to help the person in need, how likely they believe their fellow students would be to help (or not), and whether males or females would be more or less likely to help. What I do next is to predict my students' expectations for their own behavior, for their peers', and for males' and females' potential helping. My numbers accurately foresee the students' predictions because my numbers are based on data collected from past classes. I then present the actual results of the study, which deviate strongly from students' intuitions, as so many social psychological findings do. These outcomes make obvious points: Human behavior is predictable, but scientific psychology's findings can challenge students' naïve beliefs and provide students with new ways of thinking about human behavior.

I'm ready to turn to my last beginning claim, that Carleton is a great school. Let's treat the claim as generic: X is a great school (where $X =$ your institution). The point is that students have an opportunity they ought not take for granted: to study at an institution of higher education. They are attending college for greater ends, and a single course in psychology or even a major in psychology serves as only a part of the larger striving a degree represents. I want to remind my students of their good fortune and serious obligations; I want students to think about the skills and appreciations they ought to be cultivating (e.g., writing, critical thinking, quantitative reasoning); I want them to recognize how their work in my course might contribute to their overall intellectual development; I want them to realize that they need to take responsibility for their own education. I know of no finer enumeration of what an education can provide intellectually than that offered by William Johnson Cory, a master at Eton over 100 years ago, which I, in turn, share with my students.

[You] . . . go to a great school not for knowledge so much as for arts and habits; for the habit of attention, for the art of expression, for the art of assuming at a moment's notice a new intellectual posture, for the art of entering quickly into another person's thoughts, for the habit of submitting to censure and refutation, for the art of indicating assent or dissent in graduated terms, for the habit of regarding minute points of accuracy, for the habit of working out what is possible in a given time, for mental courage and mental soberness. Above all you go to a great school for self-knowledge. (1861, pp. 6–7)

And so I end my beginning class, having both told and shown my students why I believe they ought to see their course in psychology as worth taking.

There is a danger in what I do and what I am recommending. Friedrich and Douglass (1998) recognized the danger when they wrote, "an awareness of how persuasion occurs in an instructional context carries with it a corresponding need to reflect on the ethics of such influence" (p. 553). We need to articulate in some form the potential value of what we teach, but we also need to exercise suitable caution in what we claim and how we make claims. How do we convey potential meaning with integrity in a manner that is open, self-critical, and true to the state of a discipline's knowledge and controversies? One suggestion is to present claims of meaning as questions. To what extent and in what ways are psychological processes responsible for our subjective experience of the world? How possible is it to study psychological phenomena scientifically? What is the potential value of psychology? In sum, I recommend beginning purposefully but with discretion.

Endings in the Contents of Psychology

Did you know there are literatures in psychology on endings that might inform our own endings? I want to identify topics and references that support the teaching of endings and to argue that you can do your students a service by teaching them about these endings. Moreover, as people navigating life's wanted and unwanted transitions, we may have much to gain from reflection on the psychology of endings. The bottom line is this: If endings are ubiquitous in human affairs and if they are particularly powerful elements in human experience—both of which I suggest are true—then they ought to be present in the study of human behavior called psychology.

Here's the back story for the above. Over 20 years ago, I began developing a course on the psychology of endings based on literatures in psychology, sociology, English, and the arts addressing endings (e.g., the endings of conversations, relationships, sports careers, and poems). I designed the course for advanced psychology majors and have typically taught it during students' final term. The course is described as examining the psychology of endings, including those associated with psychotherapy, social interactions, personal relationships, social roles, literature and the arts, and life itself, and as addressing when and how endings occur, how we experience endings, and what makes an ending good or poor.

The Psychology of Endings has proven to be quite popular, in part because students have experienced, or at least recognize, the importance of endings. Most have ended relationships painfully; some have lost family members and friends; most are ending their college careers. Students find it reassuring to see that others have struggled with these endings and interesting to learn what psychological science can tell us about endings. The course also provides closure to students' work in the major. In this course I challenge students to recall what they have learned over their careers, encourage students to use their knowledge to generate new insights, demonstrate the power of psychology in interaction with other disciplines, place psychology in a meaningful context, and orient students to the future, a future that students now more strongly recognize will include important life endings. (For additional detail on the course, see the syllabus portal, Lutsky, 2008.)

It is not necessary to teach a course on the psychology of endings to incorporate content that addresses endings in psychology, even in introductory psychology. What ends in psychology? Here are examples. Therapy ends, and a literature (e.g., Firestein, 2001; Schlesinger, 2005; Ward, 1984) suggests that counselors and clinicians need to attend to the special needs associated with that phase of treatment. Relationships end (e.g., Drigotas & Rusbult, 1992; Weber, 1998) and lives end (e.g., Boss, 1999; Didion, 2005), and these terminations not only generate common presenting problems in therapy but they also raise basic questions about the nature of social relationships (Rusbult & Buunk, 1993) and about fundamental social motivation (Solomon, Greenberg, & Pyszczynski, 2000; Yalom, 1989). Roles change (e.g., Ebaugh, 1988), and these transitions have implications for identity, well-being, and interpersonal interaction. Conversations end, and those endings prove to be highly regularized (Albert & Kessler, 1978; Goffman, 1971), typically involving statements that review an interaction, justify its termination, plan for continuity, and express positive affect and well-wishing.

Endings may have a particularly powerful presence in human memory and experience. Kahneman and his associates (e.g., Fredrickson & Kahneman, 1993) have demonstrated the disproportionate influence of ending phases on remembered affective evaluations of events. More generally, endings may influence the narratives we create of human intentions and values, meaning in life, and the nature of existence after events have unfolded. As the literary critic Marianna Torgovnick has written,

> In part, we value endings because the retrospective patterning used to make sense of texts corresponds to one process used to make sense of life: the process of looking back over events and interpreting them in light of "how things turned out." (1981, p. 5)

In other words, endings have the power to transform how we remember and evaluate parts of our lives and how we tell the stories of our lives.

Endings are also emotionally laden, as the literature on grief suggests (e.g., Harvey, 2002). Even commonplace conversational endings can be seen as involving rituals that mitigate or mask potential feelings of rejection and loss. Edward Said captured this concern in his autobiography, *Out of Place*, where he noted, "In all cases, though, the great fear is that departure is the state of being abandoned, even though it is you who leave" (1999, p. 218). Life's more lasting endings also potentially leave deep imprints on us. As Robert Weiss observed, "Loss is inescapable. Deaths, estrangements, and separations are part of life.... Most of us have character structures influenced by partial recovery from loss." (1988, pp. 50–51).

To recapitulate, endings in the human affairs psychologists study and treat, and participate in, are signal phenomena. They deserve a presence in the psychology classroom in topics treated across the curriculum, possibly, in the form of a capstone seminar (e.g., see the chapters in the Endings section of this volume).

What Makes for a Good Ending?

We're almost there! You might be looking for specific suggestions on how to end a course well, and I can assure you those are coming. First, however, I want to step back to abstract generalized characteristics of good endings from the endings literatures mentioned above. These proffered attributes of good endings may be even more useful than specific techniques because each of us is faced with the challenge of crafting endings specific to the characteristics of the particular courses and students at hand. General guides, then, may help orient that needed creativity.

Here are five attributes I suggest are characteristic of good endings:

1. *A good ending retains our attention and interest.* We are driven to the ending by curiosity about what happens next, and the ending ultimately satisfies that curiosity.

2. *A good ending has integrity.* It is meaningfully related to and consistent with the character of the thing ended. It fits the whole and doesn't misrepresent or overstate what has occurred or not occurred. As Burns has written, the end should present "a rounding out of themes, without false conclusions" (2008, p. 135).

3. *A good ending conveys a lasting sense of meaning, purpose, and accomplishment.* It suggests that the goals of an activity have been realized, that the efforts and sacrifices made on behalf of the commitment were justified. This, of course, ties an ending back to the promises of a beginning. Even in those circumstances, common to our lives, where there is "losing after great striving," a good ending ties that recognition into the web of life. Here is how the sportswriter Roger Kahn (1972) framed that: "Losing after great striving is the story of man, who was born to sorrow, whose sweetest songs tell of saddest thought, and who, if he is a hero, does nothing in life as becomingly as leaving it" (p. xii).

4. *A good ending provides closure.* It conveys a sense that nothing essential remains or has been omitted, even if the ending hasn't resolved everything and answered all questions. A successful ending is *perceived* as over and embodies a "harmonious completion" (Albert, 1984, p. 159). The challenge of achieving such a closure is one the great psychologist James—Henry James, that is—appreciated. "Really," he wrote, "universally, relations stop nowhere, and the exquisite problem of the artist is eternally but to draw, by a geometry of his own, the circle within which they shall happily *appear* to do so" (1907, p. 471).

5. *A good ending makes the whole of the activity come alive again with pleasure and meaning, and then it moves on, directing our attention forward to new productive activity.* As Smith observes, "the last lines of a poem, like the finality of the last chords of a sonata, seem to confirm retrospectively, as if with a final stamp of

approval, the valued qualities of the entire experience we have just sustained" (1968, p. 4). A good ending furthermore both allows and prepares us for new beginnings; it conveys a sense of the value of what has ended for what lies beyond its own borders.

Techniques for Ending Courses in Psychology

With the above themes in mind, how then can we bring about successful endings in our courses (or in the major or particular class sessions)? Perlman and McCann (2002) suggested that the literature lacks "useful information on good ways to end courses" and that "many faculty spend little time ending a course, perhaps as little as a few minutes, and this is a valuable teaching moment lost." Teaching advice for "the last days of class" (Davis, 1993) seems to confirm Perlman and McCann's observations. It emphasizes the mechanics of endings (e.g., holding a review session, administering a course evaluation form). What then can we do to highlight the meaning and value we strive to achieve through teaching? Here is a list:

1. *Present a lecture that addresses the main themes of the course.* This is a suggestion Davis (1993) makes under the heading of "Conducting a Review Session," presumably for a final examination, but distilling the essence of a course into a short presentation for a last class may serve other functions as well. It reminds students about important insights and findings in psychology; it may allow the instructor to step back and draw connections between seemingly disparate topics; it may provide the instructor an opportunity to identify issues of current interest in the discipline and to suggest where those are pursued in particular areas of specialization and other courses in psychology.

2. *Ask students to report the one or two ideas or findings they believe to be most worth remembering (or sharing with friends) from the course.* Davis (1993) refers to this as "debriefing." I use this technique in final classes as well as a variant of it on course evaluations, where I'll ask students to list some number of things they believe they learned from a course, reading, or assignment. This ending technique can serve teaching and learning as well as debriefing or assessment purposes. Giving students this assignment in class or prior to the final class will encourage them

to review their notes and readings. Students can then report their selections in class or submit them in written or electronic form. An instructor and the class can work with the specific ideas and findings cited to identify broader themes and to draw connections between items in the set the class developed. In other words, an adept instructor can enlist the class in creating that final presentation discussed in (1) above. Moreover, having the class work to identify what's important or memorable may add a stronger imprimatur to a list than an instructor's selection.

3. *Return to the themes presented at the beginning of the course.* Echoing a course's beginning at its close has the potential to tie the course together for students. I'll ask students if they remember the overarching ideas I discussed in the first class of the term. A surprising number do; others hurriedly consult their notebooks. I then ask students to identify specific examples from the material we have covered that illustrate those themes or, possibly, challenge them. This task helps students appreciate the coherence of psychology and gives them a sense that the course they are now ending was designed from the outset with certain purposes in mind.

Reflecting a beginning at an end is a powerful means of bringing about closure. Klein (1995) reports posing the same question at the beginning and end of a course in philosophy to show students how much more sophisticated their understandings have become. I encountered a beautiful example of a reflective end years ago in a talk by Robert Marrs, a professor of rhetoric at Coe College in Iowa. He began a presentation on teaching with a quotation from Kenneth Burke on "the unending conversation" in academia; he ended his talk by repeating the exact same quote. That return not only signaled the end of the talk; it allowed the listener to appreciate how much he or she better understood the quotation in light of what had transpired from first hearing it. The quote was identical in words but not meaning, and the repetition led the listener to discover how he or she had gained insight from the talk now ending. Would that each of our students walk out of our final course class having recognized the same!

4. *Provide opportunities for students to demonstrate mastery of the material.* This ending was one of the most common intentional strategies professors cited when responding to the question "Do we end with a whimper?" in the 1995 issues of *The Teaching Professor* (Weimer). Having students complete knowledge games (e.g., crossword puzzles, *Jeopardy*), create course collages, act out content in games of charades, or present the findings of projects all serve to draw attention to what has been gained over a course of study. These activities mark the close of a course as consisting of something other than regular class sessions, remind students of significant course content, and, at their best, actively involve students in using the skills and understandings they have developed over the term. As a result, students may leave the course with a stronger sense of intellectual self-efficacy and a richer appreciation for the contributions the course made to their education.

5. *Don't bring brownies.* What kind of advice is this, you ask? How can anyone argue against brownies (or other food equivalents)? In truth, I'm not wholly against brownies, and I recognize that food can be a means of expressing positive affect for our students, something we strive to do more generally in interpersonal endings. The point I want to make is that what we feed our students in courses is primarily cognitive in character—the contents, disciplines, and values we intend them to gain from those courses—and how we end should celebrate the virtues and, possibly, recognize the limitations of what we have offered. Good feeling that derives from reflections on educational accomplishment maintains the integrity of the professional relationships we have with students and demonstrates consistency with the character of the activity now ending.

6. *End with endings.* Why not use the proximity and relevance of ending as a vehicle for showing how the study of psychology can illuminate, self-reflectively, its own passing? I capitalize on students' experiences when scheduling my Psychology of Endings seminar and have found that students easily link what they are learning to what they are feeling and observing as their time at college comes to a close. The last session of a course

likewise provides a ready phenomenon to which students or faculty can apply the analytic tools of psychology. What are functions of a closing class session? How are closing sessions typically structured? What makes for an effective and memorable closing of a course? The literatures mentioned earlier in this chapter represent possible beginning points for a teacher who is structuring a class session on endings. In my experience, students are likely to find that such a class demonstrates powerfully and meaningfully the ability of psychology to illuminate central experiences in their own lives.

Why End?

Endings can be difficult if not dangerous. If a beginning asserts potential value, an ending may call into question whether that value has been realized, as promised. If a beginning asserts potential value, an ending may suggest that value has been exhausted, that there are other potentially more fetching investments now available for an alternative commitment. Thus, even if I kept on writing about endings ad infinitum, or if I tried to encourage students to ignore the end of the term and continue meeting regularly to study introductory or some other psychology, the student's choice to end may signal to me that my value is spent. Better to cite compelling external reasons for ending, such as the 20 page limit imposed on this chapter or the end of the term required by an institution's calendar. The rituals of ending, then, may help us all save face.

But there is another reason to end rather than stop. If what we do has value for students and if what students have done in a course has value for them, then it is useful to help them recognize that value and to prompt them to consider how what they have learned might inform or gird their lives in the future. Needless to say, it may also be useful to us as teachers to remind ourselves of the value of our own commitments and sacrifices and to hone our future choices on the stone of meaning. Learning how to survive and even thrive with the tension between constructing value and calling that value into question may be the most important reflective gift we can give our students and ourselves through the work that we do. Ultimately, whether we attend to endings with our students and how we end the efforts and encounters we have jointly assumed may determine whether we each leave with a sense of accomplishment that prepares us to begin anew.

Recommended Readings

Albert, S. (1984). The sense of closure. In K. J. Gergen & M. M. Gergen (Eds.), *Historical social psychology* (pp. 159–172). Mahwah, NJ: Erlbaum.

Davis, B. G. (1993). *Tools for teaching*. San Francisco: Jossey-Bass.

Firestein, S. K. (2001). *Termination in psychoanalysis and psychotherapy*. Madison, WI: International Universities Press.

References

Albert, S. (1984). The sense of closure. In K. J. Gergen & M. M. Gergen (Eds.), *Historical social psychology* (pp. 159–172). Mahwah, NJ: Erlbaum.

Albert, S., & Kessler, S. (1978). Ending social encounters. *Journal of Experimental Social Psychology, 14,* 541–553.

Boss, P. (1999). *Ambiguous loss: Learning to live with unresolved grief.* Cambridge, MA: Harvard.

Burns, C. (2008). *Off the page: Writers talk about beginnings, endings, and everything in between.* New York: W. W. Norton.

Cory, W. J. (1861). *Eton reform.* London: Longman, Green, Longman, & Roberts.

Davis, B. G. (1993). *Tools for teaching.* San Francisco: Jossey-Bass.

Didion, J. (2005). *The year of magical thinking.* New York: Knopf.

Drigotas, S. M., & Rusbult, C. E. (1992). Should I stay or should I go? A dependence model of breakups. *Journal of Personality and Social Psychology, 62,* 62–87.

Dunn, F. M. (1996). *Tragedy's end: Closure and innovation in Euripidean drama.* New York: Oxford University Press.

Ebaugh, H. R. F. (1988). *Becoming an EX: The process of role exit.* Chicago: University of Chicago.

Firestein, S. K. (2001). *Termination in psychoanalysis and psychotherapy.* Madison, WI: International Universities Press.

Fredrickson, B., & Kahneman, D. (1993). Duration neglect in retrospective evaluations of affective episodes. *Journal of Personality and Social Psychology, 65,* 45–55.

Friedrich, J., & Douglass, D. (1998). Ethics and the persuasive enterprise of teaching psychology. *American Psychologist, 53,* 549–562.

Goffman, E. (1971). *Relations in public.* New York: Harper.

Gray, P. (1993). Engaging students' intellects: The immersion approach to critical thinking in psychology instruction. *Teaching of Psychology, 20,* 68–74.

Harvey, J. H. (2002). *Perspectives on loss and trauma.* Thousand Oaks, CA: Sage.

James, H. (1907). Preface to *Roderick Hudson.* In J. Auchard (Ed.), *The portable Henry James* (2003, pp. 469–475). New York: Penguin.

Kahn, R. (1972). *The boys of summer.* New York: HarperCollins.

Klein, E. R. (1995, May). Do we end with a whimper? In M. Weimer (Ed.), *The Teaching Professor,* 2.

LaVere, C. (1941). It's all in your mind [Recorded by Jay Ungar & Molly Mason]. On *The Lovers' Waltz* [CD]. New York: Angel (1997).

Lutsky, N. (2008). Psychology 382: The psychology of endings (Course Syllabus). http://www.acad.carleton.edu/curricular/PSYC/lutsky/Lutsky.html

Perlman, B., & McCann, L. I. (2002). What we need to know about teaching and teachers. In W. Buskist, V. Hevern, & G. W. Hill, IV (Eds.), *Essays from e-xcellence in teaching, 2000–2001* (chap. 10). Retrieved June 15, 2008, from the Society for the Teaching of Psychology Web site: http://teachpsych.org/resources/e-books/eit2000/eit00-10.html.

Rusbult, C., & Buunk, B. (1993). Commitment processes in close relationships: An interdependence analysis. *Journal of Social and Personal Relationships, 10,* 175–204.

Said, E. W. (1975). *Beginnings: Intention and method.* New York: Columbia University Press.

Said, E. W. (1999). *Out of place: A memoir.* New York: Vintage.

SandlotScience. (2005). Top hat illusion. http://www.sandlotscience.com/Distortions/Lincolns_Hat.htm.

Schlesinger, H. J. (2005). *Endings and beginnings: On terminating psychotherapy and psychoanalysis.* Hillsdale, NJ: Analytic Press.

Smith, B. H. (1968). *Poetic closure: A study of how poems end.* Chicago: University of Chicago.

Solomon, S., Greenberg, J., & Pyszczynski, T. (2000). Pride and prejudice: Fear of death and social behavior. *Current Directions in Psychological Science, 9*(6), 200–204.

Torgovnick, M. (1981). *Closure in the novel.* Princeton: Princeton University.

Wald, M. L. (2004, April 7). Motor-vehicle-related deaths will increase, study predicts. *New York Times.*

Ward, D. E. (1984). Termination of individual counseling: Concepts and strategies. *Journal of Counseling and Development, 63,* 21–25.

Weber, A. L. (1998). Losing, leaving, and letting go: Coping with nonmarital breakups. In B. H. Spitzberg & W. R. Cupach (Eds.), *The dark side of close relationships* (pp. 267–306). Mahwah, NJ: Erlbaum.

Weimer, M. (Ed.). (1995, February, May, June/July). Do we end with a whimper? *The Teaching Professor.*

Weiss, R. S. (1988). Loss and recovery. *Journal of Social Issues, 44,* 37–52.

Yalom, I. (1989). *Love's executioner.* New York: HarperCollins.

Part III

Coda

21 Developing Scientific Reasoning Skills in Beginning and Ending Students

Suzanne C. Baker, Maureen A. McCarthy, Jane S. Halonen, Dana S. Dunn, and G. William Hill, IV

Morgan and Johnson (1997) asserted that psychology has no central paradigm that can be tested, which complicates the establishment of benchmarks for psychology education. . . . Curriculum scholars, however, converged on the importance of instilling scientific reasoning skills through studying a diverse set of content areas as a fundamental objective of psychology.

— HALONEN ET AL. (2003, P. 197)

The journey that students make through the psychology major transforms them intellectually, particularly with regard to their ability to reason scientifically. At the outset of the major their novice enthusiasm for the discipline may be based at least somewhat on misinformation (and before they declare a major in psychology or enroll in the introductory class, their knowledge about behavior is best described as "pre-novice"). Among the misperceptions are the notions that all psychologists are therapists and that psychology has little to do with science. Often, the challenge for psychology programs involves the design of appropriate learning experiences in a curriculum that will not only move students from "novice" to "expert" but will also deal effectively with deconstruction of erroneous ideas.

The purpose of this chapter is to explore the role that departments and their faculty play in moving students from declaring psychology as a major to mastering the concepts, theories, and ways of thinking of psychologists at a baccalaureate level. We examine best practices that departments and faculty can adopt to facilitate optimal outcomes for both the students and the faculty who deliver the program. We begin before the story officially starts to unfold—with students who have little or no awareness of the whys and where-fores of psychology as a contemporary science.

Dealing with Student Preconceptions: Understanding Pre-Novices

How should we characterize those first- or even second-year students who have many ideas about psychology but who have not yet taken a college-level psychology course, particularly given that many of these students will not have completed a psychology course during their secondary education? We refer to these students as pre-novices to reflect the fact that their "knowl-edge" of psychology as a discipline is apt to be second- or even thirdhand, as well as somewhat biased by cultural prejudice, misperceptions, and even misinformation. Pre-novices may see most, if not all, psychology through the lens of clinical phenomena. In addition, the assumptions they draw from television shows or films about such phenomena may grossly underesti-mate the true complexity of behavior, distorting the accuracy of their conclusions.

Halonen et al. (2003) characterized the scientific reasoning of typical pre-novice students as "untrained" and largely superficial. In other words, they do not engage in critical thinking (e.g., Dunn, Halonen, & Smith, 2008; Halonen & Gray, 2000). Pre-novice students are not aware that psychology is a science devoted to the study of all behavior, whether overt or covert. Instead, these students persist in the belief that psychology deals largely with abnormal or atypical behaviors and even paranormal phenomena. Pre-novices anticipate that such behaviors can be explained through simple means (e.g., "too little or too much love," "not enough attention," "low self-esteem") grounded in familial or social relationships or individual adjustment and are not, for example, a result of some combination of genetics, cognitive or behavioral disorders, rearing factors, strain due to limited economic resources, and a broad array of other complex psychological factors. Indeed, Halonen et al. made note of the disappointment and frustration pre-novices often display when their presumptive and favored explanations do not possess sufficient (if any) explanatory power.

More recently, Wade (2008) suggested that many people, including stu-dents, fall prey to confirmation bias, or a propensity to recall facts that verify what we already believe, simultaneously forgetting information counter to our beliefs. Wade's observations regarding how uncritical thinking can instill false beliefs in professionals can apply as well to beginning psychology students.

Table 21-1 lists the eight skill domains described by Halonen et al. (2003) with an eye to what reasoning skills pre-novices are apt to display. A quick glance at the contents of Table 21-1 reveals that pre-novices generally engage in pre-scientific reasoning. To be fair, a given student's responses are not likely to be entirely unscientific, but we prefer to err on the side of caution when characterizing the reasoning skills of most beginning students, some of whom may never take any psychology course at all. These pre-novice responses would be characterized as *underdeveloped* in the benchmarking approach advocated by Dunn, McCarthy, Baker, Halonen, and Hill (2007) for evaluating content areas of undergraduate psychology programs. The term *underdeveloped* is used to refer to qualities (here, reasoning skills) that offer no, or even a counterproductive, contribution to undergraduate learning in psychology.

Given the pre-scientific reasoning of many pre-novice students, psychology educators have their work cut out for them. Is there anything instructors can

Table 21-1

Characterizing Pre-Novice Skills in Eight Domains of Scientific Inquiry in Psychology

Skill domain	Samples of pre-novice proficiency
Descriptive	Superficial, imprecise, intuitive description of behavior
Conceptualization	Relies on "pop" psychology accounts rather than theory
Problem solving	No use of scientific method, statistical reasoning; open to biased interpretations
Ethical reasoning	Rudimentary awareness of discipline-based ethics; often assumes psychologists are ethically challenged
Scientific attitudes & values	No reliance on research findings; objective or simple accounts are favored
Communication	Personal experiences, popular press, selective or anecdotal evidence color written or spoken arguments
Collaboration	No collaborative experiences, only solo ventures
Self-assessment	Reactive rather than planful; engages in little self-reflection

Adapted with permission from Halonen, J. S., Bosack, T., Clay, S., & McCarthy, M. (with Dunn, D. S., Hill, G. W., IV, McEntarfer, R., Mehrotra, C., Nesmith, R., Weaver, K., & Whitlock, K.) (2003). A rubric for authentically learning, teaching, and assessing scientific reasoning in psychology. *Teaching of Psychology, 30*, 196–208.

do to promote scientific reasoning in pre-novice students and help them make the intellectual transition to become novices? Dealing with students' preconceptions about psychology as a discipline, an area of science, and a diverse archive of facts about all kinds of behavior requires us to expose them to positions and perspectives that differ from their own. Our approach must be friendly, engaging, and ongoing across settings; sarcasm, claims of authority or experience, and any form of I-am-more-educated-than-you-are kinds of responses will not improve students' openness to new ideas (e.g., Benson, Cohen, & Buskist, 2005; Keeley, Smith, & Buskist, 2006; Wilson, 2006).

Psychologists who teach should take every opportunity to remind student audiences (in and outside the classroom) not to accept explanations without supporting evidence, to avoid jumping to quick and convenient conclusions, and to learn to become tolerant of ambiguity. Of course, the most difficult challenge is to convince pre-novices to be accepting of diverse views regarding psychological phenomena, especially when those views require them to learn to accept counter-evidence and alternative explanations. This challenge cannot be satisfactorily met until the pre-novice becomes a novice.

Launching the Novice Learner: Best Practices for the Introductory Course

Introductory psychology is arguably the hardest course to teach in the psychology curriculum. A typical class comprises three fairly distinct groups. The largest group includes students who are fulfilling a general education requirement. The other two groups represent students who are either already committed to psychology as a major and those who may gravitate toward the major because they become engaged in the discipline as the result of their introductory course experiences.

Typically, the majority of students in the beginning course take introductory psychology to fulfill general education requirements; they often select introductory psychology believing it to be an easy option. They may express sentiments such as, "It's about people. How hard can it be?" Many of those students express shock when they recognize the depth of effort the course requires for them to be successful. Many will inevitably experience blows to their grade point averages unless they can adjust their expectations and work habits to correspond to the standards that most introductory teachers require.

Students who arrive at college committed to the psychology major come from different pathways. Many were fortunate enough to have a competently designed and delivered course in high school, particularly in Advanced Placement or International Baccalaureate Programs. They embraced the idea of majoring in psychology because their pre-college experience produced genuine excitement about the major. Ironically, the most successful students with this background will not be found in the college introductory class as their performances allow them to advance to more sophisticated course work.

Many students, including those who declare the major at the outset of their studies or succumb to the pull of the major as the result of a well-taught introductory class, are oriented toward the goal of helping people. They may have enjoyed portrayals of professional helpers in the media. Some students who have had a troubled adolescence or problematic family background may naturally be drawn to the notion of helping people. These students may have encountered admirable therapists. It is less likely that they will have interacted with the idea of psychology as science rather than as a helping profession. Therefore, the introductory psychology instructor will need to help new learners recognize the broader base of activities conducted in and contributions made by the discipline.

The mix of students suggests that the skilled teacher of novices must design a course that will appeal to students with variable motivations for being on the class roster. In effect, they must manage a two-tiered classroom. Many students will see the course as the exciting foundation for a satisfying professional future. On the other hand, the majority of students may be harder to engage. The contribution of the introductory course is the development of basic scientific thinking skills, an appropriate contribution whether the student is establishing a major or merely getting a general education course "out of the way."

Halonen et al. (2003) captured the essential characteristics of the novice psychological thinker, as shown in Table 21-2. Generally speaking, novice learners demonstrate a limited capacity to engage in scientific thinking, primarily because of their reliance on personal experience to make sense of behavior. They find the infrastructure and procedures of science to be cumbersome and unnecessarily fussy. They may resist our encouragement to think precisely about behavior. Novice students may appreciate controlled comparisons as a scientific approach but more comfortably retreat to firsthand experience to explain behavior unless forced to be scientific. They prefer

Table 21-2
Characterizing Novice Skills in Eight Domains of Scientific Inquiry in Psychology

Skill domain	Samples of basic proficiency
Descriptive	Begins to notice and describe behaviors consistent with scientific, objective standards
Conceptualization	Compares how scientific theories fit with personal beliefs
Problem solving	Recognizes power of controlled comparison and personal biases in making cause-effect judgments
Ethical reasoning	Accepts ethical parameters of psychological practices; identifies gross ethical violations
Scientific attitudes & values	Accepts scientific findings that fit with personal belief; prefers simple, nonambiguous explanations
Communication	Argues from personal experience rather than research evidence; struggles with role and value of APA conventions
Collaboration	Cooperates in collaborative projects but may become ineffective in conflict situations
Self-assessment	Capable of global but not refined strengths and weaknesses present in own work

Adapted with permission from Halonen, J. S., Bosack, T., Clay, S., & McCarthy, M. (with Dunn, D. S., Hill, G. W., IV, McEntarfer, R., Mehrotra, C., Nesmith, R., Weaver, K., & Whitlock, K.) (2003). A rubric for authentically learning, teaching, and assessing scientific reasoning in psychology. *Teaching of Psychology*, 30, 196–208.

simple answers to messy ones and show little tolerance for ambiguity. Novices may challenge their need to learn the conventional expressions required by the American Psychological Association (APA) format as unnecessarily constraining their expression. Although novices recognize that ethics should be part of scientific practice, they tend to regard ethical protocols, such as oversight by institutional review boards, as obstacles to progress rather than protection of rights.

What are some best practice strategies that departments and instructors can use to help launch psychology majors while at the same time providing the experiences in psychology that will address the general education needs and requirements for students who will not have another psychology class in their future?

Employ the best faculty in the introductory role. Because the constituent groups are so variable, faculty members need to show respect for and patience with those who are not naturally enthusiastic about psychology. General studies students who are not certain about their majors can be converted to psychology majors when the introductory course is well taught and inviting. As a consequence, departments may need to give special consideration to hiring introductory course specialists who understand and can succeed in making unique contributions to their departments by delivering on the promise of good general education while simultaneously retaining and recruiting talented majors.

Promote the advantage of scientific explanations over personal theories of behavior. Those making untrained interpretations of behavior tend to rely on personal experience and conclusions about motivation rather than a description of behavior and more systematic consideration of variables. Providing engaging examples in which students feel some investment can facilitate further critical thinking development. For example, arguments about a person's motivation to get a tattoo may provide fertile ground for demonstrating how expert psychologists would approach this complex problem in contrast with someone with an untrained approach.

Create active learning situations that produce tailored critical thinking challenges. When prompted, novice learners can spot design flaws in research if the design flaws are large enough (Halonen & Gray, 2000). Presenting badly designed experiments that violate good design principles in obvious ways can empower novice learners to enjoy the critical analysis that will be essential to spotting problems with research designs, with arguments about behavior, or even with commercial claims.

Model tolerance of ambiguity. Instructors should not rush to answer student questions. Students typically seek simple answers to behavioral questions that they pose in class. Such opportunities allow for a free flow of ideas and the multiple points of view that allow a parade of variables to be identified. Supporting rich discussions of all the possibilities encourages critical thinking. This practice underscores why simple answers will not be satisfying in the long run.

Require practice of professional communication skills on a small scale. Asking students to track down an article in an area that they find interesting is a good way to introduce them to the nature of scientific literature in psychology. Summarizing the key points and identifying the article using APA conventions provide a taste of the activities that will lie ahead in the major. Students will be more successful if they practice on articles that are straightforward and relatively simple rather than complex empirical studies in which they may drown in the statistical analyses.

Address the role of psychology in the students' futures. Conducting an in-class discussion about the way that learning introductory psychology can be important in their future endeavors can help students understand that knowledge from the course can be personally relevant. In addition, a class period devoted to this activity can be designed to include only the majors, so that instructors can provide more concrete answers to the specific questions emerging majors will have about what will happen to them following their first course.

Managing the Middle: Developing the Scientifically Literate Student

As students move from novice to developing status in the major, the population of students in these courses becomes more homogeneous in some respects. Most now have a solid foundation based on their introductory course experiences. In general, instructors who have the challenge of the courses "in the middle" will generally find that their students will be easier to engage because they have made a commitment to some kind of career path in psychology by declaring the major. Students at this stage have developed some basic skills relevant to scientific inquiry in psychology.

Table 21-3 provides examples of skill levels for students at this middle stage. In the developing stage of scientific reasoning, students begin to recognize bias and begin to value objective approaches to investigation. Students at this stage can recognize multiple points of view and have developed some capacity to critique their own viewpoint. They are more skilled at using APA communication styles than novice students.

Most programs offer a wide array of options to help students become scientifically literate in psychology. Although this book focuses on introductory and capstone experiences, developing a scientifically literate student requires a structured sequence of experiences across the curriculum. We intentionally reference experiences rather than courses because the focus should be on development of scientific skills, regardless of the specific courses that might be present on a campus. Structured experiences should take into account the intellectual scaffolding that needs to occur between the introductory and capstone courses. How do we ensure appropriate experiences in the

Table 21-3

Characterizing Developing Skills in Eight Domains of Scientific Inquiry in Psychology

Skill domain	Samples of basic proficiency
Descriptive	Observes and carefully distinguishes behavior from interpretation
Conceptualization	Identifies objective constraints of theory
Problem solving	Recognizes influence of bias and confounds in framing questions
Ethical reasoning	Accepts and adheres to ethical protocols
Scientific attitudes & values	Distinguishes objective from subjective reality; recognition that perceptions of reality differ between individuals
Communication	Develops plausible arguments; inconsistently uses APA conventions
Collaboration	Shares in collaborative projects and fulfills responsibilities
Self-assessment	Capable of judging one's own work

Adapted with permission from Halonen, J. S., Bosack, T., Clay, S., & McCarthy, M. (with Dunn, D. S., Hill, G. W., IV, McEntarfer, R., Mehrotra, C., Nesmith, R., Weaver, K., & Whitlock, K.) (2003). A rubric for authentically learning, teaching, and assessing scientific reasoning in psychology. *Teaching of Psychology*, 30, 196–208.

course work that is sequenced between the beginning and end of the student's time on campus?

Identify a set of structured writing assignments across the curriculum. Written assignments might take place in only one writing-intensive course, or more likely, students may complete a set of assignments across courses. A well-designed writing program provides students with incremental learning experiences, so that earlier assignments focus on foundation skills and assignments later in the major require increasingly advanced skills. Assignments should be clear in their goals, and assessment of competence should provide the basis for department assessment plans (e.g., Halonen, 2002). In addition to developing basic writing skills, the department can specify proficiencies for the use of the APA publication format, such as reference citation format. Departments can optimize student development by adopting a common rubric for assessing student writing, regardless of the topic or course context.

Legitimize the ubiquitous use of quantitative reasoning in psychology. Many students resist the essential role of measurement in psychology. The role of statistics as a critical tool in answering complex questions must be a common theme that should be emphasized for developing students. Promoting activities that reinforce comfort with quantitative skills will serve these students well.

Create authentic learning experiences. Between the time that students advance beyond the novice level of scientific literacy and completion of their degree, a program is engaged in imparting knowledge about content and in developing a set of skills. The standard practice of using traditional testing methods to assess content knowledge provides an important measure of scientific literacy as the student progresses through the curriculum. However, it is equally important to create innovative assignments that require students to apply their scientific literacy skills consistent with the "developing" level of proficiency. For example, an assignment at the introductory level may entail the use of psychological principles to write a letter to an appropriate audience (e.g., editor, school board, legislator) advocating an empirically based argument. It is incumbent upon the department to ensure that students have opportunities to apply empirical techniques to everyday problems (cf. Dunn et al., 2007).

Design sequenced opportunities for student presentations. Presentation skills at the novice level are virtually nonexistent, yet we expect students to be proficient in these skills when they reach the capstone course. If students must present a formal paper as a culminating experience at the end of the program, then students should be engaged in brief presentations throughout the program. For example, asking students to conduct a brief presentation about psychological content in specific courses helps them to build this skill set. It may also be worthwhile to incorporate opportunities for students to conduct a group presentation, thus creating an opportunity to advance collaboration skills.

Review syllabi of contributing courses to facilitate program coherence. Well-run programs rely on course structures that express their mission and provide students with appropriately rigorous standards. Departments that engage in systematic review of the courses in the middle promote a more coherent experience for the developing student.

The Beginnings of Expertise: Graduating Psychology-Literate Students

What should psychology majors look like at the end of their undergraduate careers? What skills and knowledge should they have, and what course and extracurricular experiences can programs provide that will "send them off" with a set of useful academic and intellectual tools for their "toolkits"? Table 21-4 (based on Halonen et al., 2003) provides examples of skills that characterize advanced undergraduates in psychology.

Students at this level have advanced to the point that they recognize the importance of relying on data rather than personal experience when interpreting psychological phenomena. They are better at tolerating ambiguity, and they recognize that explanations of complex behaviors are likely to be complex themselves. Their scientific literacy and communication skills have advanced to a sophisticated level, and they are able to more accurately critique and judge their own reasoning and performance.

What are some ways that programs can help students practice advanced skills and learn to function as beginning professionals in the field?

Table 21-4

Characterizing Advanced Undergraduate Skills in Eight Domains of Scientific Inquiry in Psychology

Skill domain	Samples of basic proficiency
Descriptive	Systematically relies on data rather than personal experience for interpretation
Conceptualization	Tolerates counterintuitive findings; compares and contrasts relative contributions of theories
Problem solving	Independently selects and applies appropriate statistics
Ethical reasoning	Identifies how ethical standards constrain or enhance research
Scientific attitudes & values	Understands that explanations of behavior will be complex; tolerates ambiguity
Communication	Creates coherent and integrated arguments based on research evidence; uses APA format more consistently
Collaboration	Exercises leadership to contribute to positive group processes and outcomes
Self-assessment	Makes accurate judgments about quality of work; uses deep criticism to improve quality of future work

Adapted with permission from Halonen, J. S., Bosack, T., Clay, S., & McCarthy, M. (with Dunn, D. S., Hill, G. W., IV, McEntarfer, R., Mehrotra, C., Nesmith, R., Weaver, K., & Whitlock, K.) (2003). A rubric for authentically learning, teaching, and assessing scientific reasoning in psychology. *Teaching of Psychology*, 30, 196–208.

Require a formal endpoint in the program. Many departments may not provide a curriculum structure that incorporates a formal endpoint experience. Stoloff, Sanders, and McCarthy (n.d.) found that 41% of all four-year programs in psychology offered a specific integrative capstone course. Without the opportunity to integrate prior learning in some kind of formal context (e.g., internship, capstone, advanced general course), it may be difficult for students to fully develop their skills. Clearly, capstone experiences should challenge students to flex their intellectual muscles in ways they may not have done up to this point as undergraduates. This volume provides numerous examples of strategies for engaging students at the end of their undergraduate career. Although the specifics of well-designed capstone experiences may differ, they all focus on the development and refinement of advanced skills in psychology. A well-designed capstone experience based on the department's mission statement and assessment plan is one of the most important contributions the department can make to optimal student development (for ideas, see Dunn and McCarthy, this volume).

Consider multiple options for the capstone. Just as students enter into the psychology major with varying motivations and goals, senior-level students differ in how they plan to use their psychology skills and knowledge following graduation. Some of them plan to enter human services or applied careers; others are headed toward research or advanced study in psychology; and still other students will enter the workforce or graduate study in some field not directly related to their psychology major. Providing students with capstone options that are related to their future plans can be a strong motivator for skill development. Possibilities include intensive field placement or research experiences, or advanced seminars focused on specific topics.

Exploit differences in emerging expertise. By the time students reach their capstone course, as instructors, we should have an understanding of the skills they have been developing and the content they have been exposed to through the rest of the major. In a well-designed curriculum, all students at the capstone level should have had somewhat similar learning experiences and should bring similar skills to the course. In reality, though, there may be quite a bit of variability in specific content that students have encountered. If students have a choice of courses to fulfill certain curriculum objectives, they may not all have similar content knowledge of different areas of psychology. Although this situation can be problematic in an advanced course, the fact that students have different subsets of content knowledge about psychology can be exploited to strengthen the course experience.

Individual students can bring different knowledge to class discussion and can collaborate on projects with students who have taken a different path through their psychology major.

Require practice and application of high-level scientific reasoning skills. This goal might be accomplished through a thesis experience or participation in faculty-led research, or through in-class critical evaluation of research literature and theories. Faculty should challenge students engaged in practicum experiences to connect their experiences of psychology in real-world settings to what they know about theories and empirical data. Advanced students can serve as mentors and tutors to students who are at earlier stages in the major. At the program level, active student participation in research colloquia conducted by resident or visiting faculty can engage students' scientific reasoning skills.

Foster student collaboration skills. Group assignments that gradually give the students more responsibility for dividing up work to accomplish tasks efficiently can help students learn to work together in ways that take advantage of the talents of the group as a whole. Assignments in which each student in a group must take a turn serving as group leader require all students, even the less motivated and less skilled, to learn to work as a team.

Provide multiple opportunities to practice and demonstrate professional communication skills, both written and oral, at an advanced level. Required papers, in-class presentations, and presentations at professional meetings are all potential ways of developing the communication skills that the APA endorsed in its *Guidelines for Undergraduate Psychology* (2007). A program-wide student symposium, at which students make formal presentations, or a department-run research journal showcasing student papers are other options.

Build in systematic opportunities for student self-assessment and reflection on learning. Capstone courses should include activities that require students to make nuanced judgments about their own work and assess their individual progress across their academic careers. In the students' own views, have they met their academic goals? Have they achieved the program's learning objectives? These types of reflections can be combined with career-related discussions and planning for the future, as students assess what skills they have gained and how they plan to apply them.

Facilitate realistic career goals. Students at the capstone level do not all have identical motivations regarding their major, and at most institutions, they have widely varying post-graduation plans. Students who are heading toward graduate school or a career in psychology may be highly motivated to hone their research and scientific communication skills. Those who are planning a career in a non-psychology-related field may not see the value of practicing the details of APA format or of getting experience critically evaluating research in the discipline. In some ways, then, the task of the capstone instructor mirrors that of the introductory psychology instructor—how to make the class a relevant and engaging challenge both for students who intend to continue on in the discipline and for those who do not. Connecting skills in the major to the students' "real-world" post-graduate plans should be part of the agenda for a capstone experience.

Showcase high-quality student performance. Ensuring that graduating students have achieved the goals of the major should be a program-wide focus. Department functions at which senior-level students present research and reflect on their academic careers can be an important component of professional development for graduating students and an occasion for celebration of their accomplishments. Program-wide awards ceremonies, "senior day," and similar activities can give students (and faculty) a sense of accomplishment as students complete their undergraduate careers.

Use the full range of student performance quality as a stimulus to improve the program. Assessment experts (e.g., Walvoord, 2004) stress that student performance can provide feedback to the department about continuous improvement needs. Capstone contexts are ideal places to determine whether the department is performing in a satisfying manner to achieve its promised missions. Competent departments conscientiously and systematically collect data on the quality of student achievement and conduct ongoing conversations about what the quality of student performance tells them about potential new directions the department might take.

Conclusion

Graduating well-educated psychology majors requires attention to the specific challenges of both beginnings and endings. To do the best job for our students, to help them meet their goals and objectives, and to achieve our own aspirations as teachers, we should tailor our curricula and programs for the developmental tasks our students face as they complete their undergraduate careers. Departments that focus on providing a coherent experience in the major from start to finish will be the ones that distinguish themselves from their peers (see Dunn et al., 2007).

References

American Psychological Association. (2007). *APA guidelines for the undergraduate psychology major*.Washington, DC: Author. Retrieved from www.apa.org/ed/resources.html.

Benson, T. A., Cohen, A. L., & Buskist, W. (2005). Rapport: Its relation to student attitudes and behaviors toward teachers and classes. *Teaching of Psychology, 32,* 237–239.

Dunn, D. S., Halonen, J. S., & Smith, R. A. (Eds.). (2008). *Teaching critical thinking in psychology: A handbook of best practices*. Malden, MA: Wiley-Blackwell.

Dunn, D. S., McCarthy, M., Baker, S., Halonen, J. S., & Hill, G. W., IV. (2007). Quality benchmarks in undergraduate psychology programs. *American Psychologist, 62,* 650–670.

Halonen, J. S. (Ed.). (2002). *Suggested learning outcomes and goals for the psychology undergraduate major*. Washington, DC: American Psychological Association. Retrieved January 1, 2004, from http://www.apa.org/ed/pcue/taskforcereport2.pdf.

Halonen, J. S., Bosack, T., Clay, S., & McCarthy, M. (with Dunn, D. S., Hill, G. W., IV, McEntarfer, R., Mehrotra, C., Nesmith, R., Weaver, K., & Whitlock, K.). (2003). A rubric for authentically learning, teaching, and assessing scientific reasoning in psychology. *Teaching of Psychology, 30,* 196–208.

Halonen, J., & Gray, C. (2000). *The critical thinking companion for introductory psychology* (2nd ed.). New York: Worth.

Keeley, J., Smith, D., & Buskist, W. (2006). The Teacher Behaviors Checklist: Factor analysis of its utility for evaluating teaching. *Teaching of Psychology, 33,* 84–91.

Stoloff, M., Sanders, N., & McCarthy, M. (n.d.). *Profiles of undergraduate programs in psychology*. Washington, DC: American Psychological Association. Retrieved September 10, 2008, from http://www.apa.org/ed/pcue/profiles_intro.html.

Wade, C. (2008). Critical thinking: Needed now more than ever. In D. S. Dunn, J. S. Halonen, & R. A. Smith (Eds.), *Teaching critical thinking in psychology: A handbook of best practices* (pp. 11–21). Malden, MA: Wiley-Blackwell.

Walvoord, B. (2004). *Assessment clear and simple: A practical guide for institutions, departments, and general education*. San Francisco: Jossey-Bass.

Wilson, J. H. (2006). Predicting student attitudes and grades from perceptions of instructors' attitudes. *Teaching of Psychology, 33,* 91–95.

Name Index

Subject Index